With a Clear Conscience

Business Ethics, Decision-Making, and Strategic Thinking

EDITOR
Gregory G. Andres

AUTHORS
W. Jim Jordan
Andrew Stumpf
Chris Wass
Vanessa Correia
Dylon McChesney
Jamie Sewell
Sara Weaver

WITH CONTRIBUTIONS FROM
Bill Abbott
Sandie DeVries

OXFORD
UNIVERSITY PRESS

OXFORD
UNIVERSITY PRESS

Oxford University Press is a department of the University of Oxford.
It furthers the University's objective of excellence in research, scholarship,
and education by publishing worldwide. Oxford is a registered trade mark of
Oxford University Press in the UK and in certain other countries.

Published in Canada by
Oxford University Press
8 Sampson Mews, Suite 204,
Don Mills, Ontario M3C 0H5 Canada

www.oupcanada.com

Library and Archives Canada Cataloguing in Publication
Title: With a clear conscience : business ethics, decision-making, and strategic thinking / editor,
Gregory G. Andres ; authors, W. Jim Jordan, Andrew Stumpf, Chris Wass, Vanessa Correia, Dylon
McChesney, Jamie Sewell, Sara Weaver ; with contributions from, Bill Abbott, Sandie DeVries.
Other titles: Business ethics, decision-making, and strategic thinking
Names: Jordan, W. Jim, author. | Stumpf, Andrew, 1979- author. | Wass, Chris, author. | Correia,
Vanessa, author. | McChesney, Dylon, author. | Sewell, Jamie, 1982- author. | Weaver, Sara,
author. | Andres, Gregory G., editor.
Description: Includes bibliographical references and index.
Identifiers: Canadiana (print) 20200308041 | Canadiana (ebook) 20200308254 | ISBN 9780199038398
(softcover) | ISBN 9780199038404 (ebook)
Subjects: LCSH: Business ethics—Textbooks. | LCGFT: Textbooks.
Classification: LCC HF5387 .J67 2021 | DDC 174/.4—dc23

Cover image: © iStock/erhui1979
Cover design: Sherill Chapman
Interior design: Laurie McGregor

Oxford University Press is committed to our environment.
This book is printed on Forest Stewardship Council® certified paper
and comes from responsible sources.

Printed and bound in Canada

1 2 3 4 — 23 22 21 20

With a Clear Conscience

BRIEF CONTENTS

CONTENTS

CHAPTER 3 Ethical Decision Making 49

CHAPTER 4 Corporate Social Responsibility 74

CHAPTER 7 Environment, Ethics, and Business 142

CHAPTER 8 The Power of Advertising 166

LIST OF BOXES AND CASE STUDIES

BACKGROUND BOXES

CASE STUDIES

PREFACE

I have been teaching business ethics for well over a decade now. Business ethics was not my area of specialization in grad school, but rather something I fell into once I started teaching. I graduated with my Ph.D. in 2007 just as American financial institutions started imploding under the weight of sub-prime mortgage defaults, precipitating the global Great Recession. Wanting to understand what was happening and why all the academic jobs in philosophy had vanished overnight, I began reading every economics and finance book I could get my hands on. Around the same time, I was teaching a course in decision theory and game theory, and a course in business ethics. The intersection of these three areas of curiosity—economics, decision and game theory, and business ethics—formed a perfect storm and transformed my thinking. Business ethics quickly became one of my favourite courses to teach.

Business ethics tends to get a bad rap from two fronts. If I got a nickel for every time I have heard someone proclaim that "business ethics is an oxymoron," I could retire a very wealthy person. Though understandable, this is a very corrosive attitude. The news is filled with sto-ries about businesses that have been caught in some sort of antisocial behaviour: deceptive accounting practices, lying to shareholders, wanton destruction of the environment, reckless endangerment of others—the list goes on. Dismissing business ethics as oxymoronic simply normalizes the perception that one must throw ethics to the wind in the pursuit of unholy mammon. Normalizing this perception must stop.

The second front is from within academia itself. It is not uncommon to come across the sentiment that business ethics is not "real" ethics because it is applied ethics and not theor-etical ethics. Theoretical ethics is the "real" ethics that requires doing "real" philosophy. This form of gatekeeping is dangerous and regrettable. Learning how to think through problems is a necessary skill; learning how to reason our way through ethical issues is a necessary skill; developing the metacognitive ability to reflect on how we are thinking is a necessary skill. The good news is that we can learn these skills and develop them over time. Studying philosophy teaches us how to think rigorously and systematically, and we do well when we apply this way of thinking to the ethical decisions we must make in business and the workplace.

The Department of Philosophy at the University of Waterloo takes teaching seriously. As part of their professional training, Ph.D. students are given teaching opportunities as they near the end of their program. More often than not, the first course that they are given to teach is business ethics. One part of my job is to mentor Ph.D. students who teach business ethics for the first time. This has given me the opportunity to work with a lot of very smart people who are incredibly dedicated to scholarship and pedagogy.

As the years have progressed, everyone who has been involved in the course started feeling a disquiet about how the course was evolving, and it became evident that the material we were covering in the course was quite different from material covered in the many good textbooks available on the market. Taking the advice of one our colleagues at the time, we started batting around the idea of putting into writing what we were actually teaching in the classroom. At some point, we decided to take the leap and started writing.

Our book has many sources of inspiration. We immediately recognized the significance of Joseph Heath's work on adversarial ethics and a market failures approach to business ethics, and have incorporated his big ideas into this textbook. We also came to appreciate how the formal tools of game theory can be used to analyze pernicious social problems that are fuelled by a narrow conception of self-interest. Humans trade, and we are better off for doing so. Yet too often we treat trade as a zero-sum game and fail to recognize that we can create incredible value through co-operation and collaboration. Further, we would be shirking our duty to philosophy and our students if we did not encourage them to develop rigorous and systematic ways of thinking about ethical issues in business and the workplace. Persons who are unreliable, unprincipled, and unwilling to make good decisions in the workplace are liabilities to their employers. As such, learning how to make sound and ethically defensible decisions in the workplace is a career-building skill.

Acknowledgments

There are many people to thank and acknowledge, people without whom this work would not have been possible. To all those who suffered through our muddled ramblings as we formulated and refined our ideas, our deepest gratitude. To our colleagues who encouraged us and challenged us, thank you for your input and insights.

We also wish to thank the many peer reviewers, both named here and anonymous, who gave valuable feedback on drafts of this book: Julius Bankole, University of Northern British Columbia; Shawna DePlonty, Sault College; Michelle Inness, University of Alberta; Karen McMurray, Coast Mountain College; Glen Melanson, University of Prince Edward Island; Lois Nantais, Lambton College; Bill Reid, Fanshawe College; Chris Street, University of Regina; and Kira Tomsons, Douglas College.

Now for a personal note. To all the contributors to this project, my sincere indebtedness. You have all been amazing to work with! Each of you has brought an important perspective to the project, and what we have now is something that we can be collectively proud of. I have enjoyed every minute working with you.

But this book is not just about us. Fittingly, then, we dedicate this labour of love to our students. Understanding that you will face challenges we cannot anticipate, we want to unlock your ability to think clearly about them. Consequently, we acknowledge that you will be the ultimate judges of our work here. Knowing that we will not see the fruits of our labour did not hold us back.

The world needs good thinkers. Old ways of thinking need disruption. Possibilities need critical examination. We hope that this text will inspire in you a life of learning and discovery. As we seek to equip you to think well and for yourself, we hope the future will be kinder to you than we can see right now. The world needs people like you who want to be ethical and do good in the world.

Gregory G. Andres
Lecturer and Course Coordinator for Professional and
Business Ethics at the University of Waterloo

A NOTE TO INSTRUCTORS

The structure of this textbook can be understood in a couple of ways. From one perspective, the textbook should be seen as having a two-part structure: the first six chapters develop the conceptual framework and tools needed to function as ethical disruptors, and the remaining five chapters apply the framework and tools to concrete areas where ethical issues arise in business (environmental concerns, advertising, corporate governance, negotiating, and whistle-blowing). The goal is to use the theory to think toward practical solutions and make good decisions in response to ethically relevant issues like these.

From another angle, the textbook should be seen as a tapestry of interwoven threads. The four main threads include:

1. The market-failures approach to business ethics. We develop this in Chapter 1 and apply it throughout the rest of the textbook.
2. Business ethics as applied critical thinking. The key aspects of this are developed in Chapters 3, 6, and 10.
3. Balancing fiduciary duties with corporate social responsibility. We discuss this in Chapters 2, 4, 9, and 11.
4. Training as ethical disruptors. Throughout the textbook, abundant examples give opportunities to apply practical skills and learn from positive business examples.

These two descriptions of the textbook's structure are not intended to be mutually exclusive; the two perspectives overlap and reinforce one another. Understood in this way, it is our hope that we have produced a textbook that will help you motivate and benefit your students by helping them develop both the understanding and the practical skills needed to live as ethical disruptors in whatever part of the world of business they may find themselves.

FROM THE PUBLISHER

Oxford University Press is pleased to introduce *With a Clear Conscience: Business Ethics*, *Decision-Making, and Strategic Thinking*, an inspiring new text that provides students with the theoretical background and practical tools they need to make ethically informed decisions in business and the workplace. Written by scholars with extensive experience teaching business ethics, and classroom-tested by hundreds of students, *With a Clear Conscience* puts forward an approach to ethical decision-making that values collaboration, cooperation, and fairness.

Features

CHAPTER 6
Social Action Problems

By the end of this chapter you should be able to
- Explain what a social contract is.
- Describe some of the tensions between acting in one's self-interest and acting co-operatively.
- Identify ways in which co-operation can be beneficial to a business.
- Use game theory to analyze various social action problems, including the prisoner's dilemma and free-rider problem.
- Compare the concepts of moral hazard and the principal–agent problem.

a ©iStockphoto / Somi Sart

Learning goals provide students with an overview of the concepts that will be covered.

Summary of Ethical Theory

We have considered some of the main perspectives actively discussed by ethical theorists today. So what does this overview add to the market-failures approach to ethics? This chapter's survey of ethical theories provides a basic introduction to the language and concepts of ethics. When explaining to others the ethical reasons for our decisions, it is helpful to be familiar with the terminology of duties, rights, utility, character, care, capabilities, and so forth. The different theories we have covered emphasize different aspects of ethical reality, and so they offer us a plurality of conceptual tools that can be used to deal with various ethical problems we may encounter.

CASE STUDY

Autonomous Vehicles and the Trolley Problem

The trolley problem is one of the most famous problems in contemporary moral philosophy. First put forward by Philippa Foot in 1967,[11] the problem asks you to imagine yourself standing at a control switch with an out-of-control train hurtling down the track. If you do nothing, the train will continue on its current trajectory and kill five unaware workers on the tracks. However, if you flip the switch next to you, it will divert the train onto a different track on which there is only one worker. Is it permissible to kill one person to save five?

Although many people would say the latter option is indeed permissible, the trolley problem is meant to make us pause and consider our intuitions about agency, innocence, and culpability. Is killing someone the same as letting someone die? It is usually assumed to be a maxim that one ought not to kill innocents; does making an exception in this particular case jeopardize that general rule? Whichever course of action you decide to take, should you feel guilty about the bad parts of the outcome that could not be avoided?

There have been many variations of the trolley problem since Foot's original presentation. Some of the more common variants substitute the switch for a person whom you can push into the train's path to derail it. Others make the person on the second track a person dear to you, such as a child. Others introduce a really cool loop-de-loop for the trolley to go on before crashing into the five victims. (On this latter view, letting five people die in an exciting way is better than killing one person in a boring way.) The original and all of these variations ask us to critically interrogate the idea that ethics is a simple math problem. There is a seductive simplicity to the idea that all we need to do is compare the harms (or utility) of the two possible options, and that doing so will clearly tell us what the "right" thing to do is.

For many years these questions were primarily of interest to academics, but in recent years there has been an increasing urgency to do more than ask questions about these types of scenarios. This urgency has been brought on by the development of autonomous (self-driving) cars. Autonomous cars are, as the name might suggest, cars that are equipped with a variety of technological implements that replicate the functions of a driver and drive themselves. The car is able to commute from place to place—the comparatively easy part of the technological problem—and, more importantly, the cars are able to react to the environment around them.

Case studies and in-text examples from Canadian, American, and global businesses show ethical concepts and issues in action.

BACKGROUND

The Monty Hall Problem

Game theory is about making good decisions on the basis of the information you have. The old television game show *Let's Make a Deal* had contestants try to find the big prize that was located behind one of three doors. Contestants would first choose a door having no information about which door held the prize. The host would then open one of the two remaining doors, making sure that this door did not hold the prize, and then offer contestants a chance to change their mind and choose the remaining door, accept a lesser prize without opening the chosen door, or stick with their original choice.

JASON SHOWS UP FOR HIS FIRST DAY OF INTRODUCTION TO GAME THEORY

Game theory tells us that the strategy that maximizes the chance of winning the large prize is to choose the remaining door. Why? The first choice had a one-in-three chance of winning the prize. The other two doors combined had a two-in-three chance of hiding the prize. After learning from the host which door had a zero-in-three chance of containing the prize, you now know that choosing the other closed door offers a two-in-three chance of winning the prize, which is better than the one-in-three chance that your original choice, which was made when you did not have this new information, has of being a winner. (If you had known which door was definitely not the winner before you made your original choice, then the chance of picking a winner is one-in-two.) This puzzle is often called the Monty Hall problem in honour of the first host of this television program.

"Background" boxes bring clarity by providing further information about particular concepts.

CONCEPT CHECK

11.3 Which of the following describes an aspect of whistle-blowing?

a. It keeps quiet matters of unethical or illegal activity.

b. It makes public unethical or illegal matters that an organization has ignored or wishes to keep hidden.

c. It raises concerns about ethical or legal matters to management.

d. It provides legal protection, since all whistles come with a warranty.

"Concept Check" boxes provide students with multiple-choice questions to help them review their understanding of what they have just learned.

	John L.	
	Co-operate	Double-cross
Thomas H. Co-operate	5 , 5	−10 , ⃝10
Double-cross	⃝10 , −10	⃝−1 , ⃝−1

Game Table 8 Responses to the Social Contract—Nash Equilibrium
The lower-right quadrant shows the Nash equilibrium. Choosing the rationally optimal strategies that result in Nash equilibrium; however, that does not mean both players will be better off. In fact, they would be better off collectively if they both chose to co-operate (upper-right quadrant.)

A Primer on Game Theory provides further explanation of how to read game tables and how to use game theory to understand social action problems (Appendix B).

APPENDIX A

Ethical Decision-Making Model Worksheets

The decision-making model set out in Chapter 3 describes a process and suggests some questions to ask as you work toward resolving an ethical issue. However, it does not tell you how to weigh the competing criteria, obligations, and constraints as you work toward a decision. The following worksheets are designed to help you capture the information you need as you work through the decision-making process. Please note that Step 2 has two worksheets.

Step 1: Identify Relevant Facts

Set out the factual statements that describe the case. (Add or remove rows as needed. Put a checkmark in the relevant box when the answer is "yes.")

Factual statement	Morally relevant? (yes/no)	Prudentially relevant? (yes/no)
	☐	☐
	☐	☐
	☐	☐
	☐	☐
	☐	☐
	☐	☐
	☐	☐
	☐	☐
	☐	☐
What questions did you ask here?		

Ethical Decision-Making Model Worksheets provide detailed steps and considerations for strategizing ethically informed decisions (Appendix A).

First page excerpt (Chapter 3)

trip us up regardless of how much we try to compensate for them. We need to pay attention to these biases because they will affect our perspective on who the relevant stakeholders are and what significant values we ascribe to them.

Moral Intuition versus Moral Reasoning

Decision making, at least by way of following a model, is deliberative. As Daniel Kahneman points out in *Thinking Fast and Slow*,[3] this deliberative way of thinking is sometimes referred to as *System 2*, or the conscious part of thought that we identify with. In contrast, many of our value judgments are quick and automatic—this is the work of *System 1*, or unconscious thought. Systems 1 and 2 are a convenient way to think about the difference between moral intuition versus moral reasoning.

Much of our ethics-related behaviour is intuitive.[4] We shake our heads at a troubling headline because the conduct it describes goes against a value we hold intuitively. We cheer for the hero who saves a life because we intuit that such an act is virtuous. These "intuitions" (which Kahneman would say are simply acts of recognition[5]) play an important role in our day-to-day lives. When we engage in System-2-style deliberation, however, our intuitions need to turn into reasons.

When we engage in moral reasoning, we should prepare ourselves for the possibility that our moral intuitions will plausibly need revision, in much the same way that our subconscious first impression of someone might need revision when we find out new information about them. Our moral intuitions or values, while important and in many cases worth defending, are often not justified in the way we need them to be if we are going to assert that they should take priority over competing values. Consequently, part of ethical decision making is

deliberative decision making
Conscious, reflective mental processing of factors relevant to choice and action. Kahneman refers to this as System 2 thinking.

moral intuition
A persistent and powerful moral belief possessed by a person immediately, without being consciously justified in terms of other reasons or factors. Kahneman calls intuitive thinking of this sort System 1 thinking.

SYSTEM 1
Intuition and instinct

95%

Unconscious
Fast
Associative
Automatic pilot

SYSTEM 2
Rational Thinking

5%

Takes effort
Slow
Logical
Lazy
Indecisive

FIGURE 3.3 **System 1 and 2.** System 1 represents our intuitions and quick assessments. System 2 represents a more deliberate process that engages our logical and rational thinking. System 1 is useful for running away from big cats and avoiding being hit by buses. System 2 is useful when we write essays or when we need to think our way through a tough problem.
Source: Daniel Kahneman, *Thinking Fast and Slow* (London: UK: Penguin, 2012); illustration of head @Blackphoto / Eugene Volter

---

Supportive pedagogy also includes a running glossary, chapter summaries, end-of-chapter discussion and review questions, and lists of further readings to enhance understanding and support further study.

Second page excerpt (Chapter 10)

protected from further distribution, or they are dropped from consideration in favour of a student who will give access to their Facebook profile. It is difficult for someone to prove to a judge or jury that a job was not offered because they did not accede to an illegal request during the interview, and trying to prove this takes more money for lawyers than a student can afford. There is no accessible legal recourse for the students who are otherwise qualified for the job but were not considered because they defended their own privacy rights.

Each student being interviewed has to make a strategic choice about how they are going to proceed, and they will proceed on the basis of how much they value their privacy and how much illegal activity they will allow the interviewer to get away with. This means the motivations for choosing how to proceed will vary from person to person. When understood as a prisoner's dilemma, this particular game has a single Nash equilibrium: every student reveals their Facebook profile to the interviewer. But this strategy is sub-optimal given that it comes at a personal cost of privacy. (As an exercise, construct the game table yourself.)

Some employers have tried less direct, more secretive ways to see candidates' Facebook profiles rather than ask outright for access to them. Jaganathan was a co-op student on a work term, and Wei was his manager. (Names have been changed to protect the parties' identities.) Wei discovered that Jaganathan's friend Paulo had applied to a co-op job for the following work term. Wei asked Jaganathan if he and Paulo were friends on Facebook. Jaganathan replied that they were. Wei then asked Jaganathan to add him as a friend so he could see Paulo's activity before deciding to offer him an interview. Jaganathan knew that he could not be readily fired for denying Wei's request. There was no fruitful negotiation to be had, since Jaganathan had a moral obligation toward Paulo to protect his information. Jaganathan asked for time to think things over. He went home and acted on his BATNA: he deleted his Facebook account.

Nash equilibrium
The best outcome a player can hope for, given the choices available to the other player(s).

See Appendix II for more on the Nash equilibrium.

For Discussion and Review

1. Has anyone tried to "game" you like the students in the opening example tried to "game" their professor (see page 205)? If so, how did you respond? Now that you have learned some things about strategy, would you respond differently? Explain how your strategy could counter your interlocutor's move.
2. Zero-sum thinking seems to be popular in the business world. What explains this phenomenon?
3. What might happen if each party in a negotiation comes to the table with both fixed-pie and zero-sum thinking? As a disinterested third party charged with ensuring a negotiated outcome occurs, what advice might you be able to give the two parties, and why would you give it?
4. How are arms-race scenarios related to moral hazard (see Chapter 6)? Explain using an example.
5. Have you or someone you know ever been able to use integrative bargaining? If so, how successful was the strategy?
6. Is any negotiation strategy inherently more ethical than others? Explain your answer.
7. Explain in your own words why it is important to have a BATNA in any negotiation.
8. Construct the game table for Facebook disclosure where the students value privacy over being considered for the position (see pages 227–8). What is the Nash equilibrium under these conditions? How is this situation similar to the example in the chapter regarding the students who all earned full marks by not writing the final exam (see pages 215–17)?

Summing Up

We must resist the temptation to think that our ethical perspectives are always right and that others must bend their will to ours. Progress in the public sphere is made through co-operation and collaborative decision making. This decision-making process will invariably involve negotiations. The principles behind successful negotiations are simple. But that does not mean that negotiations will be easy, especially when ethical conceptions of what makes an action right or wrong are brought into the mix.

In this chapter, you have seen several strategies and techniques for keeping negotiations moving forward despite obstacles. You have also seen that not all negotiations have successful endings. Some ethical disputes, for instance, are without resolution and require a more confrontational approach. Whistle-blowing, which we consider in the next chapter, is one such confrontational approach.

Further Reading

Alfredson, Tanya, and Azeta Cungu. "Negotiation Theory and Practice: A Review of the Literature." *EASYPol* module 179. Food and Agriculture Organization of the United Nations, 2008. http://www.fao.org/docs/up/easypol/550/4-5_Negotiation_background_paper_179EN.pdf.

Bazerman, Max H., and Margaret A. Neale. *Negotiating Rationally*. New York: Free Press, 1992.

Dietmeyer, Brian J., and Rob Kaplan. *Strategic Negotiation: A Breakthrough Process for Effective Business Negotiation*. Chicago: Dearborn Trade, 2004.

Dixit, Avinash K., and Barry J. Nalebuff. *The Art of Strategy: A Game Theorist's Guide to Success in Business and Life*. New York: Norton, 2008.

Fisher, Roger, William Ury, and Robert Patton. *Getting to Yes: Negotiating Agreement without Giving In*. Rev. edn. New York: Penguin, 2011.

With a Clear Conscience is accompanied by a range of supplementary online resources designed to enhance and complete the learning and teaching experiences. These resources are available at: **www.oup/he/Andres.com**

For Instructors

- An **Instructor's Manual** provides chapter overviews, learning objectives, key concepts, discussion and debate ideas, class activities and assignments, lecture outlines, suggested lecture topics, lists of further readings, and recommended videos and websites.
- **PowerPoint slides** summarize key points from each chapter and may be edited to suit instructors' needs.
- An Image Bank provides all images from the text (photos, figures, tables).
- A Test Bank provides multiple-choice, true-or-false, and short-answer questions for each chapter.

For Students

- Links to online video demonstrations of how to read game tables provide students with further explanation of game theory.

www.oup/he/Andres.com

INTRODUCTION
What This Text Is About

Insofar as our actions affect the well-being of another person, ethics has something to say. We are not islands. What we do in the public sphere will affect others, and when our decisions affect others, we must engage in ethical considerations before we act. Now the cynic will declare that they cannot afford to be ethical, because if they are, they will be poor for the rest of their lives. But this attitude is perpetuated by a fundamental confusion about the demands of ethics, the nature of business, and what it means to be a professional. The overarching takeaway of this book is that it is possible to make money—a lot of money—and still be ethical while doing it. You do not need to violate the code of ethics of your profession in order to succeed. You do not need to engage in unscrupulous business practices in order to compete. And you do not need to run roughshod over the environment in the pursuit of profit. You can succeed in life without sacrificing your ethical principles.

In this book, we argue for the claim that moral integrity and success in business go together in three ways. We begin in Chapter 1 by explaining Joseph Heath's market-failures approach to business ethics. According to this approach, businesses operating in a market economy should be interested in promoting the healthy functioning of the markets that make their business possible.

norms
General social rules that we are expected to follow. These rules tell us what kind of behaviours are or are not acceptable.

This is a "don't bite the hand that feeds you" sort of argument, and it implies that businesses should respect norms that help ensure the efficiency of the market system.

As it turns out, by respecting these market norms, businesses also end up respecting many important ethical norms as well. By aligning their activities with standards that promote the system supporting them, businesses will also often end up doing things that are ethically sound. In other words, we argue that market norms and ethical norms intersect in important ways.

Following pro-market norms, however, will not ensure that your business practice is always ethical. This brings us to our second key point: business and ethics go together because business depends on society and is accountable to social norms beyond norms of market efficiency. Market efficiency is a good thing, but it is not the only thing of value. Business exists because it serves the interests of society. Among the most central norms of liberal democratic societies are the ethical norms of justice, equality, and respect for individual rights; we take up the moral theories behind these in Chapter 2. Given the implicit social contract that exists between any given business and the society in which it functions, businesses ought to strive to ensure that they act in accordance with the central values of that society. This means that businesses, if they are sensitive to the reality of the social context in which they exist and operate, will act in ways that promote justice and equity and respect the rights of those who have a stake in their operations. Chapter 3 provides an ethical decision-making model that requires considering both the ethical norms of society and the prudential needs of business. It also includes a discussion of biases that can interfere with making good decisions, and considers the inevitable conflict of values and ethical priorities of those affected by those decisions.

The next six chapters explore various aspects of these norms and needs. Chapter 4 addresses the responsibilities that corporations have toward society, while Chapter 5 talks about fairness, justice, and discrimination and how they connect to business. In Chapter 6 we provide a formal explanation from game theory of some particular social problems that arise when each individual pursues their (usually) rational self-interest. These kinds of problems show up in activities that affect the environment (Chapter 7), influence consumer decisions (Chapter 8), and inform the principles of sound corporate governance (Chapter 9). The next two chapters bring all of this together. Chapter 10 looks at how to negotiate in a way that gets you (most of) what you want through the ethical application of strategies. In Chapter 11 we explore some of the problems of addressing moral and legal transgressions in the workplace through codes of ethics and whistle-blowing. The final chapter (Chapter 12) reminds readers of the highlights of the learning journey they have just completed.

social action problems
Situations in which everyone following their individual self-interest results in everyone being worse off than they would have been had everyone co-operated. Also known as collective action problems.

A third key point we make in this book is that business and ethics are compatible. We do this by analyzing business transactions as games, or strategic interactions. There is a particular set of problems in game theory that are called social action problems (or collective action problems)—situations in which following our individual self-interest makes us all worse off than we could have been if we had learned to co-operate. In Chapter 6 we introduce the concepts from game theory that explain how these problems arise, and in Chapter 10 we combine them with concepts and techniques from negotiation theory to help our readers think creatively about how to reach mutually beneficial situations in the business world. (Appendix B provides a primer for those who want to learn more about how game theory works.) Very often, co-operation is better for everyone and leads to increased prosperity for businesses as well as for individuals. But this is another way of saying that ethics gels nicely with success in business.

BACKGROUND

Can a Social Action Problem Be Beneficial?

Social action problems are pernicious problems, and we do well to avoid them. There is one exception, though: competition on the free market. When two businesses are forced to compete over price and product, they do what they can do to bring their respective products to market in a less expensive way. Businesses do what is in their self-interest (they attempt to maximize profit), and they are worse off for it (their profit margins shrink). This is one of the few socially sanctioned social action problems. Businesses are worse off when they are forced to compete, but society benefits by receiving a less expensive product produced more efficiently.

Features of This Book

We do not make only abstract arguments in this book; we also try to show, from real-life examples, how ethical businesses flourish, and how ignoring the demands of ethics has serious effects on a business's bottom line. To this end, we provide extensive in-text examples and case studies drawn from Canadian, American, and global business.

We also present an ethical decision-making model in Chapter 3 (with worksheets in Appendix A) that lays out steps to guide readers through their own process of ethical reflection, whether that reflection concerns cases involving others or decisions they themselves will have to make in the business world.

A good business ethics course should help students apply critical-thinking skills to business activity. To this end, in addition to the game-theory and decision-making skills, we also consider the way our ethical reasoning works and some of the biases that hinder good ethical reasoning.

Each chapter also supports student learning by providing learning goals at the start of each chapter, review questions throughout (called Concept Check), and Background boxes to give further information about particular concepts. Glossary terms are defined in the margins and compiled at the back of the book. End-of-chapter questions encourage discussion, and a list of further readings offer more learning opportunities.

Being an Ethical Disruptor

Having good ethical reasoning and being able to make good ethical decisions are abilities that matter. For one thing, employers value them. Put yourself in the shoes of an employer and ask yourself, Whom would you rather have work for you: someone who is trustworthy and makes prudentially and ethically defensible decisions, or someone who consistently makes poor decisions? The former sort of person will clearly be an asset, whereas the latter will be a liability. Your ability to make good ethical decisions may be what differentiates you in the workplace.

People studying business today are encouraged to look for ways to be disruptive innovators, that is, to find ways of introducing game-changing new technologies or approaches that shake up markets and open new possibilities for growth. The University of Waterloo, where some of the authors study and teach, prides itself on having been ranked by Maclean's magazine as Canada's most innovative university for the past two decades.[1] The buzzword-laden web page describing global entrepreneurship and disruptive innovation at the University of Waterloo states that "[i]n a global economy driven by disruption, Canada's future economic success relies on our collective ability to push the boundaries of discovery to create new knowledge, drive innovation and prepare emerging talent to be leaders of the future."[2] On the face of things, disruption is morally problematic, since any time a new technology or way of doing things reshapes the status quo in a given market, companies using older techniques now rendered obsolete by the disruptive innovation will be harmed: shareholders in the older companies will lose money, workers will face layoffs, etc. At the same time, under some interpretations of the fiduciary duty owed to investors, market disruption may be the only way to produce the value that those investors seek. Can disruptive innovation be an ethical goal for entrepreneurs to pursue? Is it possible for us to be ethical disruptors? In this text, we argue for a resounding "yes" to these questions. Developing the set of skills described and exemplified in this book will help aspiring entrepreneurs to become ethical disruptors, that is, people who can combine disruptive innovation with enough ethical savvy to be effective leaders in ethical business practice.

A Note on Game Theory and Philosophy

We use game theory frequently in this textbook. Chapter 6—the chapter on social action problems—is riddled with game tables. Chapter 10—the chapter on strategic negotiations—is also peppered with ideas rooted in game theory. Although the subject of game theory is fun to study in and of itself, we expose students to ideas from game theory because game theory is a powerful conceptual tool and is used across academic disciplines. Mathematicians, computer scientists, engineers, social scientists, economists, and philosophers all have an interest in game theory as a formal tool of analysis. We must not shy away from using formal tools if using them brings rigour to our thinking. One of the things philosophy is good at is teaching us how to think about a question. Whether we are asking What is truth? or What is justice? or Can human consciousness be downloaded onto a flash drive? philosophy encourages us to acknowledge our assumptions, challenge our established beliefs, and reflect on how we arrived at our conclusions. There is not just one way to think about a philosophical issue. To think otherwise is to cut ourselves off artificially from a rich intellectual life that we can participate in with others.

There are many ways to approach philosophical questions. Game theory is just one of those ways. In this regard the authors are pluralists about philosophical methods. This does not mean, however, that we need to accept sloppy thinking. We can be pluralists about philosophical methods and still demand rigour in our thinking. All too often we run across the misguided attitude that philosophy is nothing more than expressing one's opinions, and that all opinions are—roughly—equally good. Opinions that are not backed up with facts when facts are needed are not good opinions. Opinions that rest on questionable inferences or fallacious reasoning are not good opinions. Opinions born of biases are not

Appendix B is a primer on game theory. It will help you understand how to read and analyze all the games (that is, strategic interactions) presented in this text.

BACKGROUND

The Monty Hall Problem

Game theory is about making good decisions on the basis of the information you have. The old television game show *Let's Make a Deal* had contestants try to find the big prize that was located behind one of three doors. Contestants would first choose a door having no information about which door held the prize. The host would then open one of the two remaining doors, making sure that this door did not hold the prize, and then offer contestants a chance to change their mind and choose the remaining door, accept a lesser prize without opening the chosen door, or stick with their original choice.

JASON SHOWS UP FOR HIS FIRST DAY OF INTRODUCTION TO GAME THEORY

Game theory tells us that the strategy that maximizes the chance of winning the large prize is to choose the remaining door. Why? The first choice had a one-in-three chance of winning the prize. The other two doors combined had a two-in-three chance of hiding the prize. After learning from the host which door had a zero-in-three chance of containing the prize, you now know that choosing the other closed door offers a two-in-three chance of winning the prize, which is better than the one-in-three chance that your original choice, which was made when you did not have this new information, has of being a winner. (If you had known which door was definitely not the winner before you made your original choice, then the chance of picking a winner is one-in-two.) This puzzle is often called the Monty Hall problem in honour of the first host of this television program.

good opinions. To be good critical thinkers and to make good ethical decisions, we must be willing to do the work needed to bring rigour to our thinking. The tools of game theory allow us to do exactly that.

Our Challenge to the Reader

It has been our experience in the classroom that students want successful careers, want to make money, and want to remain true to their ethical convictions in those pursuits. For the most part, we do not wake up in the morning resolving to intentionally harm others in the pursuit of career success and financial stability. Most of us want to do good in the world, or at least be good people. Making good ethical decisions is not just a matter of common sense, for the simple reason that there is no such thing as common sense. Saying something is "common sense" is just shorthand for saying that we know about it and that we expect others to know about it too.

BACKGROUND

Common Sense

The phrase "common sense" has its origins in early philosophy of mind and perception, where it referred to the way in which each of our five main senses—physical modes of experiencing the world—were thought to provide a full representation of what we perceive by combining all of the sensory data and processing them in common, treating them an integrated whole. A course covering some of the history of philosophy of mind will explain more.

BACKGROUND

Sustaining an Ethical Mindset

MARCO BERTORELLO/AFP via Getty Images

Egan Bernal, the first Colombian to win the Tour de France.

The Tour de France is a 21-day individual and team race that requires leg strength, cardiovascular capacity, endurance, a high tolerance for pain, a knowledge of racing strategy, and a strong support team. It takes years of training to qualify for the race, never mind win it. Similarly, ethics is not something you can master through a one-semester course. Sustaining an ethical mindset in a competitive business environment takes training and practice to develop moral strength, intellectual capacity, endurance, a high tolerance for ambiguity and conflict, and knowledge and understanding of business strategy. A commitment to excellent business and moral practices also requires a strong support team.

Consider Bob, who wants to take up professional cycling, and asks Egan Bernal—the winner of the 2019 Tour de France—for some pointers. We would rightly question Bernal's response if he simply told Bob, "Cycling is just common sense." It is a disingenuous answer. Knowing how to ride in the peloton, knowing how and when to attack, and knowing how to ride down a mountain at 70 kilometres per hour on roads with switchbacks is not just a matter of common sense. One does not simply buy a bike and enter the Tour de France. Learning how to race requires thousands of hours in the saddle and tens of thousands of kilometres ridden each summer.

Now consider ethical decision making. Each one of us has a conception of the good life. Each one of us has an idea of what makes an action right or wrong, praiseworthy or blameworthy. And we do not always agree on these matters. This might be because our backgrounds are different, our beliefs are different, or our goals are different. We live in a pluralistic society where different people value different things, and sometimes these values do not mesh. This does not mean that everyone is right, or that one person is right and everyone who disagrees with that person is wrong. What it does mean is that we must take care to examine our values and beliefs and be willing to listen to others who disagree with us.

Ethical decision making is a skill that can be learned and improved upon. Ethics matters. You can be ethical, make a difference in the world, and still derive a financial gain from business as an employee, proprietor, producer, director, or investor. The rest of this textbook will show you how to do all three.

CHAPTER 1
Business Ethics and Ethical Business

By the end of this chapter you should be able to

- Describe how business and ethics relate to each other, and why business ethics matters.

- Provide reasons why ethical relativism is a problematic view.

- List Heath's ten commandments of business ethics.

- Explain the *market-failures approach* to ethics and the concept of *ethical disruption*.

BACKGROUND

Ethics and Morality

In this text, we take the words *ethics* and *morality* (and the related *ethical* and *moral*) to be functionally equivalent. In other words, when we describe an action as ethical or as moral, we mean basically the same thing. Some scholars feel the need to distinguish between ethics and morality, usually by making ethics a broader, more inclusive discipline, and limiting morality to the study of rules and norms that govern human behaviour within groups. We do not believe such distinctions are practically important, and so we will use the words interchangeably.

The discipline of ethics is the study of what is right and wrong, praiseworthy or blameworthy, permissible or impermissible, in the area of human activity. The study of ethics has a theoretical side and a practical (or applied) side. The theoretical side covers questions like *What makes an action right or wrong, in general?* and *What does a good human life consist of?* and *What basic rights and obligations do we have?* By contrast, **practical ethics** seeks to apply the concepts of theoretical ethics to real-life situations in order to provide guidance to people who might find themselves in such situations. In both cases, ethics tries to answer the question *What should we do?* Theoretical answers to this question try to provide broad, general principles concerning what human beings ought to do, while applied approaches explain what we ought to do in the concrete, specific settings of everyday life.

practical ethics
The branch of ethics that seeks to help people to use ethical concepts to make good decisions and act well in real-life situations. Practical ethics is also called *applied ethics*.

Business ethics belongs to the field of applied ethics. For this reason, the text you are now reading focuses on giving practical guidance in using ethical concepts and methods to help you work through ethical problems and situations you will likely face one day (if you have not faced them already). However, because practical ethics involves applying concepts and methods developed in the theoretical side of the discipline, we must pay some attention to theoretical ethics. We do this in Chapter 2. The present chapter covers some preliminary questions about the nature of ethics and its relation to the world of business.

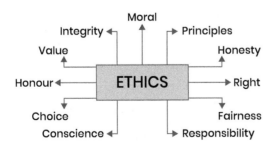

FIGURE 1.1 What ethics is about. Ethics has many dimensions; navigating the competing demands of ethics takes careful reasoning.

Source: David Degrazi, Tom L. Beauchamp, "An Ethical Framework for Animal Research," Newsday.com, 30 September 2019, https://www.newsday.com/opinion/commentary/ethical-animal-research-epa-1.37023066

CONCEPT CHECK

1.1 What do theoretical and practical ethics have in common?

a. They both explain what we ought to do.

b. Neither explains what we ought to do.

c. They both explain what I should expect someone else to do.

d. They both explain what it is legal to do.

A Modest Approach to Ethics

Ethics Is More Than Opinion

We said that ethics is the study of what is right and wrong. But according to a commonly held view, what is right and wrong can differ from person to person. Something may be right for me, given my beliefs and values and upbringing, but the same thing might be wrong for you, because your beliefs and values and upbringing differ from mine. How then can we study right and wrong as an **objective discipline**?

If the "facts" of ethics are potentially different for every person, how can one person (for example, a professor in ethics) teach others anything about ethics? In response to this view, we must start by acknowledging the obvious point that different people can and do have different opinions about what is right and wrong. But we still need to ask the further question of whether that is all we can say about ethics. In other words, is ethics ultimately just a matter of subjective, personal opinion, or is there something more to it?

Ethical Relativism

In the twentieth century, cultural anthropologists who studied different human populations pointed out ways in which cultures did things differently. For example, the Western world generally views marriage as something that holds between two partners and is based on romantic attraction, while some cultures practice polygamy (multiple wives) or polyandry (multiple husbands), and in many cultures marriages are arranged. The roles of men and women in the home and in society differ from place to place. A practice of gift-giving accepted as normal in one culture may be condemned as bribery in another. The religious ceremonies of some cultures have included drinking the blood of bears, slicing open one's head while on parade, and mixing the remains of the dead with banana soup and drinking it. These practices may seem morally wrong to those who belong to other cultures. But for the people who belong to the cultures that practise these things, they seem to be the right thing to do. Indeed, people who live there may even feel a strong sense of obligation to do them.

The fact of ethical disagreement among cultures has led some scholars to conclude that ethics depends entirely on the norms of the culture you belong to. This is a form of **ethical relativism**. According to ethical relativism, if you want to know what is right or wrong for a given individual—Sam, for instance—then you need to find out what culture Sam belongs to. If Sam belongs to culture *A*, then the cultural norms and values of *A* determine what is right

objective discipline
An objective discipline studies objective facts—that is, facts that do not depend on human perception or opinion.

ethical relativism
The view that the ethical beliefs and values people hold determine what is ethically right or wrong for those people. This is sometimes called *moral relativism*.

BACKGROUND

Kinds of Ethical Relativism

Ethical relativism (or *moral relativism*) is the view that the ethical beliefs and values cultures hold determine what is ethically right or wrong for those people. This view is a particular form of ethical relativism called *cultural relativism*.

There is another, related form of ethical relativism called *subjective relativism*, which claims that what is called ethically right or wrong is not relative to the culture you are part of, but to each individual's personal beliefs and values. Subjective relativism suffers from all the problems of cultural relativism discussed later in this section, but to an even greater extent. Subjective relativism also has fewer reasons in its favour than cultural relativism has. For these reasons, we do not take subjective relativism seriously in this text, and when we refer to ethical relativism we are referring to moral norms of different cultures.

or wrong for Sam. If endocannibalism is highly valued and seen as a mandatory practice for members of culture A, then endocannibalism is right for them, and that is all we can say. There is no room for debate.

If the moral rules governing another culture, culture *B*, reject endocannibalism, then it would be wrong for the members of culture *B* to practise endocannibalism. And again, that is all we can say about it. But now, what if we consider endocannibalism in itself, removed from the context of any particular culture? Is endocannibalism right or wrong *in itself*? There is no way for the ethical relativist to answer this question. In fact, the question does not even make sense to the ethical relativist. There is no *general* right or wrong, only right or wrong *relative* to the norms and values of a particular culture.

CONCEPT CHECK

1.2 What is the central idea of ethical relativism?

a. What is right or wrong is relative to a particular group or culture.

b. What is right or wrong is relative to what you want to happen.

c. What is right or wrong is relative to the problem at hand.

d. What is right or wrong is relative to the power one has.

In Support of Ethical Relativism

Does ethical relativism strike you as a compelling view of ethics? In a moment, we are going to indicate some serious problems with the view. But before doing that, it is worth noting that there are some strong reasons that support ethical relativism. We have already covered

incommensurate
To say that the practices of one culture are incommensurate with those of another culture is to say that the practices of the first culture cannot be measured using the standards or norms of the second culture.

liberalism
A political theory that holds individual liberty as its central value.

conservatism
A political theory that prioritizes the preservation of a certain way of life over individual liberty.

socialism
A political theory that views equality as the fundamentally important value.

Chapter 5 considers the important place of equality for liberal democracies.

self-refuting
A claim is self-refuting if the truth of the claim entails that the claim itself is false. Here is the clearest example: "This sentence is false." If the sentence in quotation marks is true, then it must be false, because it states that it is false. Philosophers call this the *liar sentence*; it leads to the logical problem known as the *liar paradox*.

one such reason: *ethical relativism takes moral disagreement seriously.* Sometimes the distinctive history of a culture's practices, and the interconnection of those practices with other facets of the culture, render it impossible for another culture (with a different history and worldview) to fully understand those practices. So sometimes we have to simply admit that some cultural practices are **incommensurate** with other cultures. In these cases, agreement about what is right and wrong may be impossible. Ethical relativism reflects this sort of scenario quite well.

A second factor that makes ethical relativism compelling is that *ethical relativism reflects a strong valuation of tolerance.* Tolerance has played a central role in the West in holding together societies composed of religiously and culturally diverse populations. The value of tolerance becomes increasingly important in an increasingly global world, where people from different ethnic and religious backgrounds mix together in various spheres of society. The value we place on tolerance explains the strong attraction many of us have to ethical relativism.

A third factor that makes ethical relativism a compelling approach to ethics for many people is that *ethical relativism resonates powerfully with individual liberty,* another core value in modern Western democracies. As with tolerance, the central place of individual liberty in Western political thought derives from a history of revolt against oppressive governance, and against the suppression of difference by the state. **Liberalism** as a political theory contrasts with **conservatism** and **socialism**, both of which minimize the value of individual liberty relative to some other goal.

A society that exalts individual liberty and autonomy requires us to respect each other and to refrain from imposing on others our own conceptions of what is right and wrong, in exchange for their extending the same attitude toward us. Ethical relativism, in urging respect for moral difference, coheres well with these basic values.

Problems with Ethical Relativism

Despite these reasons in favour of it, ethical relativism is an untenable approach to ethics. First, *ethical relativism is a self-refuting position.* An important question to ask the ethical relativist is *Does everyone (or every culture) have an ethical obligation to be an ethical relativist?* The ethical relativist cannot say "yes" to this question. Remember that for the ethical relativist, ethical truth is relative to each culture's beliefs and values. This means that there are no absolute ethical truths or principles. So ethical relativists would contradict themselves if they said that every person or every culture has an obligation to be an ethical relativist. The only way we can say that everyone has an ethical obligation to be an ethical relativist is if there is at least one absolute ethical truth, namely that everyone should be an ethical relativist. Ethical relativists cannot say this since they deny the existence of absolute ethical truths. But can ethical relativists say "no" to the question *Does everyone have an ethical obligation to be an ethical relativist?* No, they cannot. If a culture rejected ethical relativism, then the relativist would need to admit that for that culture, ethical relativism is false. So if there are two cultures, one of which accepts ethical relativism, and the other of which rejects ethical relativism, then the ethical relativist has to say that ethical relativism is both true and false. But the ethical relativist wants to say that ethical relativism is true without condition, not that it is both true and false. The conclusion of this first objection is that, no matter how the ethical relativist answers the question *Does everyone have an ethical obligation to be an ethical relativist?* ethical relativism turns out to be self-defeating.

The next objection gets at the problem with ethical relativism in a more concrete way. *Ethical relativism contradicts our strong ethical intuitions.* In the not-too-distant past, slavery was permitted in North America. Today, we believe slavery to be one of the most abhorrent human practices. Was slavery morally right for those living in the southern United States of America in the 1800s because they believed it was right? Is the only reason slavery is wrong for us today that we happen now to think it is wrong? The classic example of the atrocities committed by Nazi Germany during World War II is also relevant here. Was it right for the Nazis to round up Jews, Communists, gays, and others they found undesirable, force them into concentration camps, and kill millions of them? The Nazis believed, based on a morally bankrupt ideology, that it was right to do these things. But they were wrong! Millions of persons were killed in the Holocaust,[1] and millions of persons were forcibly taken from their homelands in Africa, sold, and abused as slaves.[2] We believe strongly that slavery and the Holocaust were morally wrong because of the grievous harm done to the victims and the promotion of hatred against particular groups of people. Yet ethical relativism would require us to say that these are only wrong *for us.* If cultural attitudes were to change, these things could become morally right again under ethical relativism, and the victims' claims of being done a moral harm would be dismissed as irrelevant. (Indeed, if ethical relativism makes these practices acceptable, there would be no talk of victims at all.) These are compelling reasons to reject ethical relativism.

The third major problem facing ethical relativism is that *ethical relativism gives up on the idea of normative ethics.* Normative ethics seeks to establish what makes something ethically right or wrong. For example, a normative theory like virtue ethics will focus on the character of a person and will tell us how a virtuous person should act.

The discipline of normative (or *prescriptive*) ethics differs from **descriptive ethics**, which simply *describes* how ethical norms differ between cultures and people groups. Descriptive ethics tells us what people *in fact* believe about what is right and wrong; normative ethics focuses instead on what people *should* believe about what is right and wrong. We engage in normative ethics because we think it is meaningful to ask what should or should not be done in various situations. We want guidance in such matters; we want to learn whether a certain

Slavery and the Holocaust are two examples of many grave injustices against particular groups of persons. The examples are meant to be illustrative of these kinds of moral wrongs, not a comprehensive list of them.

normative ethics
The study of what makes something ethically right (praiseworthy) or wrong (blameworthy). A *normative ethical theory* will tell us how we should act.

descriptive ethics
The study of what people actually believe concerning what is ethically right or wrong.

BACKGROUND

Normative versus Descriptive

The adjectives *normative* and *descriptive* describe claims, theories, and approaches to the study of particular disciplines. A normative claim is a statement about what should be the case, while a descriptive claim is about what actually is the case. A normative theory is built on normative claims; a descriptive theory is built on descriptive claims.

Normative ethics is the study of what makes something ethically right (praiseworthy) or wrong (blameworthy) and gives rise to normative ethical theories. *Descriptive ethics* is the study of what people believe is ethically right or wrong, and gives rise to descriptive ethical theories. Empirical research provides us with descriptive claims, but not normative ones.

action is the right thing to do or not. But if what makes something right or wrong is simply the fact that some culture holds it to be right or wrong, then all we really have is descriptive ethics: all we can say is that one culture believes action X is wrong, while perhaps another culture believes it is right. In other words, ethical relativism entails that there is really no such thing as normative ethics. Insofar as human beings find it deeply important to ask the questions of normative ethics (as we do in this text), ethical relativism is a non-starter.

CONCEPT CHECK

1.3 What does it mean to say that a claim is self-refuting?

a. The claim is always true.

b. The claim is also self-evident.

c. The claim leads to a contradiction.

d. The claim refutes any moral argument.

1.4 What is the difference between a normative theory and a descriptive theory?

a. A descriptive theory is relevant to ethical reasoning; a normative theory is relevant only to empirical reasoning.

b. A descriptive theory describes what I want to see happen; a normative theory describes what I think is normal.

c. A normative theory is about the way the world actually is; a descriptive theory is about what should be the case.

d. A normative theory is about what should be the case; a descriptive theory is about the way the world is.

A Middle Way: Humble Objectivism

If what we have just argued is correct, then we should not want to be ethical relativists, since ethical relativism is a highly problematic position. But we have also seen that strong reasons motivate people to accept ethical relativism. Ethical relativism resonates nicely with the core liberal democratic values of individual liberty and tolerance, and it attempts to make sense of the fact of moral disagreement. Can we find an approach to ethics that does those things as well as ethical relativism does, but without suffering from the problems that afflict ethical relativism?

Consider **ethical objectivism**. Ethical objectivism holds that right and wrong do not depend on what any particular culture happens to believe. Instead, there are moral facts that exist independently of the norms and values adopted by this or that culture, and these moral facts can be discovered in a way analogous to the discovery of empirical facts.

ethical objectivism
The view that what is ethically right or wrong is an objective matter, rather than determined subjectively on the basis of what people believe is ethically right or wrong.

BACKGROUND

Ethical Facts

Ethical objectivism holds that there are ethical facts. But it is difficult to say exactly what sort of fact makes true ethical claims like, "Nola has a moral obligation to keep her promise." To say what sort of fact makes that claim true, we would have to say what sorts of things *obligations*, *rights*, and so forth are. We might then also want to ask how we come to know the moral facts. Such questions are interesting and important, but they are beyond the goals of the present text.

As a result, a culture's beliefs about what is morally good or bad may be mistaken; we can get it wrong. On the one hand, this immediately helps us to improve on ethical relativism, since it explains our intuitions about slavery and Nazism. The norms supporting slavery in nineteenth-century southern United States of America were wrong. Slavery was not right for them, even though they believed it to be right. Instead, the norms of that society were out of touch with moral reality. But on the other hand, the claim that a culture's norms and values can be mistaken seems to put us in dangerous territory. The spectres of intolerance and bigotry raise their heads as we contemplate one culture imposing its own norms and values on another culture. People of European descent living in the Americas have a devastating history of cultural and **moral imperialism**; one need only think of the abuses of the residential schools perpetrated by the Canadian government in the name of educating Indigenous Peoples.

You can be an ethical objectivist without becoming a moral imperialist by being humble. To be humble is to have a clear, sober, realistic view of your own importance. It is the opposite of pride or arrogance, both of which involve thinking of yourself as more important than you really are. A humble person does not place themself above others in importance (and does not place themself under others in importance). It is entirely possible to believe that there are objective moral facts to be discovered, while at the same time realizing that every person (including yourself) is **fallible** and limited in their ability to know those facts. Let us call this position **humble objectivism**.

The humble objectivist's awareness of their own imperfect knowledge and limited perspective helps them to have an attitude of respect toward those with values, opinions, and perspectives that differ from their own. They do not assume that they already possess the whole truth, so they try to listen carefully to others in order to learn from them rather than trying to impose their own views on others.

The meme of several blindfolded people touching different parts of an elephant can help explain humble objectivism's approach to ethics. The idea is that each person's perspective is limited; as a result each person's knowledge of the elephant is partial. To the person touching the elephant's tusk, an elephant is like a spear. The one touching the elephant's ear describes the elephant as a big flapping fan. The person touching the tail views an elephant as some sort of brush, while the one touching its leg regards it as a sort of tree trunk. One might conclude

An excellent online resource to learn about the impact of Canadian residential schools is the National Centre for Truth and Reconciliation website.[3]

moral imperialism
The desire to hold other people—who hold moral views different from yours—accountable to your own moral standard (or to the standard of your group); the refusal to acknowledge the legitimacy of moral views when they differ from your own.

fallible
A fallible person is one who is capable of making a mistake. If we are being realistic, we will see that this includes all of us. For this reason, we should be humble.

humble objectivism
The view that there are facts about what is right or wrong, but that we are as likely as anyone else to be mistaken about these facts. In this way, humble objectivism differs from both ethical relativism and from moral imperialism.

An example of how different people can arrive at different perspectives of the same animal. No one perspective is absolutely correct, but there is some truth in each one.

from all this that knowledge of the elephant itself is hopeless, or even that there really is no elephant at all, but only the fragmented and incommensurable perceptions of different people. Or, one could urge the different people to talk to each other! If each of these individuals recognized the limitations of their own perspective, they might engage respectfully in dialogue with one another, and learn from each other's differing views of the elephant. If they talked to each other long enough, maybe they could even develop a fairly accurate view of the elephant as a whole.

If we take the elephant to represent moral reality, we can draw a lesson about how to approach ethics: different perspectives of moral reality may be limited and partial, and yet legitimate in their own way. Hence, the appropriate course of action is not to say, as ethical relativism does, that every perspective is fine on its own and that we do not need to learn from each other. But neither is it correct to act like a moral imperialist and reject the views of others whenever they disagree with our own viewpoint, since our viewpoint is surely still partial and limited. The best approach is to take the legitimacy of our own ethical intuitions seriously while recognizing the partial nature of them, and to assume that the intuitions of others have roughly as good a chance as our own at being legitimate, even when they disagree with our own views.

Humble objectivism does its best to build a complete (and objective) picture, but acknowledges that new information—perhaps from a new observation or insight—will change this picture. Humble objectivism works to provide the best conception we can have based on the information available, but does not claim to offer a complete conception or description.

CONCEPT CHECK

1.5 What can an elephant tell us about morality?

a. What we ought to do depends on at which end of the elephant we find ourselves.

b. Different perspectives of what we ought to do may be limited and partial, yet legitimate in their own way.

c. Different perspectives of what we ought to do are always incompatible with each other.

d. We can always correctly infer what we ought to do from the information available from our perspective.

ethical pluralism
Multiple distinct and potentially incommensurable views of what is ethically right or wrong can be equally warranted, and worthy of respect.

Humble Objectivism and Ethical Pluralism

Humble objectivism is a form of **ethical pluralism**, which starts from recognizing that ethical views differ, but that the merits of these views in a given situation can be discussed so as to come to an agreed view. Ethical relativism, by contrast, simply accepts that people hold views that are all right for each person or culture, and there is nothing more to say. The difference

BACKGROUND

Ethical Persuasion

How can we engage with people with whom we disagree? Charles L. Stevenson, in *Ethics and Language*, discusses the ways we try to persuade one another to agree with us when we have ethical disagreements. *Ethical persuasion* appeals to shared values and facts relevant to those values while sometimes expanding definitions and citing interesting precedents and different authorities.[4]

can be seen most clearly in the fact that pluralism leads to reasoned discussion aimed at agreement, while relativism simply recognizes a situation that does not call for discussion.

Ethics, like regulation and legislation, applies to activities in a shared world. Where we have differences, we need to think about how we act in that shared world without conflict. Driving on the right side of the road is proper and legal in Canada. Driving on the left is proper and legal in Great Britain. There is no shared driving world where these relative differences conflict. If there were a system of shared roads—if, say, Canada and Great Britain were joined by an enormous bridge over the Atlantic Ocean—then agreement would become necessary. Each side would need to explain its views and the advantages to both sides of driving on the right or on the left, and in general appeal to shared interests to come to an agreement. The discussion would appeal to consistency of views, agreed-upon facts, and accepted authorities to figure out what would work best for the whole population of drivers using the interconnected system of roads. Ethical pluralism urges us to go beyond mere toleration of the ideas of others; it urges that we should also engage in dialogue with others to learn and expand our own viewpoint. In particular, we should engage with the ethical traditions that represent humankind's most careful efforts to understand moral reality.

Learning how to engage in this type of dialogue in the context of the workplace is crucial to an organization's success. Different people will have different values. Different people will have different views of what makes an action morally right or wrong. These differences may very well hinder co-operation within the organization, which may very well get in the way of an organization's goals. Co-operation is impossible if people have fallen into an us-versus-them mentality.

In 1979, the platform of Canada's Rhinoceros Party included a staged transition to driving on the left. Only trucks and buses would drive on the left during the first year of the plan.[5]

The Place of Ethics in Business

Some people think the terms *business* and *ethics* somehow contradict one another, making business ethics an impossibility. What are some reasons for thinking that business and ethics do not go together? For one thing, business activity is inherently competitive, whereas our ordinary sense of morality favours co-operation and **altruism**. A manager who allows their company's bottom line to suffer by doing favours for competing firms would quickly be fired. It seems as though, in relation to our competitors at least, doing good business (being profitable or successful) *requires* us to act in our own self-interest, without concern for the way others will be harmed. Since ethics demands that we consider the needs and interests

altruism
A person is altruistic if they care about the well-being of someone else for its own sake, not because of how it benefits the person doing the caring.

Gavin Simms/CBC

An act of altruism. After record-breaking snowfall in the blizzard of January 2020, these community members came together to shovel out a home in St. John's, Newfoundland, after seeing an online post about the family wanting to bring their newborn baby home from the hospital.

profit motive
The desire to increase financial wealth by engaging in economic activity.

shareholder
Someone who has a financial interest in a company through the purchase (and therefore ownership) of shares.

fiduciary duty
A duty of care owed by a trustee to a beneficiary.

social licence
The idea that society permits something (for instance, particular business activities) to take place, and that society has the right to disallow that thing if it sees fit.

We talk further about fiduciary duties in **Chapters 3** and **4**.

of others in our decision making and action, ethics appears to be largely irrelevant in business.

Secondly, in a capitalist economy, business is governed by the **profit motive**. To paraphrase Milton Friedman, *the business of business is to maximize profits.*[6] For this reason, we might think business leaders cannot concern themselves with improving the environment or trying to realize social norms of fairness and equality. These goals would distract business managers from their proper task, namely increasing profits for investors. There seem to be strong reasons, then, to see business as inherently self-interested and unconcerned with the interests of others.

Clearly business managers have obligations to their **shareholders**, and the **fiduciary duty** of a manager to increase profit is a real duty. But maximizing profit is not the only obligation. We argue that the pursuit of profit is consistent with other demands of ethics. So we have to answer two questions: *Why must business honour ethics?* and *How can one be ethical while acting on a profit motive?*

Why Should Businesspeople Want to Be Ethical?

To see why business must respect the demands of ethics, we need to understand the social context that makes business activity possible. Business does not exist in a vacuum; it is embedded within a complex web of social institutions without which it could not exist, so business itself depends on society in a fundamental way. This dependence means that business owes something to society. In exchange for society agreeing to permit business to operate, business must act in ways that are responsible to society. The idea that society grants permission to business to function (and that without this permission, business cannot function) is captured by the expression **social licence**.

Although society does not literally issue licences to business owners, a business can operate only within a society whose institutions allow it to do so. And there are limits to this social licence. When the operation of a business violates the norms of the society in which it is operating, that society may take steps to punish, or even to shut down, the business. This is done through legal and regulatory means. The activities of businesses are necessarily constrained by the norms that govern those societies. The *free* in *free market* is not an unconstrained freedom.

CONCEPT CHECK

1.6 Which of the following best describes the idea of social licence with respect to business?

a. It is a legal document that permits a business to operate.

Continued

b. It is a tacit recognition that business is a function of society, and if a business is no longer good for society, that society can shut it down.

c. It is a type of licence sold by businesses that permits persons to participate in society.

d. Society and business depend on each other for prosperity.

The Social Context of Business Activity

We have provided an initial response to the question of why businesspeople should want to be ethical. To do business ethically is to simply recognize the dependence of business on society and the ability of society to shut down business when it contravenes important social norms. But let us spell out, in a little more detail, the rationale behind the idea of the social licence and the obligations it entails for business.

Business transactions (in most liberal democracies) assume a market system that is embedded in a social and political system. These market transactions rely on things like a monetary system, infrastructure (like roads, railways, telecommunication systems), a fair legal system that ensures contracts are enforceable, and other social goods (like employment insurance, pension plans, and workers' compensation). Society provides these things, and business benefits from them.

Here is a thought experiment that illustrates what we mean. Let us assume that you have just launched a start-up that makes virtual reality goggles. However, you are in a jurisdiction that does not have a monetary system. There is no money. How would you do business in this context? An obvious fallback system would be bartering, but this type of system is unwieldy at best. How many chickens and pounds of honey could you get for selling a pair of your goggles to the farmer down the road—a road that you had to build so that you could get to the farmer to sell your goggles?

The ridiculousness of this thought experiment simply highlights the social and political systems we take for granted when we engage in market transactions. No contemporary North American business could function without the **market economies** that are in place in the countries where they do business. This means that businesses, and the people who run them and benefit from them, stand in a relation of debt to society as a whole—they owe the possibility of their activity, and the benefits they derive from that activity, to the societies in which they operate. Without a society's legitimation of the market economy, the context businesses need to operate simply would not exist, so there would be no business as we know it today. But society should only permit the market economy if doing so benefits society more than some other economic arrangement: a **planned economy**, for instance. In other words, the existence of the market economy requires a social justification. If the existence of the market economy as a whole depends on being justifiable to society, then the businesses whose operations are made possible by that economic institution also depend on society to justify their existence.

So how does society benefit by allowing businesses to compete in an open market economy? The main social benefit of such a system comes from competition itself, which the open market makes possible. Competition means that different providers of goods or services seek to outdo each other and achieve a greater market share. This puts pressure on individual

market economy
An economic system in which the competitive interactions of businesses control prices and distribution of goods within society.

planned economy
An economic system in which a centralized government dictates prices and the production and distribution of goods within society. This type of economy is also known as a *state-owned* or a *command economy.*

efficiency
An activity or a system is efficient if it attains its goal(s) without wasting time or resources.

businesses to operate efficiently to ensure the quality of their products, and to set their prices at a reasonable level.

All of these factors promote the good of society. The members of society benefit directly from having needed goods and services available at affordable prices and from having high-quality products. The benefit of efficient business operations is less direct; it means that the resources needed to generate products (both material and human resources) will not be wasted, which means those resources are available to society for other purposes. These benefits of competition between distinct companies within a market provide (at least an important part of) the social justification of the free-market economy. If the market economy proves not to yield these benefits, that would call into question whether society should continue to allow it to operate, or should move instead to some other economic arrangement. All of this goes to show that capitalism, or the ability of businesses to generate profit for investors, stands in need of a sufficient social justification. Those running businesses and generating profit within the social context described above, if they are being realistic, will recognize and acknowledge their indebtedness to society's allowance of the free-market conditions that make their activities possible.

Later we will describe more specifically what businesses owe to society. But first, here is another angle on the same idea we have been developing. Businesspeople are also part of society; as such they are affected by the activities of business on society and have an interest in not being harmed by those activities. Accepting a permissive culture that expects little or nothing from business in the domain of ethics would mean accepting a culture where I, as a citizen, stand to lose quite a lot from the unethical activities of businesses. As the market-failures approach described later in this chapter demonstrates, it is in everyone's best interest, as members of society, to see that businesses adhere to standards that minimize the amount of social harm they will generate through their activities. Since the category *members of society* includes those running businesses in society, this is another way of stating the point that businesspeople should care about ethics.

market-failures approach
According to the market-failures approach to business ethics, which derives from Joseph Heath, businesses are obligated to respect norms that promote the efficient functioning of the market. A market failure occurs when something or someone causes a market to operate less efficiently than it could have.

The Social Responsibilities of Business

We have just shown that society's allowing of market-based business activity is not a given. The free-market economy, and the pursuit of profit by businesses operating within that economic system, are not necessary social institutions. Businesses exist because they are socially justified by the benefits they bring to society. But what exactly do businesses owe to

BACKGROUND

Legal Obligations and Ethical Objections

Legal obligations derive from the formally encoded rules that constitute a society's laws; *ethical obligations* result from social norms that are not necessarily encoded or written down. What is legal and what is ethical may overlap, but there are ethical obligations that are not encoded in law, and some legally encoded obligations may be inconsistent with ethical norms. Ethical considerations sometimes demand that society's laws be changed.

society in exchange for the social licence that permits them to function? What responsibilities to society do businesses have, given the relationship of indebtedness to society in which they stand?

At a minimum, businesses are obliged to obey the law of the land. A business must not act in ways that are contrary to the laws that pertain to its operations within society. But avoiding criminal activity is not a particularly high expectation, and it can be justified by an appeal to pure self-interest (the desire to avoid punishment) rather than anything in the realm of ethics. Can we legitimately expect anything more from businesses than this? Some theorists, following Albert Z. Carr, would argue that beyond the minimal requirement of following the law, society can make no further legitimate demands on the activities of businesses. Carr argues that ethical standards not captured by the law, like the *Golden Rule* for example, simply do not apply to the domain of business.[7] As long as business managers keep to the strict letter of the law, they can (and should!) lie, manipulate, bully, spy, or do anything else they deem necessary to fulfil their obligation to increase profits. As Carr puts it,

> I think it is fair to sum up the prevailing attitude of businessmen on ethics as follows:
>
> We live in what is probably the most competitive of the world's civilized societies. Our customs encourage a high degree of aggression in the individual's striving for success. Business is our main area of competition, and it has been ritualized into a game of strategy. The basic rules of the game have been set by the government, which attempts to detect and punish business frauds. But as long as a company does not transgress the rules of the game set by law, it has the legal right to shape its strategy without reference to anything but its profits. If it takes a long-term view of its profits, it will preserve amicable relations, so far as possible, with those with whom it deals. A wise businessman will not seek advantage to the point where he generates dangerous hostility among employees, competitors, customers, government, or the public at large. But decisions in this area are, in the final test, decisions of strategy, not of ethics.[8]

We consider Carr's argument in greater detail in **Chapter 4**.

We, along with other business ethicists, disagree with Carr and believe that the responsibilities of business go beyond the bare minimum of following the law. This leads us to the second question that we said we would answer: *How possible is it for a profit-oriented business to be ethical?*

BACKGROUND

The Golden and Silver Rules

The *Golden Rule* tells us to do to others what we would have them do to us. The *silver rule* tells us not to do to others what we would not want them to do to us. In a liberal democracy, most of our civil liberties rest on the silver rule; we refrain from interfering with other people as long as they refrain from interfering with us.

The Market-Failures Approach to Ethics

Profit-seeking businesses can fulfill their (ethical) obligations to society in part by acting in accordance with the internal norms of the market. In doing this, a business respects the underlying justification of the market economy that makes this institution acceptable to society. Joseph Heath develops this market-failures approach to business ethics in his book *Morality, Competition, and the Firm.*[9] The view starts from the observation that the ethics appropriate to the domain of business in Canada (or in the USA) should be compatible with a capitalist, market-based economy—a system entrenched in North American society. Inspired by Heath, we assume that many key ethical insights and principles continue to be relevant for businesses operating within a capitalist economic system that favours a free market.

Everyday Norms and Business Norms

At the centre of Heath's market-failures approach, we find an analogy between business and competitive sports. We allow certain sorts of behaviour in competitive sports that we would not tolerate in everyday life. In hockey, for example, it is legitimate to forcefully hit other people and cause them to crash into the boards surrounding the rink in order to steal a puck from them.

The same behaviour in a park or alleyway would warrant charges of assault and theft. But the rules of the game and the competitive structure of the sport create exemptions for the players from the norms that govern everyday interactions with other people. In general, athletes competing with one another attempt to defeat and even to crush their opponents in ways that are very non–co-operative and even antisocial. Why, in the context of competitive sports, does society allow such behaviour, when it would normally be considered immoral? It does so because of the benefits the sports industry produces for the rest of society: the excitement of the game, the sense of camaraderie in cheering for one's home team, and the ability to see human beings pushing the limits of what is physically possible. Without competition, none of these social gains would be possible.

THE CANADIAN PRESS/Darryl Dyck

A fight between Matthew Tkachuk of the Calgary Flames and J.T. Miller of the Vancouver Canucks in February 2020. Hockey has a set of norms around the use of physical violence during a game. A hockey player who makes a bone-jarring hit, even if it is clean, can expect some kind of retribution. But even hockey limits which forms of violence are acceptable.

By analogy, business, like sport, is a competitive enterprise in which the "players" are exempted from some general ethical norms for the sake of social benefits. We have already described some of these benefits of competition in business—increases in quality of goods and services available for consumption at more affordable prices, and a more efficient use of resources. But competition brings with it a set of norms distinct from the everyday co-operative norms that constitute morality in everyday social interactions. As a result, Heath believes, we need to describe a distinct, competitive ethics appropriate to business. He derives this ethics from the norms internal to the market.

The Ten Commandments of Business Ethics

What do the *norms internal to the market* consist of? In a general way, they can be understood as analogous to the components of the concept of *being a good sport*. Heath names four components of the concept of being a good sport: constrained competitiveness, no cheating, no gaming, and taking the high road.[10] An athlete who is a good sport knows how to differentiate their (competitive) activity within the game from their (co-operative) activity outside it. When the whistle blows, they interact with their opponents according to ordinary co-operative social norms. A good sport respects the rules of the game; for business, this entails respect for both the letter and the spirit of the laws and regulations governing the operation of their business within society. For this reason, a good sport does not use competitive strategies that exploit loopholes allowing them to do things that are not strictly ruled out, but that are contrary to the general intention of those laws and regulations. Finally, a good sport does not give in to the temptation to behave in unscrupulous ways even in the face of pressure to do so because their opponent is doing so, which puts them at an unfair disadvantage. A good sport in business limits their pursuit of profit to competitive strategies that are consistent with the proper functioning of the market.

Why should we care whether the market functions properly? Because improperly functioning markets are inefficient; they are wasteful. The **First Fundamental Theorem of Welfare Economics** states that resources in a perfectly competitive market will be distributed efficiently. In other words, allow people to trade in an unconstrained setting, and they will continue to do so until it is no longer possible to satisfy any one person's preferences without detracting from the preferences of someone else.[11] The point of this idea

> The idea of being a good sport anticipates the distinction between private and public morality discussed in **Chapter 3**.

> **First Fundamental Theorem of Welfare Economics**
> Resources will be distributed Pareto-efficiently in a perfectly competitive market. In other words, trading will make the distribution of resources socially optimal.

CONCEPT CHECK

1.8 What best describes the market economy?

a. It is a system that predicts future actions of individuals and businesses acting on their preferences.

b. It is a perfect indicator of the preferences of individuals and businesses.

c. It is the definitive arbiter of what, when, and how individuals and businesses should consume.

d. It is a system where economic decisions are guided by the sum total of individuals and businesses acting on their preferences.

The claim that meeting preferences is morally good resonates with utilitarianism, one of the ethical theories we will consider in **Chapter 2**.

is that waste (the inefficient use of resources) is a bad thing. Markets exist to facilitate the satisfaction of human wants and needs, and any situation in which more wants and needs are satisfied should be preferred over a situation in which fewer wants and needs are met. This basic goal of markets prohibits practices that detract from proper market functioning. Such practices cause market inefficiencies, or market failures. Market failures are bad because they prevent society from meeting its members' preferences as well, that is, as

CASE STUDY

Keeping Bombardier Afloat

Bombardier began in 1937 with a single snowmobile for sale. Over time, it grew to what it is today: a global transportation manufacturer that builds trains and planes around the world. Its headquarters are in Montreal, Quebec, and it does business in over 28 different countries. With revenues of over $16 billion in 2018, Bombardier is a key player in the Canadian economy. In 2018, Bombardier employed just over 68,000 people worldwide.[12]

Bombardier is far from the stable, well-running company that these numbers suggest. Their 2018 profit margin was a mere 2 per cent and they had an order backlog of $48.8 billion plus 97 units of commercial aircraft,[13] which can cost over $1 million each. In Toronto alone, Bombardier has had unfulfilled contracts since 2008.[14] During 2019, Bombardier shed around 8000 employees, added $3.3 billion to their order backlog, and had a margin of negative 10 per cent.[15]

The company has had financial difficulties going back as far as 1966. Since then, the company has received over $1.1 billion in 48 separate payments from Industry Canada to stay afloat; $55 million were in grants and the rest were conditionally repayable loans, where Bombardier agreed to repay the loan upon completing a sale.[16]

The debate is whether the Government of Canada should subsidize struggling businesses. The reasoning behind subsidizing businesses like Bombardier is to keep them running, which benefits the economy, consumers, employees, and the government itself through taxes. However, the need for government subsidies demonstrates a failure on Bombardier's part to keep itself viable and competitive. Market mechanisms would dictate that companies like Bombardier should fail. Government subsidies represent a manipulation of the market by governments to keep a company running that would otherwise close its doors.

For Discussion

1. What pressing social need is there to keep Bombardier afloat?
2. What other kinds of businesses might need ongoing public subsidies?
3. Consider a manufacturer in a province that regulates the price of electricity. Is offering a fixed, discounted price on electricity a manipulation of the electricity market? A manipulation of the market for the manufacturer's products? A form of public subsidy? Explain your reasoning.

Pareto-efficiently as it could have done. And since meeting preferences (generating utility) is a morally good thing, market failures are immoral, by this standard.

What sorts of practices generate market inefficiencies? Heath lists ten general rules prohibiting different sorts of practices that lead to market failure and promoting activities that preserve a healthy market:[17]

1. *Minimize negative externalities.* A negative externality is an uncompensated cost imposed by one party onto another. Do not externalize the cost of doing business onto a third party. Pollution is the clearest example of a negative externality.
2. *Compete only through price and quality.* Do not engage in underhanded tactics (like paying bribes) to outdo competitors.
3. *Reduce information asymmetries between firm and customers.* Be transparent with your customers. Do not hide non-sensitive information that will inhibit the customer from making a fully informed decision.
4. *Do not exploit diffusion of ownership.* Fulfill your fiduciary duties. This is not simply about being a loyal employee; it is a matter of law in many jurisdictions.
5. *Avoid erecting barriers to entry.* It is impossible to have a competitive market if competitors are prevented from entering the market. This is not a matter of being nice to potential competitors; it is a matter of abiding by anti-trust laws, which apply to all businesses.
6. *Do not use cross-subsidization to eliminate competitors.* Assume Company *X* makes products *A* and *B*, and assume Company *Y* makes only product *B*. Company *X* must not use its profits from *A* to subsidize its production of *B* in order to undercut Company *Y*.
7. *Do not oppose regulation aimed at correcting market imperfections.* A perfectly competitive market is an idealization, much akin to a frictionless plane in physics. Regulations are a way to correct market inefficiencies and stimulate competition.
8. *Do not seek tariffs or other protectionist measures.* Do not try to influence the state (through lobbying, for example) to keep out potential competitors.
9. *Treat price levels as exogenously determined.* Prices should be set by supply and demand. Do not fix prices.
10. *Do not engage in opportunistic behaviour toward customers or other firms.* This covers a wide range of exploitative behaviour. A few examples include price fixing, fraud, aggressive and deceptive advertising, predatory marketing, and high-pressure sales tactics that put people off their guard through violating social norms.

Even though these ten are only *examples* of the kinds of restrictions placed on the activities of businesses by the internal norms of the market, they are fairly comprehensive in scope. We will therefore refer to them as the ten commandments of business ethics from a market-failures approach.

This section has only introduced and explained the general rationale of these ten principles; later parts of the text will consider them individually and develop market-based approaches to avoiding them. The market-failures approach to business ethics provides the first part of our answer to the question of how a business can be ethical while retaining the profit motive. Since the market is justified by its benefits for society, and business is only possible because of the market economy, businesses ought not to act in ways that thwart the proper

Pareto efficiency
A particularly stringent form of efficiency, in which all resources are allocated and no one can be made better off by trading without making someone else worse off.

ten commandments of business ethics
A list of ten rules given by Joseph Heath that express requirements of the market-failures approach to business ethics.

functioning of the market. If they do, society has ample justification for opposing or even dismantling them. Businesses, at least as far as they engage in transactions in the marketplace, have been granted certain exemptions from ordinary social expectations by being allowed to pursue profit in a competitive context. In return, the "good sport" in business will respect the rules of the game by refusing to act in ways that lead to market inefficiencies.

CASE STUDY

Glybera: The Million-Dollar Drug

Lipoprotein lipase deficiency (LPLD) is a genetic disorder that prevents a person from digesting fat. As a result, fat particles collect in the bloodstream, and can cause a severe and painful inflammation of the pancreas. The disorder affects about one in a million persons worldwide,[18] but in the Saguenay region of Quebec, the disorder affects approximately one in 5000 persons.[19]

Michael Hayden and John Kastelein discovered the genetic defect causing LPLD while working at the University of British Columbia, and came up with the idea of modifying a virus to deliver the missing gene so the body would start producing lipoprotein lipase.[20] Universities, however, are not in the business of making drugs, so the methods developed (often with public money) need to be sold to companies that are willing to take on the work of conducting trials, convincing regulatory agencies of the drug's effectiveness, producing enough of the drug to meet anticipated demand, and marketing the treatment. Kastelein, who had returned home to the Netherlands, joined with other scientists to form Amsterdam Molecular Therapeutics to do just that.[21] The initial human trial in the Netherlands 2005 and subsequent trial in 2008 in Quebec demonstrated the treatment's effectiveness, and so plans were made to bring the treatment to market under the name Glybera.[22]

LPLD is so rare that randomized controlled trials are too small to be convincing to most regulatory agencies. Because it took so long to gain regulatory approval, Amsterdam Molecular Therapeutics ran out of money and could no longer afford to move forward with commercial production. They sold the production technology to uniQure, who partnered with Italy's Chiesi Farmaceutici, giving Chiesi the rights to Glybera in Europe. In 2015, Chiesi set the European price for Glybera at the equivalent of US$1 million per dose.[23]

When Hayden and Kastelein, who were no longer involved in the development and commercialization of Glybera, heard about the price, they were shocked. Said Hayden, "I was not happy. I did not know what they were going to charge. . . . To be quite frank, this was not something I was particularly proud of, that the pricing of this made it out of the reach of the patients."[24] Kastelein observed, "By the time there's a pricing, we're gone already. We've done the science and the clinical work and everything, and then it's the commercial and financial people that determine the price."[25]

Sander van Deventer, the chief scientific officer of uniQure, defended the pricing because it treated the cause of LPLD, unlike treatments for other deficiencies that supplement or replace what is missing. Some of those therapies are priced at $300,000 per year.[26] "It's not a crazy price. . . . [I]n the end, all of these products, even priced at $1 million, are going to be generally cheaper than replacement therapy."[27] But at that price, only one dose was sold. When the market for Glybera failed, the three remaining doses in stock were sold for one euro, and Chiesi returned the European rights to Glybera to uniQure.[28]

Continued

uniQure has no plans to offer Glybera for sale again.[29] Asked if he would lower the price, van Deventer replied, "Why would we? Pricing shouldn't be a political decision. It should be a rational decision based on merits and values. Hundreds of millions of investor money has gone into the company, and if there is no return for those investments, there will be no new drugs because nobody's going to do that in the future, right?"[30] Even Kastelein admitted in resignation, "It's kind of the law of nature.... If it's not commercially viable to produce a certain therapy, in our Western society, it does not happen."[31]

The public cost of health care is an important part of social policy. It plays an important part in a discussion of fairness and equality in Chapter 5.

For Discussion

1. LPLD affects roughly one in a million people. There is a global market, then, of about 8000 doses if the treatment needs to be administered only once. Is this enough of a market to justify the renewed production of Glybera?
2. Explain how Glybera serves as an example of a market failure. Which of Heath's ten commandments are broken?
3. In Canada, we benefit from (partially) publicly insured provincial health-care systems. But the cost of drugs, especially new or expensive ones, is not typically covered under these plans. If no person with LPLD can afford the $1 million to purchase the drug, and fewer than a dozen people in a province need it to have any kind of quality of life, is it reasonable for the government to purchase it on behalf of those persons? Explain your reasoning.
4. Van Devinter is correct in saying that uniQure has an obligation to work toward providing a return to investors. Do you think that justifies the price Chiesi set for Glybera? What other factors do you think need to be considered, and why?

Summing Up

Business has a social function—it serves the social purpose of facilitating trade so that resources can be distributed efficiently. Because of its social function, business activity is appropriately constrained by market-based norms, laws, ethics, and other social norms, all of which serve as safeguards against the excesses and abuses of the market system. Recognizing these facts about the nature of business and its relation to society helps us to understand why businesspeople ought to constrain their activity according to various norms, including ethical norms.

We have introduced you to some important concepts and crucial distinctions in this chapter, and have given arguments as to why business ethics is important. We will come back to these concepts and use these distinctions over and over in this text. We highlight them here because we think they are of utmost importance when thinking about the demands of professional and business ethics. But perhaps the most important take-away for now is this: insofar as our actions affect the well-being of another person, ethics has something to say.

For Discussion and Review

1. Describe how humble objectivism differs from moral imperialism.
2. What is the main take-away from the story of a group of people touching different parts of an elephant?
3. Outline the argument against ethical relativism. Do you think the argument works—that is, do you agree that the inferences are clear and justified, and that the premises (assumptions) are likely to be correct? Explain why or why not.
4. Is it really possible to be a humble objectivist without becoming a moral imperialist?
5. Efficiency is a value. Is it the greatest value in business, or are other values more important than efficiency?
6. What is the core idea behind the market-failures approach to business ethics?
7. Heath makes an analogy between competition in sport and competition between businesses. Does this analogy work?

Further Reading

Carr, Albert Z. "Is Business Bluffing Ethical?" *Harvard Business Review* 46 no. 1 (Jan./Feb. 1968): 143–53.

Donaldson, Thomas, and James P. Walsh. "Toward a Theory of Business." *Research in Organizational Behaviour* 35 (2015): 181–207.

Marino, Patricia. *Moral Reasoning in a Pluralistic World.* McGill-Queens University Press, 2015.

Moriarty, Jeffrey, "Business Ethics." *Stanford Encyclopedia of Philosophy.* Fall 2017 edn. Edited by Edward N. Zalta. https://plato.stanford.edu/archives/fall2017/entries/ethics-business/.

von Kriegstein, Hasko. "Oxymoron: Taking Business Ethics Denial Seriously." *Journal of Business Ethics Education* 16 (2019). Preprint available at https://www.academia.edu/39750521/Oxymoron_Taking_Business_Ethics_Denial_Seriously.

CHAPTER 2
Thinking in Ethical Terms

By the end of this chapter you should be able to

- Explain the main differences between deontological and utilitarian ethics.

- Compare leading normative moral theories and identify their strengths and weaknesses.

- Use the language of ethics appropriately, including terminology such as duties, rights, utility, care, and capability.

- Reflect on how your own values relate to normative theories and whether they would pass the *light-of-day* test.

How can businesses be ethical while retaining an orientation toward increasing profits? The first part of our answer to this question—which we gave in Chapter 1—is that profit-focused businesses can be ethical by respecting the norms internal to the free-market economy in which they operate. As we have noted already, these norms (summarized in Heath's ten commandments of business ethics) put some significant constraints on what counts as acceptable business behaviour. Although these ten commandments are not strictly ethical requirements, in the sense that they are not justified by or traced to standard ethical theories or principles, the principles of the market-failures approach overlap with traditional ethical conclusions (for example, the market-efficiency-based requirement to reduce information asymmetries overlaps with the ethical requirement that people not lie to or otherwise deceive each other). Might these constraints not then sufficiently delimit the sum total of the responsibilities of business? If they did, the job of the business ethicist would be relatively easy. As long as we agree that the market economy is a good thing, the market-failures approach would follow and would generate the entire moral framework with which businesses need to concern themselves. We could then state the responsibilities of business without having to involve ourselves in disputes over contested issues in theoretical ethics.

> We introduced Heath's ten commandments and the market-failures approach to business ethics in **Chapter 1**.

There are at least three reasons why a consideration of ethical theories remains important for business ethics, even a business ethics that follows a market-failures approach. First, the principles of the market-failures approach receive their ultimate justification from intuitions that are ethically sound. When we ask, *Why should we value the free-market economy or respect its norms?* we are asking a question whose answer will involve ethical reasons. (We noted in the last chapter that market failures are bad because they prevent people from utility gains they might have achieved otherwise.) Second, it is debatable whether the market-failures approach can account for all of the moral obligations of business. If there are obligations beyond those that flow from the internal norms of the free market, then we need to be familiar with ethical terminology to state what those obligations are, and to explain why businesses are required to pay attention to them. Third, students of business ethics need a general understanding of traditional ethical theories because human beings (including yourself as well as those you will deal with as co-workers or as clients) care about ethics. Given the kind of rational and social animals we are, ethical reasons matter to us. For these reasons, it is worthwhile to become familiar with some of the best attempts people have made to explain what the basic ethical reasons are, and the source of their sway over human thought and action.

The two ethical theories covered in nearly any applied ethics text you can read are *utilitarianism* and *deontological ethics*. The difference between these two approaches is important: while utilitarianism takes consequences or results to be the most important measure of ethical action, deontology sees ethics as a matter of reasoned understanding and following your duties regardless of what the results of your actions will be. We will discuss these two theories in this chapter, as well as a few other concepts and approaches that contemporary applied ethicists take seriously: moral rights, virtue ethics, ethics of care, and the capability approach.

Each ethical theory offers a general answer to the ethical question *What should we do?* Once we have this general answer in place, we can then ask how to apply it to specific real-life situations we encounter. Applied ethics, then, involves taking the conclusions of theoretical ethics and showing what they imply for human decisions and activity in different spheres of life.

CONCEPT CHECK

2.1 Why do we need to study traditional moral theories?

a. It is unlikely that market norms exhaustively account for all of the obligations of business.

b. There is a legal obligation to do business in an ethical way.

c. They give definitive guidance on what to do in every situation.

d. It is a moral requirement for being a responsible citizen.

Deontological Ethics: Duty, Principles, and Rights

Deontological theories of ethics come in a few different forms, some of which focus on duty, and others on rights. Despite their differences, all forms of deontology seek to express the demands of ethics in the language of rules to be followed. We will examine three major theories of deontological ethics: categorical imperative, prima facie duty, and rights-based. The word *deontological* comes from *deon*, the Greek word for *duty*, together with the Greek *logos*, *science* or *study of*. Classic deontological ethics focuses on figuring out what our basic ethical duties or obligations are, and seeks to express these obligations in the form of ethical rules. In response to the ethical question *What should we do?* deontological ethics tells us to find out what rule applies to the situation we are in, and follow it.

deontological theories of ethics
Theories that claim ethically right actions are those that fulfill one's duty.

Kant's Categorical Imperative

According to the German philosopher Immanuel Kant, there is one basic ethical obligation, which he called the **categorical imperative**. The categorical imperative is an absolute ethical demand. It is unconditional and does not depend on any other goal. There is no condition under which you can forgo your ethical duty—the categorical imperative is something that you must do simply because it is your duty to do it. Kant stated the categorical imperative

categorical imperative
According to Kant, the most basic or fundamental rule expressing our ethical duty.

BACKGROUND

What Is Duty?

Deontological theories of ethics claim that ethically right actions are actions that fulfill one's duty. *Duty* is synonymous with *obligation* or *responsibility*; these terms all refer to something that is required or demanded of us. If the demand is of an ethical nature (something that ethics requires of us), then the duty in question is an ethical one. Some versions of deontology also say that right actions must be chosen solely for the reason that they fulfill one's duty.

in a variety of ways; we present only the two most famous formulations here. The first—the **universalizability formulation**—goes like this: "Act only on that **maxim** through which you can at the same time will that it should become a universal law."[1]

To paraphrase, Kant thinks the most essential moral rule tells us that we can only do things that we could rationally allow everyone else to do too. Consider how this applies to lying. Suppose I am trying to sell a computer, and I know the operating system suffers from a defect that frequently causes the computer to crash. The person who wants to buy the computer from me does not know about this defect, and asks me, "Do you know of any serious problems with how this computer runs—does it crash often, for instance?" I know that by telling the buyer it has no problems I am more likely to close the sale. The first formulation of Kant's categorical imperative serves as a test of whether or not my decision to lie is ethically acceptable. Can I rationally accept that everyone would lie in circumstances similar to my own, when they would benefit from doing so? Kant thinks not, because if everyone lied in such situations, no one would believe another's claims about the products they are selling, and so it would no longer be possible to get what you want by lying to potential buyers. In other words, a maxim or rule of action that told people to lie when they could benefit from doing so would be self-defeating, and would therefore be irrational. This formulation of the categorical imperative is similar to the Golden Rule—do to others what you would have them do to you. Accordingly, Kantian ethics prohibits us from making exceptions for ourselves. It commands us never to do things that we would not allow everyone else to do as well.

The second famous formulation of the categorical imperative is the **humanity formulation**. It says, "Act in such a way as to treat humanity, whether in your own person or in that of anyone else, always as an end and never merely as a means."[2] An *end* is a goal, or something that is valued. So in this context, to respect a person as an end is to value their dignity and autonomy; you do not use the person simply because doing so enables you to get something you want. If you use a person for your own purposes without respecting their **intrinsic value**, then you are treating that person merely as a means. In other words, treating a person merely as a means is to treat them as if they have no value in themselves, but are only **instrumentally valuable** to the extent that they help you to get something you want. And this, for Kant, is against the demands of morality.

For Kant, we are not only ethically obligated to carry out our duties in line with the categorical imperative, but we must also choose to do our duty purely because doing so is the right thing to do, and not because of benefits we might obtain by doing our duty. Many have seen Kant's approach to ethics as overly rigid. We tend to think that there can be exceptions to certain ethical rules. For instance, in some situations it seems acceptable to lie when by doing so we might save the lives of our friends from danger. Despite doing a good job expressing some of our basic intuitions about ethics, Kant's theory often is criticized for its inability to deal with exceptions.

universalizability formulation
The version of the categorical imperative that states that one may act only on a maxim that one can will to become a universal law. In other words, if we want a maxim to be applicable universally, then acting in accordance with that maxim must be a rational exercise of moral duty for everyone, without partiality or exception.

maxim
A general action-guiding rule or principle.

humanity formulation
The version of the categorical imperative that states that one must always treat a human person as an end in themselves and never merely as a means.

intrinsic value
Something that is valued for its own sake, not because it is useful for some other purpose.

instrumental value
Something that is useful to achieve some goal. For example, money has instrumental value because it is useful for purchasing food.

We say more about intrinsic value in **Chapter 7**.

CONCEPT CHECK

2.2 What is the moral focus of deontology?

a. self-interest

b. duty

c. responsibility for others

d. rationality

Ross's Prima Facie Duties

Kant believed that there is one basic moral duty, even if it could be formulated in different ways. Kant's approach to ethics is called **deontological monism**. By contrast, W.D. Ross developed a version of deontological ethics called **deontological pluralism**, which holds that there are many distinct basic moral obligations. Ross termed these basic obligations **prima facie duties** because none of them are absolute. Ross listed seven such duties:[3]

1. *Fidelity.* This involves keeping promises and acting in good faith toward others.
2. *Reparation.* This involves undoing (at least some of) the effects of a harm.
3. *Gratitude.* This involves being grateful for the kind acts of others.
4. *Justice.* This involves doing that which promotes fairness.
5. *Beneficence.* This involves acting in a way that benefits others.
6. *Self-improvement.* This involves life-long learning and developing a virtuous character.
7. *Non-maleficence.* This is the simple duty not to harm others.

Each of the basic duties identified by Ross places a real demand on us, but may be overridden in situations where conflicting duties pull us in different directions. For example, say I have borrowed my friend's axe, so that I have a duty of fidelity to keep my promise to return the axe once I am done using it. But when I go to their house, I find them screaming about how they need their axe so they can murder their neighbour's family. In that situation, my duty to prevent harm (non-maleficence) to the family in question overrides my fidelity duty to return the axe. Ross's pluralism is more flexible than Kant's monism, and so many people find it to be a preferable deontological approach to ethics.

deontological monism
The view that there is a single, absolute, ethical duty. For Kant, this is the categorical imperative.

deontological pluralism
The view that there are multiple, distinct basic duties.

prima facie duty
A duty that is binding on us but that may be overridden by the demands of other duties in certain circumstances. *Prima facie* literally means *on the face of things*, and so a prima facie duty is accepted as holding on the face of things, or until proven otherwise.

CONCEPT CHECK

2.3 What is deontological monism?

a. It is the view that there are multiple complementary moral duties.
b. It is the view that we have moral duties only to ourselves.
c. It is the view that the only moral duty is to money.
d. It is the view that there is one fundamental moral duty.

Rights-Based Deontological Ethics

A more familiar version of deontological ethics focuses on the concept of **moral rights** as opposed to moral duties. **Rights-based deontological ethics** is commonly used to express the demands of ethics in Western liberal democracies. A *right* is a justified and recognized claim or entitlement to some object or form of treatment. The Universal Declaration of Human Rights, adopted by the United Nations in 1948, opens with the following statement: "Whereas the recognition of the inherent dignity and of the equal and unalienable rights of all members of the human family is the foundation of freedom, justice and peace in the world . . ."[4]

(moral) right
A justified claim or entitlement to have something or to be treated in a certain way.

rights-based deontological ethics
An approach to ethics that links the idea of duty to ensuring that people's rights are respected.

Canadian legislation, in the Charter of Rights and Freedoms, presents a similar perspective, guaranteeing its citizens various democratic, mobility, legal, and equality rights in addition to a number of fundamental freedoms.

Why have we included the rights-based approach to ethics as a form of deontological ethics, when the focus of deontology is the concept of moral duty? We have done so because rights-based ethics express our moral obligations in terms of rules that must be followed. Furthermore, the concept of a right makes no sense without the corresponding concept of duty. An essential part of what it means to say that one person has a right is to say that some-one has a duty to respect that person's right. Rights, then, entail duties that are expressed as rules. My right to vote in a federal election entails the duty of those officiating the election (and of anyone else in Canada) not to hinder me from voting, which can be expressed as the rule, "You must not try to prevent this person from voting in the election." The right to vote, like many other rights (the right to life, the right to liberty, the right to property, etc.) is a **negative right**, because it only entails duties *not* to interfere with the individual's exercise of the right in question, that is, to refrain from acting in ways that would violate the individual's right. By contrast, a **positive right** such as a right to education or a right to health care entails duties *to* do something positively for the person whose right we are considering. If, for example, children have a right to education, and a government refuses to establish an education system for the children of its citizens, then that government has violated the rights of those children

negative right
Requires other people to refrain from interfering with your actions or possessions. Examples include property rights and the rights to life, freedom of religion, and freedom from slavery.

positive right
Entails that other people have an obligation to do something for you or provide you with something. Positive rights include the rights to education and health care, among other things.

©WARREN TODA/EPA-EFE/Shutterstock

Canadian citizens who are 18 years old or older have the right to vote in a federal election. The right to vote is a negative right, and interfering with the right of others to vote is a serious offence.

because those rights required the government to act in certain ways, and it has not done so. Rights-based ethics is a minimalistic approach to ethics. It tells us the minimum of what is required of us (do not violate the rights of other people), and leaves room for a great deal of freedom beyond that, which is a positive way of saying that it gives us little guidance about how to live a good life.

Utilitarianism

Utilitarianism, made popular in the eighteenth and nineteenth centuries by Jeremy Bentham and John Stuart Mill, takes a consequentialist approach to ethics in that it measures the moral rightness or wrongness of actions by weighing the positive and negative consequences (or results, or effects, or outcomes) of those actions. For the utilitarian, what is morally good is promoting social utility, which can be understood as pleasure, taken in a broad sense. Correspondingly, the moral bad is *disutility* or pain, understood in a similarly broad way. The utilitarian answers the ethical question *What should we do?* by telling us that we should always act in ways that promote the greatest net utility for all interested parties.

For the act utilitarian, when deciding what course of action to follow, we should consider who will be affected, whether negatively or positively, by each possible course of action. Each course of action will generate a certain total amount of utility for those affected by it, along with a certain sum of disutility for those same affected parties. After estimating these totals, we should subtract the total disutility produced by each course of action from the total utility it would produce, and pick the action that yields the greatest overall social benefit. That action, then, is the morally right action according to utilitarianism.

It is important to see that utilitarianism urges us to focus on the interested or affected parties. On the one hand, this means that we do not have to think about the way our actions will potentially benefit or harm every single person in the entire world, or even in the society we live in. It is enough to limit our considerations to those people who will be directly affected

utilitarianism
An ethical theory that sees the right action as the one that maximizes the net utility of the relevantly affected parties.

social utility
Utility measured across the whole of society, accounting for both the benefits and harms that come from the action.

act utilitarianism
The version of utilitarianism that directs us to weigh and compare the utility of individual actions. See *utilitarianism* and *rule utilitarianism*.

BACKGROUND

Making Sense of Utility

It is hard to define *utility* without simply using synonymous terms. Something has utility for a person if it is useful, beneficial, valuable, profitable, or helpful for that person. The utilitarian takes pleasure and pain as the measure of utility. Does something maximize the pleasure of the relevant affected parties? Then it is good. Arguing that because pleasure and pain are hard to quantify, some economists and politicians measure social utility in strictly monetary terms. We believe, however, this is too narrow an understanding of social utility, because a sense of individual financial well-being, for example, typically plateaus at a certain level of income.[5]

in significant ways by our decisions. On the other hand, utilitarianism clearly requires us to take very seriously the interests of people other than ourselves.

Calculating the likely net utilities of various courses of action and assigning them numerical values is probably not realistically possible, for a variety of reasons. For one thing, we are not always very good at knowing in advance what the results of our actions will be. Furthermore, in order to assign utilities we would have to know the values and preferences of each affected person, but such information is not always readily available to us. Finally, there is the problem of comparing values; since there are so many kinds of pleasures and pains and these are experienced differently by different people, it is hard to know how to measure them against each other.

These, among other reasons, have driven people away from act utilitarianism to **rule utilitarianism**, a position that allows us to use general rules to guide ethical action, for instance, rules like *Do not kill innocent people* and *Do not manipulate people in order to get your way*. Despite appealing to rules—which is a defining feature of deontological ethics—rule utilitarianism is considered to be a form of utilitarianism because the rules are justified by the fact that behaving according to them tends to yield greater utility than acting in ways that violate the rules. The problem remains, however, that it is difficult to know with any level of certainty what rules will yield the greatest net utility, other than some very obvious ones.

rule utilitarianism
The version of utilitarianism that requires us to follow rules that tend to promote high levels of net utility. See *utilitarianism* and *act utilitarianism*.

CONCEPT CHECK

2.4 What is the moral focus of utilitarianism?

a. greatest personal happiness

b. greatest net happiness

c. greatest market opportunity

d. greatest duty of care

Virtue Ethics

virtue ethics
An ethical theory according to which good action has to be understood in relation to good character and to the overall purpose of human life.

character
The sum of a person's various dispositions to act in ways that enable their *flourishing* (*virtues*) or hinder their flourishing (*vices*).

virtue
A good or positive character trait that contributes toward human flourishing.

vice
A bad or negative character trait that inhibits human flourishing.

Virtue ethics refers to an approach that began with the ancient Greeks—Socrates, Plato, and Aristotle—and provided the main framework for philosophical ethics in the West right up until the modern era. Virtue ethics answers the ethical question by turning our attention away from the actions we should perform to examine instead the kind of people we wish to be. For this reason, **character** is the central idea of this approach, where character refers to the sort of dispositions or habits we have to behave in certain ways. Good character traits are called **virtues**, while bad character traits are called **vices**.

The Greeks presented four central virtues that they understood as the core of a good character: prudence (or practical wisdom), justice, courage, and self-control. Each of these virtuous dispositions can be understood as a kind of mean or middle between two opposed vices. For instance, the virtue of courage has to do with how we handle fear. A courageous person fears only the things they truly should fear, unlike the coward who fears things that should not be feared and the reckless person who does not fear the things they should. Similarly, the self-controlled person keeps their appetites in a healthy balance; in relation to diet, they eat neither too little nor too much, but the quantity that enables them to flourish. In virtue ethics, the ideal of flourishing (or happiness) guides our understanding of what character traits are virtues. Good character traits are those that lead to human **flourishing**. To flourish is to live the fullest human life possible, that is, to realize our natural capacities as human beings to the greatest extent we can manage.

Unlike deontological ethics, virtue-centred approaches take our desires as important guides to what is right. Rather than being a matter of obedience to rules, ethics according to virtue theory has to do with becoming the best version of ourselves we can be, by following our deepest desires for self-realization. For the utilitarian, ethics applies to isolated individual actions and decisions, measuring each according to the quantity of pleasure or pain each generates. By contrast, virtue ethics urges us to take a bigger picture of our lives as a coherent whole, understanding the trends and patterns of living that lead us to fulfillment or to unhappiness. One of the greatest problems with virtue ethics concerns the lack of agreement among human beings about what human happiness or flourishing consists of. Since there is such diversity in conceptions of the good life, some see virtue ethics as leading to ethical relativism, where different things are good or bad for different people depending on their conceptions of human happiness. On the other hand, virtue ethics can become a form of moral imperialism if it turns one person's or group's understanding of happiness into a standard by which to judge others.

flourishing
The Greek word *eudaimonia*, used by Aristotle, is often translated as *happiness*, but *flourishing* better captures its meaning. To *flourish* is to realize your human potential to its full extent—in other words, to actualize yourself as the kind of being you are or are meant to be.

We discuss moral imperialism in contrast to relativism and humble objectivism in **Chapter 1**.

CONCEPT CHECK

2.5 What is the moral focus of virtue ethics?

a. action

b. outcome

c. character

d. intent

Ethics of Care

As its name suggests, an **ethics of care** (or *care ethics*) emphasizes caregiving and care receiving as the key facets of morality. The aim of care ethics is to maintain and improve relationships by "promoting the well-being of care-givers and care-receivers."[6] Care ethicists see the world's moral terrain as comprised of networks of relationships as opposed to individuals standing alone. This is one reason care ethicists reject the idea of universal moral principles (for example, Kant's categorical imperative); embedded in the idea of universal moral principles is the assumption that what counts as a moral harm or good can be universalized to all persons. Rather, care ethicists hold that what makes something a moral good or harm will

ethics of care
An ethical theory that holds care and caring relationships as the central ethical value. Also known as *care ethics*.

Live Music Now

What does it mean to care for the elderly? A holistic approach to care can include initiatives such as "Live Music in Care" in the UK, which brings music into care homes. This type of initiative contributes to the well-being of both the facilitators and those who are there simply to enjoy the music.

justice approach
Ethical theories that emphasize impersonal and universal determinations of rights and merits while neglecting the personal and relational aspects of ethics.

vary to some extent depending on the nature of the relationships among the individuals involved. Thus, unlike most justice approaches, care ethics allows room for both partiality in moral reasoning and for emotion, since feeling love or empathy toward someone is crucial for effective caring.

In the 1970s and 1980s, care ethicists were critical of what they saw to be an over-emphasis on justice-oriented approaches in ethics (for example, Kantian ethics and consequentialism). These approaches, they pointed out, neglect or undervalue traditionally "feminine" moral domains such as care and relationships, and are overly individualistic. Early theorists in the ethics of care (in particular, Carol Gilligan, Nel Noddings, and Sara Ruddick) sought to bring into the moral arena issues that were once thought to be merely "private" concerns, as they were said to be largely the concerns of women: issues like mothering; caring within intimate relationships; caring for the elderly, sick, or disabled; and abortion decisions. Care ethicists argued that excluding these domains was essentially to exclude from moral consideration deeply integrated aspects of human life.[7] We all have relationships, care for others, and have been cared for. These features of our lives have a significant influence on how we get along with one another and make decisions that have moral impact. We ought to pay attention to them and work out how they can or should factor into our moral reasoning.

Some care ethicists have argued that because justice-oriented approaches neglect domains such as care and relationships, it is male-biased. For instance, Carol Gilligan (a psychologist) criticized Lawrence Kohlberg's hierarchically ordered five stages of moral development, a then-prominent tool for assessing a person's moral reasoning abilities. Research in the 1970s that used Kohlberg's assessment tended to claim that women were morally "weaker" than men because they could only reach level 3 on average (maintaining interpersonal relationships), whereas men could reach levels 4 (maintaining social order by following authority) and 5 (social-contract reasoning).[8] Gilligan argued, however, that Kohlberg's stages are male-biased because they undervalue interpersonal (that is, "feminine") moral goods, such as care, responsibility, emotional judgment, and relationships in favour of more abstract, impersonal (that is, "masculine") moral goods such as justice, autonomous moral agency, and impartial, universal principles.

Critics have charged care ethics as being gender essentialist. Early care ethics was especially thought to be essentialist because it was likened to a "feminine" ethics.[9] As such, its theories were taken to imply that women are inherently more care-orientated than men. Critics point out that not only is this empirically inaccurate, but valorizing care as a "feminine" virtue also acts to justify women's overrepresentation in underpaid, under-appreciated caring social roles and occupations. Contemporary care ethicists have attempted to avoid essentialism in a variety of ways.[10] For instance, some now frame care as a "symbolically" feminine virtue rather than an actual one. Others situate the "femininity" of care in a socio-historical context, and are careful to explain that care is only feminine insofar as patriarchal social structure makes it so. Still others investigate care as an ethic from a gender-neutral standpoint.

Nonetheless, the ethics of care does add to the things we ought to consider when making moral judgments. First, the ethics of care moves from abstract and ideal principles to how those are relevant to caring for the person at hand—in other words, if ethics is going to do any good, it has to do good *for people*, and that means taking note of how a person's interests are being served.[11] As Margaret Little describes it,

> from the valorized position of dispassionate detachment we are often less likely to pick up on what is morally salient. Emotional distance does not always clarify; disengagement is not always the most revealing stance. To see clearly what is before us, we need to cultivate certain desires, such as the desire to see justice done, and the desire to see humans flourish, but we must also, more particularly, work at developing our capacities for loving and caring about people.[12]

Virginia Held, noting the value of the empirical psychological work done by Gilligan and others, observes, "The ethics of care, as a normative guide, is based on lived experience, experience open to all, and across very different cultures. But it requires evaluations and judgments, not only empirical findings. So the work of developing the ethics of care continues."[13]

Critics have also charged that care ethics is too narrow in its scope. Because care ethics promotes partiality and emotion in moral reasoning, some have charged that it falls short in being able to tell us how we should treat and think about people we do not know, or people we are not moved to care about. As such, some think moral issues in politics and international relations reside outside care ethics.[14] Since the 2000s, however, care ethicists have made numerous attempts to make care ethics a global ethic. For instance, some theorists use an ethics of care to explore the ways in which social, political, and economic institutions are responsible for ensuring adequate support to caregivers and care receivers. Others consider how an ethics of

autonomy
A person's capacity to make decisions about their own life, in line with their own beliefs and values.

gender essentialism
The view that certain observed behavioural differences between men and women are rooted in biological or psychological traits, unique to what is thought to be male and female. Gender essentialism is problematic for several reasons.

The concern for persons and relationships is also reflected in stakeholder theory, which we discuss in **Chapter 3**.

care could act as a moral guide for managing and evaluating long-term relationships among countries,[15] or for alleviating global poverty.[16] While the ethics of care is still developing as a normative theory, it offers something of value for all of humanity. In that sense it is a feminist ethic, not a feminine or emasculated one.

CONCEPT CHECK

2.6 Who are the moral focus of the ethics of care?

a. those who have responsibility for us

b. those for whom we have responsibility

c. those who provide care to others

d. those who care about ethics

The Capability Approach

capability approach
An ethical theory that focuses on promoting human abilities to attain the elements of a good life.

The **capability approach** is an imperfect set of ethical principles, messily applied, but with an eye to achieving social equity. The focus of this approach is on promoting the freedom and well-being of humans. Each one of us has a conception of what it means to live well. And we likely have a vague sense of what we need (and what we need to do) to live well. So a good life will look different for each person, which means that different people will need different things to flourish. The capability approach has us ask, *What is needed for us (as individuals) and others to become the best versions of ourselves?* Because of this, the capability approach is pluralistic with respect to what people hold as valuable.

The capability approach has three fundamental commitments: treating each person as an end in themselves, promoting choice and freedom rather than achievements, and being pluralistic with respect to values.[17]

Capabilities

In broad strokes, capabilities are actual opportunities that people have to be the person they strive to be and to do the things they value.[18] There are two senses in which we can talk of capabilities. In the first sense, there are *basic capabilities*, which have some semblance of access to basic social goods. They are opportunities that are needed for a person to survive in a minimal sense.[19] In the second sense, capabilities are real opportunities that allow a person to flourish rather than merely survive. For example, if we consider the capability to nourish ourselves, we can think of a basic sense where people would have enough to survive, meeting a threshold requirement of that capability. But we can also think of it as something more robust. We may consider being able to buy organic, wholesome foods as an important capability, though not necessarily tied to survival in the same way as mere sustenance-level access to food.

While some moral theories maintain a sharp distinction between the means and ends of actions, the capability approach recognizes that, in practice, the distinction is blurry at best. This is because, while there is a moral focus on the outcomes (or ends) of our actions, those ends could simultaneously act as means to developing another capability. For example, being in good health is an important end, but also serves as a condition for travelling—those who are sick may not have the capability to travel as a result.

Which Capabilities?

When adopting any version of this approach, two immediate question arise: *How are capabilities selected as relevant in decision making?* and *Of the relevant capabilities, which take priority in our decision making?* There are a few different ways that moral theorists try to answer these questions. Some argue that all human capabilities are relevant and so should count.[20] Most argue that the selection of capabilities as morally relevant, good, or bad poses no problem at all, since justice demands that we distinguish between morally relevant and morally irrelevant capabilities, and similarly between morally good and morally bad capabilities.[21] Further, the selection of which human capabilities are relevant would differ depending on the moral problem being considered. For example, we might take certain capabilities as relevant when deciding how to spend a charitable donation, while others might be important when deciding how to care for a family member.

To aid in our thinking about human capabilities, Martha C. Nussbaum, who developed the most influential version of the capabilities approach, created a list of ten central human capabilities required for a dignified life. Although the list is incomplete, it includes:

- life
- bodily health
- bodily integrity
- senses, imagination, and thought
- emotions
- practical reason
- affiliation (personal and political)
- other species
- play
- control over one's environment[22]

If these capabilities can be agreed on by most people as minimal components of a good or dignified human life, then we will have avoided the problem of virtue ethics, which seemed to lead to either relativism or absolutism.

CONCEPT CHECK

2.7 What is the moral focus of the capability approach?

a. care for those for whom we have responsibility

b. developing the capability to do virtuous things

c. freedom and well-being

d. increasing my capability to be happy in the future

Summary of Ethical Theory

We have considered some of the main perspectives actively discussed by ethical theorists today. So what does this overview add to the market-failures approach to ethics? This chapter's survey of ethical theories provides a basic introduction to the language and concepts of ethics. When explaining to others the ethical reasons for our decisions, it is helpful to be familiar with the terminology of duties, rights, utility, character, care, capabilities, and so forth. The different theories we have covered emphasize different aspects of ethical reality, and so they offer us a plurality of conceptual tools that can be used to deal with various ethical problems we may encounter.

CASE STUDY

Autonomous Vehicles and the Trolley Problem

The trolley problem is one the most famous problems in contemporary moral philosophy. First put forward by Philippa Foot in 1967,[23] the problem asks you to imagine yourself standing at a control switch with an out-of-control train hurtling down the track. If you do nothing, the train will continue on its current trajectory and kill five unaware workers on the tracks. However, if you flip the switch next to you, it will divert the train onto a different track on which there is only one worker. Is it permissible to kill one person to save five?

Although many people would say the latter option is indeed permissible, the trolley problem is meant to make us pause and consider our intuitions about agency, innocence, and culpability. Is killing someone the same as letting someone die? It is usually assumed to be a maxim that one ought not to kill innocents; does making an exception in this particular case jeopardize that general rule? Whichever course of action you decide to take, should you feel guilty about the bad parts of the outcome that could not be avoided?

There have been many variations of the trolley problem since Foot's original presentation. Some of the more common variants substitute the switch for a person whom you can push into the train's path to derail it. Others make the person on the second track a person dear to you, such as a child. Others introduce a really cool loop-de-loop for the trolley to go on before crashing into the five victims. (On this latter view, letting five people die in an exciting way is better than killing one person in a boring way.) The original and all of these variations ask us to critically interrogate the idea that ethics is a simple math problem. There is a seductive simplicity to the idea that all we need to do is compare the harms (or utility) of the two possible options, and that doing so will clearly tell us what the "right" thing to do is.

For many years these questions were primarily of interest to academics, but in recent years there has been an increasing urgency to do more than ask questions about these types of scenarios. This urgency has been brought on by the development of autonomous (self-driving) cars. Autonomous cars are, as the name might suggest, cars that are equipped with a variety of technological implements that replicate the functions of a driver and drive themselves. The car is able to commute from place to place—the comparatively easy part of the technological problem—and, more importantly, the cars are able to react to the environment around them.

Furthermore, since these theories systematize the ethical intuitions many people operate with on a daily basis, a grasp of their basic contours can also help us to better understand the values and motivations of people we interact with. We may not always agree with the ethical views of people we encounter at our workplace or in the marketplace, but knowing the basics of ethical theory can help make us better listeners and better communicators. Finally, these ethical theories offer us ethical principles and ideals that can serve as guides to anyone interested in being an ethical disruptor. We can sum up the guidance each theory offers as follows:

1. Deontological ethics reminds us that we must always do our ethical duty, no matter how great the gains we could make by compromising them.

Enabling the cars to react to circumstances presented to them has required a number of technological challenges (sensors, image recognition, and the like), but there is also a moral question to be asked: *In situations like the trolley problem, what should the car be programmed to do?* If there is insufficient time to stop and no safe alternative to redirect toward, should the car kill one pedestrian to save five others? Should it take into account other factors such as whether the pedestrians were jaywalking or appropriately using the sidewalk? Should the ages of the pedestrians matter? What if the only way to save the five pedestrians is to steer the occupant(s) of the car into danger? Would you buy a car that does not protect you above all other individuals on the road?

These questions may seem far-fetched, but one pedestrian has already been killed by a self-driving car.[24] On 18 March 2018, Elaine Herzberg was struck and killed during the prototype testing of such a vehicle. Assigning moral blame in this case is difficult. We could blame the human safety-backup driver for failing to notice the pedestrian. We could blame the regulators who allowed an immature technology on public roads. We could blame those who programmed the computer. We could blame Herzberg herself, who was crossing the avenue outside of a designated crosswalk. We could also blame city planners who—wittingly or unwittingly—create infrastructure that is hostile to pedestrians.

Autonomous cars are not widely available in the market yet, but the future is coming faster than we think, and many trolley-style questions remain unanswered.

For Discussion

1. Consider the following claim: *An autonomous vehicle that prioritizes the safety of the vehicle's occupants over other road users (like pedestrians or people on scooters) is an unjust way to externalize the cost of responsibility.* Do you agree or disagree? Explain.
2. Would you buy (or even ride in) an autonomous vehicle if you knew that it did not prioritize your safety over the safety of other road users?
3. Should companies be allowed to test autonomous vehicles on public roads? If so, under what conditions? Explain.
4. What would you do in the trolley problem? Would you pull the lever? How would the different moral theories answer the problem?

2. Utilitarianism emphasizes the complementary insight that results do matter, and that an ethical person is sensitive to the ways their actions can benefit or harm themself and others.

3. Virtue ethics points out that, while individual actions are important, ethics also concerns the bigger picture of a human life with its history, tendencies, and overall trajectory toward or away from a state of flourishing.

4. Ethics of care highlights the fact that the concrete relationships in which we find ourselves embedded have ethical significance.

5. The capability approach expands on and combines some of the insights of other ethical theories to produce a more practical and concrete set of guidelines for ensuring the well-being of ourselves and others.

CONCEPT CHECK

2.8 What is one reason (mentioned in this chapter) to study traditional moral theories?

a. Studying different moral theories lets us decide which are right and which are wrong.

b. Studying different moral theories gives us the vocabulary with which to become better listeners and communicators.

c. Studying different moral theories makes us moral persons.

d. Studying different moral theories makes it easier to make a moral decision.

Living with Your Decisions: A Clear Conscience

In **Chapter 3** we discuss a model intended to help you work through concrete and practical ethical decision making.

How do we move from understanding the contours of ethical theory to being able to make well-informed and ethically justifiable decisions in our everyday lives? In some sense, the entirety of the rest of this text is our effort to help you think through that transition from theory to practice. But in concluding the present chapter, we want to make a few brief remarks that will begin to bring the idealism of these ethical theories down to earth.

Private and Public Domains

Each of us has a set of beliefs and values concerning what is right and wrong. We inherit many of our ethical beliefs and values from the socialization we receive through our parents and guardians, teachers, mentors, and peers, and we hold others based on our own thoughtful reflection. Our individual ethical orientation can affect the way we behave inside and outside the domain of business transactions. Let us call this personalized set of ethical beliefs and values our **private morality**.

When we take on a public role as representatives of a profession we belong to or a company we work for, we sometimes have to set aside our private morality. Our employer, co-workers, or

private morality
The personal ethical norms and values of an individual.

TABLE 2.1 Some Principal–Fiduciary Relationships

Principal	Fiduciary (Agent)
client	lawyer
patient	physician
ward	guardian
child	parent
shareholder	corporation
board of directors	executive officers

client base may hold ethical views that differ from our own, and to carry out business effectively we may have to act in ways that are contrary to our own preferred views. To act as an agent on behalf of others is to act as a **fiduciary**. The word fiduciary derives from the Latin *fides*, which means *faith* or *trust*. A *fiduciary relationship* is a relationship of trust, in which a **principal** (the person whose interests are being acted on) entrusts certain tasks or operations to an *agent* (the person who acts on behalf of the principal). The beliefs and values we are called to act on in our fiduciary capacity can be termed our **public morality**.

Many business relationships involve a fiduciary dimension, and so situations arise in which our private and public moralities clash, and we must decide which one takes precedence. The question arises to what extent we should be willing to compromise our private ethical principles when acting in a fiduciary role. This is not something that can be answered by giving a formula. To a large extent such decisions are quite personal, and different people may have different levels of comfort with allowing public morality (for example, company values) to override private morality.

Accepting Moral Tragedy

In recognizing the difference between private and public morality, we make room for moral ambiguity. Ethical issues can be incredibly complex, and there is rarely just one clear-cut solution. If we are going to develop as ethical decision makers, we must make peace with the fact that different moral obligations will pull us in different directions and that it is often impossible to act in a way that satisfies all of these obligations. In such cases, there might be a right thing to do, but doing the right thing nevertheless comes with a moral cost, since we will have left other genuine obligations unfulfilled.

For instance, let us say that you work for a Canadian company and are competing for a contract from a business situated in another country where bribing officials happens to be common practice. You are aware that other companies competing for the same contract have given these "gifts," so to be competitive it seems as though you will have to follow suit. In fact, you seem to have an ethical responsibility to offer the "gift," since without doing so you will not be able to meet your fiduciary duty to your shareholders, who have directed you to secure the contract. What makes this a moral dilemma and legally questionable is the line between gift giving and bribery. Under Canadian law, gift giving is okay, but bribery of foreign public officials is prohibited by the Corruption of Foreign Public Officials Act, SC 1998, c 34 (CFPOA).[25, 26] You cannot offer the "gift" without violating your duty to conduct business with

fiduciary
A person commissioned to act in the interests of another party called the *principal*.

principal
In a *fiduciary relationship*, the principal is the party whose interests are formally represented by the agent acting as a *fiduciary*.

public morality
The set of ethical norms and values that constrain a fiduciary given their relationship to a principal.

moral tragedy
A situation in which a choice must be made between alternatives, each of which involves violating an important ethical requirement.

We learned in **Chapter 1** that bribing in order to compete clearly contravenes Heath's second commandment that a business should only compete through price and quality.

integrity, but you cannot withhold the "gift" without failing to meet your fiduciary obligations. This sort of situation involves a **moral tragedy** since, whatever you choose, you cannot avoid doing something unethical. The old expression "damned if you do, and damned if you don't" also captures the sentiment.

CONCEPT CHECK

2.9 What is a fiduciary duty?

a. It is a moral, but not legal, duty that one person (the agent) has to another person (the principal).

b. It is a moral and legal duty that one person (the agent) has to another person (the principal).

c. It is a moral and legal duty that one person (the principal) has to another person (the agent).

d. It is a legal, but not moral, duty that one person (the agent) has to another person (the principal).

The Light of Day and How to Sleep at Night

light-of-day test
An assessment of whether you would be comfortable with your decision or action becoming public knowledge. If not, your decision or action fails the light-of-day test.

As we just noted, there are situations where no available course of action is ethically untainted, and yet we still have to act. The **light-of-day test** is a useful way of testing how comfortable you really are with a hard or ethically fraught decision you are considering. It asks you to consider how you would feel if the details of your action were published in the news, so that everyone around you became aware of what you had done. If the idea of your actions becoming public information makes you squeamish, that is probably a sign that you are not confident in your ability to justify your action ethically. If, on the other hand, you would be untroubled by others knowing about the decision you have made, that is most likely a good indicator that you have done so with a clear conscience and are not in violation of any relevant ethical principles.

An auction to determine which life is more valuable is morally reprehensible. A decision of this sort clearly does not pass the light-of-day test.

Of course, some people simply care less than others what people think about them. With such people in mind, William S. Burroughs wrote, "Hustlers of the world, there is only one Mark you cannot beat: The Mark Inside."[27] The point is that you may be able to deceive other people and hide the reality of your immoral activity from them, but you will not be able to hide it from yourself. In the end, each person has to live with themselves and their decisions. For most of us, it would take great effort to stop caring about our moral character completely, or to give up any sense of striving to do what is right and good. Whatever you do in the domain of business is still something that you do. We cannot evade responsibility simply by appealing to the fact that everyone else is doing it, or that my manager told me to do it. Every action of yours becomes a part of your history, and contributes to the sum of who you are. To the extent that this matters to us, we should choose our actions carefully.

CONCEPT CHECK

2.10 What is the "light-of-day test"?

a. It asks you to consider how you would feel if the details of your action were published in the news.

b. It asks you to consider how society would benefit if the details of your action were published in the news.

c. It invites public comment on your decision before you act on it.

d. It determines how many lawyers will starve because you do not need their services.

Summing Up

There are many ethical theories. This chapter has touched on only a few major ones that are relevant to ground a defensible business ethic. The value in learning about these theories is that it gives us the vocabulary with which to talk with each other about ethical issues. Not everyone subscribes to the same ethical theory, and learning about the different theories can help us understand how and why our ethical judgments differ. Understanding where the other person is coming from is a necessary first step if we are to make collective ethical decisions in the public sphere.

For Discussion and Review

1. Explain how, according to deontological pluralism, there can be conflicting basic moral duties.

2. List all the different ethical theories discussed in this chapter. What is the moral focus of each theory? (e.g., *What does deontology focus on? What does virtue theory focus on?* etc.)

3. Why do we need ethical theories if we are taught right from wrong at a young age?
4. What do we do in the case of conflicting conceptions of what makes something right or wrong?
5. Choose two ethical theories discussed in this chapter. Can you think of a way to reconcile the fundamental differences between those ethical theories?
6. Is it always wrong to lie? (Compare and contrast how a utilitarian would answer the question versus how a deontologist like Kant would answer the question.)
7. *"I am right. You disagree with me. So you are wrong."* Is it possible to come to a common understanding if two people disagree about what makes something right or wrong?

Further Reading

Arpaly, Nomy. "Moral Worth." *Unprincipled Virtue*, 2002, 67–116.

Rachels, Stuart, and James Rachels. "The Challenge of Cultural Relativism." In *The Elements of Moral Philosophy*. New York, NY: McGraw-Hill Education, 2019.

Richter, Duncan. *Why Be Good? A Historical Introduction to Ethics*. New York: Oxford University Press, 2008.

Shafer-Landau, Russ. *The Fundamentals of Ethics*. Oxford: Oxford University Press, 2010.

"Universal Declaration of Human Rights." United Nations. Accessed January 20, 2020. https://www.un.org/en/universal-declaration-human-rights/.

CHAPTER 3
Ethical Decision Making

By the end of this chapter you should be able to

- Explain moral pluralism and differentiate it from ethical relativism.

- Distinguish private and public morality.

- Explain and apply the concept of *dirty hands*.

- Identify challenges with value conflicts and democratic decision making.

- Describe major cognitive biases and explain how they impair our ethical reasoning.

- Apply a six-step ethical decision-making model to problems in order to gain moral clarity.

One of the themes that we have been developing so far is that business activity is constrained in two ways. First, norms internal to the market system itself constrain what we can or cannot do when competing for resources. Second, since business cannot exist without a functioning social and political system, business is constrained by social norms—or more specifically, ethical norms.

We spent most of Chapter 2 surveying different ethical theories and spelling out what the different theories focus on. Deontological theories focus on duties, utilitarian theories focus on promoting social utility, virtue theory focuses on the character of a person, ethics of care focuses on the ethical significance of the relationships we find ourselves in, and the capabilities approach focuses on the freedom and well-being of a person. With different ethical theories focusing on different things, it might be tempting to ask which theory is the right one. If one theory tells us that lying is always wrong, and a different theory tells us that lying is sometimes permissible, it is understandable why we might think that one theory has to be right and the other wrong.

A problem with saying that one moral theory is the correct one (and that all the others are wrong) is that we close ourselves off to different ways of thinking about situations that have an ethical component. If we stubbornly commit ourselves to one ethical theory and refuse to look at an ethical issue from different points of view, there is very little opportunity for dialogue with people who disagree with us. Conversely, if we view an ethical issue through the lenses of different ethical theories, we will be in a much better position to discuss the issue openly with other people.

A key part of making sound ethical decisions in the workplace is learning how to discuss the ethical components of a decision with others. However, each one of us has a conception of what makes an action morally right or wrong, and we will not always agree on this, which leaves us open to moral disagreement. If we are unable to distinguish between private and public morality, or if we lack the conceptual framework or vocabulary with which to discuss ethical perspectives, these disagreements can persist and negatively affect an organization.

Private and Public Morality Revisited

We are many things to many people. We are individuals, employees, colleagues, customers, representatives, teammates, classmates, members of communities, and parts of families. Each of these contexts has different norms or expectations of behaviour and interaction. For example, how Dana behaves toward a business competitor will be different (hopefully) from how Dana behaves toward a romantic partner. Similarly, the claims that Dana's romantic partner can make against Dana are going to be very different from the claims that Dana's business competitor can make against Dana.

moral context
A set of relational and situational factors that yield distinctive ethical requirements on your action. The most important contexts we discuss are the personal and the professional (fiduciary) contexts.

This plurality of moral contexts suggests two important things about how we behave toward others. First, there are times when it is perfectly fine to act primarily in your own interests, and times when acting in your own interests will earn you the moral rebuke of others. The difference is whether you are operating in the role of a private individual or as an agent responsible for someone else.

Many of the day-to-day decisions that we make are personal in nature: how to get to school, where to get a haircut, when to have a nap, or what to wear Friday night. We can make most of these decisions by simply consulting our own personal values—those things that matter most to us. The moral values that matter most in these settings are part of our private morality. In contrast, when we make decisions on behalf of another person, we must consider their interests, not our own. This is the case even when the values of the person we are representing do not align with our own personal values. In such cases, our decisions are subject to the scrutiny of others and are assessed under the standards of *public morality*.

Consider the following scenario that explores how a person's public and private morality interact. Osheta values community, co-operation, non-violence, justice, integrity, and fundamental equality of all persons. She strives to live by these values in all aspects of her life, because she views these things as a duty owed to both self and others in response to the rights she believes persons have. She also teaches at a public university, and the university has other values directed primarily toward producing an educated public: research, publications, teaching, service, and collegiality. In this role, Osheta has a responsibility to act in the interests of the university. Does Osheta have to check her private values at the campus transit station as she heads to her office?

The answer is, perhaps unsurprisingly, both yes and no. Many of her personal values are compatible with the values held by the university. Community and collegiality go together. She believes that persons have a right to an education if they choose, and both she and the university are active in providing that. Publications rely on academic and research integrity along with some degree of co-operation. And most public universities proclaim some kind of fundamental equality of all persons. However, if her personal values arise from a particular religious belief, she is limited in how much she can speak of that belief in class. Turning the classroom into a preaching opportunity is a violation of public morality, because it would place her interests ahead of the ones she is supposed to serve in her role as an instructor.

But there are times when the values of an organization will differ from your own. In many companies, there is a legal requirement to give high priority to creating value for investors. The industry may have its own set of practices that do not completely align with your moral expectations. The moral norms of a business tend to be more competitive than co-operative. And while management may speak of being "family," a business does not operate under the same principles as a family household. Your work for a business, whether as an employee or as a director, falls under the expectations of public morality. Whenever you are doing work for the business, you are expected to serve the interests of the business, not your own. This means that there are times when you will be expected to act in ways that you would not in your own private life.

Continuing with the scenario above, suppose Osheta is now working for a tobacco company. The company's publicly stated values include revenue growth, integrity in its dealings, fairness to its suppliers and employees, and a pleasurable customer experience. But the phrase "pleasurable customer experience" is really just a euphemism for staving off the unpleasant symptoms of nicotine withdrawal, and the company disclaims responsibility for the unpleasant experience of treating cancers caused by smoking. When Osheta inquires about the inconsistency of the customer experience, she is told that the customers, not the tobacco company, are responsible for their addiction.

Osheta sees that the company is not acting with integrity toward its customers. She sees the company taking advantage of peoples' susceptibility to the addictive effects of nicotine. She may see this as a matter of justice, for it violates a person's right to control over their own health. She discovers an incompatibility between the moral demands of being an agent of the company and her own personal values. She chooses to resign her position as a matter of conscience.

CONCEPT CHECK

3.1 What best describes a moral context?

a. It is a zone of influence where you can teach others what is morally permissible.

b. It is defined by the expectations contained in a moral pretext.

c. It is norms of behaviour that are consistent in every context.

d. Different contexts often come with different norms or expectations of behaviour.

3.2 What is private morality?

a. the moral considerations we (must) attend to in representing and serving the interests of others

b. the moral considerations we (must) attend to in our private, personal dealings

c. the moral considerations others (must) attend to when dealing with us as private individuals

d. the moral considerations we (must) attend to whenever we are out in public

3.3 What is public morality?

a. the moral considerations we (must) attend to whenever we are out in public

b. the moral considerations we (must) attend to when we are being represented by others

c. the moral considerations others (must) attend to in their private, personal dealings

d. the moral considerations we (must) attend to when representing and serving the interests of others

Ethical Pluralism Revisited

Each moral theory differs in its moral focus, and the values that inform our private morality can differ from the values that inform our public morality. So even if everyone involved in making a decision agrees to the facts of the case, each person may still come to a different conclusion about what the right thing to do is. And it may be the case that each conclusion captures an important moral aspect to the problem at hand. In such a case we have an instance of ethical pluralism. Remember, ethical pluralism is a way of describing a situation where many ethically good things are valued and taken as central in ethical reasoning, but there is no single value that is held as absolute or given priority in all cases.

> We discuss ethical pluralism in **Chapter 1.**

Given all of this, it might be tempting to say that moral pluralism makes it really hard to resolve moral disagreements: How can we come to an agreement if we all have different opinions about what the right thing to do is? Moral agreement is only impossible if our goal is to find the one problem-free solution to a moral problem. A better way to think about moral pluralism is that it creates a parameter—or design space—that constrains our moral reasoning. These constraints may not lead to a morally optimal solution, but they may allow many good, feasible, imperfect solutions. Part of ethical reasoning, then, is to determine which ethical principles can be usefully applied in a particular situation, recognizing that there may not be an ideal outcome for all parties concerned.

CONCEPT CHECK

3.4 What is moral pluralism?

a. It is the view that there is one moral value expressed in a plurality of ways.

b. It is the view that there is a plurality of contexts in which a moral value applies.

c. It is the view that there is a plurality of moral values, none of which is held as absolute.

d. It is the view that there is a plurality of moral values, all of which are absolute.

3.5 What is a good way to think about moral pluralism?

a. The plurality of moral considerations may not allow for an optimal moral solution, but it may allow for many good, feasible, imperfect solutions.

b. The plurality of moral considerations always allows for an optimal moral solution.

c. The plurality of moral considerations makes it impossible to arrive at a good moral decision.

d. The singularity of moral considerations overrides the moral context of decision making.

Moral Disagreements

Reconciling disagreements can be incredibly frustrating, even for mundane things. Just think of the last time you and a group of your friends ordered a pizza. How did you decide what to put on the pizza? Is there a combination of toppings that you can easily agree on, or does someone have to give something up in order to join in the feast? Coming to an agreement on what toppings to order can really test the limits of true friendship.

Now think of a time when you had an ethical disagreement with someone in the workplace. Perhaps you saw a co-worker falsify their timesheet and you confronted them about it. Or maybe you have been arguing with a co-worker about the ethics of selling cosmetics tested on animals. Or perhaps a debate is raging among your colleagues about your company's refusal to make some washrooms in the building gender neutral. Ethical disagreements in the workplace can be exceedingly difficult to work through. Even if those embroiled in the disagreement can agree on what the ethical issue is and who the relevant stakeholders are, it can take a Herculean effort to come to a resolution. Reconciling moral disagreements in a way that is fair, democratic, and respectful of the interests of everyone concerned requires being honest about preferences, goodwill toward other members of the group, and the grace to accept that a second-best compromise may be all we can hope for.

This assumes, of course, that it *is* possible to make group decisions that are fair and democratic. Consider the following fictitious example.

As a Canadian corporation, the board of directors of Aggregated ReadyMix Solutions Experts must act in the interests of its shareholders, which means it must give priority to the values held by the shareholders. But what happens if the shareholders do not share the same values or vision for the corporation? (While the shareholders have a legitimate contractual right to a monetary return on their investment, it is not a right to a maximized return in pure monetary terms. This means it is possible for the investors to have different visions for the corporation.)

To keep the example simple, we will say the corporation has three investors: Ahmed, Jasna, and Laurel. Ahmed values maximizing profit and would like the corporation to restructure and reduce its labour force. Jasna values social responsibility and would like the corporation to support community initiatives like the local food bank. Laurel, on the other hand, believes the corporation needs to play the long game and would like the corporation to focus on environmental sustainability. What hope do these investors have in coming to a fair and democratic agreement? Unfortunately, it is impossible to guarantee that we can convert individual preference rankings to one that represents the will of the collective. Whether or not we can all depends on how the three investors rank their preferences.

Assume the three investors rank their preferences as outlined in Table 3.1. If the investors have agreed that a majority vote among them wins, then it is not possible to reconcile the preference rankings of all three investors. A close inspection of the three individual rankings will reveal that there are three majority preferences between pairs of objectives. For example, compare the preference rankings for Ahmed and Laurel: both prefer maximizing profit over social responsibility. But the same is true for the other two objectives: social responsibility is favoured over sustainability, and sustainability is favoured over maximizing profit.

The moral of this example is that it is not always possible to reconcile the preferences of the three investors. This result is an instance of the **Condorcet paradox**: aggregating rational individual preference orderings can produce conflicting (circular) collective preferences. So unless one of the investors can be convinced to change their mind, making a group decision will involve overriding someone's interests, even though everyone involved in the decision is being rational, honest, and civil.

Condorcet paradox Aggregating rational individual preference orderings can produce circular (irrational) collective preferences.

FIGURE 3.1 An example of circular preferences.

TABLE 3.1 Individually Rational Preference Orderings

Priority	Ahmed	Jasna	Laurel
1	Maximizing profit	Social responsibility	Sustainability
2	Social responsibility	Sustainability	Maximizing profit
3	Sustainability	Maximizing profit	Social responsibility

The Condorcet paradox can arise whenever three or more voters have three or more alternatives to rank based on preference. This paradox is a corollary of the more general **Arrow's impossibility theorem**. It turns out that unless a voting system is dictatorial, it can be manipulated.[1]

Since no preference-vote scheme is free from manipulation, voters have to trust that every other voter is being honest about their preferences and not trying to rig the vote, and not violate that trust themselves; otherwise the voting method will be suspect. As a result, good collective decision making on the basis of voting could very well mean someone's preferences will be overridden. The question will be whether those preferences were captured fairly with respect to the other votes.

Arrow's impossibility theorem
Arrow's theorem shows that an ideal voting structure (a reasonable procedure for forming a collective ordering of preferences in relation to alternatives) is impossible.

CONCEPT CHECK

3.6 **What best describes the Condorcet paradox?**

a. What is true of the group is necessarily true of the individual.

b. A majority's preference ordering may be circular, and therefore irrational.

c. A majority's preference ordering is always going to be circular, and therefore irrational.

d. It is impossible to be honest about one's preferences.

stakeholder
A party with an interest in the decisions and actions of a business.

Stakeholders: Whose Interests Matter?

To make a good decision that affects other parties, you have to identify which parties matter. These parties are often referred to as **stakeholders** in the process, because they stand to gain or lose something of value to them as a result—they have something significant *at stake*. But not all stakeholders are created equal. The parties who are negatively affected may be affected only because of increased competition or other circumstances, not because they are unjustly harmed, and some of the parties who are positively affected may receive that benefit as a side effect of a decision.

We can classify stakeholders' interests along two distinct axes: proximity of effect and genuineness of claim. A stakeholder who will be directly (perhaps not immediately, but closely) affected by a decision is said to have a **proximal interest** in the outcome, while one who will be affected only indirectly has a **distal interest** in the outcome. For example, if a company chooses to open a new facility that will employ 50,000 workers, the community and province have a proximal interest compared to the interests of local realtors who will have an influx of people looking for housing. The realtors' interest is derivative, and therefore distal.

Determining whether a party's claim to be a stakeholder is genuine takes more work. Parties whose rights are infringed or whose status in a relationship will change have a **genuine interest** in the outcome. However, there are those who will complain if something of value is going to be distributed without them getting a cut, or if something to

We talk more about stakeholders in **Chapter 4**, **Chapter 9**, and **Chapter 10**.

proximal interest
A person has a proximal interest in a decision if their well-being is directly affected by the outcome of that decision.

distal interest
A person has a distal interest in a decision if their well-being is only indirectly affected by the outcome of that decision.

genuine interest
A person's claim or interest in a decision is *genuine* if the decision infringes on something they are entitled to.

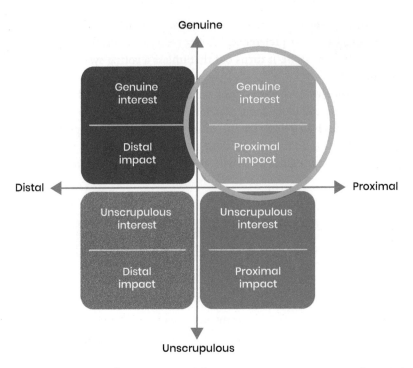

FIGURE 3.2 Stakeholder interests and impacts. We can categorize stakeholder interests in four quadrants. The upper-right quadrant represents the interests of a stakeholder that are proximal and genuine. Stakeholder interests of this type should be given priority over stakeholder interests that are distal and unscrupulous—which are represented in the bottom-left quadrant.

which they have an attachment but no entitlement is being withdrawn. Claims like this are **unscrupulous interests**.

unscrupulous interest
A person's claim or interest in a decision is *unscrupulous* if the decision does not infringe on anything they are entitled to.

Here is an example of an unscrupulous claim. Restaurateurs in Canada have complained that food trucks compete unfairly because they do not have to pay rent or maintain a building, and so the restaurateurs have argued that food trucks should not be permitted to compete directly against them.[2] The claim of unfair competition is unscrupulous, however, because the restaurateurs are trying to protect their businesses from the effects of an emerging, market-disrupting food-service model. When Canada's Competition Bureau examined the matter, they found that food trucks did not provide unfair competition; rather, they were filling a demand in the food-service marketplace that restaurants were not providing. Nonetheless, many Canadian cities still impose strict restrictions on food trucks, such as how close a food truck can be to a traditional restaurant, or how many food trucks are allowed to operate. The unscrupulous interests of the restaurateurs have resulted in a barrier to competition, which violates the fifth of Heath's ten commandments.

Armed with these two sets of distinctions (proximal/distal and genuine/unscrupulous), you can determine whose interests matter. The parties with interests that are both proximal and genuine need to be given consideration first. The other parties holding genuine interests have lower priority; those claiming unscrupulous interests need attention only insofar as they take steps to prevent you from implementing your decision.

David Giral / Alamy

Food trucks (pictured here in the Old Port of Montreal) provide a quick alternative to eating in a restaurant. Some restaurateurs claim food trucks have an unfair advantage and should therefore be banned because of unfair competition.

CONCEPT CHECK

3.7 Who is a stakeholder?

a. A stakeholder is anyone who wants to complain about how someone benefits from a decision.

b. A stakeholder is someone defending a board of directors from a vampiric investor.

c. A stakeholder is anyone who stands to gain or lose something of value when a decision is made.

d. A stakeholder is anyone who is directly affected by the outcome of a decision.

3.8 What is an unscrupulous claim?

a. It is an unjustified claim to an entitlement.

b. It represents a distal interest in a decision.

c. It is a morally justified decision to act against another party.

d. It is a claim that facilitates making a moral decision.

Continued

3.9 Who has a distal interest?

a. Someone has a distal interest if they are directly affected by a decision.

b. Someone has a distal interest if they are indirectly affected by a decision.

c. Someone has a distal interest if they do not have a proximal interest in a decision.

d. Someone has a distal interest if they have an unscrupulous interest in a decision.

Value Conflicts

When engaging in a decision-making process (following a model like the one we present later in this chapter), you will have to contend with the practical implications of conflicting values, and not just the theoretical ones. Dealing with these potential conflicts is an important skill in the workplace, so it is worth examining some important points about resolving them. In *Giving Voice to Values*, Mary Gentile notes that, especially when working with groups of people from diverse cultures, inquiring about people's values while not expecting automatic conformity with one's own is a good starting point.[3] Such an inquiry allows people to identify what values they have in common, and this common starting point can facilitate a respectful exploration of values that are not shared but still matter.

> Identifying common values is an important aspect of integrative bargaining, which is discussed in **Chapter 10**.

The striking thing is how quickly we seem to be able to express these values. As Gentile notes, we are adept at "pre-scripting"; that is, developing and rehearsing rationalizations or strategies in advance for dealing with hypothetical situations.[4] When these pre-scripted rationalizations include some expression of our values, then we have a way to articulate those values and why they matter in a particular context. All we have to do is deliver the script that we have been using to justify to ourselves what we want to do, and invite the other relevant stakeholders to do the same. This is not an argumentative step, but an informative one. Moreover, gently inquiring about stakeholder values, rather than immediately resorting to something like a priority ranking of the values we as decision makers believe should matter, can create a learning atmosphere. In this kind of atmosphere, there is less need for us and our interlocutors to resort to other pre-scripted defences about not wanting to cause offence or be disruptive. Not only will the values that are significant to the context come to the fore, but the willingness to listen will also establish the mutual respect for and goodwill toward all parties in the conflict. In turn, the rest of the conversation, even if it is difficult and impassioned, will help us arrive at a defensible decision that respects the values of our interlocutors.

Making Ethical Decisions

The cognitive features that come along with being human also affect how we reason in the moral dimension. This means that we must be aware of two particular human factors that can help or confound our ability to make good decisions. The first is understanding that we have two different "thinking" systems (unconscious/intuitive versus conscious/deliberative), each with a distinct benefit in particular contexts. The second is understanding the biases that can trip us up regardless of how much we try to compensate for them. We need to pay attention to these biases because they will affect our perspective on who the relevant stakeholders are and what significant values we ascribe to them.

Moral Intuition versus Moral Reasoning

Decision making, at least by way of following a model, is **deliberative**. As Daniel Kahneman points out in *Thinking Fast and Slow*,[5] this deliberative way of thinking is sometimes referred to as *System 2*, or the conscious part of thought that we identify with. In contrast, many of our value judgments are quick and automatic—this is the work of *System 1*, or unconscious thought. Systems 1 and 2 are a convenient way to think about the difference between **moral intuition** versus moral reasoning.

Much of our ethics-related behaviour is intuitive.[6] We shake our heads at a troubling headline because the conduct it describes goes against a value we hold intuitively. We cheer for the hero who saves a life because we intuit that such an act is virtuous. These "intuitions" (which Kahneman would say are simply acts of recognition[7]) play an important role in our day-to-day lives. When we engage in System-2–style deliberation, however, our intuitions need to turn into reasons.

When we engage in moral reasoning, we should prepare ourselves for the possibility that our moral intuitions will plausibly need revision, in much the same way that our subconscious first impression of someone might need revision when we find out new information about them. Our moral intuitions or values, while important and in many cases worth defending, are often not justified in the way we need them to be if we are going to assert that they should take priority over competing values. Consequently, part of ethical decision making is

deliberative decision making
Conscious, reflective mental processing of factors relevant to choice and action. Kahneman refers to this as System 2 thinking.

moral intuition
A persistent and powerful moral belief possessed by a person immediately, without being consciously justified in terms of other reasons or factors. Kahneman calls intuitive thinking of this sort System 1 thinking.

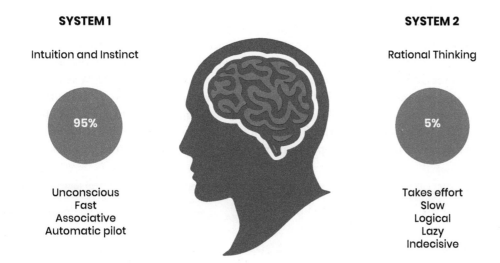

SYSTEM 1

Intuition and Instinct

95%

Unconscious
Fast
Associative
Automatic pilot

SYSTEM 2

Rational Thinking

5%

Takes effort
Slow
Logical
Lazy
Indecisive

FIGURE 3.3 System 1 and 2. System 1 represents our intuitions and quick assessments. System 2 represents a more deliberate process that engages our logical and rational thinking. System 1 is useful for running away from big cats and avoiding being hit by buses. System 2 is useful when we write essays or when we need to think our way through a tough problem.

Source: Daniel Kahneman, *Thinking Fast and Slow* (London, UK: Penguin, 2012); illustration of head ©iStockphoto / Eugene Valter

recognizing the psychological factors involved in the System-1 style of value acquisition versus the System-2 style of analysis and moral reasoning. This text provides you with tools to help with your moral reasoning, but other psychological factors can get in the way of the successful employment of such tools.

Bias and Decision Making

Despite our best efforts to be rational beings, a large number of well-established cognitive biases affect how we evaluate, plan, and execute decisions in the workplace and beyond. Biases distort our worldviews and cause us to make poor inferences; as such, they hinder our ability to make good decisions. With this in mind, it is worthwhile to examine some particularly harmful biases. Our examination will focus primarily on how these biases affect decision making.

Self-Serving Bias

self-serving bias
An excessively favourable view of oneself that results in inaccurate thinking or perception.

The **self-serving bias** affects how we think about and attribute successes and failures. To illustrate how this bias works, think back to a time where you did a great job at something. Now think back to a time where you failed at something. In what ways did you attribute the success versus the failure? The self-serving bias makes us more likely to attribute our successes to *internal reasons*, such as our hard work or the masterful execution of our skills. On the other hand, we are more likely to attribute our failures to *external reasons* such as bad luck, unfair conditions, or even taking the deterministic view that success was literally impossible. To illustrate this further, consider an example that is likely all too familiar by this point: academic testing. The self-serving bias means that students are likely to attribute high test scores to their perceived efforts, aptitude, and knowledge. But under the effects of the same bias, students are likely to attribute personal underachievement to poorly written questions, unfair expectations, or malicious grading practices.

How might the self-serving bias affect our decision making? Well, consider the primary role of a manager or supervisor. Every manager or supervisor eventually has to make decisions regarding the termination of underperforming employees. Managers and supervisors are part of teams, yet have to shoulder the responsibility of their team's performance. When it is time to take that responsibility or deflect it, the self-serving bias means higher-ups are more likely to blame employees (an external factor) for negative outcomes rather than, say, take responsibility for problematic managerial skills (an internal factor). Likewise, the self-serving bias means that people in positions of power are more likely to attribute positive outcomes to their

BACKGROUND

Internal and External Reasons

Roughly speaking, *internal reasons* are things that have to do with us, while *external reasons* are things outside ourselves or beyond our control. For example, if Greg underperforms in a triathlon race, it might be because he undertrained (an internal reason), or because the weather was awful and he had three flat tires (external reasons).

personal wisdom and skill, simultaneously discounting the important contributions of other members of the team. These scenarios can easily lead to poor morale, a workplace culture of distrust and suspicion, or worse.

This was just a simple example; the self-serving bias can negatively affect a great number of aspects of decision making, and consequently is important to watch out for. You might find Step 3 of the ethical decision-making model later in this chapter to be a good place to stop and reflect about how the self-serving bias has potentially affected your own values as well as the values of others.

See Step 3 (Identify Stakeholder Values and Conflicts) of the ethical decision-making model on page 67 of **this chapter**.

CONCEPT CHECK

3.10 The team leader on a project tirelessly self-promotes and has a habit of discounting the important work of others on the team. What is a problematic consequence of this type of behaviour?

a. This type of behaviour reflects the natural hierarchy in any organization.

b. This type of behaviour establishes how year-end bonuses should be distributed.

c. This type of behaviour encourages co-operation and goodwill.

d. This type of behaviour can easily lead to poor morale and a workplace culture of distrust and suspicion, or worse.

Attribution Error

The converse of the self-serving bias is **attribution error**. Attribution errors are made with respect to others. While the self-serving bias blames external factors for our negative outcomes, the attribution error blames someone else's failures or shortcomings on internal factors—often their character or personality—and ascribes any positive outcomes that accrue to others to circumstance or luck rather than their own efforts and abilities.

Attribution errors are pernicious because they demand of others more than we are willing to demand of ourselves. Attribution errors also foster stereotypes that push those perceived as unsuccessful to the margins. Consider homeless persons or the working poor. Canadians tend to have a less-than-charitable attitude toward the less fortunate. The homeless and working poor have been called lazy and are often considered "part of the problem."[8] However, very few people are homeless by choice, and few people choose to be poor. A survey in 2011 found that 7.6 per cent of Canadians are considered part of the working poor.[9] A lot of external factors contribute to precarious working conditions. As well, mental or physical impairments can prevent people from being employed. It is unjust to label homeless and working poor persons as "burdens on society" when there are systemic structural barriers to participating in society. Moreover, if persons are not considered a part of society, it is easy to overlook their concerns as stakeholders when making decisions that affect them. Step 2 in the ethical decision-making model later in this chapter considers the interests of all who may be affected by a decision. Making an attribution error in Step 2 will result in the decision being morally suspect.

attribution error
The tendency to give too much weight to internal reasons, and too little weight to external reasons, when making judgments about other people.

In October 2018, only 70 of 795 neighbourhoods across Canada's 36 largest cities had one-bedroom apartments that cost less than 30 per cent of the monthly income of a full-time minimum-wage earner.[10]

See Step 2 (Identify Relevant Stakeholders and Ethical Issues) of the ethical decision-making model on page 66 of **this chapter**.

Confirmation Bias

Confirmation bias is the name given to the phenomenon of people being more likely to search for and interpret information in a way that confirms established beliefs rather than information that could challenge those beliefs. Perhaps this would not be a problem if our beliefs were universally true and justified; this unrealistic scenario aside, confirmation bias prevents us from gathering the knowledge needed to make properly informed decisions and value judgments.

How might this bias affect the way we make ethical decisions in the workplace? Consider how making a decision requires collecting relevant facts. If the facts collected provide an incomplete picture of the situation you are trying to assess, then the assessment will be flawed. This applies equally for evidence gathering—remember: not all facts are obvious; sometimes a great deal of evidence is required before belief is warranted. Confirmation bias narrows the scope of our inquiries and subconsciously lowers the threshold of evidence for things we happen to already believe while raising the evidence threshold for things we do not.

Imagine your boss thought you were a poor employee (possibly for reasons motivated by the self-serving bias described above). Assuming your boss was affected by the confirmation bias, they would then be more likely to focus on any negative quality or performance you exhibited while discounting or not focusing on your positive qualities and achievements. This can result in a spiral where the new negative information reinforces the boss's original impression, leading to even more scrutiny being placed on any potential misstep. Consequently, any decisions made about you would be poorly informed and unbalanced. For a different scenario, consider how a dedicated employee, who genuinely believes the business they work for is incapable of unethical practices, might overlook or discount warning signs that eventually lead to a tragic outcome. Confirmation bias affects people irrespective of their background. If a group starts with a similar belief set, it is possible that nobody in that group will notice the confirmation bias of their peers, since each person's bias would support the other group members' bias. Unfortunately, due to the blind-spot bias (discussed next), recognizing and respectfully pointing out someone's confirmation bias might be futile.

CONCEPT CHECK

3.11 A colleague believes that they are the best candidate for the promotion. They even have a spreadsheet outlining everything they have accomplished in the job, which fails to mention the time they caused significant harm to the company by trying to bribe government officials.

a. This is an example of an inverted hypothesis distribution.

b. This is an example of an attribution bias.

c. This is an example of a confirmation bias.

d. This is an example of a self-serving error.

Blind-Spot Bias

The **blind-spot bias** is perhaps the most problematic bias because it makes people insensitive to how biases affect their thinking and decision making, even when those same people understand how bias affects how other people think and make decisions.

This bias means that, at every level of a business, the decisions being made will most likely be made by people who are not aware, or simply do not believe, they are affected by things like the self-serving bias or confirmation bias. This can make both self-correction and attempts to correct others' biases difficult, especially if the target of correction is adversarial or in a position of power to jeopardize the employment or well-being of the one doing the correcting in some way. This leads us to the bigger issue of **debiasing**.

The Difficulty of Debiasing

Trying to rid oneself of biases is like trying to steer a vehicle with a toque pulled over one's eyes: the intention might be pure, but success and the safety of others is unlikely. The bias blind spot means that we are likely unaware of the many ways in which we are biased. We are very adept at convincing ourselves that we ourselves are not biased and that we do not need to heed debiasing advice.[11] What then are we left to do?

Even though self-reflection is not a sufficient debiasing measure, the good news is that there are ways to reduce bias over time. New research shows that even a single training session involving videos or games can have a substantial debiasing effect, including for the blind-spot

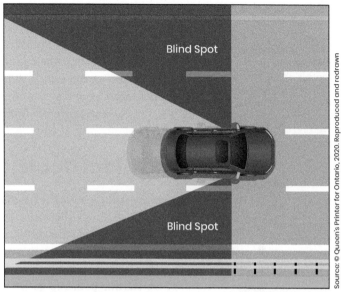

Source: © Queen's Printer for Ontario, 2020. Reproduced and redrawn with permission.

A blind-spot bias prevents us from realizing that our thinking is biased. We need to be constantly vigilant and be very deliberate in reflecting on our thought processes. Think of a bias blind spot like a blind spot in driving: if we do not deliberately check our blind spot, something can be there and we will not notice it. This oversight can lead to really unfortunate events.

blind-spot bias
Admitting that other people are affected by biases, but refusing to acknowledge the effect of biases on oneself. Also referred to as *bias blind-spot*.

debiasing
Taking intentional and reflective steps to reduce the impact of cognitive biases on reasoning.

CONCEPT CHECK

3.12 A colleague is outraged that a co-worker has just accused them of being biased. They have read a website that has a complete list of cognitive biases and so knows for a fact that they do not fall prey to biases.

a. This is an example of an attribution error.

b. This is an example of a failed hypothesis falsification.

c. This is an example of a blind-spot bias.

d. This is an example of a self-serving bias.

bias and the confirmation bias.[12] This, along with techniques like nudges[13] (small reminders or prompts) can effectively reduce people's biases, but reduction is not elimination. Assuming a business is willing to nudge or train all levels of its staff (which is a big assumption), the best-case scenario is still one where individual vigilance is needed. Although the exact number of biases fluctuates as researchers make cases for new biases or dismissing or reclassifying old ones, there are a lot of biases to worry about. We hope this serves as a nudge to stay aware of how your judgments might be affected, as well as the judgments of others with whom you work.

> The right direction to take is not always clear, and there is no guarantee that there is a single right direction rather than a collection of better and worse ones. Working through a decision-making model is only the start of the process.

prudential considerations
The factors that need to be taken into account when making decisions because they affect someone's self-interest.

An Ethical Decision-Making Model

Despite the challenges that surround the process of making good decisions, there are methods that can direct your deliberative processes toward that objective. All of these models have common features, even though the order and wording of each of the steps may be different. But none of them will give you a direct answer, and *none of them can work well without you asking relevant questions of your own*. The questions that a model asks are only suggestive. They are starting points to get you thinking about the questions that matter for the ethical issue at hand.

CASE STUDY

Ethical versus Prudential Considerations: Cyrus the Great Weighs In

Xenophon (a student of Socrates) tells a wonderfully old story about Cyrus the Great as a young child. (Cyrus the Great ruled over the First Persian Empire starting around 550 BCE.) In this particular story, Cyrus is explaining to his mother that he had learned everything he needed to know about matters of justice. He told his mother that he was asked to judge a case once where a big boy had forced another boy to trade coats with him. According to Cyrus, he judged the case incorrectly, and was punished for it. Here is the case in Cyrus's words:

> There were two boys, a big boy and a little boy, and the big boy's coat was small and the small boy's coat was huge. So the big boy stripped the little boy and gave him his own small coat, while he put on the big one himself.[14]

Basically, the big boy forced the little boy to trade coats. Cyrus thought it made sense for the big boy to do this since the result was that both boys had a better-fitting coat. And so Cyrus concluded that the big boy had done nothing wrong. The result?

> Now in giving judgment I decided that it was better for both parties that each should have the coat that fitted him best. But I never got any further in my sentence, because the master thrashed me here, and said that the verdict would have been excellent if I had been appointed to say what fitted and what did not, but I had been called in to decide to whom the coat belonged, and the point to consider was, who had a right to it: Was he who took a thing

Two types of considerations go into making a good decision: prudential considerations and ethical considerations. To act prudentially is to demonstrate care and forethought with respect to a particular objective: *Is what I am doing going to help me achieve my goal?* To act ethically is to act in accordance with principles governing right behaviour: *Is what I am doing the right thing to do?*

The goal of any ethical decision-making process is to recommend a morally and prudentially defensible course of action that addresses a particular moral issue. One way to achieve a goal is to work backward from the objective to the things needed to get there. Each of these steps may be a goal on its own, and some of these subgoals can be decomposed the same way. The goal of a defensible course of action requires having a range of options to explore. If an alternative is going to address the core moral issue, it has to consider what stakeholder values are threatened. This means identifying the stakeholders who have something to gain or lose, understanding what that gain or loss is, and discerning what the moral problem is. So the facts of the case are important because they tell you who is involved, what gives rise to the problem, and perhaps what peoples' concerns are. The normative moral theories discussed in Chapter 2 are also important because they tell you whether a situation contains a moral problem and whether a particular course of action does enough to address the problem.

ethical considerations
The factors that need to be taken into account when making decisions because they involve moral rights, obligations, issues of fairness, virtue, or other ethically relevant concerns.

ethical decision-making process
A series of steps intended to guide your thinking as you assess a situation and formulate a well-reasoned ethical decision about a best course of action in that situation.

by violence to keep it, or he who had had it made and bought it for his own? And the master taught me that what is lawful is just and what is in the teeth of law is based on violence, and therefore, he said, the judge must always see that his verdict tallies with the law.[15]

There are two questions at play here. First, *Which coat is the better fit for which boy?* This question involves *prudential* considerations. It does not make sense for either boy to have a coat that does not fit. So, Cyrus thought, just let the big boy keep the bigger coat, and make the little boy take the little coat. Again, considerations of what makes something a good fit are prudential considerations. The second question is *Who is the rightful owner of the bigger coat?* This question involves *ethical* considerations. The little boy was the rightful owner of the bigger coat, and so it was ethically wrong for the bigger boy to force the little boy to trade with him.

When making ethical decisions, we need to remember that there is an important difference between prudential considerations and ethical considerations.

For Discussion

1. Why is determining whether a coat is a good fit a prudential rather than an ethical consideration?
2. Which ethical theory from Chapter 2 helps us best explain why the question of rightful ownership is an ethical consideration?
3. In this story of Cyrus, ethical considerations take precedence over prudential considerations. Can you think of another scenario where ethical considerations take precedence over prudential considerations? Describe the scenario and explain your reasoning.
4. Can you think of a scenario where prudential considerations take precedence over ethical considerations? If so, explain why this is the case.

These normative moral theories are part of your analytical toolkit. The decision-making model assumes that you know the theories' key points (and perhaps some of the nuances) and why people think they matter. So Step 0 of any ethical decision-making process is to refresh your understanding of moral principles. Then, and only then, are you able to begin working toward a morally defensible decision.

The model set out here follows the goal-seeking method described above. The goal is a defensible resolution to a situation involving a moral issue. The model first maps out the problem space by asking you to set out what you know about the problem. Then it asks you to be creative, thinking about ways to resolve the central issue. Next it asks you to think through consequences and constraints, narrowing the range and scope of defensible approaches. This brings the feasible solutions into view, while giving you reasons to support making the decision you recommend. You can also work through the following steps using the worksheets in Appendix A.

Step 1: Identify Relevant Facts

Step 1 of the ethical decision-making model is the most straightforward: gather the facts of the case. List as many of these as you can find by asking *Who? What? When? Where?* and *How?* (Asking *Why?* comes in the next step.) Flag the facts that are morally relevant and the ones that are prudentially relevant. One way to test a fact for relevance is to ask if not having a particular fact would affect your decision.

This step has to be done carefully and thoroughly. We have a bias toward what is readily observable and tend to stop looking for facts when we have enough information to make a decision, but not necessarily a *good* decision. Gather as much information as you can within the time and resource constraints that you have.

Step 2: Identify Relevant Stakeholders and Ethical Issues

The second step in the decision-making model uses the facts of the case from Step 1 to identify who the relevant stakeholders are, what they stand to gain or lose, what the main moral issue is, and why it is an ethical problem. Ask which stakeholders are most closely affected (have a proximal interest), and which ones have a legitimate concern (have a genuine interest). You might find questions about conflicts of interest, honesty, good faith, rights, duties, harms, and protections helpful here. Then consider the normative moral theories. What about the situation is a cause for moral concern, and why is it a problem? You might find more than one

In **Chapter 2** we considered five ethical theories: virtue ethics, utilitarianism, moral rights theories (including Kantian ethics), care ethics, and the capabilities approach. Each of these ethical theories has a different focus. Virtue theory, for example, focuses on one's character. Utilitarianism, for example, focuses on promoting social utility (happiness).

See also the Ethical Decision-Making Model worksheets in **Appendix A** at the back of this book.

BACKGROUND

Prudential, Ethical, and Moral Values

A value is anything someone considers to be important, useful, desirable, or beneficial. Values are *prudential* when their value lies in the way they contribute to a person's self-interest, and *ethical* or *moral* when valued for ethical reasons—because (for instance) they satisfy a person's duty or rights; contribute to virtue, justice or utility; or increase people's range of capabilities.

moral issue here. If that happens, work with the most fundamental or serious one first. You may find that in tackling the bigger problem you also address a good bit of the smaller one at the same time.

Step 3: Identify Stakeholder Values and Conflicts

After identifying the relevant stakeholders, move on to the third step. This stage of the decision-making model explores values, the things that matter to each of the relevant stakeholders identified in Step 2.

People and organizations are motivated to action by the things that they value. For example, valuing money motivates a company to look for ways to reduce production and administrative costs. This is a prudential value because it serves the goal of making a profit. Someone who values persons' rights will work to ensure that the business provides a safe workspace free from harassment. This is a moral value, but it also has prudential implications for the business.

Sometimes there are trade-offs between values. For example, there is a trade-off between valuing charity and producing value for shareholders. Giving to charitable causes is viewed as morally good, and it enhances the reputation of the business in the eyes of the public. Some charitable donations can be used to reduce a business's tax obligations, so shareholders may derive a benefit (at least on paper). But a business cannot give all of its cash to charity because it has financial obligations to other parties, and it would be morally wrong to neglect those. Pay particular attention to these trade-offs. The moral acceptability of your decision will be determined by how you navigate the conflict of worthy values.

Ask what each of the relevant stakeholders values most in this particular situation. What do the parties want to preserve for themselves or for others? What are they willing to give up if necessary? Identifying the things that matter most to the parties lets you focus on creating alternatives that address the main concerns of each party.

Step 4: Create Resolution Strategies and Identify Consequences

Step 4 of the decision-making model is the creative step. First, set out the current state of affairs, sometimes called the **status quo**. This is the baseline. Keep in mind that doing nothing to change the situation without explaining why there is no viable alternative is not an option. Doing nothing at all without moral justification is admitting moral defeat. Then propose between three and five distinct strategies that will resolve or reduce the severity of the moral problem you are addressing. This means that the alternatives cannot make the situation worse, and they cannot shift the responsibility to address the problem to another party. Having fewer than three alternatives artificially limits your options; having more than five makes it hard to compare their drawbacks and benefits.

Once you have some alternatives to work with, think about the consequences each of them will have for the relevant stakeholders. You need to consider two different aspects here: desirability and time. Look at the negative consequences as well as the positive ones, and distinguish short-term effects from long-term ones. Think in moral and prudential terms. Which values are promoted, and which are downplayed? What is gained and lost by following this course of action? Be careful here not to rule something out prematurely. You are still at the *what if?* stage here.

> We discuss stakeholders and the different types of stakeholder interests earlier in this chapter. Revisiting **Chapter 2** will help you think through what counts as ethical issues. We will have a difficult time explaining why something is an ethical issue if we are unable to provide theoretical reasons for why something is an ethical issue.

> **status quo**
> The *status quo* is the way things are at present, and the way things will remain if nothing is done to change the situation.

> The creative process of thinking about alternatives can also be used after the fact to identify what *could* or *should* have been done to avoid an ethical failing.

Step 5: Assess the Strategies

The analytical work continues in Step 5 of the ethical decision-making model. Look at the alternative strategies you created in Step 4 and their consequences. Which alternatives best resolve the ethical issue? Which alternatives incur a moral cost? Even if an alternative is morally defensible, there may still be a moral cost to choosing that alternative. This is the concept of *dirty hands*, which we discuss later in this chapter.

Now consider the prudential, legal, and regulatory constraints around the decision. Each course of action, including doing nothing, will incur some kind of cost. These include the resources required to implement a solution. Time, material, persons, and money are the typical considerations here. Set those out for each of the alternatives, including the status quo. Of the alternatives, which will provide the best moral outcome at an acceptable prudential cost? Which one is second best? (The second-best alternative may be very different from the preferred one.) Which will have the most beneficial long-term effects, and what will it cost to get them?

The concept of *dirty hands* is explained on page 69 in **this chapter**.

If the problem is related to how the business operates in the context of a market, consider how the action satisfies Heath's ten commandments, discussed in **Chapter 1**.

Step 6: Recommend and Defend a Resolution Strategy

Step 6 is where you finally make a reasoned decision. Recommend a resolution strategy on the basis of your assessment in Step 5. Then present your reasoning—an argument—for your recommendation. What assumptions are you making that do not come from the facts of the case or normative moral theories, and why do you need to make them? What normative moral claims are you drawing on? What reasons from your analysis make this the best option given the prudential constraints? You can structure your argument from foundational points to intermediate ones to your final conclusion, or you can work from your conclusion, giving the chain of reasoning down to the basic claims about facts, values, moral norms, and anticipated consequences for the relevant stakeholders. Is this an argument you would be willing to present to the public in support of your decision? If the problem and your proposed resolution somehow found its way to the top of a national news website, would it put you and your organization in a bad light, or a good one? What parts of the reasoning would make the decision acceptable in the eyes of the public? Remember, sometimes there is no good moral outcome, but hiding that just compounds the moral wrong. Having a reasoned argument at hand can deflect some of the negative publicity because it reveals the complexity of the situation and the concerted effort the organization made to address it.

Thinking about how others will view our decisions and actions is a version of the light-of-day test we discussed at the end of **Chapter 2**.

The masthead for Colorado's *Aspen Daily News* contains the tagline "If you don't want it printed, don't let it happen."

This process cannot be rushed. You will make a better decision if you seek multiple perspectives about what matters and about what might be done. You need time to reflect about what could go wrong or right under a particular course of action. There will always be something that escapes your notice the first time through a particular step. Before you make a decision, revisit the first five steps in light of what you discovered as you analyzed the possible courses of action. This may mean changing part of your analysis, but it also means you will make a decision using better information or assumptions.

The Payoff

At the end of the process you will have a well-reasoned decision. People may disagree about the assumptions or moral priorities you have assigned, but those will not take away from the quality of the reasoning you have presented. The careful consideration you give to all relevant parties, combined with the moral reasoning and awareness of the constraints, will go a long way toward meeting the imprecise legal standard of reasonable prudence should the matter come to court.

Dirty Hands

If we think it is important to make sound ethical decisions and do the right thing, then we must acknowledge the reality of **dirty hands**. The idea of dirty hands is this: there are situations where doing what is morally required of us (or simply doing what is morally permissible) results in some kind of harm or injustice. Dirty-hands situations are truly regrettable and we should avoid them if we can, but we cannot always be so lucky. So when they do occur because of something we have done, we must accept some moral responsibility for the negative outcomes.

dirty hands
A situation where we do a morally good thing, but still end up doing some kind of harm or injustice.

Many of the cases of dirty hands come from people acting in ways required by their public roles. Dirty hands can show up in politics, for instance, when a government does something that benefits a large portion of society, but that results in a comparatively small number of people being made worse off. Consider the effects that the Canada–United States–Mexico Agreement (CUSMA) will have on Canadian dairy farmers. Under the new trade agreement, 3.59 per cent of the Canadian dairy market will be opened up to markets from Mexico and the United States.[16] This concession by the Canadian federal government was made to ensure that a new trade deal could be reached among Canada, Mexico, and the United States. Now, on the assumption that it is better to have a trade deal than no trade deal, many Canadians will be better off because of CUSMA. However, it will have a negative impact on Canadian dairy farmers, who will face lower prices and tighter competition.[17] The moral cost of doing something good for the public is to bear dirty hands because of the harm done to a comparatively small number of individuals.

Dirty hands can arise in business decisions as well. For example, the fiduciary obligation of acting in the best interest of shareholders sometimes licenses corporate boards and executives to restructure the company and permanently reduce its labour force. Even as an employee, you can make a decision that leaves you with dirty hands. One of the contributors to this book worked in industry and was the leader of a three-person development team. During a round of layoffs, this person's manager asked the team lead to identify which of the two other team members would continue on and which would be reassigned to a lower-paying position in another country. One of the two was going to be reassigned regardless of whether the team

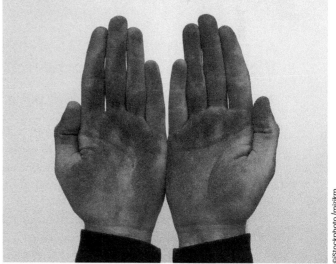

©iStockphoto/mizikm

Ethical decision making is not as clean as we want it to be. Making good ethical decisions sometimes results in dirty hands. We can still perform a morally acceptable action even though it causes some real harm to another party. The challenge is to reduce those negative effects.

lead resigned, since neither of the junior members had the knowledge required to step into the role of team lead. Both junior members had come to Canada from China; both had the same qualifications; and there was nothing the manager saw in the performance reviews that clearly made one more valuable to the development project than the other. The team lead reluctantly made a choice, knowing the decision would result in dirty hands because of the effect it would have on a trusted colleague. The words "It's just business, so don't take it personally" were of no comfort to anyone involved.

CONCEPT CHECK

3.13 What are dirty hands?

a. They illustrate the idea that everyone involved in a moral decision is blameworthy in some way.

b. They illustrate the idea that a morally justified course of action can still have a negative impact on the well-being of another party.

c. They illustrate the idea that a morally justified course of action always has a negative impact on the well-being of another party.

d. They illustrate the idea that there is no morally justified course of action to follow in the situation.

CASE STUDY

Applying the Ethical Decision-Making Model to the Video-Game Development Crunch

The video-game industry is still relatively young, so it might not be surprising to see it go through some of the growing pains of other massive media industries such as cinema. Businesses like Rockstar Games, makers of the *Grand Theft Auto* series, have repeatedly drawn controversy not just for the themes and content of their games, but also for the allegedly poor working conditions in which they are created.[18] Some of the negative experiences of employees are due to inappropriate behaviour by management,[19] but the issue of unhealthy development crunch is equally open to ethical analysis.

Unpaid overtime is commonplace in the industry,[20] as are expectations that employees will work 70- to 100-hour weeks during crunch times. Since most of these businesses are not unionized, employees who are unable or unwilling to dedicate nearly the entirety of their waking lives to work for extended periods are under constant threat of replacement with people who will. Nevertheless, employers are free to claim that the excessive work is voluntary, which complicates things. Should the video-game industry move away from the standards of crunch that currently exist? Let us apply the ethical decision-making model, but please keep in mind that we are merely demonstrating how the model is applied; we are not making substantive claims.

Step 1: Identify Relevant Facts

A large number of employees in the video-game industry are overworked during crunch periods. Reportedly 38 per cent of overtime in the industry is unpaid.[21] Consequently, employees are forced to take stress leaves or quit entirely ("stress casualties").[22] Employees have no union protection. Successful corporations that can afford to properly compensate their employees for their overtime often do not.[23]

Step 2: Identify Relevant Stakeholders and Ethical Issues

Employees and their families, retailers, and customers are all stakeholders of a kind. So is the corporation. The employees have a proximal and genuine interest.

Step 3: Identify Stakeholder Values and Conflicts

Exploitation, coercion, and manipulation of employees are value problems involving treating people as mere means to a corporation's ends, as well as potentially violating numerous rights and duties. However, if employees genuinely volunteer to work extreme hours without adequate compensation, it would be potentially disrespectful of their autonomy to insist that they stop.

Step 4: Create Resolution Strategies and Identify Consequences

Let us consider three options.

Option 1. Video-game developers could quit putting their employees through crunch periods altogether. This would be nice for employees, but likely lead to a lot of missed deadlines, which could have a negative effect on sales and the general success of the whole company.

Option 2. Video-game developers could hire temporary help for crunch periods. This might take some stress off the full-time employees, but there are significant costs involved, and it is unclear how efficient this solution would be.

Option 3. Developers could set strict limits on voluntary overtime and compensate employees for all overtime without exception. Proper compensation for overtime (voluntary or not) is sure to create a better work environment, and if the developer itself limits the amount of overtime employees take, then employees cannot be blamed or mistreated by management for wanting a healthy work-life balance. With that said, it is possible some employees would feel held back by the overtime limit. Also, while employees who are not physically exhausted would presumably work more efficiently, production deadlines that are not managed realistically still might not be met.

Step 5: Assess the Strategies

Option 1 is unrealistic and simply sidesteps the problem rather than solving it. Option 2 is probably less financially viable than Option 3, and is also likely less efficient. Option 3 is simple to implement, alleviates major ethical concerns (which results in good public relations), but potentially might be resented by some particularly driven employees who feel penalized by no longer being able to work as much overtime as they want.

Continued

Step 6: Recommend and Defend a Resolution Strategy

We will leave it to you to fill in this step. After all, the point of this text is to supply you with tools to make hard ethical decisions, not to make them for you! You may find it helpful to use the Ethical Decision-Making Model Worksheets in Appendix A (at the back of this book) as you work through this last step. Here are some questions for you to consider when constructing a resolution strategy.

Questions to Consider

1. Who else might be a stakeholder? Describe the quality and nature of their interests.
2. Which stakeholder values are prudential, and which are ethical? What normative ethical theories give support to the ethical values?
3. What do you think is the core moral issue? Explain why you think this.
4. Create one more alternative that addresses the problem without shifting the burden for resolving it to another party.
5. Part of the process is to think about both short- and long-term consequences of a particular course of action. Which alternative provides the best long-term solution?
6. Do any of these alternatives give rise to dirty hands? How?
7. Ethical decision making always takes place within a prudential context. What prudential constraints need to be satisfied by the solution?
8. What recommendation would you bring to the executives? Why did you choose this one over the others?

Summing Up

Each one of us has a conception of what it means to live well, and we quite often disagree about what that looks like. There is a very good chance that this will lead to ethical disagreements in the workplace. Seeking common ground with someone you disagree with can be challenging at best, but when you bring ethics and conceptions of right and wrong into the mix, the disagreement can be particularly ensnaring. If left unresolved, these disagreements can get in the way of the co-operation that is necessary for an organization to succeed.

Although ethical decision making is not algorithmic, there is a process to it, and we can learn that process. This chapter has provided you with a framework to use when making decisions that have an ethical component.

For Discussion and Review

1. Have you or someone you know encountered a situation that conflicted with your own ethical values? What was the nature of the conflict, and how was it resolved?
2. What matters to you more, public morality or private morality? Why do you say this?
3. What is specifically problematic with throwing up our hands in defeat and saying that since there is no one right answer to an ethical problem, there is no point in even trying to find an answer?
4. Moral defeat occurs when we refuse to acknowledge that there is an ethical issue, and we convince ourselves that we do not need to think about the ethical implications of our actions. What is the social cost of moral defeat? What will happen if everyone starts thinking this way?
5. What has been the biggest influence on your private morality?
6. Can we make good ethical decisions despite our biases? Why or why not?
7. Why be ethical if we are going to end up with dirty hands anyway?

Further Reading

Coady, C.A.J. "Dirty Hands." In *A Companion to Contemporary Political Philosophy* eds Robert E. Goodin, Philip Pettit, and Thomas Pogge, 532–40. Blackwell Publishing Ltd., 2017.

Kahneman, Daniel. *Thinking, Fast and Slow.* New York: Farrar, Straus and Giroux, 2015.

Kenyon, Timothy. "Biases with Reason." In *Clear Thinking in a Blurry World*. Toronto: Thomson Nelson, 2008.

Nagel, Thomas. "Ruthlessness in Public Life." In *Public and Private Morality*, edited by Stuart Hampshire, 75–92. Cambridge University Press, 1978.

Scopelliti, Irene, Carey K. Morewedge, Erin Mccormick, H. Lauren Min, Sophie Lebrecht, and Karim S. Kassam. "Bias Blind Spot: Structure, Measurement, and Consequences." *Management Science* 61, no. 10 (2015): 2468–86.

CHAPTER 4
Corporate Social Responsibility

By the end of this chapter you should be able to

- Define corporate social responsibility.

- Analyze four popular but problematic arguments that businesses need to be concerned only with profitability and the law.

- Describe and compare the triple bottom line, pyramid of corporate responsibility, and three-domain models of corporate social responsibility.

- Provide an argument in favour of corporate social responsibility.

In the preceding chapters, we explored the ways in which business is a function of society, different normative ethical theories, and the considerations that go into making a justified ethical decision. In Chapter 3, we talked about the potential for people's values to conflict and gave an example of three shareholders whose visions for their company were incommensurable. The example drew out the idea that some investors may want the businesses in which they have invested to give something back to the societies in which they operate. The question is, *Are corporations designed solely to make profit, or do they have additional responsibilities to society?* This is a question about **corporate social responsibility (CSR)**.

There is no question that corporations have a responsibility to their shareholders and an obligation to follow whatever statutes and regulations society, through the government, sees fit. There is also some recognition that corporations have at least some responsibilities toward society. The more difficult questions emerge when we try to determine the nature of those responsibilities. Consider the following two quotes:

> *Quote 1*
> The basic rules of the game have been set by the government, which attempts to detect and punish business frauds. But as long as a company does not transgress the rules of the game set by law, it has the legal right to shape its strategy without reference to anything but its profits.[1]

> *Quote 2*
> . . . there is one and only one social responsibility of business—to use its resources and engage in activities designed to increase its profits so long as it stays within the rules of the game, which is to say, engages in open and free competition, without deception or fraud.[2]

The first quote is from Albert Z. Carr; the second quote is from Milton Friedman. Both were very influential American economists during the last century. Though each author states that making profits is the primary focus of business, both hold making profits accountable to

corporate social responsibility (CSR) The accountability of a business to society, and the way businesses seek to promote the well-being of legitimate stakeholder groups including, but also extending beyond, their shareholders.

BACKGROUND

Businesses and Corporations

We frequently switch back and forth between talking about *businesses* and talking about *corporations*. What is the difference between them? *Business* is a very general term that primarily involves the organized (and legal) pursuit of money through trade. *Corporation* is a much more specific term. Corporations are legal entities that are given names and the right to own property and to sign contracts. The most common kind of corporation is the *limited liability corporation*, or LLC, which means that investors in the company take on a very low level of risk with regard to the activities of the corporation. For instance, investors cannot be sued or held accountable for the actions of the LLC. Because of this limited liability, many businesses choose to become LLCs when they incorporate. Because all LLCs are businesses and most businesses are LLCs, the two terms are often used interchangeably.

the "rules of the game." These rules are set out by government in laws and regulations, and that is the extent of social responsibility. For both authors, ethics does not enter into the picture.

The view that profitability and legality are the only things that matter in business is a popular view. We begin this chapter by looking at four arguments that have been made to support the sort of view held by Carr and Friedman. We then look at arguments for a different view—corporate social responsibility. CSR is the view that businesses have a social responsibility beyond just following laws and regulations.

CONCEPT CHECK

4.1 **What best describes Carr's view of corporate social responsibility?**

a. The triple bottom line addresses financial, legal, and shareholder results.

b. If it isn't illegal, it is okay.

c. If it isn't okay, it's illegal.

d. If it isn't illegal, it isn't okay.

Profitability and Legality

There are many skeptical theories within the business community proposing that the only legitimate purpose of business is to make money. The significance of these theories lies more in their popularity than in their argumentative rigour. There are four such views: *business as war*, *strong fiduciary responsibility*, *weak fiduciary responsibility*, and *the invisible hand*. We will take up each of these theories in turn.

Business as War

There is a subculture in business that projects the image that Sun Tzu's *The Art of War* is an essential read for any aspiring leader. For example, consider what a *Huffington Post* article claims: "For business leaders, reading *The Art of War* is a rite of passage; quoting from it is *de rigueur*."[3] Further, a quick Internet search will identify numerous publishers that market the book as

BACKGROUND

Business as a Battlefield

The promotional text for the Barnes & Noble Classics edition of *The Art of War* reads, "Sun Tzu's incisive blueprint for battlefield strategy is as relevant to today's combatants in business, politics, and everyday life as it once was to the warlords of ancient China." The Dover edition states more simply, "... it has ... been viewed as a valuable guide to competing successfully in business." The Thrifty Books reprint describes it as "a book which should be used to gain advantage of opponents in the boardroom and battlefield alike."

©iStockphoto / Cecilie Arcurs

Businesses can create value for shareholders by working together. A "business as war" attitude will preclude the possibility of creating value for shareholders through co-operative ventures. Do not underestimate the power of co-operation.

essential reading for business leaders. The core idea behind this line of thinking is that the highest level of business leadership involves conducting itself in accordance with military wisdom.

Whether aspiring business leaders actually read the book or not does not matter. The mindset of business as war, however, does matter, and it colours the popular perception of how business should operate. Two important lessons can be learned from the expression of this mindset. First, there are enough similarities between corporations and armies that when we, as members of the public, hear them being compared, it strikes us as plausible. If the teaching of business leadership instead centred around a different book, say Copernicus's *On the Revolution of the Heavenly Spheres*, we would find the relationship to business hard to grasp. Second, some businesses do not feel the need to deny this understanding; they are not ashamed to be viewed that way. Even if corporate executives do not literally study Sun Tzu, the business-as-war mindset captures an important aspect of how they view themselves. Chief executive officers (CEOs) are portrayed as generals, marshalling their troops to wage war against the enemy. And this mindset does capture a small piece of the truth about corporate culture: business is competitive.

There are good reasons that a businessperson might want to pursue this sort of approach. It glorifies the leaders of the company as triumphant heroes and justifies potentially unsavoury tactics in the name of the mission. There are also instrumentally useful features to a guidebook like *The Art of War* in that it commends discipline, foresight, and accountability.

Treating business as war highlights the competitive nature of the enterprise: business is a strongly goal-oriented activity in the context of a high-stakes battle. As Kevin O'Leary, one of the venture capitalists featured on the television programs *Dragons' Den* and *Shark Tank*, told students at the University of Waterloo in 2015, "Your job will be to go out and salt the earth

Treating business as war implies treating any negotiation as a *zero-sum game* in a *fixed-pie* context. This approach and the problems that can come from it are explained further in **Chapter 10**.

that your competitor walks on, destroy their market share and pour boiling oil over them. Then you will have access to more capital and create a more successful company."[4]

There are, however, good reasons to be wary of such an analogy. First and foremost, you are not allowed to kill people in business. In war (almost) anything goes; it is a violent and extreme state of affairs. In contrast, businesses must abide by rules and regulations, and are rarely justified in using violence in the provision of their goods and services. Second, war gives way to peace, whereas business begets more business. Third, in the army, soldiers are obligated to follow orders and face harsh penalties if they are insubordinate. If your boss gives you an unreasonable order at work, you are free to quit. The concepts of war and business are almost entirely dissimilar. They do not share the objectives, structures of accountability, or comparable existential stakes. There may be superficial pieces of wisdom that can be transferred from one domain to the other, but overall the business-as-war analogy is a poor one and it should worry us that anyone in the business community conceptualizes themselves in this way.

> Even war has a few rules, and violations are prosecuted as crimes against humanity.

CONCEPT CHECK

4.2 Why should we resist the analogy between conducting business and conducting war?

a. War involves atrocities against humanity. Business exists to benefit society.

b. War exists to benefit Western society. Business involves atrocities against humanity.

c. We shouldn't; business has so many analogies to war that the two are indistinguishable.

d. Both contribute to the economy, but only war advances national interests.

Strong Fiduciary Responsibility

One of the reasons that business-as-war is a poor analogy is that businesses are obliged to follow the law. But to say that business is restricted by the law turns out to be a double-edged sword, because corporations are bound by legal precedent to have a fiduciary responsibility to their shareholders. Being a fiduciary in this context means having a duty to take care of someone else's money. In the case of businesses, they were given investors' money with the understanding that the business would try to generate profits and pay out dividends to its investors. If the company does anything other than pursue profits, the shareholders might feel as though they have been denied what they deserve.

This is exactly what happened in the landmark case of *Dodge v. Ford Motor Company* in 1919.[5] Before starting the Dodge Motor Company, the Dodge brothers were investors in the Ford Motor Company. In 1916 the company's president, Henry Ford, wanted to invest that year's profits into upgrading factories and providing better wages for employees. The Dodge brothers thought that those profits belonged to them as shareholders and that Ford had no right to reallocate the money as he intended. They sued the company and won. This case established the principle of *shareholder primacy*, the idea that a company's primary obligation is to its shareholders.

There are two ways to interpret this fiduciary responsibility: a strong way and a weak way. According to **strong fiduciary responsibility**, a business has no legitimate activity other than

strong fiduciary responsibility Businesses, acting as fiduciaries of their investors, have no other responsibility than to maximize profit.

BACKGROUND

Fiduciary Roles and Relationships

Fiduciary roles and relationships can take many forms. For example, the executor of a will has been placed in a position of trust to fulfill the wishes of the departed; they have been placed in a fiduciary role. By far the most common type of fiduciary relationship, and the one discussed here, occurs when investors give their money to businesses and trust that those businesses will take proper care of it.

maximizing profit. On this interpretation, if a company donates to charity or spends a little extra on an environmentally friendly option, the shareholders could claim that this was an illegitimate use of their money and hold the managers who made those decisions accountable. The two features to notice about this stance are that, according to strong fiduciary duty, seeking profit is the only thing that companies can do and they should be seeking not just profits but *maximum* profits. Some scholars and some businesspeople still conceive of fiduciary responsibility in this way, but most hold a more moderate view. This is because trying to maintain such a strong position immediately encounters a major empirical hurdle: *businesses do not act this way*. Businesses engage in charitable and environmental initiatives all the time, and they do so while staying within the bounds of fiduciary responsibility.

There are two ways in which fiduciary responsibility can be retained and made to cohere with the actual behaviour of actual businesses. Both of these are weak versions of fiduciary responsibility.

CONCEPT CHECK

4.3 What is strong fiduciary responsibility?

a. It is the view that the only business of business is to minimize externalities.

b. It is the view that the only business of business is to minimize worker integrity.

c. It is the view that the only business of business is to maximize profit.

d. It is the view that the only business of business is to monopolize the market.

Weak Fiduciary Responsibility

The first way to think of weak fiduciary responsibility is to reject the premise that pursuing profits is the only legitimate activity in which business can engage. That is not to say that businesses should not be mindful of profits. Rather, profits are held up as one goal among many. As long as profits are considered and earnestly sought, one could say that the fiduciary responsibility has been fulfilled. How to balance the pursuit of profits with the pursuit of other objectives will be discussed later in this chapter.

The second way to think of weak fiduciary responsibility is to reject the idea that we know with any certainty what will maximize profits. Take the Ford case, for example. Ford could have

weak fiduciary responsibility
In addition to their fiduciary responsibility to maximize profit, businesses can have additional important obligations and goals.

The idea that a business can have multiple legitimate pursuits is another type of pluralism—no single objective takes absolute precedence over the others.

made the argument that by investing in the factories and paying the workers a better wage, they would expand the company's capacity and reduce turnover costs, therefore maximizing profits in the long run. The Dodge brothers might still have disagreed and argued that such investments would not be worth the short-term loss. Whose prediction about the future would have been correct? Which course of action satisfies the fiduciary responsibility by maximizing profits? It can frequently be very difficult to know which course of action will maximize profits. It is therefore unreasonable to expect companies to maximize profits. What we can expect from them is to tell a convincing story about why they chose the course of action that they did.

This weak interpretation of fiduciary responsibility is especially important when it comes to considerations like the company's brand and the non-monetary desires of consumers. Consumers like to support companies that give to charity. How much is it worth to the company to maintain an image of being charitable? Some consumers are willing to pay more for an environmentally friendly product. Can the increased cost of producing an environmentally friendly product be offset by the higher prices those consumers are willing to pay? We cannot answer these questions with certainty until after the fact. What we can do is make educated guesses. We can tell stories about what we think might happen. If we do a good job of telling those stories, we might not have satisfied a strong fiduciary responsibility, but we will have come pretty close.

CONCEPT CHECK

4.4 What is weak fiduciary responsibility?

a. It is the view that weak agents do not owe a duty of care to their principals.

b. It is the view that seeking profit is only one goal among many for businesses.

c. It is the view that the only business of business is to maximize profit.

d. It is the view that shareholders have a duty of care to overthrow a weak board of directors.

The Invisible Hand

invisible hand
The belief that a free and competitive market will spontaneously coordinate buyers and sellers, acting in self-interested ways, in the most efficient way possible. The metaphor comes from Adam Smith's *The Wealth of Nations*.[6]

The last argument used to justify unrestrained pursuit of profit is the theory of the **invisible hand**. The invisible hand is the belief that a free and competitive market will spontaneously coordinate buyers and sellers in the most efficient way possible. This means that there is no reason for governments or any other entity to interfere in the market. The best possible outcome will be achieved by getting out of the way and simply letting buyers buy and sellers sell.

Consider two hypothetical cases involving cars. These examples are completely fictional, so let us call the car companies Ekornbur and Hamsterrad.

If both Ekornbur and Hamsterrad produce very similar cars, but Hamsterrad charges a much higher price, no one will buy from Hamsterrad. There is no need for the government to order Hamsterrad to lower its prices or intervene in some other imaginative way. The consumers will make their preferences clear by buying the cheaper product. The market will send a signal to Hamsterrad that it either must lower its prices or adapt in some other way.

This ability of the market to self-correct toward greater value for money applies to both quality and price. If Ekornbur and Hamsterrad both sell their cars for the same price, but Ekornbur cars are of a lower quality, consumers will choose to buy from Hamsterrad.

The market sends a signal to Ekornbur that it must improve its quality or adapt in some other way. Once again, the market self-corrects and there is no need for outside interference.

Consumers will make the decision that reflects their best interest. No one gives them orders regarding which car to buy; they figure it out all on their own. But as the consumers pursue their best interests, the effect on the automobile market will signal to manufacturers what customers prefer to buy. This market effect is the invisible hand that will guide manufacturers to make better products, make cheaper products, or find another line of work. The belief is that everything will work out in the best possible way if we just let markets work. The invisible hand will take care of it.

Everyone, not just businesses, should want the harmonious outcomes produced by the invisible hand. Businesses pursuing profits by competing with one another will result in the highest quality and the lowest prices possible for consumers. Moreover, these miraculous outcomes can affect more than just prices and quality. Charitable and environmental works were mentioned earlier in this chapter in regard to fiduciary responsibility. The invisible hand can intervene here, too. If two companies sell similar products for similar prices, but one of them engages in other praiseworthy initiatives, consumers will likely reward

FIGURE 4.1 An artist's conception of the invisible hand. The invisible hand is a metaphor used by Adam Smith in *The Wealth of Nations*. Markets can look planned and coordinated (as if by an invisible hand), but really there is no planning or coordination going on at all. Order in the market is simply the result of individuals doing what is in their self-interest.

that company with their business. The market sends a signal to that company's rivals that they must either increase their pro-social activities or be driven out of business. In this way the market and the invisible hand maximize positive outcomes. This is why, at least according to those who have faith in the invisible hand, there is no need for additional responsibilities. They believe that everything will be taken care of if we just get all external regulation out of the way and let the majestic, benevolent, unquestionable hand work its magic.

CONCEPT CHECK

4.5 What is the invisible hand?

a. It is the view that markets are transparent and accountable to society.

b. It is the view that free and competitive markets are bad for monopolies.

c. It is the view that planned economies are the most efficient way to stop the wasteful distribution of resources.

d. It is the view that a free and competitive market will spontaneously coordinate buyers and sellers in the most efficient way possible.

CASE STUDY

Assessing Walmart's Commitment to Corporate Social Responsibility[7]

It can be challenging to assess a company's commitment to corporate social responsibility (CSR). Take Walmart, for example. Walmart is an international conglomerate of subsidiaries that is known for its affordable goods, summarized in its slogan, "Save money. Live better." As of 2019, the company is enjoying its 13th year as the largest company in the world, and its sixth consecutive year at the top of the Fortune Global 500, which is a ranking based on revenue.[8] With over $500 billion in annual revenues and 2.3 million employees, Walmart provides economic growth and jobs all over the world.[9]

The company has had its fair share of ethical issues. Walmart has been the subject of unflattering news articles and events that have changed the way consumers think about shopping. For example, in November 2012, there was huge fire in a Bangladesh factory that made clothes supplied to Walmart, among other fashion retailers. At least 112 people died in the incident and investigations showed that the high death toll was due to there being no emergency exits in the building. Walmart had previously audited the building in May 2011 and gave it a "high risk" categorization, followed by a "medium risk" categorization in August 2011; however, no details were given as to the nature of these risks, or what—if anything—had been done to address them. Walmart had continued to do business with this factory.[10]

Walmart has also been at the centre of a highly publicized six-year-long bribery case related to the behaviour of its subsidiary in Mexico. On April 21, 2012, *The New York Times* broke the story of accusations of bribery in Walmart de Mexico. The bribes were paid to obtain building permits, construction permits, and other documentation that would help Walmart de Mexico expand quickly. After a former executive accused the subsidiary of paying bribes and provided vast amounts of detailed information relating to the bribes, Walmart opened an internal investigation. They found over $24 million in suspicious payments and evidence that executives at Walmart de Mexico knew about the bribes and tried to cover them up. The evidence was enough for the investigators to conclude that "[t]here is reasonable suspicion to believe that Mexican and USA laws have been violated."[11] After the case went back and forth between Walmart's headquarters and its executives in Mexico, the case was handed off to the lawyers at Walmart de Mexico, the very subsidiary that paid the bribes. The investigation was quickly terminated after concluding that there was no wrongdoing on the part of any employees.[12]

The US Department of Justice became involved due to the potential breach of the Foreign Corrupt Practices Act that prohibits companies from paying bribes to officials in foreign countries. According to Bloomberg, American authorities conducted their own investigation. In 2017, Walmart and the Justice Department had a preliminary agreement on a $300 million settlement.[13] In June of 2019, as part of the settlement, Walmart agreed to pay $144 million to the Securities and Exchange Commission and $138 million to the US Department of Justice.[14]

On the flipside, Walmart has been investing significantly in its sustainability efforts. Many of its vehicles run on alternative energy and the company is on track to reach zero waste from its operations in 2025.[15] To tackle food waste, for example, the company keeps prices low for all food and discounts non-optimal foods for quick sale. Walmart donates extra food to local food banks as well. Walmart also aims to reduce plastic waste by minimizing the amount of plastic packaging used for its products and removing plastic bags from circulation, while making all remaining plastic packaging recyclable. As of 2019, Walmart stores were well on their way to reaching the company's sustainability goals, reducing greenhouse gas emissions by 28,000 tonnes of carbon dioxide due to investments in energy infrastructure. Currently, 87 per cent of waste is being diverted from landfills, including 11 million pounds of food donated to local food banks throughout Canada.[16]

Looking at Walmart's CSR statement is important when considering this contradiction. Its 2018 Global Responsibility Report Summary describes Walmart's mission to save its customers money so they can live better lives, including goals with respect to safe food, enhancing economic opportunities, and environmental sustainability.[17] On the one hand, Walmart has demonstrated some unethical behaviour and decision making that contradicts the substance behind how many of us understand— and how Walmart itself articulates—CSR. On the other hand, the company's dedicated effort to be a more sustainable, less wasteful company has produced real results and lives up to its CSR goals. What does this contradiction tell us about how a company like Walmart incorporates CSR into its business model and practices? How do you approach these opposing behaviours in a triple-bottom-line reporting context?

For Discussion

1. Consider the following claim: We must not allow some of the unethical things a company does to stop us from praising the same company for the good things it does. Do you agree or disagree? Explain.
2. Heath's first commandment is to minimize negative externalities (see Chapter 1). Describe how dangerous working conditions for factory workers overseas is a negative externality.
3. Consider the claim that factory workers overseas would not have any work at all if companies did not buy from those factories, as dangerous or abusive as those factories may be. Does this economic benefit to the factory workers justify helping Canadian customers live better by saving them money?
4. Does a company's commitment to CSR influence whether you do business with them? Explain.

Theories of Corporate Social Responsibility

The four arguments that we just examined all emphasize seeking profit and attempt to minimize the social responsibility of corporations. In contrast, CSR is the view that the responsibility of business extends beyond the interests of the shareholders to stakeholders broadly conceived. Three distinct expressions of corporate social responsibility have gained traction: the triple bottom line, the pyramid of corporate responsibility, and the three-domain model.

Applying Stakeholder Theory: Triple Bottom Line

The idea of **triple-bottom-line reporting** was first set out by John Elkington in 1994. Triple-bottom-line reporting is an accounting framework that considers three distinct categories of accounts, each with its own bottom line: the *people account*, the *planet account*, and the *profit-and-loss account*.[18] The idea behind triple bottom line is that a business's success should be measured not just according to the traditional or financial bottom line, but also according to its social, ethical, and environmental performance.[19]

Triple bottom line is a practical application of **stakeholder theory**,[20] which is the idea that companies must take into account the interests of various others besides shareholders who might have a financial stake in their business. So, for instance, local communities, customers, employees, governmental bodies, or the environment might count as a business's stakeholders depending on how their interests relate to that particular business. Triple-bottom-line reporting is a concrete way in which businesses can fulfill their obligations to those stakeholders who do not directly profit from the business, but who nonetheless have legitimate interests at stake.

Triple-bottom-line reporting gained traction at the turn of this century in the wake of a decade in which cost-cutting was the number one business priority.[21] Western consumers started to notice the hidden social and environmental costs associated with big business, such as atmospheric pollution and the abuse and exploitation that often accompanies outsourced labour. Growing awareness of and outrage at these issues forced some companies such as Tesco and Nike to keep a closer eye on their **supply chain** and enforce ethical standards.[22] Elkington's

Chapter 3 discusses the concept of a stakeholder in terms of when someone's interests need to be considered and when they do not.

triple-bottom-line reporting
A way of measuring success in business performance that uses social and environmental measures in addition to financial profit.

stakeholder theory
The view that businesses should strive to satisfy the interests of all important stakeholders.

The ethical decision-making model in **Chapter 3** requires giving consideration to stakeholders and their interests.

supply chain
The various stages and parties involved in generating a product and getting it to customers.

BACKGROUND

Shareholders versus Stakeholders

A *shareholder* is someone who has a financial interest in a company through the purchase (and therefore ownership) of shares. A *stakeholder* (also described in Chapter 3) is anyone who is potentially affected by the activities of a business. The concept of stakeholder may include, but is by no means limited to, investors, employees, customers, communities, and governments. Shifting from a narrow focus on shareholders to a more inclusive conversation about stakeholders has been one of the major successes in business ethics over the last few decades.

triple bottom line was an attractive model for businesses like Tesco and Nike, which were on the hook to be able to showcase new and improved sustainability and ethical practices.

Since the 1990s, triple bottom line has gained in popularity. By 2006, over half of the global Fortune 500 companies and just under half of Standard and Poor's 100 companies boasted triple-bottom-line reports.[23] Even many governments at both the federal and local levels now issue something like a triple bottom line.[24] The popularity of triple-bottom-line accounting among some of the largest and most successful companies clearly shows that there does not necessarily need to be a trade-off between profitability and taking one's ethical responsibilities seriously.

Despite its popularity, triple bottom line has its critics. One recurring issue with triple bottom line is the difficulty many have with actually trying to quantify social and environmental costs.[25] While there are some commonly used cost units (for example, charitable contributions, electricity consumed, etc.), not many are standardized. What is more, social and environmental costs cannot always be measured in workable cost units like dollars. For instance, how do you assign a dollar value to a business's efforts to support its employees' work–life balance? This makes rating or comparing businesses based on their triple-bottom-line practices difficult.[26] Wayne Norman and Chris MacDonald wrote a scathing critique of the ambiguity surrounding triple-bottom-line reporting in 2004. They argue that triple bottom line is nothing but public relations, and dangerous public relations at that, since it offers a reassurance to consumers and the general public that is not actually there.[27]

sustainability
A business is sustainable if it can be maintained for the long term in an appropriate balance with important financial, social, and environmental constraints.

A challenge with triple-bottom-line reporting is the difficulty in quantifying social and environmental costs, such as a company's efforts to support its employees' work–life balance.

Still, triple bottom line remains lauded by most. Some have responded to criticisms like those launched by Norman and MacDonald by pointing out that triple bottom line has nevertheless met with real success. Even Norman and MacDonald concede that some of the big companies that practise triple bottom line, like Shell and BP, have made truly remarkable changes in their organizations' cultures as well as improvements to human-rights issues and emissions reductions. Defenders of triple bottom line point to successes like these as a reason not to abandon triple bottom line just yet. They remind us that it is important to be aware of and to continue to try to resolve the difficulties that come along with putting triple bottom line into practice, and to always be sure to interpret triple bottom line public relations cautiously. But these caveats are not so great that we should simply give up on the ethical potential of triple bottom line. Triple bottom line represents a real movement in the business world toward heightened transparency and holistic sustainable practice.

CONCEPT CHECK

4.6 Which of the following is one of the bottom lines in the triple-bottom-line accounting framework?

a. the incongruent person's account

b. the insolvency account

c. the pollution account

d. the people account

4.7 What is one difficulty with applying the triple bottom line?

a. It will make business lose money.

b. It is not immediately obvious how to quantify social and environmental costs.

c. It is not immediately obvious how to price goods and services.

d. It involves resorting to a barter system. And there is no clear way to determine how many chickens a kilogram of honey goes for.

Pyramid of Corporate Responsibility

Archie B. Carroll first introduced his four-part definition of CSR in 1979. He listed four responsibilities of business: *economic*, *legal*, *ethical*, and *discretionary* (or *philanthropic*). Economic responsibilities recognize that a business's first responsibility is to generate profit; otherwise, all other areas of CSR become moot. Legal responsibilities require businesses to generate profits within the bounds of the law. Ethical responsibilities are actions that are expected of a business but are not legally required. Finally, discretionary responsibilities are social actions that a business can choose to perform but are not expected of a business.

Though we have described the four parts of CSR separately, they are dynamic and sometimes fulfilled simultaneously; typically, legal and economic responsibilities are often satisfied at the same time. For example, a pharmaceutical company that recalls a drug due to adverse side effects may be simultaneously fulfilling its economic, legal, and ethical responsibilities.

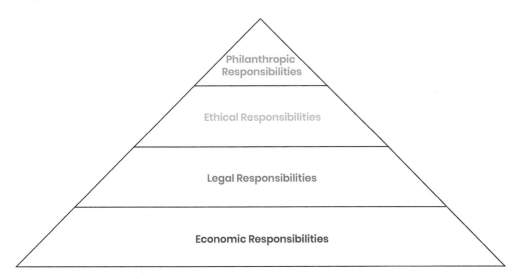

FIGURE 4.2 Carroll's pyramid of CSR.

Source: Based on Archie B. Carroll, "The Pyramid of Corporate Social Responsibility: Toward the Moral Management of Organizational Stakeholders," *Business Horizons* 34, no. 4 (July–August 2003): 39–48.

Further, ethical responsibilities push the boundaries of legal responsibilities, such that actions that we think are ethically required often become codified in regulations. The four parts of CSR are heavily intertwined.

Carroll later characterized these four aspects as a **pyramid of corporate social responsibility**.[28] The pyramid depicts economic responsibilities as the foundation of the pyramid to show that these responsibilities are most important for the firm to fulfill. Next come legal responsibilities, then ethical responsibilities, and finally philanthropic responsibilities. Carroll argued that philanthropic actions are those that make a firm a good corporate citizen. Again, the four parts of CSR are presented separately but are intertwined in reality.

Carroll's pyramid of CSR has several shortcomings.[29] First, the use of a pyramid might lead one to think that philanthropic responsibilities are most important because they are at the top of the pyramid. In fact, this is the opposite of what Carroll intended, as he says that economic responsibilities are the most fundamental. Further, a pyramid does not depict the overlapping nature of these CSR domains. Third, philanthropic responsibilities are ill-defined and often subsumed under ethical responsibilities. This is because it is difficult to differentiate between ethical and philanthropic activities, and philanthropic actions could be based purely on economic interests.

pyramid of corporate social responsibility Responsibilities of business are organized hierarchically with economic obligations as the foundation, followed by legal, ethical, and finally, at the top of the pyramid, discretionary or philanthropic obligations.

CONCEPT CHECK

4.8 According to Carroll's pyramid of corporate responsibility, why is a business's first responsibility to generate profit?

a. If a business is not profitable, it cannot fulfill its ethical and discretionary responsibilities.

Continued

b. If a business is profitable, it cannot be ethical.

c. Without profit, there is no possibility of embezzlement.

d. If a business is not profitable, it cannot file taxes.

Three-Domain Model

three-domain model
A presentation of the responsibilities of business as three interconnected domains: economic, legal, and ethical.

Building on the ideas from Archie Carroll's pyramid of CSR, the **three-domain model** attempts to address the shortcomings addressed at the end of the last section. Namely, the three-domain model aims to show the interconnectedness of the economic, legal, and ethical responsibilities of business.

The economic domain is defined as any direct or indirect activity meant to maximize profit or share value. Most of a business's actions are expected to fall under the economic domain.

The legal domain is split into three categories: *compliance*, *avoidance of civil litigation*, and *anticipation of the law*. Compliance is further subdivided into three categories: *passive* compliance, *restrictive* compliance, and *opportunistic* compliance. Passive compliance occurs when a business is doing what it wants to do and happens to be complying with the law. Restrictive compliance occurs when a business performs an action that it would not perform if it were not for the legal requirement. Finally, opportunistic compliance occurs when a business finds a loophole in the law or operates in a certain area because of the particular legal requirements in that area. Avoidance of civil litigation occurs when a business performs an action to avoid future litigation for negligence. Voluntary recalls or ceasing environmentally unfriendly activities fall under this category. Finally, anticipation of the law occurs when a business changes its practices due to upcoming or expected legislative changes.

See the discussion of normative moral theories in **Chapter 2**.

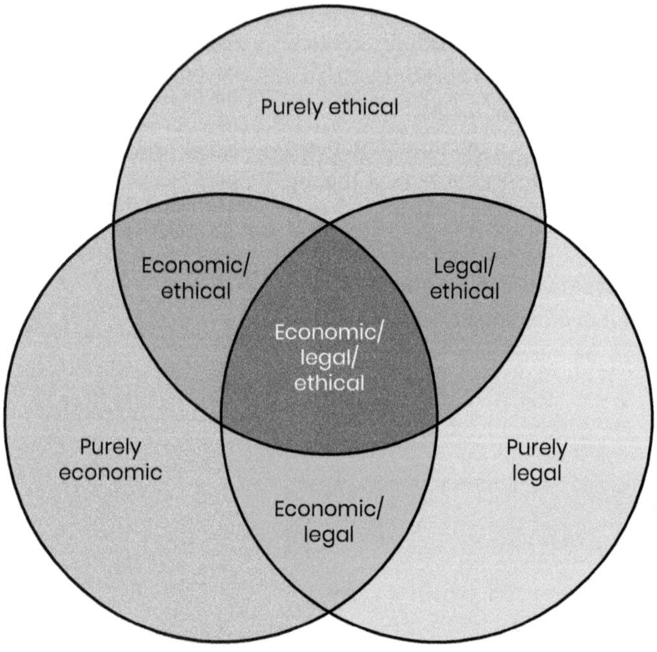

The ethical domain refers to *conventional*, *consequentialist*, and *deontological* ethical standards. Conventional standards refer to the norms for ethical behaviour in a given organization, industry, profession, or society. Consequentialist standards encompass activities that promote the general good of society by creating the greatest net benefit or lowest net cost to society. Finally, deontological standards refer to duty-based ethical standards, including, but not limited to, those of moral rights and justice.

The three-domain model of CSR clearly shows that the three domains overlap and provide a myriad of possible combinations of the three domains to describe one particular behaviour. The different orientations of the model show how the model is flexible enough to depict the CSR orientations of different corporations or departments.

FIGURE 4.3 The three-domain model of CSR.

Source: https://www.researchgate.net/figure/The-three-domain-model-of-corporate-social-responsibility_fig2_303465263

CONCEPT CHECK

4.9 According to the three-domain model, what is opportunistic compliance?

a. A business undergoes an existential recalibration.

b. A business complies with equal opportunity.

c. A business finds a loophole in a law or regulation.

d. A business adjusts its profit margin to reveal its regulatory compliance.

CASE STUDY

Public Statements of CSR: TD Bank Group

One of Heath's ten commandments is to reduce informational asymmetries between firm and customer. (See Chapter 7 for more on information asymmetries.) This does not mean that a company must tell its customers everything. For example, a company is not obliged to release proprietary information to the public. However, there are some things a company can—and should—make public. For example, a company can be transparent around its commitment to corporate social responsibility. TD Bank Group (TD) is an example of this.

In September 2019, the TD Bank Group was the only Canadian bank listed on the Dow Jones Sustainability World Index; this was its sixth consecutive year on this list.[30] This index is one of the Dow Jones Sustainability Indices (DJSI), which are "a family of best-in-class benchmarks for investors who have recognized that sustainable business practices are critical to generating long-term shareholder value and who wish to reflect their sustainability convictions in their investment portfolios."[31] TD was listed for its "strong performance in the areas of Corporate Governance, Risk Management, and Talent Attraction and Development."[32]

Earlier in 2019, TD was also included in the Bloomberg Gender-Equality Index (GEI) for the third year in a row.[33] The 230 companies listed in the 2019 GEI also included Bank of Montreal, CIBC, National Bank of Canada, Royal Bank of Canada, and Scotiabank. (Note: Walmart and Walmart de Mexico were also included in this index.) The GEI tracks the performance of public companies committed to "transparency in gender reporting and advancing women's equality in the workplace."[34]

TD stated its commitment to CSR publicly in its *2018 Environmental, Social and Governance (ESG) Report*. The report describes the bank's sustainability goals, including investing $100 billion into low-carbon programs and initiatives by the year 2030. As well, TD's 2018 Ready Challenge offered ten $1 million grants to help people build job skills for the future economy. The bank also provided consultation for 3000 small-business owners in 2018 as part of a $3 million partnership with the National Foundation for Credit Counselling.[35] Finally, TD appeared in the number one or two spot on *Global Finance* magazine's ranking of the World's 50 Safest Commercial Banks in 2018 and 2019.[36]

Continued

A comment we often hear from students is that they think the phrase "business ethics" is oxymoronic—a contradiction in terms. This sentiment is no doubt fuelled by news stories that report the awful things done in the pursuit of profit: sweatshops, child labour, environmental destruction, and so forth. So when a positive story comes out about a company's commitment to doing business ethically, it is easy to let our skepticism guide our analysis.

The *2018 ESG Report* is the first of its kind from TD and covers three very broad categories: environmental, social, and corporate governance. Although we might want to consider this type of self-reporting to be self-serving, insofar as companies sharing it likely do so to highlight their achievements and thus their reliability or impressiveness to clients, TD has been recognized by others for its efforts, in particular its attention to corporate governance, as mentioned above.

So what do we do when a company states its commitment to doing things ethically and releases a report outlining its environmental, social, and economic performance? Do we take them at their word? If we demand that a business be transparent and then dismiss everything the company reports as an exercise in self-serving public relations, we miss an opportunity to read reports like the one from TD with a critical eye and base our judgment on verifiable evidence. Consider what the evidence suggests about a company's efforts and achievements. Has the company done work that merits recognition? If it has, then recognition is due.

At the same time, when you consider the evidence itself, you might ask, *Where does it come from?* In our case, who oversees, organizes, and develops the standards for indices such as the DJSIs and the Bloomberg GEI? Both are overseen by financial conglomerates specializing in global markets and financial analytics—they seem well-suited to measure the performance of a company like TD. But where do these giants of finance get their benchmarks and who stands to benefit from them? The Bloomberg GEI, for example, notes the following: "While all public companies may submit supplemental gender data for their company's investment profile, at this time only companies with a market capitalization over US$1 billion are eligible for index inclusion."[37] The Bloomberg GEI monitors and reports on a particular slice of the professional world; inclusion in its annual index is evidence of achievement, but a critical review of the index itself shows that its scope is limited to a coterie of extremely high-worth global companies. We can value a company's transparent reporting of its performance and still think critically about the circumstances. In this sense, a critical eye involves considering evidence as well as a host of complex relationships, interactions, and priorities without lapsing into cynicism, dismissal, or too much praise.

For Discussion

1. Which is better for business: doing business ethically but not saying anything about it publicly, or doing business ethically and making it known through things like an ESG report? Explain why.
2. Is the goodness of a deed diminished if the person who did the good deed talks about it? Does your answer change if it is a business talking about its ethical commitments? Explain.
3. Is the information in an ESG report important for investors to make sound investment decisions? Explain.
4. Explain how the exclusion of companies with smaller market capitalizations from these surveys and indices distorts the public perception of companies' reputations. Is this a kind of dishonesty? Why or why not?

An Argument for Corporate Social Responsibility

We have presented three ways to think about CSR, but we have not yet given an argument for it. One approach is to give an empirical argument and demonstrate that businesses that adopt CSR policies fare better, everything else being equal, than businesses that do not. A second approach, which relies on the first approach, is to give a decision-theoretic argument demonstrating that it is in a business's narrow self-interest to adopt CSR policies. A third approach is to give a normative argument for why businesses *should* adopt CSR policies. We will focus on this third approach.

There are two broad reasons why businesses should adopt CSR policies. The first reason was already developed in Chapter 1: namely, there are norms internal to the market system itself. Recall that Heath's ten commandments of business ethics focus on fairness in competition, which has to do with everyone playing by the same rules of the game. Who sets the rules of the game? For Carr and Friedman (mentioned at the beginning of this chapter), this is the government's job. But we argue that the job of setting the rules extends beyond the government. What is the government, if not the agent of society? So who sets the rules? We do. Society does. This leads to the second reason businesses should adopt CSR policies.

Business serves at the pleasure of society, so to speak. The relationship between society and business is mutually beneficial and mutually dependent. Without business, there is no society. Without society, there is no business. It is in the interest of business to contribute toward the society that sustains it, lest society fail and take business down with it. As we will see in Chapter 9, if business fails to live up to its end of the tacit mutual bargain, including the rules of fair competition, there are a variety of steps that society can take to address the breach.

Finally, consider this quote from Joseph Heath:

> The most persuasive argument in support of the market economy has always been that it facilitates cooperation, enabling individuals to engage in mutually beneficial interactions that otherwise might not occur.[38]

If Saresh were able to produce everything he consumes—from vegetables to cell phones—he would not need to trade with anyone. Saresh would be self-sufficient. But no one is smart enough, energetic enough, or industrious enough to be self-sufficient. The self-made person is a myth. Humans are social animals and benefit greatly from trading with one another. Trade makes us better off, and markets facilitate trade. But these markets are constrained by social norms—norms that include bearing some responsibility to (at least) not cause unjust harm to members of society. Insofar as our actions affect the well-being of another person, ethics has something to say.

The claim that the government is the agent of society assumes that we are dealing with a democratic state with just institutions. We acknowledge this assumption (and others we have not mentioned), but cannot develop or defend it here.

CONCEPT CHECK

4.10 What does it mean to say that the self-made person is a myth?

a. No one can trade with anyone else.

b. No person is smart enough, energetic enough, or industrious enough to be self-sufficient.

c. When you trade with someone, you'll always be worse off for it.

d. Markets necessarily require a minimum of two people to trade.

Summing Up

Answers to the question *What responsibility does business have to society?* will run the gamut of political and economic responses. In this chapter, we have argued against the minimalist view that the only responsibility of business is profitability and legality. While we support the idea of economic and legal obligations, ethical obligations and discretionary responsibilities are also important for sustainable business. Business exists to benefit society, and cannot exist without society's social licence. Anti-social behaviour violates that licence and may very well harm business in the long run.

For Discussion and Review

1. Why have CSR statements become popular in the business world?
2. Is CSR enough to guide a business to perform ethically? Why or why not?
3. The "business as war" analogy is problematic. We discussed some ways in which business differs from war. Can you think of other ways that war and business are different?
4. Albert Carr claims that legality and profitability are the only legitimate constraints on business. What is a counterexample to the *If it is not illegal, it is ethically okay* attitude?
5. What is the central idea behind stakeholder theory?
6. Do we really need ethics? Why can we not allow the free market to weed out unethical businesses?
7. One of the criticisms of Carroll's pyramid of corporate social responsibility is that philanthropic responsibilities are ill-defined and often subsumed under ethical responsibilities. Is this a strong criticism of Carroll's position?
8. Does a business deserve praise if it accidentally does the ethically right thing?
9. A good business does good business. Does it matter if a business is ethical just so that it can make more money? Do intentions matter?

Further Reading

Carr, Albert Z. "Is Business Bluffing Ethical?" *Harvard Business Review*, August 1, 2014. https://hbr .org/1968/01/is-business-bluffing-ethical.

Heath, Joseph. "Business Ethics without Stakeholders." In *Morality, Competition, and the Firm: The Market Failures Approach to Business Ethics*. New York: Oxford University Press, 2014.

Heath, Joseph. "The History of the Invisible Hand." *In Morality, Competition, and the Firm: The Market Failures Approach to Business Ethics*. New York: Oxford University Press, 2014.

Heath, Joseph. "The Just Price Fallacy." In *Filthy Lucre: Economics for People Who Hate Capitalism*. Toronto, ON: HarperCollins Publishers, 2009.

"The CEOs of Nearly 200 Companies Just Said Shareholder Value Is No Longer Their Main Objective." CNBC. August 19, 2019. https://www.cnbc.com/2019/08/19/the-ceos-of-nearly-two-hundred-companies-say-shareholder-value-is-no-longer-their-main-objective.html.

CHAPTER 5
Fairness and Non-Discrimination

We begin this chapter by tying together some of the themes we have developed so far. The *free* in *free market* is not an unconstrained freedom. Business has an obligation to society and is constrained by both market norms and social norms. The market-based norms that we considered in Chapter 1—Heath's ten commandments—are internal to a well-functioning market economy itself. While the goal here is market efficiency, it is important to note that efficiency is not the only thing of value. We value things like fairness as well. To this end, business is expected to follow the law of the land. However, *being legal* and *being ethical* are not the same thing, so the legal constraints on business only go part of the way in ensuring fairness in the market. The other part involves ethics.

Equal Opportunity as Fairness

What does fairness in society look like? Consider the following two claims.

> Claim 1: A society that treats everyone *equally* is fair.
> Claim 2: A society that treats everyone *equitably* is fair.

Claim 1 and Claim 2 mean very different things. A society that focuses on **equality** will ensure that everyone has the same rights and the same access to social goods like education, health care, the justice system, and public infrastructure (like roads). In contrast, a society that focuses on **equity** will recognize that just because everyone has equal shares of resources, it does not follow that each person will able to use those resources effectively to live a meaningful and dignified life.

To better understand the difference between equality and equity, consider the following two societies: Society One and Society Two. Let us assume both societies provide social goods on a user-pay basis. If you use the social good, you pay for it directly. If you do not use the social good, you do not pay for it. Consider Society One first.

> Society One has two citizens: Citizen *A* and Citizen *B*. To help them successfully enter the labour market, the state has given each citizen 20 social vouchers. The citizens can spend their vouchers to access whatever social goods they want, including health care, education, roads, transit, the justice system, and so forth.
>
> Citizen *A* is 21 years old and in good health. They have no mobility issues. They have just joined the labour market and only needed to spend 10 of their social vouchers to do so.
>
> Citizen *B* is 21 years old as well, but has had chronic health issues and is confined to a wheelchair. Since they are in a wheelchair, they have to pay for special access to public buildings, transit, etc. They need 25 social vouchers to enter the labour market, but only have 20. They have used all of their social vouchers and are unable to enter the labour market.

Society One treats its citizens equally in the sense that everyone in the society gets 20 social vouchers each, regardless of their circumstances in life. But notice this conception of equality—where everyone is treated the same—results in a society that is inefficient. Citizen *A*

equality
Individuals have equality if they have the same rights and the same opportunity to access social goods such as education, health care, the justice system, and public infrastructure.

equity
Individuals are treated equitably if they are given what is needed for them to realize a full human life, considering their circumstances.

has a surplus of 10 social vouchers while Citizen *B* ran out of theirs and still needs 5 more in order to live a dignified life.

So Society One has spent a total of 40 social vouchers, but not everyone is flourishing. Now consider Society Two.

Society Two has the same two citizens described above, Citizen *A* and Citizen *B*, but Society Two is structured around the idea of equity. This means that different people get different numbers of social vouchers. The number of vouchers a citizen gets is determined by their circumstances. Under this structure, Citizen *A* is given 10 social vouchers, and is still able to successfully enter the labour market. Citizen *B*, however, is given 25 social vouchers, which allows them to enter the labour market as well.

Society One treats its citizens *equally* but not *equitably*. Society Two treats its citizens *unequally* but *equitably*. Two questions arise. First, which society is more efficient with social resources? Second, which society is fairer? To answer the first question, note that Society Two is more efficient because it has spent fewer resources than Society One. Perhaps surprisingly, the society where everyone is treated equally is less efficient. This is summarized in Table 5.1. But again, efficiency is not the only thing of value in a society. A well-functioning society also values fairness. Not only is Society Two the more efficient society, it is the fairer one as well, because it has given everyone in that society the opportunity to convert resources into real opportunities to achieve a fully realized life. Further, it has accomplished this without disadvantaging anyone else in that society. This example demonstrates that efficiency and fairness are not contradictory social objectives.

CONCEPT CHECK

5.1 What is the difference between equality and equity?

a. Equality is about sharing, whereas equity is about taking what isn't yours.

b. Equality is about being equal, whereas equity is about the value of a company's shares.

c. Equality is about having the same quantity or value, whereas equity is about fairness.

d. Equality is unnatural, whereas equity is natural.

TABLE 5.1 Comparison of Favouring Equality or Fairness in Two Hypothetical Societies

	Vouchers needed to qualify for the labour market	Society One		Society Two	
		Vouchers granted	Labour market participation	Vouchers granted	Labour market participation
Citizen *A*	10	20	100%	10	100%
Citizen *B*	25	20	0%	25	100%
Total	35	40	50%	35	100%

Rawls on Justice as Fairness

We can think of equity as the starting point for an efficient distribution of resources and the fair treatment of others. This way of thinking about fairness and resources is closely linked to the work of John Rawls on distributive justice as fairness. In his 2001 book *Justice as Fairness: A Restatement*,[1] Rawls theorizes about what makes a perfectly just society. Specifically, he states what the basic political and economic structure of society should be to ensure that every citizen enjoys equal opportunity to lead a good life, and for the society to be just.

For Rawls, constructing laws and public policies should be done behind a **veil of ignorance**. Rawls argues that to ensure fairness we ought to be ignorant of our own social position relative to policies so that when we reason through the associated benefits and burdens for community members, we will not know how the law or policy would affect us personally. Presumably, this would encourage the creation of formal systems that do not unjustly disadvantage any social group or its members. Behind the veil of ignorance, we could not serve our own interests by structuring laws in our favour because we could envision ourselves in socially vulnerable positions (and in need of protection) just as easily as we could in whatever social position each of us currently occupies. Ideally, constructing formal systems in this way would promote protections for all, but with a focus on protections for the most vulnerable community members.

For Rawls, a just society requires not only formal equality but also real opportunities. Formal equality means that no one should be excluded from participating in society to their fullest simply because of their race, ethnicity, socio-economic status, religion, gender, degree of (dis)ability, age, and so forth. Having real opportunities means having the resources to participate in society together with the power to use these resources to have a fair chance to succeed. If we are outcome-oriented, then we must recognize the fact that there is often a significant difference between treating everyone equally and treating everyone fairly. Moreover, extrapolating from Rawls, we are reminded that fairness involves taking stock of the social conditions in which business decisions are made to ensure that everyone has adequate, though perhaps not always equal, resources to succeed. When our attempts at equality and equity fail, the resulting harms are often significant.

veil of ignorance
A hypothetical state of ignorance, in which people thinking about what a just society would look like imagine they do not know what their own place in society will be.

A course in political philosophy will address Rawls's ideas, among others, in more detail.

CONCEPT CHECK

5.2 What best describes Rawls's view of formal equality of opportunity?

a. Formal rules should exclude others from achieving personal goals, particularly if they are lazy.

b. Formal rules should not exclude anyone from achieving personal goals on the basis of arbitrary characteristics like race or socio-economic status.

c. Formal rules should exclude anyone from achieving personal goals on the basis of arbitrary characteristics like race or socio-economic status.

d. Formal rules should not exclude others from having an equal share of resources, even if they are lazy.

The Harms of Injustice

So far, we have talked a lot about foundational concepts in ethics and underscored the importance of fairness. But we have not yet explained how an unfair social structure can do real harm to real people. When people point out social injustice, they usually point out instances in which people or groups of people are left out or disadvantaged by that social system. An unjust social and political system will give rise to people being harmed materially, physically, and psychologically.

The *material* harms of injustice include unjustified restrictions on access to resources, employment opportunities, equitable pay, access to justice, and participation in the political process. Concretely, insufficient pay can inhibit one's ability to meet minimum requirements for a decent life, or limit one's ability to meet one's financial needs. Another example of a material harm is voter suppression. If you are eligible to vote but cannot because your name has been removed from the voter list, you will be unable to participate fairly in the democratic process.[2]

The *physical* harms of injustice include diminished access to resources such as health care, dental care, mental health, and nutritious food. People who are paid lower wages have to work more hours or second jobs just to survive.[3] This increases both physical and mental stress, and decreases leisure time. These factors also contribute to psychological harm.

Psychological health is also impacted by social injustice. Cases of overt discrimination often result in a decreased sense of self-worth, a lowered confidence in ability, and the internalization of negative stereotypes. The realization that one is consistently regarded and treated as less valuable than others because of irrelevant characteristics is understandably infuriating, stress-inducing, isolating, and demoralizing. These psychological effects often produce stress-induced physiological effects, such as increased blood pressure.[4]

Recognizing the severity of these harms provides ample motivation to guard against inequality whenever possible, and certainly in business. Discrimination that happens at school, in the workforce, in the health-care system, or by law has the highest potential to effect such harms since much or most of our well-being and livelihood depends on these institutions.

social injustice
Social injustice exists where people or groups of people are left out or disadvantaged in a social system such that they do not have the opportunities they are owed.

overt discrimination
Discrimination that takes place openly, in a way that is acknowledged and perhaps even formally encoded into policies.

CONCEPT CHECK

5.3 Which of the following is an example of a physical harm of injustice?

a. A company eliminates the health benefits it offers to its employees and instead puts a foosball table in the lunchroom.

b. A company forgets to pay its taxes.

c. A company tells employees that they cannot take time off work to vote in the federal election.

d. A company has to pay a fine for illegally dumping toxic waste in a sugar bush.

Workplace Inequalities

Business ethics is most concerned about the inequality that results from discrimination in the workplace. Discrimination in the workplace happens when an individual receives negative and unfair differential treatment in a workplace context because of their sex, gender, age, race, ethnicity, religion, ability, sexual orientation, or any other feature that ought to be irrelevant in a work or performance context. Such discrimination can occur at any level, sector, rank, or geographical location in the business world. A person may encounter discrimination during the hiring process because some employers have prejudicial beliefs about certain groups of people and do not want to hire a member of that group. Discrimination has taken place during the review and promotion cycle if a qualified person has been passed over not because of their performance but because of some irrelevant feature about their appearance or background. Harassment is also a form of discrimination. When someone harasses another person, they are disadvantaging that person by making their work environment distracting, uncomfortable, and sometimes even threatening. Harassment often results in the victim developing high levels of stress and activating increasingly severe avoidance mechanisms. This can affect their work performance and mental and physical health.

> **harassment**
> According to the Canadian Human Rights Commission, harassment "includes any unwanted physical or verbal behaviour that offends or humiliates you."[5]

In short, inequality in the workplace has the potential to cause serious and unjustified harm to workers. Businesses have an obligation to know what these harms are so as to avoid them or to deal with them if they arise. In what follows, we discuss issues in business that illustrate systemic injustice. Some belong to informal social institutions, and others show how laws need to be changed to achieve greater equity in formal institutions.

Wage Gap

Differences in wealth do not always constitute an injustice. There is a strong consensus in capitalist countries that differences in wealth among individuals are justified when, for example, wealth results from a difference in experience, responsibility, training, or expertise. Wealth disparities among individuals are not justified, however, when they are based on individual characteristics *irrelevant to one's ability to do one's job*. When this happens, the irrelevant characteristics driving wealth disparities are typically socially salient ones like gender, race, religion, age, ability, physical attractiveness, accent, and others. The bulk of work done on unjust wage gaps is focused on gender, though racial wage gaps are typically just as large, and in some cases larger.

> **gender wage gap**
> The difference in average wages between women and men, all else being equal. The gap can describe the average difference in a given workplace, a sector, or over the whole of a country's economy.

There is some debate as to the usefulness of measuring wage gaps rather than wealth gaps, the most important indicator of financial health and security,[6] because wage gaps account only for the average hourly wage, whereas wealth gaps consider debt levels and assets to give researchers a clearer picture of how financially secure individuals or populations are, rather than simply measuring how much income is earned. In simpler terms, where the income gap "provides a huge hurdle to equality, the wealth gap presents a mountain."[7]

> **wealth gaps**
> Wealth gaps are calculated by adding total assets, then subtracting financial liabilities. From this we can measure net worth.

Whether we focus on wage gaps or wealth gaps, the findings are equally concerning. The popular perception of racial wage gaps is that they are small, when they exist at all. In terms of wealth gaps, recent studies in both Canada and the USA show that most racial wealth gaps are far larger than gender wealth gaps. Moreover, in the American context, studies reveal that the general public largely believes that the institutionalized systemic racism of the

BACKGROUND

The Jim Crow Era

The *Jim Crow era* refers to the period of US history between 1877 (when the reconstruction period after the American Civil War ended) and 1968 (when the Fair Housing Act was passed). During that time, all of the states that opposed the abolition of slavery, along with some of the others, passed laws specifically intended to prevent the accumulation of wealth by black citizens and keep them segregated from the white community. The name *Jim Crow* comes from a song typically performed by white minstrel performers wearing blackface. Canada had similar legislation with respect to Indigenous persons, not for segregation as much as for eradication of Indigenous practices. The Indian Act of 1876 denied citizenship to many Indigenous persons (in particular, those living on lands reserved for First Nations). It was only in 1960 that these persons gained the legal freedom to vote, own a house, or own a business.[8]

Jim Crow era is squarely in the past. The suggestion here is not that overt systematic racism has continued uninterrupted, or that our current social systems have not changed from pre–civil rights movement North America, but instead that there is an extreme, unexplainable, and reliable disparity among the average wealth of white, black, and Latin American citizens and families in both Canada and the USA.

CONCEPT CHECK

5.4 **What is the difference between a wage gap and a wealth gap?**

a. A wealth gap is a measure of difference in how much a person gets paid, whereas a wage gap is a measure of difference in net worth.

b. A wealth gap is a measure of difference in net worth, whereas a wage gap is a measure of difference in how much a person gets paid.

c. A wealth gap is caused by symmetrical problems, whereas a wage gap is caused by asymmetrical problems.

d. A wealth gap is something I have, whereas a wage gap is something my neighbour has.

According to 2010 American census data, for every $100 in white family wealth, black families hold, on average, only US$5.04.[9] Statistics Canada has not published corresponding wealth-gap data, but there are a few reports on racial wage gaps in Canada. A 2011 report from the Canadian Centre for Policy Alternatives shows that the largest wage gap in Canada in 2006 existed between registered reserve-resident Indigenous men and white men of British origin, about 50 per cent, though in major urban centres the disparity was often smaller—ranging from

THE CANADIAN PRESS/Nathan Denette

An eight-year-old girl plays on a swing in Attawaspiskat, Ontario. A 2019 study of Canada's 2016 Census revealed that 53 per cent of Indigenous children living on First Nations reserves were living in poverty. This is directly connected to the wealth gap between Indigenous and non-racialized non-Indigenous families.[10]

approximately 11 per cent in Halifax, Nova Scotia, to 41 per cent in Saskatoon, Saskatchewan.[11] A more recent report using data from the 2016 Census of Population paints an equally bleak picture. The report states that the income gap between Indigenous women and non-Indigenous men is at a significant 45 per cent. Further, the average income gap between Indigenous and non-Indigenous people in Canada is 33 per cent.[12] A 2017 report from the Conference Board of Canada (a private research organization) on racial wage gaps neither discusses nor accounts for Indigenous persons at all.[13]

BACKGROUND

Institutionalized Indigenous Invisibility

The Auditor General of Canada, in its Spring 2018 report to Parliament, presented the scathing observation that Indigenous Services Canada "did not adequately measure well-being for First Nations people on reserves," and that this government department "could have used the volumes of available data from multiple sources to more comprehensively compare well-being relative to other Canadians and across First Nations communities, but did not."[14]

It is important to remember that both wage and wealth disparities are differences that remain after all other information is controlled for. In brief terms, this means that wage disparities exist among persons categorized by race despite:

- having the same kind and amount of education
- being recognized as having the same level of experience in a given field
- working in similar (and sometimes even the same) companies
- taking the same amount of time off work
- working in the same or similar fields
- having similar family commitments
- having the same type of job

The harms created by unjustified wage gaps are multiple. The most immediate and obvious harm is that unjust wage gaps leave those who are discriminated against with fewer resources to meet their needs or achieve long-term financial goals. Further, being paid comparatively less than your professional counterparts because of characteristics irrelevant to the performance of your job is degrading and disrespectful to the person being paid less for doing the same work. The message is that because you are this *kind* of person, your work is not as valuable, and so we do not have to pay you as much. More long-lasting than the immediate feeling of disrespect is the potential for messages like "Your best is not good enough" or "Your work is not valuable" to be **internalized**, further reducing the confidence, self-esteem, and ambition of victims of discrimination.

internalization
The internalization of a belief or attitude takes place when that belief becomes a stable part of one's psychological makeup or character.

Correcting for wage gaps is primarily an equality-based solution to injustice. The goal is to pay everyone equally, though that initiative is limited by the kind of work one does. It is not some radical socio-economic agenda seeking to give each worker the same "cut" of the economic pie, but rather a recognition that those with the same job, expertise, seniority, and the like—those doing work of equal value—should be paid the same. Correcting for wealth gaps, however, is an equity-based solution. Observing wealth gaps and recognizing their impact on relative chances of success might mean that we, as a society, agree to increase the minimum wage, or set higher wages for certain sectors of the economy that are over-represented by members of certain groups. For example, if systemic racism leads to visible minorities being disproportionately hired for lower-paying jobs, increasing a minimum wage to increase overall wealth of workers in the service sector, for example, would help correct for this injustice—though being anti-racist in how we conduct business is the obviously preferable solution.

Implicit Bias and the Workplace

Attitudinal biases are the automatic, unreflective tendency to associate two or more things with each other. An example of this is the tendency to associate the words *cat* and *dog* with each other, or *cat* and *mouse*. We create automatic associations between all manner of things: colours with feelings, like *red* with *anger*, and emoji images with various emotions. In this way, a bias is simply a cognitive mechanism that helps sort through information by associating concepts with other concepts, or anything else one's brain might pick out as relevant. Biases are strong when the tendency to associate two or more things is also strong; we observe this when people reliably and automatically, though subconsciously, associate two or more things. Biases are weak when the association between two things is not as automatic or not as reliably

BACKGROUND

Cognitive and Attitudinal Biases

We must disambiguate the word *bias. Cognitive biases* are dispositions or tendencies to think in certain ways. Some cognitive biases are discussed in Chapter 3. An *attitudinal bias*, by contrast, is a prejudice in favour of, or against, a person or thing. Cognitive biases and attitudinal biases quite often travel together.

associated in one's mind. We also tend to make automatic and unreflective associations between things and our feelings about them.

To have a bias in favour of something or someone is not, in itself, a problem. For example, a person is biased when they claim that their sister is the best singer in the world. In this case, their biased evaluation is not harmful because their taste in singers does not matter to anyone else. However, the harmful potential of a person's bias exists if, for example, they judge singing contests in which they are responsible for awarding prizes for great singing. In contexts where their evaluations have authority, the harm comes from their automatic (and often stubborn) positive evaluation of one person's voice over others, despite the quality of the performances. Similarly, bias in business has potential to harm when the tendency to associate certain ideas, people, or groups with feelings and concepts impedes the ability to impartially evaluate some problem, performance, or someone's potential.

Biases can be explicit or implicit. When a bias is **explicit**, the person holding the biased view knows that their judgment is partial in some way. **Implicit biases**, on the other hand, are tendencies of association that the holder of the bias is not aware of. The hardest biases to identify are typically those we learn from our culture, families, religions, and media. For example, the strong tendency to associate *man* with *breadwinner* is a bias that contributes to the relatively higher starting salaries often offered to male job applicants. While the strength of this association is slowly waning, it has not yet disappeared.[15] The assumption is that when a man works, it is to support his family, and when a woman works, it is to supplement the income of her household, rather than to function as the primary breadwinner. This bias is harmful not just because it runs counter to the just requirements of equal pay for equal work, but also because the association does not track reality. As one writer noted, "In 2017, . . . 41 percent of mothers [in the USA] were the sole or primary breadwinners for their families."[16] This attitude is particularly harmful when the worker is a single mother.

explicit bias
Tendencies of association that the holder of the bias is aware of.

implicit bias
Tendencies of association that the holder of the bias is not aware of.

CONCEPT CHECK

5.5 Which of the following is an example of an explicit bias?

a. A professor gives an A+ on an essay written by a particularly keen student despite not having read the essay carefully.

b. A supervisor gives a warning to an employee for being late for work.

Continued

c.   A customer thinks that anyone who wears a blue shirt and black pants is a worker at the store.

d.   A police officer gives a traffic ticket to a cyclist for failing to stop at a red traffic light.

Biases do not have to be as specific as in the previous example. Instead, the association can be between a general feeling and an idea, solution, person, or group. Stereotypes offer illustrative examples here. In a frequently cited experiment,[17] researchers sent over 5000 resumés in response to approximately 1300 job postings in Boston, Massachusetts, and Chicago, Illinois. The aim of the experiment was to test for racial bias in hiring, and so traditionally "white" names and traditionally "black" names were used to indicate the racial identity of the applicant to potential employers. To each job posting, the researchers sent one high-quality and one low-quality resumé with "white" names (for example, Emily Walsh and Greg Baker), and one high-quality and one low-quality resumé "black" names (for example, Lakisha Washington and Jamal Jones). Resumés were sent to employers over a large spectrum of different jobs, from low-paying service jobs to management and sales positions.[18] The results were clear:

> Applicants with White names need to send about 10 resumes to get one callback whereas applicants with African-American names need to send about 15 resumes. This 50 percent gap in callback is statistically very significant. Based on our estimates, a White name yields as many more callbacks as an additional eight years of experience . . .
>
> Race also affects the reward to having a better resume. Whites with higher-quality resumes receive 30 percent more callbacks than Whites with lower-quality resumes, a statistically significant difference. On the other hand, having a higher-quality resume has a smaller effect for African Americans. In other words, the gap between Whites and African Americans widens with resume quality.[19]

From this example, and from other large-scale experiments of the same sort, we see reliable trends in biased hiring across a large number of industries. A study on gender bias in symphony orchestra auditions found that after large orchestras adopted a policy of "blind" auditions to conceal the identity of the auditioning musician, the likelihood that a female musician would be chosen increased by just over 30 per cent, and the number of successful female musicians rose from just 6 per cent to 21 per cent across the five most prestigious orchestras in the United States.[20] Given the low turnover rates in symphony orchestras, this increase is substantial.

In both examples, there is a stable trend of bias in favour of one group of applicants to the detriment of other groups. In the first example, the general association between "white" names and whatever positive attribute the companies were seeking in applicants held stable until resumés with "black" names demonstrated at least eight additional years of relevant experience than the resumés with bearing "white" names. By no means did the trend tip in favour of "black" applicants at that point; however, the statistically significant trend of racial bias disappeared, meaning that with eight additional years of relevant experience, resumés with "black" names on them were given equal consideration.

Holding anonymized auditions works well to control for bias in hiring musicians, but how does that help in the case where resumés are submitted? Some companies have instituted practices through their human resource departments where resumés are received and then stripped of all identifying features to enable hiring committees to assess resumés impartially. This strategy is helpful in mitigating the effects of bias in hiring, but is of little use in eliminating bias in promotion or evaluations once the applicant has secured the job.

Bias impacts many aspects of business decision making, from deciding who gets hired, to how much employees will be paid, to assessments for promotion, to who gets what kind of job, and so on. Businesses will do well to control for bias whenever possible.

Employees, however, are not the only people who are impacted by bias. Bias can impact the way companies and employees treat customers, too. Think of the racism experienced by Donte Robinson and Rashon Nelson, who were arrested in a Starbucks in Philadelphia in 2018 while waiting for the third member of their party to arrive for a business meeting.[21] One of the men asked to use the washroom while they waited, and was informed that washroom access was for paying customers only. (The men had not made a purchase yet.) When the man sat back down, the manager asked them if they wanted drinks or water; the men said they had brought their own water and were waiting for a colleague. Two minutes after the men arrived, the manager called the police, and within eight minutes of police arriving, the two men were arrested. Both Mr Robinson and Mr Nelson were charged with trespassing and creating a disturbance, despite the fact that none of the witnesses had reported that the men had misbehaved.[22] Starbucks dropped the charges, issued an apology, and instituted a company-wide afternoon training session to educate employees and managers about bias and racial profiling.[23] Starbucks's limited response was criticized at the time, as many people felt an afternoon education session was insufficient to deal with deeply embedded racial bias. Starbucks also reached an undisclosed financial settlement with Robinson and Nelson and agreed to fund their college degrees. In addition, the city of Philadelphia designated $200,000 for a pilot program (with involvement from Robinson and Nelson) for high school students who aspire to be entrepreneurs.[24]

The injustice of implicit bias includes many of the harms previously mentioned in this chapter. Receiving consistently low evaluations of performance, being offered lower starting salaries, having to apply to 50 per cent more jobs to get a callback—all can have a lasting effect on one's sense of self-worth, and unjustly limit access to financial resources and opportunities. So too can having one's potential assessed by irrelevant characteristics.

But there is an additional and unfortunate layer to implicit bias that makes it tricky to control for: when a bias is implicit, the bias is hard to spot. This is both because we do not know that we are being biased, and because people do not want to recognize their own biases—generally, we want to feel like good people. The disincentive to acknowledge a bias, combined with the fact that biases are hard to identify, means that there is a culture of wilful ignorance of, and general resistance to, identifying and controlling for bias.

See the discussion of the self-serving bias and the blind-spot bias in **Chapter 3**.

Tips to Control for Bias

Here are some tips to control for bias in the workplace:

1. Anonymize resumés and any other materials for review when possible to control for gender, racial, or other biases. Where resumés are not anonymized, applicants with, for example, traditionally "female" names could include only the initial of their first name, making it impossible to associate an applicant with a gender identity.
2. Control for bias in policy development and implementation by making managerial boards demographically representative of their wider communities.
3. Encourage employees to offer self-assessments in advance of performance reviews so that large discrepancies between employer and employee assessments can be identified and investigated.
4. Include bias training as a part of the hiring process for successful applicants and require ongoing education for all employees and managers.
5. Survey employees and managers regularly to invite comments on policies, office culture, managerial strategies, and so on. Make sure that the surveys are anonymous to get the most impactful feedback, while demonstrating that employee perspectives matter. Comparison between employee and manager surveys is important to show misalignments in perception and experiences of bias.
6. Make decisions with other people. Bias is far more likely to go unchecked if one person makes the decision. Adding as many diverse perspectives to policy development and evaluations as is appropriate will help expose bias in decision making.

Accommodation

So far, we have been discussing discrimination with respect to race and gender. Another form of discrimination is independent of these, and will likely affect every person as they age: disability. Some persons are born with a disability, and others acquire them at different points in their lives. Taking the concept of a "fully abled" person as normative is mistaken because no one meets the ideal all the time, particularly when invisible impairments arise. There is, then, a need to **accommodate** persons with various types and degrees of disabilities.

Accommodation is an excellent example of an equity-based approach to justice because it often includes the allocation of resources in ways that make it possible for everyone to participate in some activity, or to gain access to a program or service. Each Canadian province has regulations for businesses and requirements for employee education and compliance standards with respect to accommodating various disabilities. For example, Ontario's **accessibility** laws and standards are aimed at helping businesses become accessible for people with disabilities by 2025.

accommodation
A fairness-based approach to justice that aims to make full participation in society possible for everyone.

accessibility
The degree to which a business or service is available to be used by all intended audiences.

See page 116 later in **this chapter** for references to legislation setting out specific accessibility requirements.

CONCEPT CHECK

5.6 Why is accommodation considered an example of an equity-based approach to justice?

a. It is important for everyone to have adequate accommodations while on a business trip.

Continued

b. It is important for everyone to be equal, which can only be achieved through equitability.

c. Being disabled is not the exception; everyone is simply temporarily abled.

d. It often includes the allocation of resources in ways that make it possible for everyone to access some service or program.

Providing access to persons with disabilities opens up a large potential market for products and services. A report commissioned by a Canadian bank discovered that "persons with disabilities have an estimated spending power of 25 billion dollars annually across Canada."[25] Accessibility also unlocks a largely untapped source of labour (broadly understood). A mobility impairment, for example, does not necessarily mean a cognitive impairment. Such a person could be a customer-service agent, an engineer, or a corporate officer, depending on training and experience.

Barriers to Access

Physical Barriers

The first barriers to full participation in the everyday life and culture of the workplace are often physical. One class of physical barrier affects persons with mobility aids such as wheelchairs, scooters, and walkers. Doorways and hallways are often too narrow to safely navigate with these aids. Most desks are built to a height that suits people who can sit in an office chair, but not all office workers can use one. Another barrier involves usability. For example, a simple doorknob can be a challenge for a person who has no grip strength in their hand. A doorknob like that closes off access to a part of the building for that person. Environmental factors such as poor lighting—either too bright or too dim—can not only make it impossible for persons with certain visual impairments to work effectively, but also affect the ability of persons who are hard of hearing to sign or read speech.[26] These are just a few examples, but they are enough to illustrate how benign assumptions about the design of spaces and fixtures can lead to the unintentional exclusion of a portion of the population. Accommodation in the workplace requires making all spaces employees are expected and invited to use, including meeting rooms, washrooms, and interior and exterior common areas, accessible.

Procedural Barriers

In contrast with physical barriers, procedural barriers are not physical in nature. Attitudes, policies, practices, assumptions, and beliefs that discriminate against persons with disabilities are procedural barriers. For example, when persons with disabilities encounter attitudes held by co-workers who assume a person with a disability is inferior, or encounter an assumption that a speech impairment indicates lack of understanding,[27] it becomes clear that the workplace is not a safe environment for those persons. It is important that the policies and practices of a workplace require professional, civil conduct among co-workers.

Company policy should support accommodations explicitly and encourage an inclusive work environment that is respectful of persons' differences. Inviting employees with disabilities to come forward to speak about the ways the workplace may be disabling will help to avoid the attitude that providing an accommodation is doing a "special favour" and encourage all employees to engage in accommodation processes in good faith.[28]

Other unintentional barriers to accessibility can prevent individuals from participating fully in the activity of the organization. For example, workplace policies that require all employees to attend meetings—or even communicate with colleagues—in person unfairly discriminate against persons with mobility, sensory, and social disabilities.[29] Communication and meeting attendance should be possible through various means to allow for varied interpersonal interaction styles, abilities, and comfort.

Persons with sensory disabilities require special attention with respect to communication and technology, particularly with respect to sending and receiving information. Some technological barriers can be resolved through an assistive device, but not all forms of information can be presented through such a device. For example, image-only PDF documents cannot be read by a screen reader. Video recordings of training materials need transcripts and descriptions to be accessible.[30] Even the choice of typeface on written documents can be problematic. A typeface that is too small or too visually complex cannot be read easily, even if the reader is wearing corrective lenses.

Flexible working hours seem like a good idea, but can easily be transformed into a means of discrimination. For example, an overly flexible workday where the flexibility favours the employer often does not allow employees to decide their workweek with sufficient advance notice.[31] Moreover, it can set up an unofficial culture of last-minute overtime requests. Many employees have varied external commitments that require strict schedules.[32] However, requests for overtime often arise within a power relationship, which can make it difficult to say "no" and can threaten job security when employees do refuse overtime offers. Workplace policies should be made with the needs of persons with disabilities and external commitments (such as necessary medical appointments) in mind.

CONCEPT CHECK

5.7 Which of the following is an example of a procedural barrier?

a. Company policy states that all employees must use the same template for presentations, but the colour scheme makes the template difficult for people with blue-yellow colour blindness to use.

b. City workers go on strike during a major snow event.

c. A company gives employees the option of having a standing desk in their office.

d. A company allows (and provides the necessary equipment for) office employees to work from home during a flu outbreak.

Religious Accommodation

Under the Ontario Human Rights Code, it is against the law to discriminate based on religion. Justice requires all persons to have access to the same opportunities and benefits. Religious practices, beliefs, and observances are protected under the law, but personal moral, ethical, and political views are not. It is important to note that, while religious protections are encoded in law, these protections do not extend to any religions that promote violence or hate toward others or violate criminal law.[33]

Before Canada's Lord's Day Act (1906) was struck down as unconstitutional in 1985, businesses in Canada were required to close each Sunday for observance of the Christian sabbath. The law clearly privileged the religious freedoms of Christians over other religious groups, and disadvantaged other people for whom the day meant nothing, and so wanted to keep their businesses open. Large corporations and business owners of other faiths complained that having to close on Sunday meant loss of profits, especially for store owners who closed their shops on other days for their own religious observances. For some of these store owners, having to close shop for two days was a significant financial strain.

Since the Act was stuck down, Canada has taken a more pluralistic stance to the protection of religious freedom. However, some business norms continue to disproportionately constrain the practices of some religions while informally privileging others. For example, most stores are closed on the statutory holidays Christmas Day and Easter, but remain open for Orthodox Easter, Yom Kippur, and Eid al-Fitr, for example. Protection for some religious holidays is encoded in Canadian law, while people who practise other faiths must choose between observing their religious practices and receiving pay deductions for missed work, or using a personal or "sick day" to avoid financial penalty. These kinds of choices present a double bind where choices are limited, and neither outcome can be seen as fair treatment. While individual businesses cannot change the law, formal practices within companies and organizations can be changed to protect religious freedoms equally.

Changes could include adding additional days off for members of religious groups without sufficient legal protections for time off around important holidays. It could also mean decorating communal spaces for a variety of holidays (if appropriate), not only one or two. Making people feel valued is part of protecting their interests. For example, changing static break times to flexible ones permits every person needing to observe religious practices during work hours to do so. Similarly, small changes to office spaces to allow for prayer rooms where no shoes are to be worn or to company traditions—for example, ditching the pig roast picnic in favour of a variety of foods, some of which satisfy kosher, halal, and Jain diets—go a long way to valuing and protecting everyone's religious rights equally.

Sexual Harassment

In the wake of the #MeToo campaign raising awareness and calling out harassers across a variety of industries, harassment has become one of the most publicized issues in business ethics. At its most basic, harassment is conduct that intimidates or pressures others. In the context of **sexual harassment**, it is the use of coercive or bullying language or behaviour of a sexual nature that is unwanted and unwelcome. There are two basic types of sexual harassment.

The first type of sexual harassment turns a formal power relationship into an abusive relationship. It occurs when someone in a position of authority offers incentives to someone in a subordinate position to tolerate unwanted sexual advances, comments, and activities. The trade-off can be communicated as a reward, where a bonus or promotion might be offered in exchange for sex, or as a punishment, where the employee might be threatened with demotion, termination of employment, or some other unwanted consequence if they do not comply.

sexual harassment
The Canadian government defines sexual harassment as "any conduct, comment, or contact of a sexual nature that is likely to cause offence or humiliation to any employee; or that might, on reasonable grounds, be perceived by that employee as placing a condition of a sexual nature on employment or on any opportunity for training or promotion."[34]

BACKGROUND

The #MeToo Movement

CBC

Demonstrators at the Women's March in Toronto in January 2018.

The #MeToo campaign began in October 2017 and quickly became a powerful global movement that encourages women to come forward and share how the harms of sexual harassment have negatively affected their lives. The movement has been lauded as a major advancement in gender equality, and the effects of it have been very pronounced in Canada. For example, the calls to rape crisis centres across the country have significantly increased,[35] with calls to the Ottawa Rape Crisis Centre increasing by 100 per cent in 2018.[36] Although the #MeToo movement has generated many important conversations locally and nationwide, a lot more needs to be done in Canada to change social attitudes about women who come forward to report sexual harassment and sexual assault.

hostile work environment
A work environment is hostile when discriminatory behaviour makes it uncomfortable or frightening for individuals to work in that environment.

The second type of sexual harassment does not involve formal power relationships but occurs in the larger workplace community. It is one in which language or behaviour of a sexual nature creates a **hostile work environment**, impairing the victim's ability to do their job. Typically, sexual harassment of this sort must be persistent for a harassment claim to receive consideration, but if the language or behaviour is severe enough, this condition can be dropped, so even one-time offences can also count as harassment.[37] It is important to recognize that this kind of harassment can be *direct* or *indirect*. In other words, harassing behaviour need not target one person in particular. Using sexually charged language, derogatory terms, posting sexually explicit material in the workplace, and telling sexist or sexually inappropriate jokes can create a hostile work environment for people regardless of whether or not the behaviour is directed at them specifically.

Anyone can create a hostile work environment. Even though employers and managers may not be involved in creating such a workplace, they have an obligation to investigate and respond when they become aware of harassment,[38] and they may be implicated if they do not respond appropriately to reports of sexual harassment.

CONCEPT CHECK

5.8 Which of the following is an example of a manager failing in the duty to respond appropriately to a report of sexual harassment?

a. After an employee makes a formal complaint about sexual harassment in the workplace, the manager dismisses it as "just a joke."

b. After an employee makes a formal complaint about sexual harassment in the workplace, the manager follows company policy to ensure that the complaint is dealt with appropriately.

c. A manager checks to see if the company's sexual harassment policy complies with provincial and federal human rights laws.

d. A manager takes proactive steps to make sure their subordinates clearly understand the company's sexual harassment policies.

Ethnocentric Harassment

Often called *racial harassment*, this form of discrimination is connected with the second type of sexual harassment outlined above. The term **ethnocentric harassment** better captures the range of identity markers this kind of discrimination connects with than does the term *racial harassment*. While racial harassment might include discrimination based on perceived racial identity and extend to **shadism**, which discriminates based on the relative lightness or darkness of a person's skin, ethnocentric harassment includes more. Harassment under this name includes threatening or offensive conduct related to race, colour, ancestry, place of origin, ethnic origin, creed, or citizenship.[39] Offensive conduct can come in the form of racial slurs, "jokes," posting offensive material that degrades a racialized or ethnic group, and mocking accents.[40] The harms of ethnocentric harassment are similar to those discussed above: harassing behaviour makes people uncomfortable, feel threatened, and reinforces a divisive "us and them" culture at work. In short, harassing behaviour is upsetting, distracting, and unfairly impedes the victim's ability to work. While work environments are the focus here, it is important to note that harassment occurs outside of work environments, too. Harassment can happen at home, in public, and wherever people access services.

One of the most effective means of shutting down harassing behaviour is through **bystander intervention**. Often, when co-workers experience or notice harassing conduct—be it "jokes," the use of slurs, or something else—they tend to ignore it. Because harassment makes people uncomfortable, there is a tendency to try to ignore the offence, make light of it, or sometimes offer quick agreement to satisfy the offender and redirect the conversation. But none of these responses directly address the problem, and none indicate to the harasser that their co-workers will not tolerate their behaviour.

Instead, those of us who witness harassment should speak out against it. The zero-tolerance message will come through. The harasser will know that there is a social expectation of fair and respectful treatment, and any continued harassment will be met with

ethnocentric harassment
Harassment that targets the race, colour, ancestry, place of origin, ethnic origin, creed, or citizenship of the individual being harassed.

shadism
A form of personal discrimination based on the relative lightness or darkness of a person's skin. This is distinct from racism, but is just as pernicious.

bystander intervention
Active opposition to discriminatory behaviour given by someone who is not themself the target of the behaviour but who observes it.

resistance by their peers. The responsibility of bystanders to intervene should not extend to situations that risk their personal safety, and those targeted by harassment should not bear the responsibility of speaking out because it puts them at further risk. The greater responsibility should be left to managers and employers (when they are not the harassers) and to those who are not the intended targets of the harassment. Why is this? Harassers already demonstrate a clear lack of respect for those they harass. It is unlikely that harassers will take seriously the feelings of those whom they do not care about. Additionally, if the aim of the harassment is to make the target feel uncomfortable or threatened, harassers may take instances of resistance or requests to stop as indicative of their success. Disapproval from peers—from people whom the harasser likes and respects—will serve as a far greater deterrent.

CONCEPT CHECK

5.9 Which of the following counts as discrimination in the workplace?

a. Siddhant's supervisor gave him a "satisfactory" work evaluation instead of a "very good" evaluation.

b. Siddhant's supervisor makes him work on Saturdays.

c. Siddhant's supervisor mocks him constantly by talking in a fake accent.

d. Siddhant was passed over for a promotion. The promotion went to someone else.

Why Should I Care?

The sheer magnitude of systemic unjust inequality can be overwhelming. Sometimes, when faced with problems of this scale, it is hard to see how our own actions can have a positive effect on the workplace, business, and other social systems in which we participate. Complex problems of this scale cannot be fully and sustainably addressed by a handful of individual actions alone. Any solutions that will adequately address systemic problems are themselves systemic. It is the collective effect of policies and enforcement, attitudes, individual actions, and sustained efforts to expose and resolve inequality that will promote lasting change.

A possible reason for the backlash against the movement toward equality comes from fearing a loss of unjustified personal privilege. It is important to understand that a reduction in this kind of privilege is not a moral harm.

Motivating everyone to do their part can sometimes be challenging. An important part of the reason for this is that, for every person or group of people who are disadvantaged by inequality and discrimination, another person or group is made better off by it. For example, job candidates with traditionally "white" names benefit from overt racism and implicit bias when candidates with traditionally "ethnic" names are not seriously considered.[41] There are many ways that systemic inequality privileges certain people, and getting those who benefit (either knowingly or unwittingly) from racism, sexism, classism, ableism, and so on to recognize their privilege can be challenging. But there are many reasons why even those of us who benefit from inequality should care.

Personal Affect

There are good reasons why people should care about inequality. Some of those reasons are related to how we feel about ourselves, and the impact of our attitudes and behaviour on others. Promoting equality feels good; almost no one wants to feel like they are treating others unfairly. Standing up for yourself and being equitable in your treatment of others means you are valuing people, promoting the self-esteem of those around you, and showing that others can trust your dealings with them.

Corporate Profit

Some arguments against the rigorous enforcement of equity initiatives focus on the negative impacts to business. Arguments like these typically claim that regular operating costs might go up if under-qualified candidates are hired, or that valuable resources will need to be allocated to the development, implementation, and monitoring of equity policies. What many, though not all, who make these claims are actually trying to say is that women, or visible minorities, or neuro-atypical folks, because of the kind of person they are, will not be up to the task. This privilege-protective stance ignores the potentially huge benefits that promoting equity (and, in turn, diversification and inclusion) can have:

equity initiatives
Programs and policies aimed at increasing and promoting equity.

- Diversification has become a social expectation, and companies that embrace it will be more competitive than those that do not.[42]
- Companies with diverse leadership have been shown to have higher net profit margins than those with homogenous leadership.[43]
- A diverse team may offer insight into the needs of diverse consumer groups, allowing businesses to identify under-explored market opportunities, and fulfill the needs of a wider consumer base.[44]
- Collaboration among employees with different sets of experiences, expertise, knowledge bases, and values can promote innovation, and increases potential for the development of new solutions for old problems.

Moral Obligation

The strongest reasons to care about inequality and discrimination are moral. No matter the moral theory, be it consequentialism, deontology, care ethics, capabilities, virtue ethics, or something else, justice requires, at the very least, that we treat each other as worthy of equal moral consideration. (The ethics of care might appear to be an exception because it favours certain persons, but it does not deny anyone the right to have that kind of care.) This can mean respecting others' autonomy, protecting the physical integrity of others, listening to others and valuing their contributions, or something more robust, like acting in ways that help promote the interests and development of others. Acting in a way that demonstrates the equal moral worth of all people sounds demanding, and it can be. For example, valuing the interests of someone you may not like can be challenging, but failing to do so communicates more than mere dislike. It also communicates that the other person is not worthy of equal respect, and that you believe yourself to be in a position to judge their value. Isolated incidents of unjust behaviour such as this can be damaging, but in business, treating people unjustly can unfairly limit access to resources, chances for success, and self-esteem.

Chapter 2 describes these moral theories in more detail.

Personal Protection

Finally, there are important self-interested reasons to uphold equality and promote transparent and fair decision making in business. You may find yourself the target of discriminatory practices. The same formal rules and codes of conduct are in place to protect everyone. If you find yourself a victim of discrimination, harassment, or other unjust attitudes and behaviours, the legal protections available are important tools to address injustice.

CONCEPT CHECK

5.10 Which of the following is an example of an inequality that is prohibited under Ontario human rights law?

a. Bob's feet are a different size than Irene's.

b. Irene is receiving social assistance for a disability and no landlord is willing to rent her an apartment.

c. Abdul abstains from drinking alcohol on the job.

d. Johannes lost his job because he was stealing office supplies.

CASE STUDY

Initiatives for Providing Equal Access to Capital

Banks are a vital part of Canadian business infrastructure. One of the important functions of a bank is to provide capital to entrepreneurs who are growing their businesses. In 2015, women led almost half of new small-business start-ups in Canada, and the number of females in professional roles increased by 35 per cent between 1995 and 2015.[45] In 2017, 15.6 per cent of small to medium-sized businesses were owned by women, particularly in the realms of retail, food services, tourism, and accommodation.[46] Women are a significant part of Canada's business landscape.

Having a secure source of capital is important for any entrepreneur to develop their business; this capital often comes in the form of bank loans or lines of credit. From 2015 to 2018, Bank of Montreal (BMO) set aside $2 billion in credit for female entrepreneurs, in addition to the credit that they had already made available to entrepreneurs of all types, including women.[47]

Then in February 2018, Carleton University, BMO Financial Group, and Beacon Agency released a study titled "Everywhere, Every Day Innovating: Women Entrepreneurs and Innovation Report" that identified barriers facing female entrepreneurs, including a perception by financial institutions that they are high risk; policies and programs that value technological innovation rather than innovation in the sectors where women are more likely to be involved (such as services); and issues related to child care and aging (such as programs targeted to 18- to 39-year-olds, which results in excluding women who start businesses after child-rearing).[48]

In June 2018, BMO announced another three-year initiative to earmark $3 billion of credit for female entrepreneurs.[49] (Scotiabank also announced a $3 billion initiative in 2018, called the Scotiabank Women's Initiative.[50]) BMO undertook these initiatives to invest in female entrepreneurs because of an awareness of challenges facing women-owned businesses, and an understanding of the positive contribution these businesses make to the Canadian economy, such as job creation. These initiatives also make good business sense for BMO because they open up underdeveloped capital markets. In 2019, Andrew Irvine, the head of Canadian business banking at BMO, said, "We're doing this for a number of reasons . . . one is that we're very conscious that women are starting more businesses. Globally and certainly in Canada the number of women-owned enterprises is increasing at a faster [pace] than other business strata."[51]

For Discussion

1. Think about what you would need to start your own business. How would being denied access to bank financing affect the viability of the business?
2. How might banks benefit from encouraging women entrepreneurs?
3. How might society benefit from encouraging women entrepreneurs?
4. What would you say in response to a charge that a bank is being discriminatory by setting aside capital specifically for female businesspersons?

Resources

We have discussed at length some of the problems of unfairness and discrimination in different contexts, and suggested some ways to reduce the impact or eliminate the harm. Here we point you to some of the legal resources and institutional policies for identifying instances of inequality and discrimination, and protecting those who are discriminated against. These resources will help you develop a clear understanding of the legal requirements of businesses, their agents, and their staff, and equip readers with resources to protect themselves and others against the harms of inequality and discrimination.

Canadian Charter of Rights and Freedoms

Section 15 of the Canadian Charter of Rights and Freedoms states, "Every individual is equal before and under the law and has the right to the equal protection and equal benefit of the law without discrimination and, in particular, without discrimination based on race, national or ethnic origin, colour, religion, sex, age or mental or physical disability."[52]

Canadian Human Rights Act

The purpose of the Canadian Human Rights Act is to extend Canadian legislation such that "all individuals should have an opportunity equal with other individuals to make for themselves the lives that they are able and wish to have and to have their needs accommodated, consistent with their duties and obligations as members of society, without being hindered in or prevented from doing so by discriminatory practices."[53]

Canadian Human Rights Commission

The Canadian Human Rights Act created the Canadian Human Rights Commission, which investigates and settles claims of discrimination.[54] If claims are not settled by the Canadian Human Rights Commission, the claims will be judged by the Canadian Human Rights Tribunal. Canada's provinces have similar legislation and commissions.

Employment Equity Act (2010)

The Employment Equity Act, originally enacted in 1967 under Prime Minister Lester Pearson, was drafted during a period of increased immigration to Canada. It was intended as a response to, and protection against, long-standing xenophobic and racist norms in Canadian business practices. The Act also included protections for women, persons with disabilities, and Indigenous Peoples, noting particularly that "employment equity means more than treating persons in the same way but also requires special measures and the accommodation of differences."[55]

Federal and Provincial Accessibility Legislation

Upwards of 22 per cent of Canadians over the age of 15 have a disability that affects how they conduct their daily lives.[56] In absolute terms, this means that over 6 million Canadians find it challenging to access businesses, services, education, and labour markets, among other things. To address this reality, federal, provincial, and territorial governments have taken recent steps to facilitate access to these types of social goods.

In summer of 2019, the federal government of Canada passed Bill C-81, which introduces accessibility requirements for all organizations that fall under federal jurisdiction. This includes "banking, telecommunications, transportation industries and the Government of Canada itself."[57]

Some Canadian provinces also have accessibility laws. For example, the Accessibility for Ontarians with Disabilities Act (AODA) sets out the impairments and disorders that require workplace and public accommodation. These include sensory, mobility, developmental, mental, linguistic, and learning impairments, regardless of how or when the impairment began. A full definition appears in section 2 of the Act.[58] The Act establishes standards in five broad areas: communication, customer service, employment, public spaces, and transportation. Manitoba and Nova Scotia have similar legislation in place. British Columbia is working on an initiative, originally called "Accessibility 2024," which has the goal of making the province "truly inclusive" for people of all disabilities by 2024.[59]

Occupational Health and Safety

The federal government of Canada, along with each province and territory, has legislation outlining the rights and responsibilities of both employers and employees. Federal legislation, as outlined in Part II of the Canadian Labour Code, applies to Crown corporations and other agencies that fall under federal jurisdiction. This includes things like railways, highway transport, pipelines, ferries, and some grain elevators and feed mills. Part II of the labour code states that every employee within federal jurisdiction has the right to know about potential hazards in the workplace, the right to participate in identifying workplace hazards, and the right to refuse to do dangerous work.[60]

Provincial and territorial occupational health and safety legislation applies to workers in those jurisdictions, with some exceptions. Generally work done within a home by the "owner, occupant, or servants" does not fall under safety legislation.[61] Similarly, farm labour is generally exempt from labour laws. The provinces and territories are responsible for the enforcement of their respective safety laws and regulations.[62]

International Labour Organization

The International Labour Organization (ILO) was established in 1919 under the terms of the Treaty of Versailles that ended the First World War.[63] It became a United Nations agency in 1946. The ILO, as an advocate for peace through social justice, "brings together governments, employers, and workers of 187 member States, to set labour standards, develop policies and devise programmes promoting decent work for all women and men."[64] These standards and policies include a convention declaring that participating states will eliminate discrimination in the workplace.[65]

Summing Up

To ignore the wrongs of inequality and discrimination is to admit moral defeat. We have assumed in this chapter that inequality and discrimination are bad things. We have not given arguments to support this position, but that is because to do so would take us beyond the scope of this textbook. There are plenty of philosophy courses that one can take that address these social, political, and economic concerns.

What we have done in this chapter is discuss the harms of inequality and discrimination, and why we should take care to redress these harms, particularly in the context of the workplace. We must know what our rights and obligations are. These rights and obligations are there to protect everyone's interests and to ensure that everyone has a fair chance at being the best versions of themselves that they can be.

For Discussion and Review

1. Could issues of equity and privilege be dealt with appropriately through CSR (introduced in Chapter 4)? Explain your reasoning.
2. Which normative ethical theory (covered in Chapter 2) best deals with issues of equity and privilege? Why do you think this?
3. Are issues of equality primarily issues of public or private morality? (See Chapter 3 for the distinction between public and private morality.) Explain your answer.
4. Rawls suggests that those who design a society should do so from behind a "veil of ignorance." What do you think the outcome of this process would be for a person who cannot see? For a person who uses a powered wheelchair? For someone who is easily overwhelmed by loud or repetitive sounds?
5. "If we make an accommodation for you, we have to do it for everybody." Is this a problem? Why or why not?

6. Consider the distribution of social resources on the bases of equality, fairness, and efficiency. Which one would you favour in your ideal society, and why? How would you address the matter of those who, for reasons beyond their control, need more social support than others?

7. How are wage gaps and wealth gaps related? Which is the better indicator of socio-economic well-being, and why?

8. "Privilege is when you think that something's not a problem because it's not a problem for you personally."[66] Discuss.

Further Reading

De Houwer, Jan. "What Is Implicit Bias?" *Psychology Today*. Last updated 13 October 2019. https://www.psychologytoday.com/us/blog/spontaneous-thoughts/201910/what-is-implicit-bias.

Government of Canada. *Guide to the Canadian Charter of Rights and Freedoms*. Last modified 18 June 2019. https://www.canada.ca/en/canadian-heritage/services/how-rights-protected/guide-canadian-charter-rights-freedoms.html.

Morris, Stuart, Gail Fawcett, Laurent Brisebois, and Jeffrey Hughes. "A Demographic, Employment, and Income Profile of Canadians with Disabilities Aged 15 Years and over, 2017." Canadian Survey on Disability Reports. Statistics Canada, 2018. https://www150.statcan.gc.ca/n1/en/pub/89-654-x/89-654-x2018002-eng.pdf.

Ontario Human Rights Commission. *Guide to Your Rights and Responsibilities under the Human Rights Code*. Government of Ontario, 2013. http://www.ohrc.on.ca/sites/default/files/Guide%20to%20Your%20Rights%20and%20Responsibilities%20Under%20the%20Code_2013.pdf.

Ward, Susan. "Statistics on Canadian Women in Business: What Women Entrepreneurs in Canada Are Like." The Balance Small Business. Last modified 28 February 2019. https://www.thebalancesmb.com/statistics-on-canadian-women-in-business-2948029.

CHAPTER 6
Social Action Problems

By the end of this chapter you should be able to

- Explain what a social contract is.

- Describe some of the tensions between acting in one's self-interest and acting co-operatively.

- Identify ways in which co-operation can be beneficial to a business.

- Use game theory to analyze various social action problems, including the prisoner's dilemma and free-rider problem.

- Compare the concepts of moral hazard and the principal–agent problem.

Pick up any introductory textbook to economics and within the first few pages you will see the claim that people are rational maximizers. According to economists, a person will only choose a course of action if the marginal benefits of that action outweigh the marginal costs. People do what is in their self-interest. If this is true—that humans are self-interested—then we can be forgiven for thinking that business is all about making decisions that are ruthlessly self-serving. Yet this principle seems to contradict our claim earlier in this text that business has a responsibility to society. We started this text by examining what is needed to make free and competitive markets work. Competitive markets that are free and fair only work if those operating within the market system recognize that businesses and markets are society's creations. This means that business operates in a context of social norms, expectations, and requirements that businesses cannot ignore if they wish to continue functioning. In some sense, business must be pro-social.

Can we have it both ways? Can we agree that humans are self-interested, and that business must have some sort of pro-social disposition? The short answer is *yes*, but the longer answer requires nuanced thinking about self-interest and co-operation.

The Social Contract and Enlightened Self-Interest

Co-operating with other people requires seeing things from their perspective, and adapting to their preferences—at least temporarily. To co-operate with another person, we must make decisions with their needs and wants and goals in mind, not just our own. So what is the motivation to co-operate? What if we do not want to adapt or change our actions and goals to reflect this bigger picture?

One significant motivation for co-operating with others is the realization that if we do not co-operate, we ourselves often end up worse off than we would have been if we had co-operated. In other words, it can be in our self-interest, broadly construed, to co-operate with others, even if it is not in our narrow self-interest to do so. Thomas Hobbes, a seventeenth-century political philosopher, famously captured this idea in his view of the origin of governments.

BACKGROUND

Co-Operation and the Social Contract

Hobbes's *Leviathan* was published in 1651. In it, Hobbes describes how civil society would emerge from the "state of nature"—a state in which there is no morality or rule of law. Hobbes conceived of civil society as a voluntary and co-operative association, where members are bound by a mutually agreed-to contract. According to Hobbes, this contract (now often called the *social contract*) is the basis of morality and the rule of law.

According to Hobbes's view, people agree to live together under laws in a civil society as a sort of second-best condition. Acting out of narrow self-interest, each individual would seek to get as much as they could without concern for the well-being of others. But life in a hypothetical "state of nature" where everyone acted like that, Hobbes says, would be "solitary, poor, nasty, brutish, and short,"[1] and a war of all against all.[2] In other words, individuals following the principle of narrow self-interest would only end up stealing from and killing one another.

But, Hobbes thought, when such individuals realize what their narrow self-interested actions will lead to, if they are rational, then they will also see that a violent free-for-all is not the best thing for themselves. Everyone has to sleep at some point. The idea that it can be in our own considered best interests to *refrain* from doing what we want or feel like doing is the basis for what is called enlightened self-interest. Enlightened self-interest is, in part, simply a way of describing a person who is aware of a broad range of factors that impact their interests— including the interests and well-being of others. The other part involves having the patience and self-control to forgo what is in your narrow self-interest in order to achieve what is in your enlightened self-interest when doing so would be advantageous to you. Sustained co-operation is only possible if people act out of enlightened self-interest.

According to Hobbes, rational beings following their enlightened self-interest in the state of nature would agree to give up some of their freedom in exchange for a guarantee that others would also constrain themselves in the same way. For example, I can say that I will not steal other people's things in exchange for the assurance that they will not steal mine. This agreement frees each of the participants from the need to protect their stuff from each other so they can give their attention to more productive activities. To that effect, rational individuals will make a covenant or social contract with one another.

narrow self-interest
What is best for oneself, irrespective of the interests of others.

enlightened self-interest
What is best for oneself, including consideration of the interests of others.

social contract
The idea that people mutually agree to forgo what is in their narrow self-interest for the sake of what is in their enlightened self-interest, namely to give up some of their individual liberty in exchange for social security and stability.

CONCEPT CHECK

6.1 According to Hobbes, life in the state of nature would be:

a. nasty, brutish, and short.

b. pleasant, collegial, and long-lived.

c. rashy, irritable, and foul-smelling.

d. belligerent, contemptuous, and disputatious.

6.2 What is enlightened self-interest?

a. It ignores things like the interests of others, thereby making it lighter than regular self-interest.

b. It takes the interests of others into consideration.

c. It is the view that selfishness and self-interest are the same thing.

d. It involves projecting one's desires and ideals onto the infinite.

But there is a catch. If I am one of the individuals who is about to enter into a contract with others, how can I be sure that they will not break the covenant, ignore their promises, steal my things, and even kill me if doing so helps them get what they want? We can use

In game theory, a *game table* is also known as a game matrix. See **Appendix B** for a primer on how to read game tables.

John L.

	Co–operate	Double–cross
Co–operate	Safe and secure , Safe and secure	Murdered , Complete dominance
Double–cross	Complete dominance , Murdered	Nasty, brutish, short , Nasty, brutish, short

Thomas H.

Game Table 6.1 **Responses to the Social Contract**

game theory
A formal system for modelling the actions of rational decision makers (the *players*) in strategic social interactions (*games*). The outcome depends on the combined actions of all of the players. The players individually choose the action each will take on the basis of the information each has available and the outcomes each is willing to accept.

See **Appendix B** for more explanation of Game Table 6.1 (Responses to the Social Contract).

game theory to analyze this type of dilemma. Consider the potential outcomes shown in Game Table 6.1.

Thomas and John must decide if they will enter into a social contract with each other. If neither of them co-operate and instead double-cross each other, they will remain in the state of nature and their lives will be nasty, brutish, and short (this outcome is illustrated in the lower-right quadrant). If both Thomas and John decide to co-operate, both will be safe and secure (this outcome is illustrated in the upper-left quadrant). It may seem obvious what the decision should be, for who would choose a life that is nasty, brutish, and short over a life that is safe and secure? Unfortunately, there is more to the decision than this. Consider what happens if John is willing to co-operate, but Thomas decides to double-cross him (the lower-left quadrant)? Things go well for Thomas, but the outcome is fatal for John. A similar thing happens if Thomas chooses to co-operate but John decides to double-cross him (the upper-right quadrant).

If Thomas were to ask for our advice, we would rightly point out that no matter what John decides to do, he (Thomas) is better off if he decides to double-cross John (we come to this conclusion by doing a column-by-column analysis of Thomas's outcomes). Now the cruel reality of the situation sets in when John asks us for advice. If John were to ask for our advice, we would rightly point out that no matter what Thomas decides to do, he (John) is better off if he decides to double-cross Thomas (we come to this conclusion by doing a row-by-row analysis of John's outcomes).

The outcome of their decision is not good. Both Thomas and John decide to double-cross each other, neither enter into the social contract, and both live lives that are nasty, brutish, and short. This result is frustrating on so many levels, and we may feel like screaming at Thomas and John that they should just both co-operate. Why choose to double-cross each other if they are collectively better off if they choose to co-operate? The answer is that Thomas and John have become trapped in a *social action problem*.

BACKGROUND

Governing the Social Contract

How did Hobbes resolve the trust issue that plagues the social contract? For Hobbes, assurance of security rests in entrusting absolute power to a sovereign, a king or ruler responsible for enforcing the laws according to the social contract. By this reasoning, Hobbes believed himself to be showing that a government with the power to compel people by force is rationally justified, and even rationally necessary, given the conditions of human life. The sovereign (that is, the government) will use compulsion, including punishment for those who are noncompliant, to ensure that the citizens of the state keep the terms of the social contract (the laws of society). Such compulsion is just, in this view, because to violate the covenant is to undermine the basis of your own protection and security.

Social Action Problems

A **social action problem** is a situation where, if each individual in that situation does what is in their self-interest, the result would be that everyone is worse off than they would have been had each individual acted otherwise. The basic idea is that there are social contexts where the interests of each individual conflict with the interests of the group. In such contexts, everyone (collectively) would be much better off if they co-operated with each other, but there is no *incentive* to do so. In fact, in many social action problems there is a *disincentive* to co-operate. The fact that social action problems have a logical structure that pretty much guarantees that people will not co-operate with each other is what makes these problems so pernicious.

social action problem
A situation where, if each individual in that situation does what is in their self-interest, the result will be that everyone is worse off than they would have been had each individual acted otherwise.

BACKGROUND

Incentives and Disincentives

An *incentive* is designed to motivate a particular behaviour. For example, offering a reward for the safe return of a lost pet serves as an incentive for people to look for that pet. By contrast, a *disincentive* is designed to discourage a particular behaviour. For example, fines for speeding are meant to be a disincentive against exceeding the speed limit. Sometimes pairing an incentive with a disincentive is called a carrot-and-stick approach: the incentive is to keep pursuing a goal in the same way a working animal pursues a food reward, while the disincentive is the threat of being punished by being hit with the stick.

The Prisoner's Dilemma

prisoner's dilemma
A prisoner's dilemma is a scenario in which two alleged criminals, acting rationally and according to their self-interest, confess to the crime (that is, defect) and end up with longer jail sentences than if they had simply kept quiet (that is, co-operated with each other).

socially optimal outcome
The result of the players' choices that yields the greatest utility available to them collectively.

The **prisoner's dilemma** is often the go-to example of a social action problem. Here is the scenario. The local police have charged Sid and Velma with committing two crimes: one major, the other minor. The pair are brought in for investigation and interrogated in separate rooms. The investigating officer tells both Sid and Velma that the police have conclusive proof that the two committed the minor crime, and offers each of them the following deal respectively: If Sid confesses to the major crime, but Velma keeps quiet, then Sid will go free after one year, but Velma will get a ten-year prison sentence; similarly, if Velma confesses, and Sid keeps quiet, then Velma walks after a year, but Sid gets ten years in the slammer. The catch is, if both Sid and Velma keep quiet, they can only be indicted on the minor offence, and both will get two years in prison. However, if they both confess, then each of them ends up with a five-year jail sentence. We can illustrate this scenario using Game Table 6.2.

The **socially optimal outcome** of this game is the upper-left quadrant, which results if both Sid and Velma keep quiet. If both Sid and Velma keep quiet, each will spend two years in prison. However, the socially optimal outcome will not be the actual outcome of this scenario. If both Sid and Velma act out of self-interest, the actual outcome of this scenario will be the lower-right quadrant, where Sid and Velma each spend five years in prison. What generates the social action problem is that each person has a strong disincentive to keep quiet (to co-operate with each other) and a strong incentive to confess (defect). To see this, consider that if Velma keeps quiet, then it is better for Sid to confess since one year in prison is better than two years in prison, and if Velma confesses, then it is still better for Sid to confess since five years in prison is better than ten years in prison. So no matter what Velma does, Sid does better by confessing. The same type of analysis for what Velma should do will result in a similar conclusion: no matter what Sid decides to do, Velma does better by confessing.

Even though the prisoner's dilemma seems highly contrived and extremely unlikely to occur in any actual police investigation, we do ourselves a disfavour if we dismiss it as such. There is great value in using game theory to model the logic behind the prisoner's dilemma.

		Velma: Keep Quiet (co-operate)	Velma: Confess (defect)
Sid	Keep Quiet (co-operate)	2 years in prison , 2 years in prison	10 years in prison , 1 year in prison
Sid	Confess (defect)	1 year in prison , 10 years in prison	5 years in prison , 5 years in prison

Game Table 6.2 Prisoner's Dilemma

BACKGROUND

Calculating the Socially Optimal Outcome

The socially optimal outcome is calculated simply by summing the utilities of both players for a given outcome. Consider Game Table 6.2. The top-left quadrant is the best outcome for everyone since it only results in four years in prison collectively. This is the best outcome that both players can hope for collectively. Contrast this with the social outcome represented in the bottom-right quadrant. In this outcome, both players spend ten years in prison collectively.

Once we have generalized the problem and identified the key features of the model, we can use it in our conceptual analysis of other social action problems, which can and do occur in all areas of life, including in business and the workplace.

The Free-Rider Problem

The prisoner's dilemma helps to explain why individuals—even though they would do better if they co-operated—make decisions that are collectively self-defeating. Knowing this, we can see that it is in everyone's (enlightened) self-interest that we find ways to prevent defection in prisoner's dilemma scenarios. If we could only learn to co-operate with one another, each one of us doing our part, things would end up so much better for all of us. How might we go about ensuring the co-operative outcome? One strategy we can try is to adopt a **default co-operative attitude** toward others.

If everyone adopted a co-operative attitude toward other people, then everyone would end up co-operating, and we would find it much easier to reach the socially optimal solution to social action problems. Large-scale social co-operation has the potential to dramatically increase utility gains for everyone, and if we value utility (which we all do!), then we should all be very interested in generating co-operative outcomes.

Co-operation can be extremely beneficial. But a group of people co-operating with one another creates the conditions for **free-rider problems** to emerge. A free-rider is a person who takes advantage of the benefits of co-operation without paying the cost required for the co-operative situation to exist. The free-rider gets a "free ride" on the co-operative bus that everyone else is paying for.

To illustrate, consider any situation where you are part of a group that must accomplish some task together. If the members of the group are co-operators, each will do their fair share of the work, and will (if all goes well) reap the benefits of their individual contributions by getting a good grade on the assignment (for group work at school), or secure other benefits for themselves (for group work in an employment or other business setting). But notice what unfortunately happens all too often: one member of the group sees that the rest of the group members are highly motivated co-operators, and realizes that if one member shirks their responsibility, the other group members will likely pick up the slack. So the group member in question decides to become a free-rider and enjoys some extra time to watch videos or catch up on sleep, assured of a share in the benefits of the project without having to fully (or fairly)

default co-operative attitude
The strategy of playing co-operatively unless the other player defects from the co-operative strategy.

free-rider problem
A free-rider problem emerges when someone (the free-rider) benefits from the co-operative activities of others without themself contributing to produce the benefits. This puts a strain on the rest of the group and threatens to undermine the co-operative outcome.

contribute to produce that outcome. A social action problem quickly emerges when everyone in the group starts thinking like a free-rider.

CONCEPT CHECK

6.3 What is a social action problem?

a. Everyone (collectively) does something, and someone else is punished for their behaviour.

b. Everyone (individually) acts selflessly and everyone (collectively) is better off for it.

c. Everyone (individually) does what is in their self-interest, and everyone (collectively) is worse off for it.

d. Everyone is made better off, and no one is made worse off for it.

6.4 Which of the following scenarios is an example of a free-rider?

a. Bob has a student card that allows him to ride the local buses and trains for free.

b. Bob lives alone and uses paper dishes because he hates doing dishes.

c. Bob enjoys taunting fate by jaywalking.

d. Bob does all the work for the group project since no one else did any of the work.

Free-rider scenarios are obviously not good for the group. For one thing, it means more work for the other group members. For another thing, consider what the outcome would be if all of the group members decided to act as free-riders. Once again, we can model the scenario envisaged here using a game table as shown in Game Table 6.3. To make things simple we will assume there are only two group members.

If you and your partner choose the free-rider strategy (shirk responsibility and let the other person do the work), both of you end up in the lower-right quadrant (0, 0), which is a

	Partner	
	Work (co–operate)	**Shirk (defect)**
Work (co–operate)	2 , 2	−3 , 5
Shirk (defect)	5 , −3	0 , 0

Game Table 6.3 Free-Rider Problem

BACKGROUND

Numbers in a Game Table

The numbers in the quadrants simply represent the utility each group member receives if that outcome obtains. Referring to Game Table 6.3, if you decide to work and your partner decides to shirk, you receive −3 units of utility (which is equivalent to losing 3 units of utility, or receiving 3 units of disutility) and your partner gets 5 units of utility. The numbers here are simply a convenient way to represent things like time spent on the project, effort, happiness, frustration, etc.

sub-optimal outcome compared to the upper-left quadrant (2, 2). Nonetheless, whatever your partner does, you do better by not working (in the case where your partner works, you get a reward valued at 5 rather than 2, and in the case where your partner shirks, you get a reward of 0 rather than −3). However, when you and your partner do what is in your own self-interest, then you both end up with a worse outcome (the lower-right quadrant) than you could have if you had simply co-operated with each other.

A close comparison of the prisoner's dilemma (Game Table 6.2) and the free-rider problem (Game Table 6.3) should convince us that the two scenarios share the same logical structure: there is a strong incentive to defect despite the fact that co-operation would lead to the better collective outcome. These types of social action problems are pernicious because there is no straightforward way to solve them. Any attempt to resolve a social action problem will be fraught with the risk of defection—of people engaging in what looks like self-defeating behaviour. Moral hazard is a clear example of this.

Moral Hazard

The phenomenon of **moral hazard** arises when a person believes they are protected from the full consequences of their actions.

Think about how our behaviour changes while walking outside during an ice storm. Our behaviour changes to compensate for our perceived risk of personal injury: the focus

moral hazard
The phenomenon known as moral hazard emerges when people who believe they have protection from the full consequences (though not necessarily full protection from any consequences) of risky behaviour will take more risks.

BACKGROUND

Moral Hazard and Insurance

Moral hazard was first observed in fire-insurance markets, where those who were insured were more likely to have fires than those who were uninsured.[3] The term now refers to any situation where there is the opportunity or incentive for someone to engage in risky behaviour because someone else bears most of the consequences.

BACKGROUND

Moral Hazard and Risk Compensation

We present the hockey-helmet example as a hypothetical thought experiment for the following reason. Even though there is widespread agreement in the literature that risk compensation in sports is a real phenomenon, there is less agreement about where and under what conditions the phenomenon will occur, and even less agreement about what types of policies and safety regulations should be put in place as a result.

of our attention changes, our gait changes, our willingness to jaywalk on a busy street changes, and so forth. We become more careful because the potential for serious injury is greater.

Now think about how our behaviour could change if we think that we are protected against a perceived risk. Consider the following thought experiment. Helmets were first introduced in hockey to reduce the number of head injuries sustained by players. But when the players starting wearing helmets, they felt less concerned about protecting their heads (or those of other players) from injuries than they did previously. As a result, body checking became rougher,

CASE STUDY

Moral Hazard and Perverse Incentives

Canadian provinces' publicly funded health-insurance programs pay physicians to attend births in hospitals. There is typically a base fee paid for an uncomplicated vaginal delivery on a weekday, with a premium paid for attending a weekend delivery—50 per cent in one particular province. This premium is not exorbitant and is consistent with the premium in other jobs where overtime is paid. The weekend premium is designed to ensure that women who go into labour on Saturday or Sunday can receive the care that their taxes and provincial insurance fees have purchased. In one province, this premium translated to an extra $249.35 for each weekend birth.

One doctor, finding that he had less money after a divorce than he was used to having, and who had a "sterling reputation" and privileged status within the medical community, found a way to increase the number of his patients delivering on weekends.[4] Without the patients' consent—or even knowledge—he gave them a drug that would induce labour a couple of days later. The drug was in pill form, so he could administer it secretly by placing it in the patient's vagina during pre-delivery examinations late in the workweek. The drug had not been approved for this purpose, and such use was judged by medical authorities (including the hospital where the doctor worked) to be risky and even dangerous. Alert nurses discovered the situation and informed the director

and there were more passes above the waistline. The outcome was, despite having to pay the extra expense of the helmets, there were roughly the same number of head injuries with helmets as there had been without them.

Ensuring that we are protected from things like head injuries is a good idea. But once we are protected, we might tend to act more recklessly than we would have done if we had no protective equipment. If we do, we have fallen prey to moral hazard.

The effects of moral hazard can contribute toward the existence of a social action problem. If everyone takes steps to protect themselves from things like head injuries and, as a result, everyone becomes more willing to take risks, the result is sub-optimal compared to the initial situation where people were not protected, but took fewer risks.

Circling back to the free-rider problem, we can use moral hazard to explain why someone might choose to be a free-rider. Imagine that a group of co-op students working for the same company have been given a task during their first work term. Even though everyone in the group wants an outstanding work-term evaluation, someone in the group might think they can get away with doing less work and still get a favourable evaluation. Moral hazard helps us explain why. If the other group members pick up the slack and the project is ultimately successful, there is little risk to free-riding. The free-rider essentially uses the other group members as an insurance policy to ensure a glowing evaluation.

How we perceive and assess risk can change if we think—rightly or wrongly—that we are shielded from the full consequences of our actions. One of the lessons to take away from this discussion is that we have good reason to pay attention to the presence of moral hazard

of the hospital.[5] Thus a policy intended to guarantee safe and appropriate medical treatment of patients was perversely rewarding one rule-breaking doctor who put his patients' health at risk, and worse.

For Discussion

1. Explain what a perverse incentive is.
2. After this discovery the hospital increased the kinds of records it kept, so that any such activity would be noticed. How does accurate and impartial record-keeping important help to avoid perverse incentives?
3. Hospitals have top-down administrative structures, somewhat like the police and the military, where subordinates have little authority and are supposed to be quietly subservient. Explain (in general terms) why it is important to have mechanisms by which subordinates can report the illegal and unethical behaviour of their superiors.
4. What alternative ways of structuring incentives for weekend medical service can you think of that would not lead to perverse rewards such as this?
5. Do the medical professionals in your country/province/state have an enforceable code of ethics? If so, what would it say about the type of situation described in the case study?

and to find ways of mitigating its effects if possible. If we do not, we can get ourselves into some really sticky (and potentially dangerous) situations. The game of chicken is an example of this.

CONCEPT CHECK

6.5 What is moral hazard?

a. People take responsibility for their actions.

b. People act in overly risky ways because they are shielded from the full consequences of their behaviour.

c. People act in overly risky ways, thereby endangering those around them.

d. An individual refuses to do the tasks assigned by the group leader.

The Game of Chicken

game of chicken
A game-theory depiction of a situation where the competing players have little to gain by winning and a great amount to lose by losing, and are motivated toward mutual self-destruction by perversely preferring to maintain their pride or reputation for being "tough."

A social action problem with tragic results is the game of chicken. The scenario is this: two people in trucks are driving at top speed toward one another, and whoever swerves first loses. That is, the driver who swerves first is the chicken. Consider Game Table 6.4.

If both James and Dean swerve at the last moment before impact, they remain alive and neither of them looks any more "chicken" than the other in the eyes of their friends and any potential romantic partners who might be watching. This outcome is represented in the upper-left quadrant of the game table. However, no one wins the game either. The only way to win the game is if one person swerves and the other does not. James is the chicken if he swerves and Dean does not (upper-right quadrant). Similarly, Dean is the chicken if he swerves and James does not (lower-left quadrant). Tragically, though, if neither swerve, both end up dead, an outcome that is near the very bottom of most people's preference rankings (lower-right quadrant).

		Dean	
		Swerve	**Don't Swerve**
James	**Swerve**	Lucky , Lucky	Chicken , Victor
	Don't Swerve	Victor , Chicken	Dead , Dead

Game Table 6.4 Game of Chicken

The choices do not look great in the game of chicken. In order to "win" under the rules of the game, you have to be more willing to risk death—your own and that of someone else—than your opponent. By playing the game of chicken, you put yourself in a situation where choosing not to die (by swerving and avoiding collision when it is still possible to do so) is the "losing" choice. The "co-operative" outcome in this case will be hard to achieve, since it involves very precise timing, and the game is not set up to encourage coordination in swerving. Instead, the goal is to bluff that you will keep driving straight convincingly enough so that your opponent believes you, and swerves before you do.

We should wonder why anyone would put themselves into a situation like this. Part of the problem is that the preferences driving the game are perverse. A person acting rationally should not prefer mutual destruction over a loss of honour, especially when honour is measured in this way. To use the language of virtue ethics, it is not courageous to almost kill yourself and someone else in a car crash willingly for no real gain. It is reckless or foolhardy—an example of the vice that involves not fearing and avoiding things that should be feared or avoided. But this foolhardy behaviour is exactly what the game of chicken urges people to do! Something has gone seriously wrong here.

Social Action Problems in the Wild

We have now considered four different types of social action problems: the prisoner's dilemma, the free-rider problem, moral hazard, and the game of chicken. Thinking through the underlying logic of these problems can help us better identify the psychological and situational factors that generate such problems. In what follows we look at some concrete examples of social action problems.

Unhealthy Competition

As was noted when discussing the game of chicken, being overly competitive can contribute to a social action problem with potentially dire consequences. The game of chicken models the kind of situation where a desire to win the game is out of line with more important values like personal safety and fair play. However, winning at any cost is not the sort of thing we should desire for its own sake. This kind of unhealthy competition can show up in team sports, where players might be willing to engage in behaviours that endanger the health of their opponents.

In football, cut-blocking (driving your shoulder into your opponent's knee) is (surprisingly still) technically legal, but it can also cause injuries like torn ligaments, broken legs, and broken ankles.[6] Some of these injuries can end a player's career. Joe Bugel, who spent more than 30 years as an offensive line coach in the National Football League, has said, "There is no way a guy can protect his knees against cut-blocking. Keep getting cut; sooner or later you're going to be in hospital having surgery."[7] Yet some coaches push their players to cut-block. Les Steckel, another long-time offensive coach, told a reporter, "I'd say 'Go cut 'em,' and they'd say 'But they have a career like me.' And I'd say, 'Well, they're trying to take your career away from you.'"[8] If we take both coaches at their word, we can see that some coaches want their players to believe that they have to cut-block to keep their jobs, while others believe it is a play that is disrespectful of other players since it introduces unfairness to the competition.

The issue comes down to one of values. If an offensive coach values winning at all costs over fair play and the well-being of the opposing players, the coach will instruct the players to cut-block, since there is a competitive advantage in injuring an opponent's defensive lineman. However, if the offensive coach values player safety more than ending an opposing player's career, then fair play dictates that cut-blocking should not be used as a strategy.

CONCEPT CHECK

6.6 What is a problem with unhealthy competition?

a. It detracts from a healthy sense of self-worth.

b. It makes it harder for bookmakers to set odds.

c. It easily leads to adopting a win-at-all-costs attitude.

d. People lose sight of the big picture and set unattainable goals.

Unhealthy competition shows up in many contexts. High-performance athletes who use steroids to boost their performance may (if they get away with it) make themselves more likely to win a medal. But fair sportsmanship demands that we not violate the rules of the game for the sake of winning—and for this reason athletics associations have no tolerance for those who do get caught. In the political world, we can see that the real-life results of unhealthy competition can have very serious consequences, as in the case of the nuclear arms race. The escalating threats made by the Soviet Union and the USA during the Cold War (1947–1991) were not just a case of misplaced bravado—the lives of millions of people were at stake.

A more recent example of unfair competition comes from the state of Pennsylvania, where the popular vote has been divided roughly evenly between the Republican and Democratic parties. The unhealthy aspect of the electoral competition arises when partisan legislators select their voters by the demographics of geographical areas, rather than allowing the voters to choose their legislators to reflect the will of the people.[9] (Reshaping electoral districts for the purpose of guaranteeing a winning election result for a particular party is known as gerrymandering.) Every ten years the map of congressional electoral districts in Pennsylvania is redrawn by the state government. The map drawn in 2011 focused on lumping large clusters of Democratic voters into a small number of districts, leaving the rest of the districts with a large plurality of Republican supporters. The boundaries of one electoral district (the 7th) were so distorted that it became known as "Goofy kicking Donald Duck" because of the way it looked on the map (see the 113th Congress in Figure 6.1). This map was used for congressional elections in 2012, 2014, and 2016. Each of those elections resulted in 13 seats for the Republicans and only 5 for the Democrats—a congressional delegation that did not reflect the political makeup of the state, but was engineered to preserve a Republican majority. A court challenge forced Pennsylvania legislators to use a less distorted, more competitive map for the 2018 election. With this revised map, the Republicans and Democrats each won 9 congressional seats.

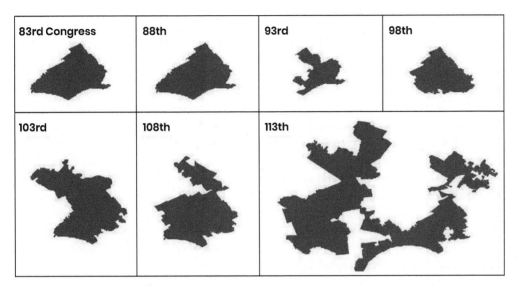

FIGURE 6.1 The evolution of Pennsylvania's seventh district. This illustration shows the shape of Pennsylvania's seventh congressional electoral district every ten years from 1952 to 2012. In 1992 (103rd Congress), the district's boundaries started being drawn to encompass supporters of a particular party rather than a compact geographical area with a representative voter orientation.

The Principal–Agent Problem

In the corporate world, moral hazard needs to be taken very seriously as its effects can be detrimental to the well-being of a firm. A significant possibility for moral hazard to arise in a business context has to do with the way corporate executives can be shielded from the consequences of their actions. The business owners want their executives to be free to take the risks necessary to bring about success for the firm, but the executives will be disinclined to do so if they are solely responsible for the negative consequences of their decisions. Incentive structures need to balance the owners' desire for the executives to take appropriate risks on behalf of the firm, and the executives' desire not to be fired because of risky decisions that harm the company.

> This is one form of the principal–agent problem. We explore this problem in more detail as one of the risks associated with corporate governance in **Chapter 9**.

CONCEPT CHECK

6.7 Which of the following is an example of the principal–agent problem?

a. A shareholder sells all their shares of a company at the most inopportune time.

b. Bob is the principal of University Heights Elementary School. And he has a problem.

c. A worker works overtime, but does not get paid.

d. A manager acts in a way that is not in the best interest of the firm.

Dirty Dishes

This example might be a little "closer to home" for the average undergraduate student. Everyone knows the feeling of being a bit too busy to wash your own dishes. Sometimes you just have to leave them in the sink for a while—with every intention, of course, of coming back and doing them later. This approach can lead to serious relational and practical problems, especially if you have several other housemates who think in the same way. Once four or five people have left a few dishes in the sink, it becomes complicated to try and do your own dishes. "Is that my fork?" "That might be my cup, but the orange slime sitting in it did not come from me!" Before you know it, where there used to be a counter and sink, you have a mountain of unwashed dishes that no one is willing to touch. If everyone had spent two minutes taking care of their own dishes, everyone would still have a functioning kitchen. But because everyone went for the small benefit of putting off washing their dishes until later, everyone is now much worse off than they would have been.

The potential benefit of this free-rider strategy comes, of course, if one of your roommates has had enough and does everyone's dishes. But since no one ever wants to be the chump, this does not actually ever happen.

Pre-Emptive Strikes

Sometimes, anticipating that the person we are dealing with is going to use a non-co-operative strategy, we reason that we should play non-co-operatively from the outset. We think, "If I don't take advantage of them, then they will take advantage of me." This approach does not tend to lead to mutual co-operation. Instead, it more or less ensures that if the conditions are right for a social action problem to develop, then that problem surely will develop. Even thinking of our

©iStockphoto / CamiloTorros

The problem of the dirty dishes. If everyone took the time to wash their own dishes, everyone in the group would have access to the sink.

competitors as opponents can lead to social action problems. If we see every interaction with our competitors as a zero-sum game in which there can only be one winner, then we prevent ourselves from being able to secure co-operative benefits before we even get started.

This kind of thinking has slipped into social events as innocent and simple as children's Easter egg hunts. The children who participate typically must be in the care of a responsible adult, so the event organizers do not have to police the children's behaviour as closely as a parent would. But must the event organizers police the parents?

The answer turns out to be *yes*. At least one community Easter egg hunt was cancelled because parents, no longer content with helping their children locate eggs by standing at the edge of the playing field and pointing, raised the stakes by going and taking the eggs themselves.[10] One parent at the 2011 event in Colorado Springs, Colorado, told a reporter, "You better believe I'm going to help my kid get one of those eggs. I promised my kid an Easter egg hunt and I'd want to give him an even edge."[11] That hunt was cancelled the following year.

In 2012, organizers in Easthampton, Massachusetts, scattered 18,000 plastic eggs containing small toys or candy in the field. Part of the field was set aside for children of age four or younger, and those children could be accompanied by parents. But two toddlers were knocked down by older children while parents invaded the field where the older children were expected to hunt. There was no need for parents to ensure their children got something, because the organizers had extra eggs to make sure no child went away empty-handed. Afterward,

organizers posted a message saying parents were rude and used swear words when asked to get off the field and control their older children, little ones were knocked over and the bunny, who usually arrives in a fire truck, had to be brought in an ambulance instead.[12]

Easthampton held the hunt again the following year, but recruited more volunteers to restrain the parents.

Now consider what could happen if businesses acted in the same way. The first company to make an underhanded move to gain an unjust competitive advantage would inspire other companies to do the same in order to neutralize that advantage. The rules of fair play go out the window. Just as the parents who jumped in to collect eggs violated a tacit social norm, a corporation that violates market norms can cause a descent into chaos when other corporations join in. This behaviour will ultimately reduce investor value by eradicating consumer trust.

If we find ourselves affected by these sorts of attitudes, we need to take a step back and ask ourselves whether a shift in perspective might not prevent us from a situation where everyone ends up worse off. Are there ways of rethinking the relationship that make co-operation viable?

zero-sum game
A game in which any gain for Player *A* involves an exactly proportionate loss for Player *B*, and vice versa.

Refer to **Chapter 10** for a more detailed explanation and examples of zero-sum games.

CONCEPT CHECK

6.8 What is zero-sum thinking?

a. It is a strategic interaction in which everyone loses. Zero people win.

b. It is a strategic interaction in which the winner wins exactly as much as the loser loses.

c. It is a strategic interaction in which everyone wins. Zero people lose.

d. It is a strategic interaction in which some people win and others lose. Zero people tie.

CASE STUDY

Cheating: The Fallacy of Success at All Costs

In 2012, more than a hundred students at Harvard University were suspected of cheating on a take-home final exam. The exam instructions permitted students to use course resources and the internet, but they excluded getting help from other people.[13] The instructions overlooked the internet's facilitation of interactions with other people, and one way of reading the instructions would allow the reading of material shared by other students in online discussion boards and chat rooms. The students made the looser interpretation, but given that face-to-face collaboration with other students was explicitly forbidden, the looser interpretation presumed it was the means of collaboration that mattered, not with whom they collaborated.

Harvard was criticized for punishing the students who collaborated using the internet. After all, the chances of succeeding in a business venture increase when the parties work collaboratively.[14] However, the criticism overlooks the fact that this occurred in an academic setting, where individual abilities are assessed. While there is a strategic advantage to this kind of collaboration, unless this collaboration is managed well, it allows persons to claim individual credit for the collective performance. The collaborating students took the benefits of working together for a better collective outcome and each represented that as their individual work, undermining the instructors' ability to provide a fair and honest assessment of individual students. Collaborating gave these students an unfair advantage on the assessment over the students who worked individually, and the collaborators recognized this. Afterward, Harvard professor Howard Gardner wrote,

> [S]tudents told us that they admired good work and wanted to be good workers. But they also told us they wanted—ardently—to be successful. They feared that their peers were cutting corners and that if they themselves behaved ethically, they would be bested. And so, they told us in effect, "Let us cut corners now and one day, when we have achieved fame and fortune, we'll be good workers and set a good example."[15]

Some of the Harvard students were found guilty of plagiarism, which went beyond collaborating on the question to copying answers almost word-for-word. This kind of cheating takes someone else's work and claims it as your own.

In 2014, 17 per cent of Harvard's graduating class said the incentive to cheat outweighed the risk of being caught.[16] This underscores Gardner's point: for some, the measure of success is having the best score, and that means getting it by any means necessary. Unfortunately, these students felt that ethics can wait.

For Discussion

1. Explain how widespread cheating at your university would diminish the value of your degree.
2. What policies at your university deal with issues of academic integrity? Explain what the policies say about academic integrity.
3. According to the policies at your university that deal with academic integrity, what are the specific consequences of cheating?
4. Explain one problem arising from a success-at-all-costs attitude.
5. Would you be willing to report cheating to your professor if you found out that your peers were cheating? Explain why or why not. Bring your answer to question 1 above into your explanation.

"But They're Doing It!"

Imagine you are taking a course and you know that the exam has been leaked, and that other students in the class are using it to cheat. You may very well feel like you must cheat as well. If everyone is cheating, you think, then surely I can be excused for cheating. But there are ways of resisting this conclusion. Instead of cheating, you could report the leaked exam to the course instructor. That way, you avoid the degradation of your own education and of the value of your degree. If everyone cheats when the opportunity arises, and no one does anything about it, the eventual effect will be that your school earns a reputation for having very low educational standards. As a result, the public will not see a degree granted by your institution as being valuable or meaningful, since it no longer represents the achievements of the students who attain the degree; this is an outcome where everyone suffers. Enlightened self-interest alone (to say nothing about morals!) should lead us to resist the power of peer pressure to collaborate in producing outcomes that make things worse for everyone.

Cheating has its consequences, even if the cheater is not caught. Each time a person cheats, it becomes easier for that person to do it again and not be bothered by it. It can become a habit, and habits are hard to break. The problem with the success-first attitude is that the cheating required to be successful according to that narrow measure will not go away. If a person thinks they must cheat to stay level with their peers now because they believe their peers are cheating, they will continue cheating to stay level with their peers in the future simply because they believe that their peers are likely to continue cheating, and any cheating peers will be thinking along the same line. This points to a second problem: a person who sees that someone has successfully cheated without being caught may think that they have a justified reason for doing the same thing. This kind of thinking is not a useful line of defence should this person be caught. The need to cheat in this way arises because the ideas of success and failure are mistakenly used as personal attributes: "I have to be a success in order to not be a failure."

People succeed or fail in activities, but that does not make those people successes or failures themselves. When someone starts thinking of success or failure in personal terms, the need to be perceived as a success (particularly when it becomes a matter of personal pride or a competition with others) compels them to reach for a top standing by any means—including dishonest ones.

Turning to the world of business, what if you are doing business in a country where offering bribes to government officials is common practice for anyone to secure a contract? Should you offer the bribe, knowing that in doing so you are supporting a corrupt system? In such

BACKGROUND

The Cost of Being Ethical

Refusing to cheat is an action where doing the ethical thing has a cost, at least according to some measures. (Chapter 11 on whistle-blowing describes another costly action.) The desire to do the ethical thing has its own benefits, many of which cannot be measured but nonetheless have value. Yet there is at least one measurable outcome: cultivating the habit of not cheating means being less likely to have to pay a lawyer to get you out of trouble than someone who gets caught.

BACKGROUND

Canada's Efforts to Fight against Foreign Bribery

As you learned in Chapter 2, Canada has foreign anti-bribery legislation that makes it a serious offence for Canadians and/or Canadian companies to bribe foreign government officials. Canada has also been involved in examining reports in preparation for the implementation of the OECD Convention on Combating Bribery of Foreign Public Officials in International Business Transactions.[17]

See Heath's ten commandments for preserving a healthy market (and prohibiting practices that lead to market failure) in **Chapter 1**.

cases, we are tempted by the thought that, since everyone else is doing it, we need to do it too. If we do not, we are just cutting ourselves out of the competition. But that does not make bribery okay. As you read in Chapter 1, bribery is a clear violation of Heath's second commandment of business ethics: compete only through price and quality. Bribery is unfair because it disrupts market signals that are needed for an efficient distribution of resources.

Conducting business honestly requires stepping back from dishonest means and being satisfied with receiving less than what you might get by cheating. It also means understanding that your value as a person does not depend on whether your projects succeed or fail, or whether your goals are met. You can still claim success if you have done what you set out to do, even if doing things dishonestly could have earned you more money or prestige. Moreover, you can learn from a failed endeavour and carry that new knowledge into your next venture. Furthermore, the habits you develop as you bring projects to successful completion will help you bring future projects to a satisfying end.

Trust, Coordination, and the Benefits of Co-Operation

We probably cannot realize all the benefits of co-operation or build an ethical society on the basis of enlightened self-interest alone. As long as people are motivated purely by their own interests, they will take the opportunity to do unethical and even illegal things whenever they think they can get away with it. Unfortunately, a lot of times people can and do get away with unethical things, undermining the potential for co-operative gains by their pursuit of narrow self-interest. There is no guarantee that what is in a person's enlightened self-interest will always align with the right or ethical thing to do.

Nevertheless, enlightened self-interest can often bring us a long way in the direction of what is ethical. The recognition of **reputational capital** is a great example of this. A business might not value doing the right thing because it is the right thing to do, or because it values co-operation for its own sake, but it might see that being perceived as ethical by society has a direct impact on its financial bottom line. Seeing that it is in its self-interest to act according to ethical norms, the business might establish rules governing its operations that will ensure its behaviours are in line with the co-operative norms of society. After all, the most straightforward way of getting a reputation for being ethical is to consistently act ethically!

reputational capital The way the reputation of a business, organization, or an individual acts as a factor that increases profitability.

A firm might codify and enforce such rules in a code of ethics or a code of conduct designed to produce a co-operative ethos. Such behaviour is called self-regulation. Reputational capital is so valuable that most professions (physicians, accountants, engineers, etc.) and industries (Canadian diamond mining, broadcasting, etc.) invest large amounts of resources into self-regulation, precisely with the aim of ensuring the trust of the public toward their members. Beyond self-regulation, regulation by government agencies is a further mechanism used by society to ensure co-operative outcomes and counteract the tendency for people to defect from co-operative behaviours.

The purpose of regulation, whether by firms, industries, or governments, is to create an atmosphere of trust in which different parties can engage in co-operative behaviours without the worry of having the gains of their co-operation undermined by others who choose to defect and act solely in their own narrow self-interest. Trust is the foundation of co-operative interactions; when each party in an interaction trusts that the other will behave co-operatively, each can, in turn, act co-operatively with confidence.

code of ethics
A set of principles intended to guide the members of a profession or organization in carrying out their roles in accordance with ethical norms.

code of conduct
A set of rules specifying the behaviour expected of the members of a profession or other organization, in addition to disciplinary measures the organization may use in case of code violations.

self-regulation
The activities of a profession or an organization aimed at ensuring compliance of its members with legal and ethical standards.

CONCEPT CHECK

6.9 What best describes the value of reputational capital?

a. It is something that a business can use to repay a bank loan.

b. It is instrumental to monetizing human dignity and moral conscience.

c. It gives a company a free pass for its next public-facing ethical disaster.

d. It gives assurance that an organization will likely continue to do business in good faith, reducing the perceived risk to customers and investors.

Summing Up

It would be great if we could all just get along, but sadly we often do not. As a result, we often lose out collectively on gains we could have secured because we failed to see that it was in our enlightened self-interest to co-operate. Studying social action problems from a game-theory perspective can help us to appreciate the dynamics involved in various troublesome social situations, and to begin to reflect on ways to steer ourselves away from tragic outcomes toward co-operative solutions. This chapter has argued that it is always better to act in your enlightened self-interest rather than in your narrow self-interest. When we broaden our perspective to include the goals and interests of other people we are working with, we begin to see the possibilities of co-operative gains that are in everyone's interests, including our own.

Doing what is in our enlightened self-interest is the ethical bare minimum. Ethically speaking, it is much better than pursuing your narrow self-interest, and the outcome will often be similar to that which results from following properly ethical principles. But living by enlightened self-interest alone is kind of like doing the dishes but only washing the outside of the cups and bowls. In the process some of the insides might accidentally get cleaned out as well by the splashing soapy water. Since cleaning the inside of the dishes is generally much more important to us, dish-cleaning methods that focus only on the outsides are not reliable. Ethics involves the rights and interests of other people in a fundamental way; these things must be respected in their own right. Further, there is no guarantee that actions guided by a principle of enlightened self-interest will yield the same results as actions guided by ethical principles. If the interests and well-being of others factor into your decisions only when you perceive some benefit to yourself, then ethical results will be hit-or-miss, like happening to get the inside of the dish clean as you wash its exterior. If we change our preference structures to value other person's rights and well-being (at least those of persons we directly impact) as important to us in themselves, we will attain ethical or co-operative outcomes much more reliably.

For Discussion and Review

1. Describe what a social action problem is.
2. Describe the common features of the prisoner's dilemma and the free-rider problem. Explain how the prisoner's dilemma and the free-rider problem are examples of social action problems.
3. Explain how moral hazard is an example of a social action problem.
4. Explain why it is important to have fiduciary laws given that principal–agent problems exist.
5. Suppose you were sitting in the first lecture of a course when a classmate stood up and proclaimed, "It's OK if I cheat!" How would you respond? How do you think you should respond? Give reasons for your answers.
6. How might moral hazard be connected to the blind-spot bias? (See Chapter 3 for an examination of biases.)
7. What strategies might we adopt to promote an attitude of co-operation if the incentive is to defect? Explain why you think the strategies you suggest are plausible.
8. From mechanical doping in professional cycling to sign-stealing in professional baseball, unsporting behaviour ruins the game for players, fans, and spectators alike. Using concepts from this chapter, explain why it is important for everyone to follow the same rules in sport. (Alternatively, describe what a sport would look like if there were no rules. Would you play this sport? Perhaps think back to Hobbes's state of nature.) Now apply your answer to a business context. Explain why it is important that everyone agree—even if only implicitly—to a set of rules that everyone must follow. (To answer this question, we encourage you to research what mechanical doping is and what sign-stealing is. We also encourage you to read up on Calvinball.)

Further Reading

Binmore, Ken. *Game Theory: A Very Short Introduction*. Oxford University Press, 2008.

Canada. Canada Business Corporations Act. RSC, 1985, c. C-44. https://laws-lois.justice.gc.ca/eng/acts/c-44/fulltext.html. (Search the document for "fiduciary.").

Heath, Joseph. "Incentives Matter." In *Filthy Lucre: Economics for People Who Hate Capitalism.* HarperCollins, 2010. 44–64.

Heath, Joseph. "Personal Responsibility." In *Filthy Lucre: Economics for People Who Hate Capitalism.* HarperCollins, 2010. 117–46.

Hedlund, James. "Risky Business: Safety Regulations, Risk Compensation, and Individual Behavior. *Injury Prevention* 6, no. 2 (2000): 82–9. http://dx.doi.org/10.1136/ip.6.2.82.

CHAPTER 7
Environment, Ethics, and Business

By the end of this chapter you should be able to

- Distinguish between instrumental value and intrinsic value.

- Evaluate the various "green" and hybrid approaches to balancing business and good environmental practices.

- Assess the Coase theorem as a negotiation strategy for resource distribution.

It is hard to avoid news stories about the environment. From global climate change, water shortages, and unprecedented wildfires to species extinctions and deforestation, the news is filled with bleak outlooks and dire warnings. So how do we approach the important business questions pertaining to the environmental calamity that is befalling our planet? We must consider how we value the environment, some strategies we might employ to redress the environmental concerns facing us, and the potential role business plays in these solutions.

environment
The surroundings within which something exists. Typically this refers to the natural habitat, including land, water, atmosphere, and climate, but can also refer to political or economic circumstances, or a particular setting in which events and activities occur.

The Value of Nature

Why should we value the environment? This question is difficult to answer for two reasons. First, it is difficult to define what constitutes *the environment*. On the one hand, your home constitutes an environment. It has topographical features, physical properties such as temperature and humidity, and many creatures that live there and engage in various biological processes to sustain their lives. On the other hand, the planet Earth is also an environment; one with a much greater mass, complexity, and diversity. But these clearly are very different types of environments. One might have an *environmental concern* for the local level of noise pollution and songbird population, or one might have an environmental concern for global levels of carbon emission and the depletion of farmable soil through mismanagement and urban sprawl.

These different types of concerns, and many more in between, are all legitimate environmental issues. However, this makes it difficult to offer a tidy definition of what constitutes the *environment* or an *environmental concern*. That said, both types of concerns are legitimate and important. Environmental concerns can be for one's own backyard or for the continued feasibility of life on earth. We will adopt an inclusive conception of the environment for the purposes of this chapter.

Two Types of Value

Why should we value the environment? As we discussed, the word *environment* can apply to a wide variety of things, and we value those things for different reasons. For example, the reason Eszter values a good season for growing apples is very different from the reason she values grizzly bears. Eszter wants to eat apples, which is why she values a good apple-growing season. In contrast, Eszter values the bear as a living being despite the fact that the bear would have no

BACKGROUND

Environmental Concern

The phrase *environmental concern* has two distinct senses. One sense reflects an attitude of awareness with respect to the environment, or a particular aspect of it. For example, someone might be concerned about improving recycling capture rates as a part of making responsible use of natural resources. The second sense gets at the idea of something that may cause harm to the environment. For example, someone might be concerned about the release of arsenic from the process of refining gold.

problem eating her. With these very different notions of value, we must look for more general categories into which we can group and orient our thinking about the value of the environment.

Values can be grouped into two major categories: *instrumental value* and *intrinsic value*.

Instrumental Value

instrumental value
Something that is useful to achieve some goal. For example, money has instrumental value because it is useful for purchasing food.

Instrumental value applies to objects that we value insofar as they help us achieve some other goal or objective. An easy illustration to help understand this type of instrumental value is a tool such as a can opener. For example, Eszter does not value a can opener itself; rather, Eszter values the can opener because it lets her open cans and access the delicious food within. Eszter values the food, and because the can opener is (usually) necessary to open cans, the can opener has instrumental value.

It is common to think that nature has instrumental value. For example, over the last few decades, the Louisiana bayous (swampy wetlands found along the coastline and rivers) have gradually been filled in and developed so that they can be sold as real estate for commercial and residential use. But the Louisiana bayous are more than just a patch of wilderness. During hurricanes, these wetlands act as a buffer between the water and the land, absorbing much of the water that would otherwise be a menace to the buildings on the other side. An unforeseen consequence of depleting the bayous has been an increase in the damage caused by hurricanes. Therefore, local residents and governments have begun to preserve and rehabilitate the bayous. However, many of these people do not value a bayou in and of itself; rather, they value their homes and therefore value the protection that the bayou offers. This is an instrumental valuing of nature—but it is not the only way to value nature.

CONCEPT CHECK

7.1 What does it mean to say that something has instrumental value?

a. It means that the thing helps us achieve some other thing.

b. It means that the thing has sentimental value.

c. It means that the thing can be used as an instrument in a jazz band.

d. It means that the thing has value in and of itself.

Intrinsic Value

intrinsic value
Something that is valued for its own sake, not because it is useful for some other reason beyond itself.

Intrinsic value, on the other hand, applies to objects that we value for their own sake. These are the valued things that we use instruments to acquire. For example, food and shelter have the intrinsic values for which the can opener and the bayou are used. The things that we find intrinsically valuable are largely context-dependent and individualized. Keeping with our two examples, if Eszter is a vegetarian and the food in the can is meat, then the food will not be intrinsically valuable to her. Or if she is a real-estate speculator who cares only about her properties on the Louisiana coast because they will make her money, the bayou becomes instrumental to her goal of making money. In this case she does not believe that the bayou has intrinsic value.

Many things that seemingly have intrinsic value are at risk of being subjugated to the goal of making money. But what is the value of money? Money itself is only valuable because it gives us access to other things. Its value is purely instrumental. So what has intrinsic value? As mentioned before, what we consider to have intrinsic value tends to be highly context dependent and largely up to the individuals involved. But there are a few frequently recurring things to which persons ascribe intrinsic value, such as happiness, health, beauty, dignity, and life. One of the things that distinguishes intrinsic value from instrumental value is that there is no need to ask the further question of why this is valuable or good. We like beautiful things because they are beautiful. We like being healthy because we like being healthy. That is what makes these goods intrinsically valuable: we value them for their own sake.

Is the environment intrinsically valuable? Perhaps. The answer to this question will ultimately be up to the individual to decide, but hopefully with the vocabulary of instrumental and intrinsic value you will be able to sort out more clearly some of the environmental issues that you will encounter in your lifetime.

CONCEPT CHECK

7.2 What does it mean to say that something has intrinsic value?

a. It means that the thing helps us achieve some other thing.

b. It means that the thing is valuable in and of itself.

c. It means that the thing has monetary value.

d. It means that the thing has cosmic energy.

Whence Catastrophe?

How did we arrive in a situation where the environment is under such an intense existential threat? It is difficult to believe that people intentionally set out to damage the environment and threaten the possibility of life on this planet. Yet that appears to be the inescapable result of our collective actions.

The general structure of this environmental problem may sound familiar from the previous chapter. In social action problems, the collective result of everyone acting out of narrow self-interest gives rise to negative consequences. A special type of social action problem that occurs frequently in environmental contexts is the **tragedy of the commons**. The word *commons* here refers to some resource that is shared by a group of people. The *tragedy* refers to the unintended results of that shared use. We will explore what this means with a couple of examples.

tragedy of the commons
A situation in which a commonly owned or accessible resource is depleted or ruined because of overuse by individuals acting in their self-interest without regard for the sustainability of the resource.

CONCEPT CHECK

7.3 What is a commons?

a. A resource that is privately owned.

b. A resource that is shared by a group of people.

Continued

c. A resource that is infinite and rivalrous.

d. A resource that is finite and discrete.

Shared Study Space

Consider your favorite study space on campus. Ultimately someone (the school) does own that space and it will likely be cleaned at night, but during the day it functions like a commons. Everyone has access to it and no one has an explicit responsibility to care for it. What are the possible outcomes?

On a good day, everyone will use the space respectfully, being mindful of others and cleaning up after themselves. But what if a large group comes in and decides to take up all the available seats, putting their backpacks, skateboards, and the like on them? There is nothing to stop them from doing so—the space is open for anyone to use—but behaving in this way makes the space less usable for others. The same general dynamic can occur with noise or garbage. There is no rule against talking in the common space, but if one group takes advantage of this and starts to speak loudly, the people at the next table over might have to speak more loudly to carry on their own conversation. Then the people at the table next to that one will have to speak more loudly still, and so on and so forth. Soon it is a raucous environment that is no longer well-suited for studying. Finally, it is not a big deal if you absentmindedly drop a gum wrapper or do not quite get all your crumbs when you wipe off your desk, but if people start wantonly throwing garbage on the ground and food and drinks get spilled everywhere, the space quickly becomes unusable.

This example is slightly dramatized in that we recognize the litterer and the obnoxiously loud neighbour as the bad actors in this situation. But a more charitable interpretation is possible. The loud talker might just need a place to have a conversation and not notice how that contributes to a general escalation. Litterers might be in a rush or lack the materials to clean up after themselves. Frequently, people are unaware that their minor misdeed contributes to a larger problem. This is the mechanism that lies at the heart of the tragedy of the commons: individuals pursuing their own interests inadvertently reduce the usefulness of a shared resource.

CONCEPT CHECK

7.4 What is an example of the tragedy of the commons?

a. A group of people having to work together to achieve a common goal.

b. People enjoying the warm breeze of an early spring evening.

c. People picking up after their dogs in the park.

d. People littering in a public park.

Agriculture in Kansas

The tragedy of the commons can occur in broader geopolitical contexts. Consider the example of western Kansas. Western Kansas is one of the most bountiful agricultural regions in the entire USA, producing a greater amount of market value from agriculture than any other region in the nation.[1] There are two significant problems, however, that threaten agricultural production in western Kansas. The first is tied to the way water is managed in current farming practices. The reason the region can produce so much corn is that many fields are irrigated. The problem is that the rate of water consumption for agricultural purposes has significantly reduced the amount of water in the Ogalalla Aquifer. If the rate of water consumption stays the same as it is now, peak corn production will happen around 2025, after which yearly yields of corn will start to decline because of the depletion of the aquifer. However, if the anticipated efficiency gains in the way water is used for irrigation are achieved, peak corn production can be pushed back to 2040. Further, if farmers cut back on water consumption by converting some of their fields to dryland farming, **peak production** can be pushed back even further to 2070.[2] This leads to the second problem: dryland farming produces significantly lower crop yields than irrigated farming does. An irrigated crop can yield upwards of 12 tonnes of corn per hectare, whereas dryland farming yields around 4 tonnes of corn per hectare.[3]

The farmers understand that their source of water is effectively a commons: no one person owns it, and so no one person is responsible for conserving it. However, those farmers who start to reduce water consumption by moving more production to dryland farming will be at a competitive disadvantage to those farmers who continue to irrigate their fields. Let us see what this looks like in dollars and cents, taking the price of corn to be US$128.34 per tonne.[4] This means that a farmer can expect to earn roughly US$1540 per hectare of corn on irrigated land. The value of producing corn on a hectare of dry land is roughly US$513. It is reasonable to say that it would take great effort to persuade a farmer to willingly reduce their farm revenue by roughly two-thirds, particularly if they are the only farmer who decides to reduce the amount of land they irrigate. The disincentive to do the environmentally responsible thing can be represented in Game Table 7.1.

To reiterate, a farmer with an irrigated section of land can expect to make roughly US$400,000 from that land. In contrast, a farmer who grows corn on dryland can expect to make roughly US$133,000 from each section. (Put yourself in the shoes of a farmer in this

peak production
The maximum yield or production of a resource, after which point the yield will decline.

Game Table 7.1 is similar to the prisoner's dilemma, which is modelled and discussed in **Chapter 6**.

BACKGROUND

Agricultural Terms

North America's Great Plains were originally surveyed using miles and acres as measurements. There are 640 acres in a section of farmland. A section is one mile by one mile. The revenue from an irrigated section of land using January 2020 prices would be in the range of US$400,000. The revenue from a section of dryland would be in the range of US$133,000.

Wichita Eagle/Contributor/Getty Images

Irrigation systems like this provide water for the corn crops in Kansas.

See **Appendix B** for more explanation of **Game Table 7.1** (The Farmer's Tragedy).

position: would you willingly reduce your revenue by $267,000 a section?) This significant loss of revenue will have a severe domino effect on things like hired help, capital investments (like equipment upgrades), household purchases, and where farmers can send their children to school. The trickle-down effect on the regional economy would be significant if every farmer followed suit. (Of course, since the supply of corn would decrease, demand would drive up the price of corn. We will leave those calculations to the student of economics.)

Game Table 7.1 represents the tragedy of the commons that will happen if the farmers play their dominant strategy, which is to continue irrigating. Each farmer has a huge

		Farmer 1			
		Convert to Dryland (co-operate)		**Continue Irrigating** (defect)	
Farmer 2	**Convert to Dryland** (co-operate)	$133,000 per square mile	$133,000 per square mile	$133,000 per square mile	$400,000 per square mile
	Continue Irrigating (defect)	$400,000 per square mile	$133,000 per square mile	$400,000 per square mile	$400,000 per square mile

Game Table 7.1 The Farmer's Tragedy

(short-term) financial incentive to keep irrigating their fields despite the fact that this strategy is not environmentally sustainable. Everyone loses in the long run if they play their dominant strategy.

A close comparison should convince us that the prisoner's dilemma (that we discussed and modelled in Chapter 6) and the tragedy of the commons described here have the same logical structure: both players have a strong incentive to defect despite the fact that co-operating with each other would be the socially optimal thing to do. (Again, if the farmers in the region collectively agree to cut back on the rate of water consumption by converting fields to dryland, peak production can be pushed back from the year 2025 to 2070.)

Is there a way out of this tragedy for the farmers? A group of farmers in northwestern Kansas have voluntarily agreed to reduce their water usage, which is a great example of stakeholders taking an environmental concern seriously. However, a voluntary agreement is vulnerable to defectors if there is no credible enforcement mechanism to punish any farmer who decides to renege on their promise. A threat of reprisals for non-compliance is a **strategic move** meant to preserve solidarity, and any agreement to conserve water would be fragile without one.

> The use of an enforcement mechanism is an example of strategic co-operation, which is described in **Chapter 10**.

> **strategic move**
> An attempt to convince others to adopt a co-operative attitude and to thwart those who would be tempted to defect from a co-operative strategy.

CONCEPT CHECK

7.5 Concerning the farmers in Kansas cutting back on their water use, what is one potential problem with the farmers voluntarily conserving water?

a. Co-operation leads to an increased expectancy of reciprocity.

b. Voluntaristic co-operation of this sort treats water as a non-fungible resource.

c. Without a mechanism to punish defectors, there will always be an incentive to defect.

d. Without a mechanism to encourage defection, the farmers will just continue to co-operate with each other.

Reframing the Environmental Conversation

In 2008, the Business Roundtable Institute for Corporate Ethics, an independent association of CEOs of leading companies in the USA, alongside 16 expert faculty from the nation's top business schools, published a "Bridge Paper" focused on some of the major challenges facing business and the environment. The paper argues that a shift in framing values to emphasize the importance of innovation in responding to environmental problems will relieve some of the gridlock between **environmental protections** and profit seeking.[5] The paper identifies four basic strategies that emphasize the role of innovation in determining environmental strategies while also recognizing the importance of increasing profit and maintaining a competitive edge: 1) light green, 2) market green, 3) stakeholder green, and 4) dark green. We will discuss each approach in turn.

> **environmental protections**
> Initiatives put in place to protect and benefit the natural environment.

Light Green Approach

light green approach
An environmental strategy that relies on public policy to guide environmental initiatives undertaken by the company.

The light green approach resembles a regulatory mindset to the extent that businesses using this approach rely on public policy to guide environmental initiatives.[6] This does not mean, however, that companies relying solely on the letter of the law cannot also help push environmental regulations forward. Some companies can comply easily with comparatively strict regulations, and so may pressure governments, provinces, or municipalities to increase regulations in ways that make it hard for competitors to adhere to.[7] The benefits of having an environmentally progressive reputation and of being an environmental leader in their industry create opportunities for value creation. This approach works well for companies that give priority to investor interests.

CONCEPT CHECK

7.6 What best describes the light green approach to business and the environment?

a. Businesses—at a minimum—comply with government regulations.

b. Businesses try to externalize the cost of pollution.

c. Businesses lobby for exemptions from environmental regulations.

d. Businesses encourage their employees to compost food waste at their desks.

Market Green Approach

market green approach
An environmental strategy focused on responding to environmental concerns and preferences of the company's consumer base.

In the market green approach, the production and marketing strategies of a business are motivated by the environmental concerns of their current and potential consumer base.[8] This approach will lead to a variety of environmental protection approaches, especially since not all customers are environmentally conscious to the same degree. The environmental protection afforded by this approach, then, fluctuates with market expectations and with social awareness. This approach works well for businesses that place a lot of value on direct accountability to their consumer base.

CONCEPT CHECK

7.7 What is one outcome of a market green approach to business and the environment?

a. How a business approaches environmental protection will depend on the environmental awareness of its consumer base.

b. Businesses will only be environmentally conscious if their shareholders demand change.

c. Businesses will use informational asymmetries to trick consumers into buying their products.

d. Businesses will start trading carbon credits on the dark web.

Stakeholder Green Approach

Similar to the market green approach, companies using the stakeholder green approach will guide their environmental policies according to "external" expectations, though in this case the policies attend to and represent not just consumers, but also stakeholders more generally. This strategy can include suppliers, employees, investors, the public, and the like.[9] The stakeholder green approach is more demanding than the previous approach. The values that a business embraces will need to be negotiated and brought into alignment with many different stakeholder groups that potentially have very different values and interests.

stakeholder green approach
An environmental strategy that reflects the concerns not only of consumers but of stakeholders more generally.

CONCEPT CHECK

7.8 What best describes the stakeholder green approach to business and the environment?

a. Businesses try to externalize the cost of pollution.

b. Businesses lobby for exemptions from environmental regulations.

c. Businesses encourage their employees to compost food waste at their desks.

d. Businesses will create environmental policies according to stakeholder expectations.

Dark Green Approach

This is the "deepest" approach to environmental protection identified by the Business Roundtable Institute for Corporate Ethics report. Companies adopting a dark green approach allow environmental concerns to dictate policy, rather than primarily responding to the interests of consumers or stakeholders, or following existing regulations. In this approach, a business gives priority to environmental concerns and puts environmental principles front and centre in its way of doing business.[10]

dark green approach
An environmental strategy that allows environmental issues identified by experts to dictate company policy.

CONCEPT CHECK

7.9 What is the difference between a market green approach and a dark green approach to business and the environment?

a. A market green approach involves attention to what customers want, whereas a dark green approach allows environmental concerns to dictate company policy.

b. A market green approach involves a carbon tax, whereas a dark green approach allows policies to be dictated by shareholders.

c. A market green approach involves selling shares to environmentalists, whereas a dark green approach requires the divestment of fossil fuels.

d. A market green approach involves green energy solutions, whereas a dark green approach involves ignoring government regulations.

CASE STUDY

A Market Green Example: Tesla Electric Vehicles

In March 2016, Elon Musk revealed the fully electric Tesla Model 3 automobile. At the time, the Model 3 was priced more affordably than previous models. Tesla provides an interesting example for analysis of barriers to making environmentally responsible choices. These barriers include price, lifestyle choice, hidden environmental costs, and information asymmetries. We will discuss these in turn.

Price

Electric vehicles are often more expensive than comparable combustion-engine vehicles. Although the federal and some provincial governments, such as British Columbia and Quebec, have subsidized the cost of electric vehicles,[11] these subsidies (usually in the form of rebates) are not guaranteed to last beyond the government administration that put the subsidies into effect. For example, in Ontario, the Ford government ended the provincial Electric and Hydrogen Vehicle Incentive Program when it came to power in June 2018.[12] Further to this, subsidy programs can be victims of their own success. For example, Canada's planned three-year-long federal rebate program introduced in May 2019 paid out $134 million of its $300 million budget in only eight months and will likely be depleted by the end of 2020.[13] (In January 2020, the federal transport minister, Marc Garneau, said he was considering expanding the rebate program.)[14] Clearly, rebates are effective incentives for consumers to purchase greener alternatives, at least with respect to vehicles. Until the market price for electric vehicles drops substantially, however, the high financial cost for the consumer will remain a major consideration for consumers.

Lifestyle Choices

Product narratives play a huge role in how people attach to products. Potential buyers are often drawn to higher-end cars for the social status they signal. For some buyers, electric vehicles appear less powerful and less attractive than the deep-growling gas-guzzlers they compete with. If a consumer is in the market to spend $50,000 on a vehicle, they may be looking for something they have "always wanted"—a luxury car from the conventional brands. This barrier can be removed with education around the speed and power of electric cars. But one serious barrier to environmental protection for many countries in the world is the line between need and want. Luxury has become an addiction for many, so the resulting social pressure to show status through material wealth fuels excessive consumerism and, in turn, environmental damage.

   Another worry is the consumer concern that an electric vehicle will run out of charge, leaving the consumer on the side of the road with no source of power to charge the battery. This is quickly becoming less and less a concern as charging ports are being installed at major fuelling stations, malls, and other institutions, and reducing the time to charge fully is a central focus of electric vehicle technology development.[15] Tesla is working on creating a network of non-profit charging stations that can recharge the battery in the time it takes to pump a full tank of gasoline.[16]

Hidden Environmental Costs

There are worries about the energy source of electricity because, in many locales, fossil fuels are burned to produce the electricity used to power the cars. Consumers are also often unsure about the environmental costs incurred before and after they own the vehicle: for example, how is the environment affected during Tesla Model 3 production? We will look at the environmental cost of electricity production, and battery production and disposal.

Fully electric vehicles do not burn gasoline. Instead, they rely on electricity, which (depending on the particular electricity market) is predominantly produced by burning coal or natural gas. When power grids are supplied by hydroelectric dams, solar collectors, and wind turbines, charging a Tesla's battery is a deeper shade of green than charging it in a coal-based power grid.

The second hidden environmental cost of buying a Tesla is the environmental damage incurred by the mining required to access the rare metals used in Tesla production—lithium, for example, is necessary for the batteries. As Lizzie Wade reported in *Wired* magazine's article on the environmental impact of the Tesla Model 3, although the batteries can be reused for energy storage when they are no longer viable for powering the car, the relatively small number of Tesla vehicles on the road make the batteries unattractive and unlikely candidates for recycling.[17]

Moreover, the environmental impact of mining the raw material for Tesla's batteries is substantial. The rare metals required to build batteries form just 0.2 per cent of the material pulled out of the mines. The other 99.8 per cent of the material—having been contaminated in the extraction process—is left as tailings.[18] Furthermore, mining is done by large machines that depend on fossil fuels.

Given the pollution created by the production and maintenance of a Tesla vehicle, do conventional energy-efficient fossil-fuel cars make more sense? No, because once all the environmental impacts have been counted, at the end of each car's life, the Tesla Model 3 still generates only half of the emissions of an average energy-efficient gas-dependent car.[19] In the end, Tesla is a deeper green than a conventional fuel-efficient car, but the choice to buy and use a Tesla still needs to be weighed against consumer and environmental concerns described above.

While at first glance the environmental costs of some eco-friendly conventional cars seem to compare favourably against the environmental costs of a Tesla Model 3, this is actually not the case. A deeper green approach requires accounting for environmental impacts from product inception to disposal.

Information Asymmetries

An *information asymmetry* is a situation where one party has information that another party does not have. The person with more information has an advantage over the less-informed party in any kind of debate, negotiation, or transaction. (We address informational asymmetries further in Chapter 8.)

Ultimately, discovering how green a company or product is depends on knowing where it stands in relation to other competitive companies or products. Public education about electric vehicles and other eco-friendly products is a live issue, as lack of knowledge about comparison between gasoline-powered and electric vehicles can produce consumer anxiety about the introduction of new, environmentally friendly products. For example, just knowing that the battery production for the Tesla Model 3 is harmful to the environment may be enough to dissuade consumers from purchasing the vehicle, and can even prevent them from looking into the full extent of the environmental comparisons between an electric vehicle and their conventional vehicle.

It is sometimes hard to identify exactly what the barrier to more responsible production and consumption is. Take, for example, consumer attitudes toward newly available eco-products like the

Continued

Tesla Model 3. Is the barrier a lack of publicly supported education about the comparative environmental effects of products? Is the barrier poor consumer practices around consumption such that people do not feel the need to know what kinds of impacts the products they own have, and continue to have, on the environment? Or is the barrier perhaps advertising regulations, or interest groups that keep public education superficial or inaccessible in attempts to maintain the public image of conventional products that drive large sectors of industry? Perhaps it is a combination of these things and more, and so resolving informational barriers should take a multi-dimensional approach where each "link" in the chain of production and consumption—be it business, government, interest groups, consumers, advertisers, investors—has increased responsibility for the informational deficit.

For Discussion

1. What information have you heard with respect to electric vehicles compared to conventional ones? How can information asymmetries between company and consumer affect the environment?

2. One reason for the higher price of electric vehicles compared to conventional ones is the cost of new technology developed specifically for the product. While the cost of raw material used in that technology may not ever go down, the cost of manufacturing the technology likely will as processes become more efficient and as supply increases to match demand more closely. How likely is it that lower prices for electric vehicles alone will cause a market disruption? Explain your thinking.

3. While energy markets do not have much of an impact on the retail price of an electric vehicle compared to a conventional one, they do affect the operating costs of the vehicles. What effect could the declining cost of green electricity generation have on the market for electric vehicles? What about incorporating the cost of managing CO_2 emissions in the price of gasoline or diesel fuel? Explain how shifts in the energy market can contribute to a disruption in the automotive market.

4. The cost of building and maintaining roads is usually paid from public funds raised through taxation, including an excise tax on gasoline and diesel fuel. (This tax is separate from any carbon taxes or offsets.) Electric vehicle owners do not pay this particular tax because they do not buy those fuels. Is their use of public roads a kind of free-riding on the backs of conventional vehicle owners? Explain.

5. What are some of the other costs to the public of private car ownership? Does replacing a conventional vehicle with an electric one help to reduce these kinds of shared social costs? Why or why not?

Hybrid Strategies

hybrid approach
An environmental strategy that draws on particular aspects of the light green, market green, stakeholder green, and deep green approaches.

It is important to remember that there are more ways to approach environmental protection than those described here, and that **hybrid approaches** are possible. In that spirit, we are able to think of this framework as offering different styles of environmental consideration, or as a plan for environmental progress if companies choose to change or deepen their green initiatives. There is no expectation that a business will commit to using only one approach. Further, there are different benefits associated with the various approaches that may be more or less appropriate for different companies, perhaps depending on their industry or size.

Bargaining and the Coase Theorem

Disagreements about resource distribution bear significantly on our ability to protect the environment. Ownership and access to a resource sometimes have to be negotiated in ways that represent the interests of stakeholders and environmental protection. So how should ownership of natural resources be distributed? This is one of the questions that Ronald Coase set out to address in his 1960 paper "The Problem of Social Cost."[20] According to Coase, it does not matter to whom we give the ownership rights of a resource. As long as we give the rights to an agent (a person, a company, or a regulatory body), and then allow the agent to negotiate with others who want access to the resource, the interested parties will always find the most efficient distribution of that resource. This is known as the Coase theorem. The theorem assumes that there are no transaction costs and that negotiations are done within a perfectly competitive market.

The Coase theorem is used in environmental economics to demonstrate how a negative externality like pollution can be internalized through market mechanisms. In many cases the cost of pollution is "free" to the polluter but costly to those who are affected by the pollution (like unbreathable air, toxic lakes and rivers, contaminated drinking water, etc.). The Coase theorem demonstrates how a perfectly competitive market can put an economic price on pollution.

The Features of the Coase Theorem

There are two ideas at the centre of the Coase theorem: *rivalrousness* and *distribution*.

Rivalrousness

There are resources in the world that people want to use. Sometimes multiple people want to use the same resource and that resource cannot be shared without diminishing its value. In economic theory, these goods are described as rivalrous goods; that is, one person's use of a good diminishes its value to other people. How should ownership of rivalrous resources be distributed? An easy theoretical answer to this question is that they should be distributed in a way that will maximize utility. But it can be difficult to discern exactly what is meant by this answer and how to bring it about. Let us look at an example.

Imagine two radio stations that both want to broadcast at the same frequency. If they both broadcast at the same time, their signals will interfere with one another and they will both fail to get their programming out to the audience. The airwaves are a rivalrous commodity. Now we can ask, *How much does each station value its ability to broadcast on this frequency?* If Station *A* values the airwaves at $100 and Station *B* values them at $50, there is an efficient solution to be worked out. Station *A* can pay Station *B* $50 not to broadcast and have the airwaves all to itself. Station *B* will get the same level of utility by taking the payment that it would have gotten from broadcasting on that frequency, since it valued both outcomes at $50. Station *A* gets slightly less utility than it would like; instead of the $100 at which it values broadcasting, it receives only $50 worth of value (that is, the original $100 minus the $50 it had to pay to Station *B*). This arrangement maximizes utility ($50 for Station *A* + $50 for Station *B* = $100 total utility).

It might feel a little bit strange to talk about valuing things in this way. How much are radio airwaves worth? Why does one station value them so much more than the other? How

Coase theorem
In the absence of transaction costs, the participants in a perfectly competitive market will find the most efficient distribution of a resource, regardless of who is given ownership of the resource.

transaction costs
Costs incurred during an economic transaction like transferring ownership rights between agents (a person, a company, or a regulatory body). These costs derive from gathering information, establishing who the negotiating parties are, negotiating contracts, and enforcing contracts.

negative externality
An uncompensated cost that is imposed on a person by the actions of one or more other people. For example, if your neighbour hosts a wild backyard party with live music and fireworks, you will suffer the cost of air, noise, and light pollution, among other vexatious things.

rivalrous
A resource is rivalrous if one party's use or consumption of it means that another party or parties cannot consume or use it.

do you come up with a precise dollar amount for something like that? These are all difficult questions, but their answer is more intuitive than one might expect. The values are subjectively determined. That is to say, an individual in a particular situation makes a judgment about what something is worth. This judgment becomes the thing's value. This may seem like a fickle and unreliable source of value, but it is the only system available to us.

Distribution

ownership rights
The right of ownership to something. According to the Coase theorem, it does not matter to whom the ownership rights of a resource are given. Give the ownership rights to one party, and allow them to negotiate with the other interested parties, and all parties involved will come to an efficient distribution of the resource.

The second feature of the Coase theorem regards the initial distribution of **ownership rights**. According to the theorem, it does not matter who has rights to the resource in question. If we assign ownership rights to either party and then allow the parties to freely trade, they will always reach the most efficient outcome.

Let us go back to the example of the competing radio stations. Remember that the most efficient distribution was for Station *A* to be the one broadcasting. In our original scenario, both stations had equal rights to the airwaves, but according to the Coase theorem we could change those starting conditions and we would arrive at the same outcome. In this simple example there are only two ways we could assign the original ownership rights: either Station *A* owns the airwaves at that frequency or Station *B* does. If Station *A* owns them, there is no need to work out a deal with Station *B* simply because Station *A* controls them. Station *A* simply proceeds to accrue the full $100 worth of value from its broadcast. The total utility is still maximized and is the same as it was before. If Station *B* owns the airwaves, the sequence of events is the same as described above: Station *A* buys the rights to the airwaves from Station *B* and total utility remains unchanged.

This is a simplified example with only two parties and clearly divergent valuations, but the same principle should hold as we add more parties and more commensurate valuations. Say there are six radio stations, each of which values the airwaves in similar ways. The utility calculation might be more difficult to do, but the important theoretical point that Coase assures us of is that there is a most efficient outcome and that if we remove barriers to trade, the airwaves will end up in the most efficient distribution possible regardless of the starting position.

CONCEPT CHECK

7.10 What is a defining feature of the Coase theorem?

a. Negative externalities. Carbon taxes are the only way to overcome negative externalities.

b. Ownership rights. It doesn't matter to whom you give ownership rights over a resource. If you allow people to trade, they will find the socially efficient use of that resource.

c. Strategic irrationality. Markets cannot function efficiently without people behaving irrationally.

d. Negative property externalities. If you give a resource to one person, they will not trade with others.

Internalizing Externalities: An Application of the Coase Theorem

We mentioned that the Coase theorem is used in environmental economics to demonstrate how a negative externality like pollution can be internalized through market mechanisms. We will unpack what this means with the following thought experiment illustrated in Figure 7.1.

Let us say that a creek fed by an artesian well flows through property owned by Greg. Jim lives downstream from Greg and uses the creek as a source of drinking water. Let us also say that Greg quite enjoys tire fires. He loves the colour of the flames and the thick black acrid smoke that billows into the sky, so Greg puts an ad in the classifieds inviting people to drop off their old tires. Greg sees himself as providing a necessary and very beneficial service to the larger community by redirecting tires that would have otherwise been sent to the local landfill. Assured of a constant source of tires, Greg starts a beautiful and magnificent tire fire. Unfortunately, not everyone values the tire fire in the way that Greg does. For example, Jim is rather angry about the fire. The runoff oil from the fire seeps into the creek and makes the water toxic and unusable to Jim, to say nothing of the unbreathable air.

Greg's other neighbour Chris is a very industrious innovator. Chris had been thinking about building a solar heat exchanger for some time, but was not convinced that there were enough sunny days to make it worth his while. Seeing that the tire fire will be a constant

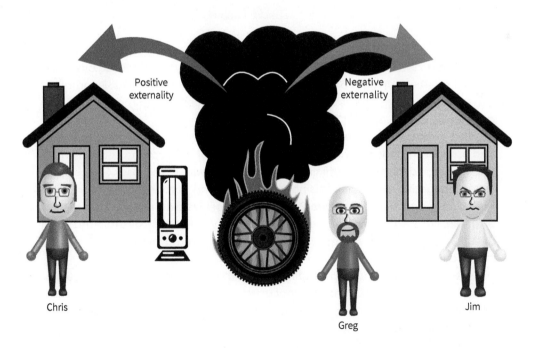

Positive externality

Negative externality

Chris

Greg

Jim

FIGURE 7.1 Tire fire.

Source: ©iStockphoto/Irina Devaeva (tire); ©iStockphoto/ONYXprj (black smoke); ©iStockphoto/bortonia (houses); Canstockphoto/ylivdesign (heat exchanger); ©iStockphoto/SENRYU (arrows)

source of heat, Chris quickly builds the thermal collector and aims it at the tire fire. Chris is very pleased with this arrangement as he now has a perpetual source of heat that he can use to heat the water for his house. Chris lives upstream and upwind from Greg, and so he is unbothered by the fire and only sees the upside.

The water in the creek is a rivalrous resource: whatever Greg pollutes becomes unusable by Jim. Since no one owns the creek, it does not cost Greg anything to pollute it. Further, Greg suffers no harm and receives only enjoyment from the fire. It is crucial to note that there is a cost to Greg's fire, but Greg does not pay it. Jim does. Jim is clearly being harmed by Greg's tire fire. The smoke wafting over Jim's property is toxic and the drinking water from the creek is now carcinogenic. As a result, the property value of Jim's land has gone down. We can think of the harm being done to Jim as a part of the **marginal social cost** of the tire fire.

Pollution is a negative externality, and we cannot expect markets to work efficiently in the presence of externalities. The reason is that if pollution is free, then by definition the social costs associated with the pollution are not accounted for through market mechanisms. This is where the Coase theorem becomes relevant—at least in theory.

To see how the theorem applies, we think about what would happen if we gave ownership rights of the creek to Jim. In this case, Greg would have to pay Jim if he (Greg) wanted

marginal social cost
Marginal social cost is greater than the direct cost of producing a unit of something. Marginal social cost takes both negative and positive externalities into account.

BACKGROUND

Externalities

An *externality* is a kind of side effect that affects one party but is caused by the actions of another party. An action can produce multiple externalities. Externalities either harm parties that are not involved in that action, which make them *negative externalities*, or benefit parties that are not involved, which make them *positive externalities*. For example, climate change, while devastating forestries and fisheries in Canada, may increase the length of the growing season on the Prairies—provided there is sufficient moisture to go with it. The loss of forests and fish is a negative externality arising from consuming carbon-based fuels, while the boon to agriculture, if realized, would be a positive externality. In the tire-fire example, Jim is experiencing a negative externality from the tire fire (air and water pollution), whereas Chris is experiencing a positive externality (heat for the water in his house).

Externalities are uncompensated; that is, the party harmed by the action is not given anything in exchange for that unwanted harm, and the party benefiting from the action is not paying anything to receive the gain. Negotiating payment for the harm caused is one way of accounting for the cost imposed on a party. This is one way of *internalizing* an externality.

to continue enjoying his tire fire. Intuitively this seems right and fair. If Greg wants to pollute, he should compensate the people he harms by his tire fire. However, we could just as easily give ownership rights to Greg. In this case, Jim would have to pay Greg to stop polluting the air and the creek with his tire fire. This likely does not feel right or fair, but remember that the Coase theorem states that it does not matter who has the ownership rights. As long as Jim and Greg are allowed to negotiate with one another—without paying transaction costs—they will eventually reach the efficient and socially optimal level of tire-fire pollution.

The Limits of the Coase Theorem

It is crucially important to understand what the Coase theorem can and cannot do. We ended the last section with a comment about Jim and Greg finding an efficient and socially optimal level of tire-fire pollution. There is no dispute that the tire-fire example is absurd, but there is a point to it. If we are going to use the Coase theorem as a model to distribute access to natural resources, we must be absolutely clear on what the limits of the theorem are and what it commits us to. An absurd example can help us make these limits and commitments explicit.

First, the Coase theorem cannot solve an environmental problem like pollution. Even if we could agree on what a "solution" to pollution looks like, the theorem can only tell us what the socially optimal market price of pollution is. Going back to our example, if Greg and Jim are willing to put a high price tag on pollution, and if Greg is able to pay that price, he will keep throwing tires on his tire fire. The Coase theorem does not tell us that tire-fire pollution is bad; it only tells us how to internalize externalities like pollution through the use of market mechanisms.

Second, free negotiations in a perfectly competitive market are a central part of the Coase theorem. The theorem, however, does not tell us who gets to be at the negotiating table. From our tire-fire example, it is clear that Jim and Greg are the primary stakeholders. Their interests are both genuine and proximal. It is not clear, however, whether Chris has a right to be part of the negotiations. Our earlier account of marginal social costs was incomplete. Marginal social costs include both negative and positive externalities. Chris is benefiting from Greg's tire fire (a positive externality) and will suffer a tangible loss if Greg extinguishes his tire fire. The elimination of the positive externality will result in a loss for Chris in that he no longer has a source of free heat. Does this mean that Greg should also compensate Chris, or that Chris should have been paying Greg for his "free" heat? An answer to this question takes us beyond the scope of this chapter, but the point to take away is that it is not always easy to determine who the relevant stakeholders are.

See **Chapter 3** for an explanation of genuine and proximal shareholder interests.

Third, the real world is messy and complicated. Theoretical modelling can only ever capture aspects of reality and never the complicated whole. The Coase theorem is an ideal theory that allows us to work out ideal solutions on paper. However, when one tries to apply ideal solutions to the real world, sticky problems quickly arise. Simplistic economic models such as the Coase theorem often fail to account for basic realities like differentials in negotiation power, access to political influence, the role of past laws, treaties, and many other things that rightly shift the ethical focus of negotiations to represent the real stake that people and groups have in resource management.

Climate Justice: Environmental Harm and Marginalized Peoples

Business and consumer responses to environmental issues must extend beyond reducing the amount of plastic that we use or the amount of carbon dioxide that we pump into the

CASE STUDY

Pipelines, Dams, and Indigenous Territory

In November 2016, Native American environmental philosopher Kyle Powys Whyte had a conversation with writer and editor David Hall for *The Pantograph Punch*, an online arts and culture journal based in New Zealand.[21] Whyte spoke about the Standing Rock Indian Reservation, where members of the Sioux tribe established a resistance to the construction of the Dakota Access Pipeline (DAPL).

The planned pipeline would transport crude oil from North Dakota to southern Illinois. This route would bring the pipeline near the northern boundary of the Standing Rock Indian Reservation and would cross beneath the Missouri River, which is the tribe's primary source of drinking water.[22] Protesters feared an oil leak or spill would endanger the tribe's drinking water, and were concerned that construction would pass through and damage their sacred sites.[23]

The protesters' rallying cry "Water is Life!" drew Indigenous peoples from around the world—including more than 300 Native American tribes, Indigenous environmentalists, and activists—to Standing Rock. The standoff lasted from April to December 2016, when the US Army Corps of Engineers halted construction by not granting an easement for the pipeline to be built under the Missouri River.[24] In January 2017, however, US President Donald Trump issued an executive order to revive the pipeline project.[25] The conversation between Kyle Powys Whyte and David Hall occurred in response to the possibility of that executive order. (The order was signed after the interview was conducted but before it was published.)

Whyte's commentary focused on the values and motivations that drove the No DAPL resistance. He explained that, from 1851 to 1868, the Standing Rock Sioux tribe secured via treaties a large area of land. However, when the US federal government wanted access to gold in the sacred area of the Black Hills, in what is now South Dakota, it reneged on the deal, and forcibly reduced the tribe's land to a small area: the Standing Rock Indian Reservation, which is a fraction of the size of the land agreed on by treaties. The United States went on to build a dam, which created a reservoir that flooded the Standing Rock Sioux tribe's best farming, agricultural, and timber-producing land. The reduction of the tribe's land does not change the tribe's values, and the surrounding land is still sacred and significant to them.[26] Whyte explains:

> For Indigenous people generally, stopping this particular pipeline is not the end. This is going to keep happening as it has in the past, where tribes are constantly having to deal with being dispossessed of their land, then being asked to host these pipelines and mines. It is the

atmosphere. Those initiatives are important, yet climate justice also demands that we redress the environmental harm that disproportionately affects historically **marginalized** communities. Here we have in mind the harm done in the name of developing and managing resources to Indigenous Peoples who live in what is now called the United States of America and Canada.

marginalization
Treating people as insignificant and not worthy of moral consideration.

constant barrage of people wanting to do stuff on your land that you do not have the governing capacity to fend off.[27]

Unfortunately, the environmental concerns of those involved in the resistance to the pipeline were well-founded. After becoming commercially operational in June 2017, the Dakota Access Pipeline leaked at least five times in 2017.[28] (One commentator later tried to brush this off by writing, "[T]he pipeline has been entirely free from significant incidents. While several minor leaks have been recorded, they were each quickly contained at the source and amounted to mere gallons, rather than barrels of volume escaping."[29]) These concerns were reinforced in late October 2019 when another pipeline—the Keystone pipeline that runs from Hardisty, Alberta, to the US Gulf Coast—ruptured and spilled 1.4 million litres of oil in North Dakota.[30]

Whyte also notes that oil pipelines are not the only threat to Indigenous Nations and their territory. Even green projects have environmental impacts. Whyte observes, "A good example is hydropower. Dams are coming back after being phased out for a long time; we're seeing major dam projects that are displacing indigenous people."[31]

For Discussion

1. Two main concerns raised by the Standing Rock protest were the risk to the environment, and the ongoing dispossession of Indigenous land that had been recognized through a treaty. Explain how the two are related from a human rights and social justice point of view.

2. Who bears the harm from a pipeline leak? Who benefits from the pipeline? (Think in terms of stakeholders as presented in Chapter 3.) Thinking in terms of negative externalities and issues of social justice, what kind of arrangement should be made to compensate the people of Standing Rock for bearing the risk of a leak?

3. The planned route of the Dakota Access Pipeline was altered so it would not cross the water supply for the city of Bismarck, North Dakota. Would you be willing to allow an oil pipeline to cross your community's source of water? Why or why not?

4. Is satisfying a demand for resources adequate justification for dispossessing and displacing people from their land? Think in terms of social licence, and explain your reasoning.

5. Green electricity generation has environmental and territorial concerns, whether it be for wind, solar, hydro, or (more controversially) nuclear generation plants. What are some of the effects and considerations that need to be taken into account before building these kinds of projects? Who might the stakeholders be, and how would they be affected?

CASE STUDY

Canada's Trans Mountain Pipeline

In 2013, the energy company Kinder Morgan Inc. filed an application with Canada's National Energy Board to build a second pipeline along the same route as its existing Trans Mountain pipeline. The Trans Mountain pipeline was built in the 1950s and stretches from Leduc, Alberta, to Burnaby, British Columbia, transporting Alberta's crude oil and refined petroleum products to the west coast so that they can be shipped to markets in Asia and the US.[32] The pipeline had already undergone a number of expansions and upgrades over the preceding decades as demand for oil increased. From the point of view of Kinder Morgan, the proposed expansion project would be a continuation of business as usual. However, a number of stakeholders felt very differently about the situation.

At least three distinct issues of concern were raised in opposition to the project. First, the existing pipeline had proven to be hazardous to public safety. Since the year 2000, the Trans Mountain pipeline had been responsible for multiple oil spills in British Columbia. Three of those spills were in excess of 1000 barrels (roughly 159,000 litres) each.[33] Second, environmentalists were concerned about the impact that the pipeline might have on both local and global scales. In addition to the well-documented effects of burning oil being a major contributor to greenhouse gas emissions, the Trans Mountain pipeline's endpoint was in the Strait of Juan de Fuca, a particularly sensitive marine ecosystem. In addition to the threat of spills, activists were concerned that increased shipping activity in the area could be dangerously disruptive to the local wildlife. Third, the proposed pipeline passed through a number of Indigenous territories. Many Indigenous groups in these regions were opposed to the expansion. Many members of those communities felt that Kinder Morgan had ignored their sovereignty and opposition to the pipeline. Several Indigenous groups organized protests, including blockades of construction sites.[34] Although Kinder Morgan was successful in convincing the police to arrest and remove the protesters, the protesters were successful in drawing national attention to the controversial project.

In April 2018, Kinder Morgan suspended non-essential spending on the pipeline, claiming the decision was intended to protect shareholders.[35] The issues discussed above (combined with falling oil prices) had brought negative publicity to the company and imperilled both their stock price and the viability of the project. This might have been the end of the project, but the federal Government of Canada stepped in and purchased the pipeline for $4.5 billion in May that year.[36] In August, however, the Federal Court of Appeal nullified the federal government's approval of the pipeline construction because it deemed consultations with Indigenous groups to have been inadequate, and said the National Energy Board (NEB) had failed to properly consider the impact of increased oil-tanker traffic on marine life.[37] Construction of the pipeline halted.

The federal government started another round of consultation with Indigenous groups, and then approved the project again in June 2019.[38] (Construction started up again later that year.) The Tsleil-Waututh Nation, Squamish Nation, Coldwater Indian Band, and a coalition of Sto:lo First Nations in the Fraser Valley brought a legal challenge against this second approval. In February 2020, the Federal Court of Appeal ruled that the federal government had consulted adequately with Indigenous peoples before reapproving the project in 2019, and said "the case law is clear that although Indigenous peoples can assert their uncompromising opposition to a project, they cannot tactically use the consultation process as a means to try to veto it."[39]

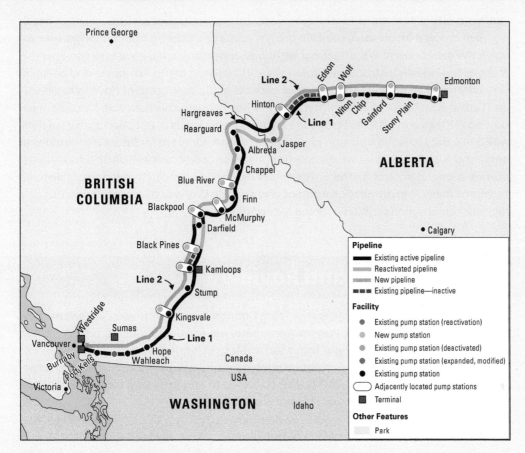

FIGURE 7.2 Trans Mountain Pipeline expansion route.

Source: Natural Resources Canada, Trans Mountain Expansion Project https://www.nrcan.gc.ca/energy/resources/19142

For Discussion

1. Do any of the original objections to the pipeline change now that the pipeline belongs to the Canadian government? Explain.

2. Research the reasons the Government of Canada gave to justify the purchase of the pipeline.

3. Do you think using public funds to purchase the pipeline from Kinder Morgan amounts to a corporate bailout? If so, is this a justified bailout? What social good does the Government of Canada's purchase serve?

4. Recall the ethical decision-making model we introduced in Chapter 3. Do some research to identify the genuine stakeholders in this pipeline dispute. Each of the stakeholder groups is expressing a set of values. What are these values, and what are each group's stated interests?

5. Was Kinder Morgan justified in suspending construction? Explain your reasoning in terms of stakeholder interests. (Recall that the company's shareholders are also stakeholders.)

Summing Up

There are no easy solutions to the environmental problems that we face, many of which we have brought on ourselves. But we are not powerless to bring about change. How we value the environment will affect our attitudes and behaviours. If we take the environment as having only instrumental value, we will approach things like waste and pollution very differently than if we recognize that aspects of the environment have intrinsic value. Further, if we take the environment as only having instrumental value for us here today, we will take very different positions on acceptable levels of pollution than if we think we have a duty to leave as much and as good an environment for future generations to enjoy and sustain life. What we do now as consumers, professionals, and business leaders has a lasting impact on the environment. To deny our impact, or to simply wish the problems away, is to admit moral defeat and engage in one of the most dangerous and reckless social action problems facing humankind.

For Discussion and Review

1. Pick two normative ethical theories from Chapter 2 and compare and contrast how each theory can deal with an environmental issue like refugees from the effect of climate change (for example, rising sea levels or extended droughts).
2. How does environmental protection relate to moral hazard? (If everyone else is taking environmental responsibility, why do I need to care and take responsibility? See Chapter 6 for an explanation of moral hazard.)
3. Can putting a price on pollution (like a carbon tax) reduce CO_2 emissions? Explain.
4. Why do you think some industries and interest groups resist the idea of putting a price on pollution? What reasons do they give?
5. Explain how the tragedy of the commons is an example of a social action problem.
6. Make a list of the things you currently do to reduce your carbon footprint. List three additional things that you can do.
7. Explain how recycling bins on your campus can quickly turn into a social action problem. (For example, what happens if someone puts a pizza box in a "Containers" bin meant for glass and plastic?)
8. To fully appreciate the nature of the tragedy of the commons facing the farmers in western Kansas, another game table needs to be constructed to overlay Game Table 7.1. This additional game table would need to explicitly model the environmental harm done by farmers if they continue to (defect and) irrigate their fields. One way to do this is to consider how imminent peak production is. Construct such a game table. (Consult Appendix B for a primer on game tables.)
9. Thinking back to the example of the farmers in Kansas, what sort of enforcement mechanism could help foster an attitude of co-operation and solidarity?
10. It is not uncommon to see the phrase "privatize profits and externalize the costs" in the comments section of online forums. Given the nature of such comments,

though, the phrase is rarely used critically (in the sense of reasoning). Instead it usually nothing more than a cynical jab at corporate greed and government bailouts of corporations. Using the language of externalities, moral rights, and justice, provide a critical analysis of the phrase "privatize profits and externalize the costs."

Further Reading

Banyan, Margaret E. "Tragedy of the Commons." *Encyclopædia Britannica*. Encyclopædia Britannica, Inc., 23 November 2017. https://www.britannica.com/science/tragedy-of-the-commons.

Baxter, William F. *People or Penguins: The Case for Optimal Pollution*. New York: Columbia University Press, 1974.

Brown, Jennifer L. "The Coase Theorem." *Encyclopædia Britannica*. Encyclopædia Britannica, Inc., 5 February 2018. https://www.britannica.com/topic/environmental-economics/The-Coase-theorem.

Rosen, Harvey S., Jean-François Wen, Tracy Snoddon, Bev Dahlby, and Roger S. Smith. "Externalities." In *Public Finance in Canada*. Toronto: McGraw-Hill Ryerson, 2008.

Siano, Alfonso, Agostino Vollero, Francesca Conte, and Sara Amabile. "'More than Words': Expanding the Taxonomy of Greenwashing after the Volkswagen Scandal." *Journal of Business Research* 71 (2017): 27–37. https://doi.org/10.1016/j.jbusres.2016.11.002.

Whyte, Kyle Powys. "Justice Forward: Tribes, Climate Adaptation and Responsibility." *Climate Change and Indigenous Peoples in the United States*, 2013, 9–22. https://doi.org/10.1007/978-3-319-05266-3_2.

CHAPTER 8
The Power of Advertising

By the end of this chapter you should be able to

- Explain why *information asymmetry* makes advertising itself an ethical issue.
- Identify ways advertisers can frame information to bypass the rationality of their target consumers.
- Provide examples of how advertising has reinforced stereotypes and promoted the darker side of human psychology via racism, sexism, and more.

Advertising is everywhere. It is on our smartphones, our televisions, and on big billboards that we cannot avoid. Advertising even parades as grassroots social media content coming from individuals who appear to have no connections to a company. Who knows if the latest Instagram celebrity was sponsored or not? Given that we are exposed to a vast amount of advertising, it makes sense to question whether any ethical issues arise from this constant bombardment.

New media brings up significant issues in advertising ethics. Content spreads to large numbers of people at a fast pace, and it lives seemingly forever on the Internet. Meanwhile, new media has reduced accountability with fewer checks and balances, and regulation has struggled to keep up. Temptation to skirt ethical lines is higher than in previous decades and the rewards for taking big risks are higher.[1] What does a person concerned about doing business in ethical ways need to know about the ethics of advertising in order to avoid moral missteps?

Ethical Issues in Advertising

Ethical issues in advertising arise because there is asymmetrical information between the seller and the buyer. **Information asymmetry** is present when one party has more relevant information than the other. In the case of advertising, the company knows all that there is to know about a product—where it was manufactured, how high the quality of the product is, and so on. As a consumer, we only know what the firms tell us and what we can infer from reading product packaging or service descriptions. This asymmetry of information leaves consumers vulnerable to the firm. It also relates to the idea of *caveat emptor*, which is a Latin phrase for *let the buyer beware*. *Caveat emptor* makes it the customer's responsibility to gain all of the relevant information about a product or service before purchasing it. For example, if you are buying a used car, it is your responsibility to ask the seller about the car's accident history, mileage, maintenance history, and so on. So long as the seller is truthful in their answers, it is not their responsibility if, for example, the car breaks down after five minutes of you purchasing it. However, *caveat emptor* does not mean that the seller is free of all responsibilities when it comes to selling a product or a service.

Caveat emptor applies even when the advertiser is telling the truth. For example, in 2014 the creators of the game *Cards Against Humanity* offered for sale—and sold 30,000 boxes of—"literal

advertising
Any means of promoting a product or service for sale to the general public or target market. Advertising is not necessarily purchased by the seller. Even the display of a slogan or an image on a piece of clothing purchased by a consumer is an advertisement.

information asymmetry
A situation where one party has information that another party does not have. The person with more information has an advantage over the less informed party in any kind of debate, negotiation, or transaction.

***caveat emptor* (buyer beware)**
It is the customer's responsibility to examine the product before purchasing it, to become aware of any defects or unsuitability of the product for their use.

Information asymmetry also plays a part in some *principal–agent problems*. See **Chapter 9** for an explanation of what this means.

BACKGROUND

The Effect of Information Asymmetry

The parties to a transaction often have different (and therefore incomplete) information relevant to that transaction. The parties' information is asymmetric when one party to a business transaction has more information than another party. The effect of this asymmetry is to render the transaction inefficient, because the trade does not take place according to the preferences of all involved parties. Once all relevant information has been exchanged, the state of information is symmetric, and both parties can make a fully informed decision.

feces, from an actual bull" for six dollars each on "Black Friday," the day when American retailers usually record their biggest sales in advance of the winter holiday season.[2] Many purchasers demanded their money back after receiving their little boxes of dried sterilized bovine scat. However, if the company had shipped something else, their advertisement would not have been truthful. The company fulfilled its obligation to the purchasers, who had received precisely what they had ordered. In this case, the expression *buyer beware* is quite appropriate.

The Canadian Code of Advertising Standards (CCAS) sets standards prohibiting advertisements from making false or misleading claims and/or omitting pertinent information; see page 170 in **this chapter**.

See the discussion of priming and deception on page 177 in **this chapter**.

CONCEPT CHECK

8.1 What does the phrase *caveat emptor* mean?

a. It is Latin for *seller beware*.

b. It is Latin for *the cave is empty and the philosophers have won*.

c. It is the Latin warning put on cans of caviar. It means *beware the caviar*.

d. It is Latin for *buyer beware*.

There are significant ethical worries when it comes to advertising. One worry is deceptive advertising. An advertisement could potentially be deceptive by making false claims, misrepresenting data, or omitting key information. The seller, however, is still responsible for providing truthful information and not omitting material information. Alternatively, an advertisement might play on a person's emotional, perceptual, or cognitive vulnerabilities.[3] For example, a funeral home might want to advertise its services in a palliative care hospital ward, but this would immorally play on grieving families' emotional vulnerabilities. Another worry is that advertising **manipulates** consumers. It is obviously unethical, however, to manipulate somebody into purchasing a product, thereby undermining a person's autonomy and ability to make sound, well-informed decisions.[4]

manipulation
To control or use someone for your own purposes, without their awareness of the fact that they are being so controlled.

Not everyone holds that advertising is necessarily manipulative. Some scholars, among them Roger Crisp,[5] think that advertising does not usually disrespect autonomy in any way. Crisp argues that so long as advertising does not create a desire that is formed due to bypassing the consumer's awareness, does not create a desire for no good reason, and allows for ordinary decision making, there is no problem with advertising.[6] Crisp admits that some forms of advertising might be wrong, such as advertising tobacco products, but by and large, there is no problem with advertising.

autonomous desire
A desire that an individual willingly identifies with or has freely chosen.

Other scholars disagree. Robert Arrington argues that an autonomous purchase must stem from an **autonomous desire**.[7] An autonomous desire is one that you want to maintain after reflecting upon it. Another way to think about autonomous desire is to consider a desire that readily aligns with your character or the person you want to be.[8] For example, you might find yourself desiring an expensive luxury vehicle but, upon reflection, realize that buying this vehicle conflicts with your deeply held value of donating to charity. The desire for an expensive luxury vehicle, then, would be non-autonomous. Arrington ultimately warns that some forms of advertising are morally wrong because they generate non-autonomous purchases.[9]

CONCEPT CHECK

8.2 What is an autonomous desire?

a. It is a rogue desire that has no genesis.

b. It is a desire that has a mind of its own.

c. It is a desire that aligns with your character.

d. It is a desire that contradicts all other desires.

Putting arguments about autonomy aside, there is still another worry over advertising. Recall Chapter 1, when we introduced you to Joseph Heath's ten commandments, which are aimed at minimizing market inefficiencies. One of the commandments is to reduce information asymmetries between company and the customer. Advertising, however, is all about creating information asymmetries. The company that puts out an advertisement has a vested interest in highlighting only the positive aspects of its product or service, and minimizing or omitting information about less favourable aspects. For example, low-cost providers of products always highlight the low price of their products instead of advertising the products' relatively poor quality. To the businessperson, this seems like an obvious and standard tactic. However, from the point of view of the market-failures approach to ethics, this information asymmetry is highly inefficient: it keeps customers from having a free choice in a fair market, wasting the customer's money on a product that will be discarded at the first opportunity. So as long as advertisers hide or omit information from consumers, advertising decreases market efficiency.

BACKGROUND

Return for the Worse

While purchasers know that many retailers will let them return a product that does not meet their needs, they do not know what happens to returned products, particularly ones bought from online retailers. In 2015, Canadian shoppers returned merchandise worth about $46 billion.[10] In the USA, roughly a quarter of all returned merchandise ends up in a landfill, producing almost 2.3 million tonnes (5 billion pounds) of waste in a year.[11] The waste from returns around the globe is estimated to be twice that.[12] This has created a new business opportunity for "reverse logistics"—managing returns on behalf of retailers in order to salvage some value through reselling the product.[13]

CONCEPT CHECK

8.3 How can advertising go against Heath's ten commandments?

a. Advertising can create or sustain information asymmetries, which contributes to market inefficiencies.

b. Successful advertising creates a barrier to entry for new suppliers.

c. Advertising creates negative externalities, as it forces consumers to make decisions about which product to buy.

d. Advertising exploits the diffusion of ownership, since the shareholders are not the ones creating the advertisements.

Canadian Advertising Regulations

Chapter 6 discusses some of the goals of self-regulation.

While the idea of *caveat emptor* assigns responsibility to the buyer for making sure they purchase what is agreed to, the seller is also responsible for not misrepresenting their product or defrauding the customer. This falls under the corresponding notion of *caveat venditor*: *let the seller beware.*

We examine subliminal messaging and its effects on pages 171–178 in **this chapter**.

In Canada, the advertising industry regulates itself and holds to the standards set by the Canadian Code of Advertising Standards (CCAS),[14] which is administered by Ad Standards (formerly Advertising Standards Canada). The CCAS explicitly addresses many of the ethical worries we have raised about advertising. For example, the CCAS states that advertisements must not make false or misleading claims and should not omit pertinent information. Price claims about sales must be genuine discounts where the product or service was sold at the regular price for a significant amount of time, or approximately six months. Terms and conditions of guarantees and warranties must be clearly stated. Reviews and testimonials must be real. These are just some provisions of the CCAS.

Ad Standards also administers the Broadcast Code for Advertising to Children (BCAC).[15] The BCAC explicitly states that advertisements directed at children must not use *subliminal messaging*. Advertisements cannot directly encourage the child to purchase products or services or ask their parents to purchase products or services. The BCAC sets out scheduling rules for how often an advertisement for the same product or service can be aired. Well-known puppets, persons, or characters cannot be used to endorse products or services. Again, these are just some provisions of the BCAC.

It is important to emphasize that Canadian advertising is self-regulated. Instead of the government being involved in regulating advertisements, Ad Standards takes on the burden of laying out the CCAS and BCAC (collectively, the Codes) and enforcing them. This is important because the self-regulatory nature of the industry helps convince the government that there is no need for the government to intervene. The advertising industry benefits from self-regulation because government intervention is often stricter and more heavily enforced. Thus, it is in the enlightened self-interest of all advertisers to adhere to the Codes, and report those who do not comply with them.

Notice that this creates a social action problem. The punishment for a Code violation is relatively mild, given that there are no criminal or legal charges for such a violation. Some advertisers might feel, then, that it is in their narrow self-interest to push the boundaries of the Codes. For example, an advertiser might gain an advantage if it pays individuals to write excellent reviews about its product, so long as everybody else adheres to the Codes. However, if every advertiser were to violate the code in a similar way, the government would likely deem self-regulation ineffective and step in with regulations that have legal consequences. This would take away the advantage of self-regulation for all advertisers.

In the province of Quebec, some advertising directed at children younger than 13 years old is prohibited under the Consumer Protection Act. Advertisements directed at children are banned on radio, television, mobile phones, print, and other media originating in Quebec. Advertising is considered directed at children if it is intended for or appeals to children, if the message is designed to attract children's attention, or if children are targeted by or exposed to the advertisement. The ban carries a fine of up to $100,000 and other punitive action. However, since the ban only applies to media originating in Quebec, which is largely produced in French, most English-language media are not subject to this restriction.

See **Chapter 6** to learn more about social action problems.

CONCEPT CHECK

8.4 How can self-regulation in the advertising industry collapse into a social action problem?

a. A social action problem will emerge if there is competition among advertisers themselves.

b. A social action problem will emerge if consumers are overwhelmed with information, forcing them to sit down and do a cost-benefit analysis.

c. There is always an incentive to push the boundaries of the advertising codes, knowing that small transgressions will likely not be punished. But if every advertiser does this, self-regulation collapses.

d. A social action problem will emerge once consumers decide which product to buy.

Bypassing Rationality

These safeguards with respect to advertising are fine with respect to the presentation of information. They do not, however, guard against the subconscious cultivation of beliefs about the product through an evocative non-informational context. That is, an advertisement does not need to present information about the product. All it has to do is create a desire for it by presenting sights, sounds, and even scents that stimulate the brain's reward system. This is often called **subliminal advertising** because its effects occur in brain processes that take place before our rational processes can evaluate the desire-producing content of the message. For example, seeing a bottle of cola dripping with what appear to be beads of condensation conveys the message that a cold, sweet, carbonated beverage is waiting for you. Such a presentation has said nothing about the product itself, so there is no information to think about and therefore no deception going on. All we have is awareness of a desire, and perhaps no idea what prompted it. This is an example of priming, one of three common ways to create beliefs about products without using explicit deception. Other ways of creating beliefs involve framing the presentation of information in a way that makes it difficult to assess value, and appealing to emotion.

subliminal advertising
Bypassing a person's critical self-reflective capacities to generate a desire for a product or service.

For more on subliminal messaging, see the discussion of priming and deception on page 177 of **this chapter**.

Framing Information

Suppose you are looking to buy a new wrist-worn fitness tracker. You are in Store *A* and notice that it has the model you are looking for on sale for $99. But you also recall seeing an advertisement from Store *B* pricing the same model at $69. Do you put down the fitness tracker and head to Store *B*? If no other considerations affect the decision (such as convenience or immediacy), most people would opt to save the $30. Now suppose you are looking at the latest curved high-resolution widescreen monitor that would complete your gaming rig. The price tag at Store *A* says $8999, but you know that your friend got one for $8969 at Store *B* yesterday. Would you head to Store *B* to save $30 on the monitor?

Notice that the absolute difference between prices at the two stores is $30 for both the fitness tracker and the monitor. The difference is that you would be saving 30.3 per cent of the higher price for the fitness tracker by going to Store *B* in person, but less than 0.4 per cent of the higher price for the monitor. The savings of $30 seems more significant for a smaller item than for a larger one, even though the difference in savings is exactly the same. We tend to think in relative terms—not absolute ones—when we assess value. People are more likely to switch from Store *A* to Store *B* for the fitness tracker than for the monitor, because the relative difference in price does not seem to offset the effort of going to a different store. We frame the same $30 difference in prices in two different ways. While we often unreflectively *frame information* for ourselves, advertisers are more than happy to do that work for us, taking advantage of the *framing effect* created by carefully limiting and crafting the presentation of information.

Brick-and-mortar businesses are limited in what types of information their customers see. The information that businesses choose to disseminate must be suitable for a broad consumer base. Determining a consumer's willingness to pay (the maximum a customer is willing to pay for a good or service) is based on assumptions about the characteristics of a *typical* potential customer.[16] Additionally, businesses have very little control over what products their customers actually look at as they browse the aisles of the store. In a brick-and-mortar context,

BACKGROUND

Framing Information

Framing describes shaping how information is presented to an audience. It is intended to influence the decisions of those receiving the information in the direction preferred by the presenter. (In politics, this is called spin.) For the presentation to succeed, it must create an uncritical *framing effect* in the mind of the audience—that is, the audience sees the information as credible, even though it is distorted. We can overcome a framing effect by taking time to think about what has been presented and filling in what has been left out. Sellers know this, too, so they will attempt to limit the amount of time you have to think about the incomplete information you were given. For example, the seller may say that there is one unit left and someone else is also interested, or they may tell you that the offer expires when you leave the (virtual or physical) shop.

it is not easy to engage in real-time dynamic pricing in ways that would not raise the ire of potential customers.

In an online environment, however, e-commerce actors *can* control what information potential customers see on their website; they *can* control what products potential customers see on their website, and they *can* engage in real-time dynamic pricing. Big data allows e-commerce actors to acquire vast amounts of information to accurately construct complex, real-time profiles of online customers. Using complex algorithms, they can then accurately predict a customer's willingness to pay and individualize the products and prices that potential customers see on their computer or devices.[17] At this point, one strategy open to e-commerce actors is to offer a "discount" on the product and then offer accessories for the product at inflated prices—that is, at higher prices than offered by their competitors. In this scenario, the e-commerce seller is banking on the fact that its "discount" has lowered the customer's incentive to check out their competitor's prices.[18] This type of behaviour is a quintessential example of *framing information*. If we are not cognizant of our online footprint, the trail of information that we leave online can be compiled and used to frame products and prices in favour of the e-commerce seller. "Deals" online are rarely that.

> Saving, in the context of buying and selling, is a euphemism. Not spending more is the more accurate phrase. If shops were genuinely interested in you saving money instead of spending it, they would not sell you more than you actually need.

CONCEPT CHECK

8.5 Which statement best describes the framing effect?

a. If you're expecting one thing to happen, but a different thing happens, you will suffer cognitive dissonance.

b. The way information is presented to consumers will affect how they make purchasing decisions.

c. The effect happens when one thing is framed in one way, and another thing is framed in a different way.

d. The effect emerges when perfectly competitive markets distribute resources efficiently.

Lease-to-own companies typically frame information in a way that hides the real cost of their items. In 2010, CBC's consumer affairs program *Marketplace* reported that Easyhome was advertising a weekly lease price of $23 per week for a 32-inch LCD television.[19] The same model sold at retail for $449. Over the three years of the lease, the television would cost $3588. Assuming a compounded interest rate of 29.9 per cent per year, Easyhome was pricing the television at a $1640 base price, more than triple the price at a regular consumer electronics store at that time. But for someone who cannot scrape together the purchase price, $23 a week seems like a bargain—until the total cost is calculated.

Special promotions may also convince a person to purchase a higher-priced item than they would otherwise. Consider a fitness club that offers the following New Year's Resolution packages in December and January:

- $260 for unlimited use of the gym and pool
- $320 for unlimited classes
- $320 for unlimited use of the gym and pool, plus unlimited classes

There are two ways to read this. Either you are getting unlimited access to classes for an additional $60 when you sign up for using the gym and pool, or you are getting the gym and pool for free when you sign up for unlimited classes. Most people would see the latter. After all, if classes cost $320 alone, combining it with a free gym-and-pool membership looks like a great deal. But come February, when almost everyone's resolutions are broken, the choices are different:

- $260 for unlimited use of the gym and pool
- $320 for unlimited use of the gym and pool, plus unlimited classes

Now people are more likely to opt for the less expensive package. But those people who saw the expensive, though low-value, classes-only membership likely signed up for the gym, pool, and classes because the promotion overstated the value of the classes. The fitness club took advantage of people's New Year's resolutions to direct them to a more expensive membership than they would have taken at another time of year.

This kind of information framing is another instance of information asymmetry. The seller is hiding information about the value—not the price—of its product in a way that makes customers believe they are getting a good deal at the time. However, once the missing information is filled in, the offers look much less appealing. Advertisers are not going to fill that information gap willingly. You have to do that hard work of research and critical analysis yourself. But since most people are not willing (and some are unable) to do that work, advertisers can get away with hiding information until someone notices.

Appealing to Emotion

If it feels good, do it. This little sentence can be understood in many ways: pursuing hedonistic physical delight, trusting a gut feeling about a difficult decision, creating a comfortable personal space, laughing with friends. Advertisements appeal to our affective faculties, not just our rational ones. Advertisers know that if they can create a positive association between a person's response to an advertisement and their product, they have shaped a part of that person's beliefs about that product. This ensures that it will be among the first of the ones considered when it comes time to make a purchase. The brewers of a particular brand of beer know that Sweden's women's ski team will not arrive at your door as soon as you open the case, but they want young men to associate their beer with the excitement of the possibility of such an unexpected adventure.

Advertisements can be more than just a 15-second video on a blog or an eye-grabbing animated billboard visible from the road. Songs and movies advertise, too. On 4 July 2013, a video featuring country music performer Will Hoge's song "Strong" was released.[20] The piece was commissioned as part of General Motors's advertising campaign for its Chevy Silverado truck, and it extolled the virtues of hard work, faithfulness, reliability, trustworthiness, friendship, and unfailing strength—features that any company would want associated with their trucks. These virtues, along with independence and self-sufficiency, are prized in the parts of the USA where pickup trucks are common. Releasing the song in Texas on Independence Day and to the rest of the USA on the eve of Major League Baseball's All-Star Game was not a coincidence. The campaign was geared around cultivating a **sentimentality** about a traditional (though mythical and romanticized) American lifestyle and associating it with Chevy trucks.

sentimentality
To appeal to sentimentality is to seek to influence people's choices by playing on their strong emotional connotations rather than giving them reasons for making those choices.

CONCEPT CHECK

8.6 **Which of the following is an appeal to sentimentality?**

a. Acadian Tire plays a Mothers' Day commercial depicting a mother receiving a pink cordless drill from her daughter.

b. Paris-of-the-Prairies Oyster Emporium gives free doughnuts to the local under-16 hockey team every time they win a game.

c. Carabella Park throws an extravagant holiday party for its employees.

d. Stereo Hut advertises its retro Colour Computer III that has a whopping 128 KB of memory.

Labatt Brewing took the appeal to sentimentality in a different direction with the 2013 film *The Movie Out Here*. It was effectively a 90-minute advertisement for its Kokanee lager brewed in Creston, British Columbia, and it formed the centrepiece of a nine-month-long promotion for the brand. The movie's crude and lewd comedy appealed to young men aged between 19 and 25—precisely the market Labatt was targeting. Though the movie was a critical failure, the campaign was a marketing success: it raised market share significantly beyond what was hoped,[21] while managing to get viewers in 30 theatres to pay $12 each to see the feature-length advertisement on its opening weekend.[22] According to Randy Stein, one of the partners in the advertising agency used by Labatt, "Branded content is becoming more accepted, especially with younger consumers—so long as it is entertaining."[23]

Some of the characters that met their demise in Metro Trains Melbourne's "Dumb Ways to Die" online advertisement. The catchy tune and whimsical animation conveyed a memorable message about safety around trains.

CASE STUDY

Coca-Cola: Bubbling with Happiness

Some advertisements do not present any information at all. Instead, they create an association of a pleasurable experience with a brand or product. The Coca-Cola Company's "Open Happiness" campaign that ran from 2009 through 2016 is just one example of such association-creating advertisements. The ads ranged from whimsical to provocative. In one, a young man dozing in a meadow has his Coke stolen by insects who work together to unlock the sweet liquid.[24] Another shows what happens among a new cohort of university students when they discover that the cap on their bottle can be removed only by pairing it with the cap from a second bottle. This forced interaction between strangers forges a human connection over the common goal of opening the bottles.[25]

Later in the campaign, an ad featured migrant labourers in Dubai who make roughly six dollars a day and who have to pay a dollar per minute to make a telephone call to their families back home. Here Coca-Cola installed a telephone that provided a three-minute call for the price of a bottle cap, which could be obtained by purchasing a bottle of Coke for the equivalent of fifty-four cents. The workers were delighted that they could speak longer with their families for about one-fifth of the cost per minute that they would ordinarily pay.[26]

Each ad in the series portrayed some kind of happiness or delight. As New York University's Marion Nestle puts it, "The advertisements are designed to sell happiness. They're not selling a drink. But on an emotional level you attach to it."[27]

Nestle goes on to explain what soft-drink companies do to stimulate demand through repeated messages that evoke emotional responses.

> [I]t's so pervasive that you don't even notice it. You're not supposed to notice it. If you start putting your critical thinking cap on and looking at all the places you see subtle or not so subtle marketing for Coca-Cola and Pepsi, you're kind of stunned by how much of it there is. But otherwise it's just kind of there. And you don't notice it, save for on some kind of subliminal level. We don't like to talk about subliminal levels, because we think we're completely rational actors in all of this. But the soda companies know better, and they use that to their advantage.
>
> That is, largely, the reason why we love soda so much.[28]

For Discussion

1. Think about the last cola ad you saw. How was the product presented? Was there a direct mention of the product in the song or dialogue? What kind of emotional content did it portray?
2. To what extent was Coca-Cola being manipulative when people needed to work with another person to open their bottles? Is this a good thing, or a bad thing? Explain.
3. The ad featuring migrant workers was controversial for two main reasons. First, it required them to purchase a bottle of Coke to make the cheaper phone call, which is a purchase the workers might not have made otherwise. Second, it did nothing to present the other injustices migrant workers face.[29] Could the advertiser have done more to promote happiness? How might these criticisms change the effectiveness of the ad?
4. What other emotions or sentiments have you experienced because of advertising? (Here are some ideas to get you started: arousal, curiosity, anger, excitement, insecurity, fear of missing out.)
5. Do you think you are immune to subliminal advertising? Explain why or why not.

Being entertained creates a positive emotional association with the brand behind the message, and humour in advertising serves the same purpose as appealing to sentimentality. Humour helped Metro Trains Melbourne's safety campaign become a cultural phenomenon of its own. In November 2012, the transit company released a song and animated video called "Dumb Ways to Die."[30] The advertisement did not appear on television, but it was seen 28 million times in the first two weeks it was online.[31] Leah Waymark, the general manager for corporate relations at Metro Trains Melbourne, told a reporter, "This campaign is designed to draw young people to the safety message rather than frighten them away."[32] The campaign spawned a series of games for mobile devices, with over 200 million downloads by April 2016. Chloe Alsop, the marketing manager, said that the two apps available by that point were "loved by young people across the world" and generated "millions of hours of engagement with the rail safety message subliminally communicated through game play."[33] A small line of merchandise followed, transforming a public safety announcement into a secondary revenue stream—an unexpected but welcome result to go alongside a self-reported reduction in incidents at level train crossings.[34]

Priming and Deception

Metro Trains Melbourne admits to subliminal communication to convey a safety message, but it is not trying to sell you anything more than that. Advertisers for products are not usually so open about the impressions they are trying to cultivate.

The effectiveness of subliminal advertising is not well understood. What is known is that if a person wants to satisfy a particular desire, a subliminal presentation of a product that will satisfy that desire is more effective than if the viewer is not interested in what the product offers.[35] For example, a subliminal presentation of the logo for a particular brand of cola will have little effect on someone who is not thirsty, but could influence the choice of someone who is. This effect can be mitigated if the viewer is warned about the possibility of being **primed** beforehand.[36]

Moderately deceptive claims in advertising are harder to filter out than highly deceptive ones, particularly when we are distracted or tired.[37] Some of the processing of claims is done in the brain automatically, before we are conscious of it. Highly implausible claims are processed quickly. Plausible and moderately implausible claims appear to receive more attention in a second level of processing, but fewer moderately implausible claims are flagged when the person is busy with another cognitive activity than when they can give their full attention to assessing claims.

It takes conscious effort to avoid the effects of subliminal and/or deceptive messaging. If a person is not able to make this conscious effort (due to either distraction or passivity), the messages can hit their target. However, treating a prospective customer as an adversary to be caught off-guard is not respectful of the right to make a clear and informed decision about a product. Rather, it is market-distorting, opportunistic behaviour with respect to the prospective customer, and violates the tenth of Heath's commandments.

While some subliminal messaging may be overcome by conscious effort, repeated subliminal messaging stays in the subconscious mind. For example, the illusionist Derren Brown invited two creative professionals from an advertising agency to create a company name, logo, and slogan for a poster advertising a chain of taxidermy stores.[38] Before Brown set them to the task, he exposed the men to a number of carefully selected images (London Zoo, a bear with a harp, angel wings) and phrases ("Where the best dead animals go"; "Creature Heaven") placed along the route that the driver followed when taking them to the meeting with Brown. To the professionals' chagrin, many of the things they were exposed to peripherally—that is, not shown to them directly yet visible enough to be noticed—on the journey showed up in their branding concept.

priming
A way of influencing people's decisions by instilling words or images in their memory. Once primed in this way, people are more likely to respond in ways preferred by the one doing the priming, under certain circumstances.

These prompts had not been hidden, and the professionals' brains certainly noticed them, but the men were not conscious of this act of noticing. Steve Genco, a specialist in neuromarketing, points out that these men became aware of the unobtrusive prompts (but not the context in which they saw them) only when "they were presented with a specific task [designing a brand], and in using their full conscious processing capabilities to perform that task, they activated and connected to the new stimuli their brains had "taken in" and "filed away" without conscious awareness."[39] Brown's experiment had captured the recollection of a nonconscious experience.

Companies want their brands and logos visible everywhere so people perceive them non-consciously and then recall them when a cognitive task brings them to conscious awareness. As Brown notes, no one is immune from this kind of messaging, since even expert marketers fall prey to their influence. There are so many messages of this kind that no one can be aware of all of them all the time. Humans simply do not have the cognitive capacity to process consciously and rationally every message they encounter. The pervasiveness of advertising messages wears us down, and we do not know what messages we have picked up until they make themselves known. The moral challenge for advertising, then, is to create a message that is memorable and informative, not deceptive and detrimental to personal autonomy.

Advertisement by Joseph Schlitz Brewing Company, 1952.

How Advertising Harms

Advertising sends messages about more than the products or services being offered. It also says something about our cultural perceptions (or at least the perceptions of a particular target demographic) and about ourselves as individuals. Advertising must be relevant to the target audience, so it must be congruent with the culture and values of that audience. But it also tries to convince people that they will not be full participants in that culture unless they have the latest item favoured by that culture. When the notional requirements for full acceptance drive people to engage in harmful behaviour against themselves or others, that messaging has crossed a moral line—the well-being of persons has been harmed.

Gender Roles

Advertisements often promote rigid gender roles, encouraging women to take up domestic pursuits while men do the paid work. In the early 1950s, an advertisement for Schlitz beer suggested it did not matter how well women did at domestic pursuits, as long as their husbands could reassure them that dinner would be just fine because the beer had not been burned.[40]

Even in the mid-2010s, gender expectations continued to show up in ads. For example, Gap Kids ran an advertising campaign showing a little boy described as a "little scholar" and a little girl as a "social butterfly" in the context of their future aspirations.[41] Critics felt the subtle message was that only the boys need to learn how to think.

Abuse

In 1973, the slogan in an advertisement from BPA Fun Center, a Detroit-area bowling alley, joked about domestic violence by making a pun of the phrase "beat your wife."[42] In 2011, Fluid Hair, a salon in Edmonton, Alberta, came under fire for an advertisement showing a woman with a black eye dressed up for a glamourous night out with her abuser alongside a slogan about "looking good" in everything you do.[43] Abuse violates a person's right to security of the person, and these kinds of advertisements undermine that right by portraying abuse as socially acceptable.

Racism

In the late nineteenth century, a soap manufacturer used a painting of a blonde-haired white girl in a clean dress and a curly-haired black girl of similar age dressed in dirty rags to promote its product. The white girl, trying to be helpful, asks the other girl why her mother does not use Fairy Soap.[44] More recently, two different health-and-beauty companies fell into the same racist pit. In 2017, one of Nivea's advertisements for a colourless deodorant (which was intended to not show on black or white clothing) showed a white woman in a white robe and proclaimed, "white is purity."[45] There was no corresponding advertisement mentioning black. Also, in 2017, Dove's three-second social media loop advertising its body wash started with a black woman pulling off a brown shirt, revealing a white woman wearing a light pinkish-brown shirt;[46] this woman pulls off her shirt, revealing a tanned (but still white) woman wearing a tan-coloured shirt. This ad was perceived as devaluing black persons. Putting the tanned woman at the beginning and the black woman second or third would have resolved the problem, as would have adding an Asian, Latina, or Indigenous woman to the loop.

Body Image and Sexuality

Ads that portray the human body are particularly powerful—after all, each one of us has a body. Ads that draw attention to human sexuality work because we are sexual beings. Healthy sexuality is a human good. However, when that sexuality is depersonalized, it becomes devoid of everything human except for the dynamic of power and submission. Ads playing on sexuality alone take something good about humanity and strip the human element away, leaving just a depersonalized object behind.

For example, Reebok's 2010 Reetone ad campaign used the human form to draw attention to depersonalized feminine legs and buttocks by depicting slim women from the waist down in underwear or skimpy shorts and their Reetone shoes at home or working out.[47] The shoes were not the focal point of the advertisements because they were not the things being sold; instead, the ad portrayed attractive legs and buttocks as objects that could belong to any woman. This leading message about body image was followed by the commercial message that a woman can get this toned figure if she lives in these purpose-designed shoes. (It should be noted that using the textbook-appropriate word *buttocks* does not adequately capture the crass sexism of the Reebok advertisement.)

CASE STUDY

Inclusivity in Advertising

Mountain Equipment Co-op (MEC) has its roots in the rock-climbing business. The company was founded in 1971 by a group of four climbers from Vancouver, British Columbia who wanted easier access to climbing gear. To bring this goal to life, they incorporated a consumer co-operative, charged just $5 for a membership share, and provided customers with easier access to gear for rock climbing, mountaineering, ski mountaineering, and hiking. The company has since grown to supply outdoor gear across Canada.

Until 1990, in the place of smiling individuals enjoying the company's products, MEC chose to showcase and capture the feeling of the great outdoors in their advertisements.[48] Covers of its lookbooks displayed silhouettes of people climbing up snowy mountains and resting in a canoe on a lake without displaying gender, race, or any other distinguishing features of the person. The focus was on wilderness, being outside, and participating in nature.

In the 1990s, MEC started to experiment with advertisements displaying both men and women against backdrops of mountains and snow. The advertisements have become increasingly diverse, with a front-page 2019 holiday seasonal advertisement displaying what appears to be an interracial family enjoying gift-giving together. MEC's advertisements continue to contain nearly equal numbers of images of men, women, boys, and girls and clearly highlight people of different backgrounds. MEC provides an example of displaying diversity in advertising in a way that is intended to unite and support families across the country.

For Discussion

1. What do you notice first about the people who appear in advertisements in general?
2. When you see an advertisement clearly showing a same-sex couple, what impression do you have? How does it change your perception of the company advertising the product or service?
3. What emotions, feelings, and desires does MEC try to evoke in its newer advertising? Explain how you think MEC does this.
4. Advertising both reflects and shapes social perceptions. What does MEC's gender- and race-inclusiveness in its advertisements do more: shape or reflect? Why do you think this is so?
5. What groups does MEC's advertising exclude? Think in terms of privilege and implicit, but not malicious, biases (refer to Chapter 5 if you need to). How could these groups be represented in MEC's advertising?

The objectification of women is pernicious, and the presentation of the "ideal" female body can have harmful and lasting consequences. The pornography industry shows how. In Australia, one of the criteria for printed pornography to be labelled "soft core" is that any visible labia minora be edited out of the photograph.[49] This has the predictable (in hindsight) but unintended effect of cultivating false beliefs about what female genitalia should look like, which has led to an increase in cosmetic labiaplasty.[50] The lesson for advertising is that using edited and depersonalized body imagery creates a false image of what the perfect body should look like, which motivates individuals to act in self-harming ways in the quest for that ideal.

CONCEPT CHECK

8.7 A building company provides an online virtual reality tour of its bathroom designs. One model contains an image of a naked woman standing seductively in an open shower.[51] What harmful message does this send?

a. Women spend too much time in the shower.

b. People do not shower with their clothes on.

c. Their bathroom designs are not gender-inclusive.

d. Women are household accessories.

Summing Up

Although advertising does serve the important function of conveying information about a good or a service, it can quickly devolve to deception, manipulation, and marginalization.

To an extent, advertising is self-regulating through its industry codes, but advertising also has some legal constraints designed to protect society from overt manipulation and false claims. Following regulations and the law is not enough, however. Advertisers must engage in ethical considerations as well. Success at advertising does not preclude following the demands of ethics. We can have advertisements that are clever, humorous, and memorable, but that still pass the light-of-day test of ethics.

For Discussion and Review

1. While there are some laws and governmental regulations directed at advertising in Canada, the advertising industry is self-regulated for the most part. What are the advertising laws in Canada? Are they the same for all provinces?

2. Has distasteful or exploitative advertising ever motivated you to not buy a product? Explain your objection.

3. How can advertisements be a benefit to society—that is, how can they be a way of increasing social utility? (See Chapter 2 for information on utilitarianism.) What elements do you think an ad would need to be considered pro-social?

4. How might implicit bias (refer to Chapter 5) affect both the creation and the reception of advertising?

5. *Caveat emptor* is Latin for *buyer beware*. To what extent does that adage hold in the Canadian marketplace?

6. Is it important to protect children from direct advertising, as Quebec does? Pick a side and argue for it.
7. How does packaging serve as advertising? Are governments right in prohibiting certain images on tobacco packaging?
8. How many advertisements do you wear or carry in a day? Include visible logos or brand names.
9. How often do you click on targeted advertising online? How can you know that you have been targeted with an advertisement? What steps—if any—do you take to protect yourself against targeted advertising? Explain.

Further Reading

Ad Standards, "The Broadcast Code for Advertising to Children." 2015. https://adstandards.ca/wp-content/uploads/2018/09/broadcastCodeForAdvertisingToChildren.pdf

Ad Standards. "Canadian Code of Advertising Ethics." July 2019. https://adstandards.ca/code/the-code-online.

Bachnik, Katarzyna, and Robert Nowacki. "How to Build Consumer Trust: Socially Responsible or Controversial Advertising." *Sustainability* 10, no. 7 (July 2018), art. 2173. https://doi.org/10.3390/su10072173.

Drumwright, Minette E. "Ethics and Advertising Theory." In Shelly Rodgers and Esther Thorson, eds, *Advertising Theory*, 2nd edn, Routledge, 2019, 503–22.

Galbraith, John Kenneth. "The Dependence Effect." In *The Affluent Society*, 40th Anniversary edn, Houghton-Mifflin, 1998, 124–31.

Snyder, Wally. *Ethics in Advertising: Making the Case for Doing the Right Thing.* Routledge, 2017.

CHAPTER 9
Corporate Governance and Perverse Incentives

By the end of this chapter you should be able to

- Detail how corporations are structured.

- Demonstrate how the principal–agent problem applies to corporate structure.

- Explain what *perverse incentives* are and provide examples.

- Identify some ways in which the structure of corporations allows for the correction of poor executive performance or high-level misconduct.

principal
In a fiduciary relationship, the principal is the party whose interests are represented by the agent acting as a fiduciary. In the context of corporations, the owners are the principals; the executives and other employees are the agents.

We described corporations, and in particular limited liability corporations, in **Chapter 4**.

incentives
Reasons for acting that appeal to a person's self-interest. *Perverse incentives* have the effect of motivating the agent to act in ways contrary to the interests of the principal(s). *Benign incentives* align the agent's self-interest with the interests of the principal(s).

As you will recall from **Chapter 3**, *prudential considerations* are the factors that need to be taken into account when making decisions that affect another person's self-interest.

We have seen how markets indicate what people are willing to purchase and for what price. The changing demands of buyers in the market influence the division of labour: labour is re-allocated to support the production and sale of the goods and services that are in demand. But a market is not the only way to manage the distribution of labour. Consider a group of individuals who want to accomplish a common goal that is beyond what any one of them can do with their own labour. They can agree to contribute to this common cause by creating a *corporation*. The agreement to form a corporation is, in a sense, a collection of contracts between an incorporator and each of the other incorporators, so this kind of corporation can be understood as a *nexus of contracts*. These contracts among the **principals** give structure to the corporation. Without this formal structure, the vision of working together can descend to infighting, chaos, and sabotage. Corporate governance is about giving clear direction to the work of the corporation and effective organization of persons so that work can be done well.

While it is fairly easy to convince people that a common goal is worth pursuing in general terms, it is harder to convince people that it is worth *personal* investment of time, effort, material, and capital to pursue that goal. **Incentives**—the promise of gaining something of personal value in exchange for activity in pursuit of a common goal—are one way to keep individuals focused on advancing corporate goals. But incentives can go awry. A person may find that their personal goals are better served by working against corporate ones, particularly if there are few negative personal consequences for doing so. We will explore some of the ethical and prudential aspects of *benign* and *perverse* incentives, and how corporate governance involves managing these incentives in a way that fulfills the organization's duties to its beneficiaries.

CONCEPT CHECK

9.1 A corporation should be understood as:

a. a nexus of contracts.

b. a paradox of personhood.

c. a market for labour.

d. a tax shelter.

BACKGROUND

Corporate Goals

Usually the common goal that drives the formation of a corporation is to make a profit for the owners by providing goods and services that are in short supply, though this is not always the case. Municipalities are typically incorporated so they can own property and provide services on behalf of their residents. Other corporations are designed as not-for-profit organizations that conduct business to serve some other value such as relieving suffering.

Corporate Structure

Each legal jurisdiction has its own rules for organizing a corporation, and the details depend in part on the amount of involvement expected from the principals. A **publicly traded corporation** with shares that can be bought and sold on a stock exchange has the most complex corporate structure, but it contains all of the features needed to understand governance in any corporate context. We will use the fictitious publicly traded corporation *Aneroid Digital Automation Manufacturer*, which is referred to by its acronym ADAM, as the continuing example for this chapter.

publicly traded corporation
A corporation whose shares are traded on a stock exchange.

Shareholders

While ADAM is a for-profit corporation, it is easy to overlook the fact that the profit is not for the people who run the company, but for those who own a share of its profits and losses. These are the shareholders, the ones who have acquired a stake in the corporation's performance by purchasing ADAM stock. Shareholders are investors, and there are contractual obligations between the individual shareholders and the collection of shareholders represented by the corporation in order to safeguard each of the shareholders' investments in the corporation.

There is a widespread belief that owning shares in a corporation means owning a part of everything the corporation owns. This is incorrect. Owning a share of the profits and losses is one thing; having control over the corporation's resources is quite another. An ADAM shareholder controls only the shares associated with their investment in ADAM, not the assets that ADAM owns as a corporation. For example, a person who owns ADAM stock cannot sell off a portion of ADAM's manufacturing plants as a personal transaction. Such a move could require ADAM to reconfigure a building and transfer (without compensation!) a sliver of property to the new owner. This imposes a cost on the corporation and consequently to the remaining shareholders. While shareholders are the ultimate beneficiaries of the corporation's operations, they do not have the rights of property ownership with respect to the corporation's holdings. If they did, one shareholder's unilateral transfer of a fractional ownership right could unjustly reduce the value of the other shareholders' property. Sole corporate ownership of assets protects not only the corporation but also the corporation's ability to continue producing value for its shareholders.

Stockholders and *shareholders* are the same thing, but we prefer the term *shareholders* to avoid confusing it with the term *stakeholders*. See Background Box "Shareholders versus Stakeholders" in **Chapter 4** for an explanation of the difference between these two groups.

BACKGROUND

Corporate Liabilities

Sole corporate ownership also extends to liabilities, which limits the financial risk borne by individual shareholders. Should a corporation become insolvent, its shareholders are free from personal responsibility for the corporation's unpaid debts. The corporation's assets will be sold to meet creditors' demands for payment. This will draw down the value of shareholders' investments to almost zero, but that is all the (non-board) shareholders can lose. The situation is more complex for board members, but they can be insured separately against personal liability.

Even though shareholders do not acquire pieces of corporate property, they do get something from the corporation in exchange for their investment. Each one of ADAM's shareholders has a measure of input into how ADAM conducts its business because the shareholders are ADAM's principals. (ADAM's profits are expected to benefit the shareholders.) The shareholders have primary responsibility for establishing ADAM's corporate goals (though this responsibility is delegated to a small number of persons), and they bear the risk of losing their investment should ADAM no longer be a viable business. Anything ADAM does as a corporation must demonstrably serve the interests of the shareholders, even if doing so does not contribute directly to the company's financial bottom line.

CONCEPT CHECK

9.2 What is a shareholder?

a.   One who shares while holding stakes for stakeholders.

b.   One who receives patronage appointments to the Canadian diplomatic corps.

c.   An owner of shares in a company.

d.   A member of an incorporated co-operative.

Directors or Trustees

Now consider the scenario where each of ADAM's thousands of investors have to make a strategic decision on whether the company should invest in small-scale electricity production to power its processing plants. How does the corporation make sense of the shareholders' diverse opinions and establish a direction on such a substantial change to its operations? It would take weeks to give every investor three minutes to speak on the matter. The problem is multiplied if each investor were to participate in something more mundane such as employees' annual performance reviews.

Most investors know this is impractical. Once the number of principals grows beyond a certain number, decision making is unwieldy and does not always produce a result that reflects each investor's preferences. Most investors also recognize that they do not have time to be involved in these kinds of internal activities. But investors also know the power of delegated authority, so they engage responsible agents to make routine decisions on behalf of the shareholders. Every year, ADAM's shareholders elect a few of their members to serve as the company's **board of directors**, and that board gives direction to the company in a way that satisfies its trust relationship with the rest of the shareholders.

The members of the board often hold a large number of shares compared to other investors, so their opinions carry more weight when it comes time to make a decision. This usually works out for the smaller shareholders because as the board members work to enhance the value of their individual investments in the corporation, they are adding to the value of everyone's investment. Thus, while the members of the board are among the company's principals, they are charged with acting as agents for the remaining principals.

board of directors
Elected representatives of a company's shareholders entrusted with the responsibility to direct the company according to the wishes of its shareholders. In some places, this board is called a *board of trustees* or a *supervisory board*.

In **Chapter 3** we discussed the Condorcet paradox and Arrow's impossibility theorem, both of which point out problems for collective decision making.

Let us return to ADAM's proposed project. Suppose the board determines that investing in small-scale electricity generation would provide good value for ADAM because generating power will consistently cost less than purchasing it. It is likely that most of the other shareholders would come to the same conclusion. The board could confidently make the decision to proceed in less time than consulting all of the shareholders would take, and it would still be acting in the interests of all of the investors. Boards provide the means for shareholders to exercise control over their corporation without each shareholder needing to continually give attention to steering it.

CONCEPT CHECK

9.3 What is the primary role of a board of directors?

a. A board of directors gives direction to the affairs of the company in such a way as to benefit all of the stakeholders.

b. A board of directors gives direction to a company in a way that satisfies its fiduciary duties to the shareholders.

c. A board of directors gives direction to the affairs of the company in such a way as to benefit the executives.

d. A board of directors gives direction to the affairs of the company in such a way as to benefit society.

Officers and Executives

Just as ADAM's shareholders cannot give continual attention to leading the company, ADAM's board members typically do not have the means to oversee all of the company's internal operations. The board, again acting in the interests of the shareholders, will recruit **corporate officers** to oversee the day-to-day business of the corporation. The most common of these is the *chief executive officer* or CEO. The CEO is ultimately responsible for keeping the corporation operating in accordance with its goals and external obligations, and makes regular reports to the board and shareholders on how well the corporation is performing with respect to those goals.

The CEO may also work with a *chief financial officer* (CFO), a *chief operating officer* (COO), and other officers responsible for different aspects of the corporation's operations, infrastructure, compliance, and management. The designation *officer* typically, but not always, refers to someone who holds a role that reports either to the CEO or board of directors, while *executive* typically describes anyone in a high-level managerial position. How this works in practice varies from corporation to corporation.

Corporate executives and officers usually receive both a salary and bonuses based on corporate and personal performance. These bonuses provide an incentive to work in the interests of the corporation while still satisfying personal goals with respect to income, investments, professional networks, challenges, skills, and experience.

corporate officers
Those in positions of the highest level of management in a corporation. These include the *chief executive officer* (CEO), *chief financial officer* (CFO), and the *chief operating officer* (COO).

Managers and Working Staff

No organization can do anything useful without people producing something of value—for example, making something that can be sold or traded, or developing a process that reduces the costs of production, sales, support, or shipping. Most of a corporation's resources should go to this kind of work. This work needs to be managed by assigning people, equipment, material, space, and time to each of the product streams. Good managers make sure that the staff working under them can do their jobs well. They do this by negotiating with executives to get what is needed to do that work. Moreover, they can explain to executives how those needs are related to corporate objectives, and to their working staff how their work contributes to meeting those objectives. But ADAM's low-level managers and working staff have little connection to ADAM's shareholders and their interests. The responsibility toward the shareholders seems distant as personal interests come to the fore.

The challenge here, as it is at higher levels of the corporation, is to ensure that the staff and low-level managers have effective motivation to work in line with corporate—and ultimately shareholder—objectives. Luís Cabral recognizes the delicate nature of this problem. He writes,

> The optimal contract between shareholders and managers is . . . one that balances the benefits from insuring the manager against risk, on the one hand, and the benefits from providing the manager with the right incentives, on the other hand.[1]

Corporations must be careful to identify and offer only meaningful, effective, and appropriate incentives for employees throughout the organization.

Principals and Agents

You have already seen the terms *principal* and *agent* in this chapter. An *agent* is any person who has been given responsibility to act on behalf of another party. That other party is the *principal* party in the relationship, because their interests are the primary ones served by that

> While working in industry, one of the authors of this text attended a divisional all-hands meeting where a corporate executive said, "You don't work for [the corporation]. You're working for yourselves and your families." The point is that the interests of the rank-and-file employees are centred around their own familial needs, and not those of the corporation.

relationship. Since one party is acting as an agent for the other, the ethical requirements of public morality govern the relationship. It is not acceptable for the agent to act in their own personal interest using the resources provided by the principal. While the payment for working as an agent should ensure that the principal's interests are protected, sometimes there is more to gain by working against the principal's interests. The presence of an incentive to break faith lies at the core of the principal–agent problem.

The Principal–Agent Relationship

The principal–agent relationship most frequently mentioned in the context of a corporation is the relationship between shareholders as principals and the board as their agent. But the board also brings in people to serve as officers acting under the direction of the board, so the directors are the principals in that relationship, while the officers are the board's agents. This continues down the line: managers become agents for executives; staff workers are responsible for acting in accordance with their managers' instructions.

> See **Chapter 1** and **Chapter 3** for more on public and private morality.

> **principal–agent problem**
> A problem that arises when the actions and interests of agents are not aligned with those of the principals. In a corporate context, usually the managers, executives, and officers are agents and the shareholders are principals. A major function of corporate governance is to ensure that the corporation does not fall prey to principal–agent problems.

BACKGROUND

The Dual-Agent Problem

A particular kind of principal–agent problem, called the *dual-agent problem*, arises when both parties to a real-estate transaction use the same realtor. In this case, the realtor will collect both halves of the commission agreed to by the seller, rather than splitting it with the purchaser's realtor (if the purchaser has their own realtor). The higher the

When purchasing real estate, a buyer can avoid the dual-agent problem by using a different realtor from the seller.

sale price, the greater the dual-agent's commission will be, and so the realtor is motivated to maximize their commission without an incentive to act in the interest of the purchaser. If the purchaser wants a realtor to act with their interests in mind, then they should use a different realtor from the seller—and ideally one from a different brokerage.

THE CANADIAN PRESS IMAGES/Richard Buchan

Principal–agent relationships show up outside a corporate environment, too. If you have a financial advisor managing your investments, you are the principal party in that relationship and the advisor is your agent. The agent can advise you to do certain things, but that advice has to be in your interest and not just in the agent's interest. If you own a building and hire someone to manage it, that person becomes your agent. These kinds of principal–agent relationships are contractual and fiduciary. They are also susceptible to principal–agent problems.

Some relationships are not governed by formal contracts, but they still function as principal–agent relationships. Others look like principal–agent relationships in some ways, but do not operate as one. Recognizing that business operates under a social licence and not out of its own autonomy means that business writ large is akin to operating as an agent for society, since any gain it makes comes from serving the interests of different segments of society. Statutes and regulations describe some of the obligations business has to society; in exchange for this, the government facilitates wide-ranging—but (importantly) not unrestricted—business activities. Understood this way, the relationship between business and society has aspects that look a bit like business serving as an agent of society. However, the inescapable mutual dependence of business and society upon each other makes the relationship more like a symbiotic one than a principal–agent one. Individual would-be principals might be able to handle their affairs without agents, but envisioning society as a principal in a fiduciary relationship with business overlooks the fact that without trade—that is, business—of some sort, there would also be no society.

> **Chapter 1** and **Chapter 4** both discuss the duties of business in relation to society, and the concept of social licence.

CONCEPT CHECK

9.5 Which of the following is an example of something that looks like a principal–agent relationship, but really is not?

a. A board of directors hires Bob as the chief financial officer.

b. Bob hires Doug as an accountant.

c. Bob hires Doug as a lawyer.

d. An aunt pays her niece to mow her lawn.

Principal–Agent Problems

A principal–agent problem arises when the agent has a greater incentive to act in their own interests rather than the interests of the principal, and when the agent is shielded to some extent from the consequences of acting against the principal's interests. This situation involves *moral hazard*. It is like the free-rider problem because the agent gets off lightly and other people pay the price for the wrongdoing. It is different from the free-rider problem because it involves the active breaking of a fiduciary duty and not just the shirking of a responsibility toward one's colleagues.

> See the discussion of moral hazard and the free-rider problem in **Chapter 6**.

The corporate structure provides fertile ground for principal–agent problems to arise. One of these problems is known as *insider trading*. Since the board of directors of a publicly traded corporation is obliged to file quarterly reports with securities regulators, the board receives information about corporate performance before the rest of the shareholders do. If the news is bad, the directors can sell off some of their holdings before the stock market can react; if it is good, the directors can acquire more stock and make a quick gain once the results are announced. This acts against the interests of the other shareholders—the ones on the outside of corporate operations—by denying them the opportunity to adjust their investment before the quarterly report becomes public knowledge. Securities regulators have a two-pronged approach for reducing the risk of **insider trading**. The first is to impose a *moratorium* on directors and officers buying and selling their corporation's shares between the time the reports are prepared and their release. The second is to make insider trading illegal in most circumstances.

insider trading
The illegal act of members of the board of directors or corporate officers enriching themselves by using their early access to information relevant to changes in share price.

CONCEPT CHECK

9.6 **What is the essential idea behind the principal–agent problem?**

a. The principle of beneficence overrules duties of care.

b. Agents have a perverse incentive to work in their own self-interest rather than in the interests of the principals.

c. Principals have a perverse incentive to act in in their own self-interest rather than the interests of the agents.

d. The main idea is that people respond to incentives in predictable ways.

Many principal–agent problems take advantage of *information asymmetry*. See **Chapter 7** for more on the concept of information asymmetry.

When corporate governance becomes functionally inverted, there are more opportunities for principal–agent problems to arise. Normally, the shareholders elect a board of directors (even though the nominees are recommended by the board), and the board gives direction to the corporation's officers. The board also receives reports and recommendations from the CEO concerning the corporation's operations. In a functional inversion of governance, the CEO also recommends candidates to replace directors whose terms have expired, and the board presents these to the shareholders for confirmation at the next annual general meeting. After a few years, this will give the CEO effective direction of the corporation since the board is now more inclined to favour the CEO's wishes, rather than respond to input from the shareholders. Any reduction in functional oversight by the board leaves the CEO with more freedom to favour personal interests over corporate ones.

Investment brokers also face the temptation of a principal–agent problem. Brokers who receive a commission for selling certain financial products may advise their clients to purchase those products, even though they products may not be the best match for the clients' risk tolerances and investment goals. This is subtler than insider trading because the investor, who is the principal in the relationship, may not ever know how the broker, acting as an agent, stands to gain from the transaction. Moreover, if the broker convinces the principal to invest in a product where the price is higher than can be justified by the fundamental measures of value and risk, the broker can collect their commission and sell part of their own investment in that same product before the overvaluation becomes widely known.

It is impossible to close off all routes to principal–agent problems. The temptation to break the trust relationship is always present, even though it may not be strongly felt. Potential

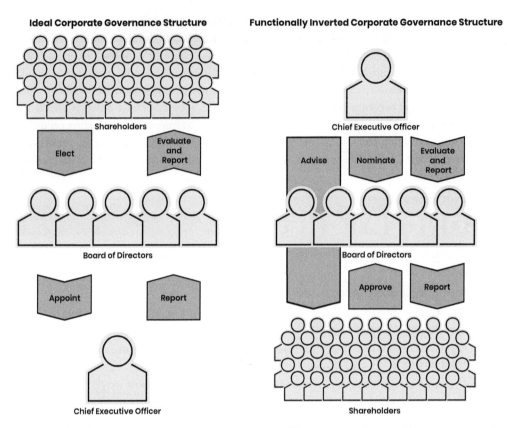

FIGURE 9.1 Corporate governance structures. Directors and executives are expected to act in the interests of the shareholders (left). However, if the board does not carry out its duties, it provides an opportunity for the CEO to take effective control of the corporation (right), leaving greater opportunity for principal–agent problems to arise.

principal–agent problems become real only when there is an incentive to break that trust and a lack of consequences for doing so. We turn our attention to incentives now.

Perverse Incentives

Setting Up for a Fall

So far we have looked at a rough outline of how a corporation is structured. Ultimately, it is owned and controlled by the shareholders, who for good prudential reasons delegate responsibility to a board of directors. The board hires executives to run the operations of the company. Those executives hire a series of managers and those managers hire workers. Finally, the workers fulfill the actual function of the company by providing some kind of good or service to the customers. There are many variations of this basic structure, but this is the general organizational layout found in all corporations. We now have to ask, *How does one ensure that the various agents will fulfill the duties laid out above?*

The simple answer to the question is this: if you want someone to do something for you, pay them. Here money acts as an *incentive*. Money is not the only type of incentive, as we will discover later, but it is by far the most common. Workers receive wages and shareholders receive dividends. It is by way of financial remuneration that the efforts of everyone within the company are directed toward a common goal—provided that the incentives are well-structured. Properly setting up an incentive structure can be difficult and frequently leads to unforeseen consequences. Consider the following example.

Imagine you are a burger-flipper at a fast-food chain and management decides that you have been flipping burgers too slowly. They offer to give you a raise if you can increase the number of burgers that you make in an hour. On the face of things, this seems like a well-thought-out incentive structure. In the minds of your managers, the ultimate goal is profitability and a good way to achieve this is by selling more burgers per hour; thus, they make you this offer. But what else might happen if you focus too much on increasing your burgers-per-hour rate? You might not assemble the burgers to the best of your ability. You might not be as attentive to potential errors, and customers might not come back if their burger is poorly assembled or they get something that they did not order. You might not keep your workstation clean when working so fast, which could become a food safety issue. You might become so focused on speed that you take shortcuts and injure yourself. All of these possibilities have the potential to backfire on management and ultimately harm the profitability that they had aimed to improve.

At the other end of the ladder, imagine you are a CEO and your yearly bonus is dependent on the company seeing a profitable return of 5 per cent annually. There are only a few days left in the fiscal year and the company has earned profits of 4.9 per cent. You could sell off a few of the company's assets to bump that total up and secure your bonus. Such a sale could hurt the company in the long run, but you would get your bonus. In this example, the board of directors is focusing too narrowly on annual profit targets, providing an incentive that encourages their CEO to mortgage the future of the company to achieve present-day success.

In all these cases, the incentive structure designed to promote the overall goal of the organization ends up doing the opposite; we call this a **perverse incentive**. Perverse incentives result in unintended and undesirable outcomes. The possibility of these perverse outcomes is a constant source of difficulty for members at all levels of the corporation. The corporation wants its burger-flippers to flip faster and its CEOs to maintain profits. The primary way to do this is by offering them incentives. By being aware of the possibility of perverse incentives and studying common mistakes, we can set up better incentive structures to achieve the actual goals of the company rather than a narrow subset of them.

perverse incentive A kind of "loophole" in a structure that allows an incentive designed to encourage beneficial behaviour to be used instead in a way that undermines the purpose of the incentive.

CONCEPT CHECK

9.7 Which of the following is an example of a perverse incentive?

a. Greg buys candy from a man in a van.

b. The authorial agreement for the authors of this text does not specify who owns the copyright. Greg (the senior editor) has the opportunity to steal the authors' work and publish it under his name only.

c. Greg accidentally spills coffee on Andrew's laptop.

d. Greg buys something from Canadian Tire instead of MEC.

Dodging the Consequences

As mentioned above, payments are by far the most common type of incentive. There are, however, two other types you should be aware of: **negative incentives** and **shielding from negative consequences**. Rather than rewarding good behaviour, negative incentives punish bad behaviour. This basic concept should be familiar from domains such as sports. In sports, referees do not reward players for following the rules; they penalize the players who violate them. These negative incentives can also be monetary in nature, taking the form of fines. Take the case of traffic laws. Police officers do not reward drivers who stop at stop signs; they penalize drivers who do not stop by issuing a ticket (fine). Thus, drivers are negatively incentivized to follow the rules.

Many corporations attempt to use negative incentive structures in their workplace. For example, it is common in the food-service industry for managers to make servers pay for broken dishes or unpaid bills (dine and dash). Although these practices are common, they are also explicitly illegal. Employers cannot make employees pay for damages that occurred incidentally during the course of their duties. So, although negative incentives are common in other domains such as sports and driving, they are less common in the business setting because they are illegal. Some businesses choose to ignore this illegality and workers are often ill-informed about their rights.

negative incentive
An incentive that threatens to punish bad behaviour rather than motivates by rewarding positive behaviour.

shielding from negative consequences
When a corporation takes on legal responsibility for its employees, it is shielding those employees from (some of) the negative consequences of their actions.

Workers in the food-service industry cannot have the cost of stolen meals or broken dishes taken from their wages. However, these costs may be taken from tips, unless tips are paid out as wages or provincial labour legislation explicitly prohibits it.

CONCEPT CHECK

9.8 What is the value of negative incentives?

a. Negative incentives encourage bad behaviour.

b. Negative incentives override bad behaviour.

c. Negative incentives explain bad behaviour.

d. Negative incentives punish bad behaviour.

The final type of incentive we will examine here is shielding from negative consequences. As just discussed, there are lots of negative incentives in the world. We used the examples of penalties in sports and tickets in driving, but these skirt around the edges of the most common negative incentive: legal ramifications. These include both criminal ramifications (jail time) and civil ramifications (lawsuits). When individuals abstain from actions, it is frequently because the action would risk legal ramifications. It may be very tempting to steal or use physical violence or any number of other criminal means to achieve your desires, but the legal system provides a significant negative incentive against pursuing such means.

It is quite common in the workplace for the company to take on a certain amount of legal responsibility for its employees. Imagine if a server trips, spilling hot soup on a patron and that patron wants to sue the server. The restaurant will likely step in and defend the server, thus shielding them from negative consequences. If companies did not take on these types of responsibilities, many employees would be hesitant to work for them and take all that risk onto themselves. This is good business practice for both the employer and the employees. But it can be taken too far.

CONCEPT CHECK

9.9 What is *shielding from negative consequences?*

a. It is a way of assigning moral blame to someone other than yourself.

b. It is the result of being self-insured.

c. It is an incentive by which a company takes on a certain amount of legal responsibility for its employees.

d. It is what happens when employees are careless.

If the business makes it clear to the employee that they will protect employees from any and all negative consequences, then the negative incentives that prevent the employee from engaging in bad behaviour will no longer be effective. To illustrate this, consider a bouncer at a nightclub. As a regular part of their duties, they will have to use physical force against patrons. It is possible that an unfortunate situation will unfold and a patron will feel the need to sue the bouncer. As above, the club ought to be obliged to step in and represent the bouncer in court. But if the bouncer knows that they will not suffer the legal ramifications of their actions, perhaps they are no longer restrained by negative incentives and begin to behave in an unnecessarily aggressive manner in the execution of their duties. Maybe they start picking fights and using unnecessary force. It can be very difficult for a business owner to strike the correct balance between these two possible outcomes. This dynamic should be familiar from previous chapters and the discussion of moral hazard. One the one hand, if businesses do not shield their employees from negative consequences the employees will be unwilling or unable to do their jobs. Yet on the other hand, if they shield employees too much they might incentivize bad behaviour. Shielding can be an effective incentive, but it can also enable bad behaviour.

CONCEPT CHECK

9.10 Shielding from negative consequences can lead to:

a. moral hazard.

b. perturbed indifference.

c. collateral invectives.

d. corporate failure.

When All Else Fails

The previous sections focused on the internal decision-making apparatuses of the corporation and how a business makes its day-to-day decisions. In most situations, these apparatuses will be sufficient to determine the objectives and activities of the corporation. Despite these many levels of responsibility and accountability, sometimes corporations engage in morally dubious activities. These are the sensational stories that we are bombarded with on the nightly news: companies dumping toxic waste into the environment, selling unsafe products, using slave labour (overseas or at home), or any number of other activities that the public finds unacceptable.

There are two things worth noting about these types of stories. First, they are newsworthy *precisely* because they are unusual. Most companies most of the time are well-run. The internal decision-making apparatuses function appropriately and morally competent individuals put a stop to these types of outrages before they become news stories. These kinds of things become news stories because something went wrong inside the corporate structure. Second, if something has gone wrong inside the corporate structure (and we know that this does happen), how else might problems be addressed? In this section, we will look briefly at three extra-corporate mechanisms that can serve to monitor the behaviour of corporations: *consumer boycotts*, *shareholder activism*, and *charter revocation*.

Consumer Boycott

The first alternative to internal decision making is the consumer boycott. As the name suggests, this involves customers becoming so outraged by the behaviour of a company that they stop purchasing that company's products or services. Without customers, the company ceases to be financially viable; it must sell something in order to have money to pay its employees and satisfy its shareholders. Consumer boycotts are quite common, but they often lack sufficient size to produce the desired result. If only a few hundred people stop shopping at a large chain, that company can afford to ignore the boycott and wait for the inciting event to be forgotten. Nevertheless, consumer boycotts remind us of a fundamental truth that often gets obscured by the anonymity of the market: corporations ultimately exist to serve some demand. We as consumers demand certain products and services in exchange for our money and the company responds to meet those desires. If we use our purchasing power to demand ethical behaviour and environmental sustainability, corporations will be forced to respond to that demand as well. If corporations do not respond, it is within our power, by way of the consumer boycott, to punish them for not meeting those demands.

Shareholder Activism

The second way in which outrage with a corporation's decision might manifest is by way of shareholder activism. Remember that our account of corporate structure began with the shareholders. They ultimately own the company and hold all of the power. However, in most cases, the shareholders have very little to do with the day-to-day operations of the company they hold shares in. They delegate all that responsibility to a board of directors and that board becomes the *de facto* highest authority in the company. But if that board and the decision-makers below it act in a way that displeases the shareholders, there are a variety of ways in which the shareholders can re-exert their dormant power.

The most direct form of activism is to sell one's shares in the corporation. If enough shareholders do this, it will negatively affect the stock value of that company. One can also merely *threaten* to sell one's shares and potentially have the same effect. Shareholders can also seek to remove board members, filibuster meetings (that is, speak at length until the time for adjourning the meeting has arrived without a decision being made), demand information from the CEO, and create a variety of other small rights-defending disturbances that can cumulatively

---

We must not fall into the confirmation bias that says all companies are morally bankrupt. Only the failures are reported in the news; as a result, we have to dig deeper to find the evidence that there are well-run companies who operate with a high degree of integrity. See **Chapter 3** for more on confirmation bias and other cognitive biases.

consumer boycott Consumers may attempt to alter the perceived negative behaviour of a corporation by refusing to purchase its products or services, thereby communicating their disapproval of the behaviour.

The market green approach to environmental concerns set out in **Chapter 7** is an example of customer-driven demand.

shareholder activism Those holding shares in a corporation may seek to alter the behaviour or direction of a corporation in a variety of ways, including submitting proposals for action for discussion at shareholder meetings, voting against director candidates nominated by the board, and so forth. Note that if a person sells all their shares, then they are not able to participate in other forms of shareholder activism.

Randy Jackson (left), dressed as CEO Brian Moynihan, and Lenina Nadal (right) have a mock boxing match symbolizing the struggle of shareholders against the board outside the Bank of America annual shareholders meeting in Charlotte, North Carolina, in 2012. Shareholder groups presented resolutions to change corporate practices on political contributions, lobbying, and mortgage foreclosure, among other things.[2] None of the proposals passed.

cause great disturbance to the operation of the company. Shareholders are technically part of the corporate structure, but they are a part that is often treated as inert, uninterested, and only concerned with dividends. This may frequently be true, but if the circumstances demand it, the shareholder can become a more active participant in the corporate structure by way of shareholder activism.

Charter Revocation

Last, it is important to remember that corporations exist within a society. They are artificial entities that are granted existence by a government when they incorporate. As such, if society feels that a company has become detrimental to society, it can revoke the privilege of incorporation and with it the very existence of that corporation. The laws that allow governments to do this are commonly known as **charter revocation** laws.

    Charter revocation laws exist in most countries but are very rarely used. Canadian law professor Joel Bakan has argued that such laws should be used more frequently given what he sees as rampant and unrepentant misbehaviour on the part of corporations.[3] When individuals commit crimes, we punish them by removing them from society and sending them to jail. Why would we not treat the artificial person of the corporation in a similar manner? If a

charter revocation
The government revoking the charter of a corporation would essentially mean the cessation of the corporation's legal existence.

CASE STUDY

Shareholder Activism: Canadian Pacific Railway and Pershing Square Capital Management

In 2011 Canadian Pacific Railway Ltd. (CP) had an operating-cost–to–revenue ratio that was higher than most other railway companies in North America.[4] Pershing Square Capital Management, an American hedge fund founded by William Ackman, saw an opportunity to improve CP's return to investors, and acquired 14.2 per cent of CP's shares, becoming its largest shareholder.[5] In advance of the 2012 annual general meeting, Pershing Square nominated Hunter Harrison, the former CEO of CP's competitor Canadian National Railways (CN), to replace Fred Green as CEO, and also nominated several new members to the board,[6] claiming that "Fred Green's and the Board's poor decisions, ineffective leadership and inadequate stewardship have destroyed shareholder value."[7] The battle for shareholder proxy votes between the existing board and Pershing Square as the largest investor had begun. (Shareholders who cannot attend an annual meeting typically designate proxies to vote on their behalf. In the normal course of business, this is the board, but in cases of shareholder activism or a hostile takeover bid, it can be any shareholder standing opposed to the board.)

Shortly before the annual meeting was to begin, Green resigned and five members of the board, including the chairman, declared that they would not stand for re-election. Pershing Square's board nominees were elected, and Harrison was named CEO.[8] As Harrison's expertise in running railroads led to operating efficiencies, CP's share price took off, moving from below $49 per share in September 2011 to above $220 at the end of 2014.[9] Pershing Square sold its investment in CP in 2016, earning a profit of about $2.6 billion.[10] The activism of the largest shareholder transformed CP into a more efficient railway company while producing a handsome return for all investors.

There is more to the story, however. Recall that Harrison was an industry insider before coming to CP. He had retired from CN at the end of 2009, but because of his intimate knowledge of CN's operations, his retirement package included a no-competition clause.[11] Further, in Canadian business at the time there was a tacit understanding that moving from being CEO of one company to becoming the CEO of a major competitor "is not quite gentlemanly."[12] Why are Canadian businesses troubled by a CEO being hired to lead a rival company? Well, CEOs have access to a lot of privileged information, trade secrets, and other confidential matters. This sensitive information belongs to the organization the CEO is leaving, and should not become available to a competitor who hires that person as their new CEO. Because this information is privileged and can cause material harm if it falls in the hands of a competitor, a CEO's fiduciary duties to their past employer often extend for a negotiated period of time following the termination of employment. Further, the leader of a company is expected to do just that—lead—and not be available to the highest bidder. Leadership requires the ability to start a project and see it through, which in this case calls for long-term commitment to a company's overall business strategy. Having CEOs jump from competitor to competitor flies in the face of this commitment.

So how did Pershing Square get away with disrupting this tacit understanding? They challenged the agreements that covered Harrison's retirement from CN, and guaranteed that Harrison would get from Pershing Square whatever retirement monies CN would not pay if Harrison was found to have breached his contract.[13] Governance researchers Yvan Allaire and François Dauphin describe this arrangement in no uncertain terms: "Ackman and Harrison are Americans who could not care less about the mores and values of the Canadian business world."[14]

This type of response reflects the complex reality that different cultures often value things differently and often give different priorities to the same values. It is important to understand that the way one culture prioritizes a value is not necessarily more ethical than the way another culture expresses and prioritizes that same value. Both American and Canadian companies value and rightfully expect loyalty from everyone in a company, executives included. It is just that in this particular case, what it means to be loyal meant one thing to Pershing Square and another thing to those critical of Pershing Square's form of shareholder activism.

For Discussion

1. CP's directors were highly regarded in the Canadian business community. But one of the criticisms Ackman levelled against them was that they could not steward a railroad company adequately because they did not understand the industry. Can a board faithfully execute its fiduciary duty to shareholders if it understands how to conduct business in general, but not the workings of the specific industry? Is this a legitimate reason for a shareholder to prompt other shareholders toward corrective action? Explain your reasoning.

2. Given a corporation's fiduciary duties toward its shareholders, should it consider hiring executives from competing companies, even though it is frowned upon in Canadian corporate culture? What are the moral and prudential values involved here?

3. Though hiring a CEO from a competitor may be considered unethical, it is still legal if certain stipulations are met. Under what circumstances, if any, is this acceptable in the business world? Think in terms of applying Heath's ten commandments (see Chapter 1).

4. It is not often that a respected executive with knowledge of an industry becomes available for recruitment by an activist shareholder. Harrison did not make the jump from CN to CP immediately, but became involved in Pershing Square's takeover a few years later. Does this time gap make a difference to your answer to the previous question?

5. Harrison was successful as the CEO of CP, at least in terms of generating shareholder revenue. If Harrison had failed to improve CP's operations and increase its stock price and dividend, would his hiring still have been justified?

6. To what extent should cultural norms shape corporate governance, particularly in the context of international investment? Could Pershing Square's disruption of Canadian business norms be considered ethical? Why or why not?

CASE STUDY

Profiting from the Wrongdoing of Others: Gotham City Research

One of the assumptions of capitalist markets is that inefficiencies will be exposed and eliminated. Part of the reason that free-market advocates are confident that this will happen is because money can be made by uncovering market inefficiencies. This can be done through short selling.

Short selling is the practice of selling shares at their current price in anticipation of the price dropping significantly in the near future so that they can be bought back at a lower price. The way that a company makes money doing this is by borrowing and selling shares that belong to someone else. But why would a shareholder lend their shares to a short seller? A short sell is basically a bet: the shareholder is betting that the shares in the company will increase in value (or at least not lose value), and the short seller is betting that the value of the shares will go down. So the short seller "rents" the shares for a defined period of time, turns around and sells them, waits for the shares to decrease in value, buys the shares back, returns the shares to the original shareholder, and pockets the difference. In essence, a short seller makes money by selling high and buying low (which is the reverse of the usual buy low and sell high).

A real-life example that demonstrates how money can be made by uncovering market inefficiencies is the company Gotham City Research LLC. Gotham's business model is based on researching publicly traded companies, identifying companies that are overvalued, short selling those companies, and then publicizing their research.[15]

Here is a simple fictional example to demonstrate how Gotham operates. Suppose you own 100 shares in Finagle Financial and those shares are valued at $10 each. Gotham approaches you and offers to pay you $50 to borrow those shares for a few weeks, at which point they will return your shares to you. After you agree, Gotham sells the shares, pocketing $1000, and publishes some shortcoming that they have discovered about Finagle Financial. This shortcoming could be any number of things, but Gotham is famous for exposing companies who have engaged in deceptive accounting practices to project an unduly positive image of the companies' finances. When this information is released, the share value of the company falls, say from $10 to $1 a share. Gotham can then buy back your 100 shares for just $100 and return them to you, walking away with $850 for its efforts. Because Gotham discovered the underlying inefficiency first, it was able profit from it.

Some people think that Gotham is doing good work.[16] There are two components to this line of thought. First, Gotham's business model is primarily based on exposing companies who are themselves engaged in bad practices. By taking down these kinds of bad actors they could be understood to be acting as a kind of market vigilante, partially fulfilling the image associated with the company's name. Second, on a more systemic level, the existence of companies like Gotham discourages companies from engaging in deceptive practices in the first place. Everyone benefits from assets being accurately priced and deceptive practices being minimized.

The practice of short selling is legal in many jurisdictions, including Canada. But the question is, is short selling ethical? As we have said throughout this text, just because something is legal, it does not follow that it is ethical. A company like Gotham makes money by short selling shares in a company and then deliberately publishing true, though damaging, public information about that company. Gotham's objective is to make money from the targeted company's subsequent loss of market value. One way to think about the ethics of short selling is to ask, *Has anyone been harmed?*

Going back to our fictitious example, is Finagle Financial harmed through the actions of Gotham? A company like Finagle Financial does not have the legal or moral right to profit from deceptively framing information that it gives to its shareholders and government regulators. It would be difficult to argue, therefore, that Finagle Financial can be materially harmed by being caught in their deception. In essence, the "harm" done to Finagle Financial is that it lost market value because it got caught, which cannot be used as a moral or legal defence.

But what about the shareholders of Finagle Financial? Yes, the value of their shares decreased, but this cannot be blamed on Gotham. The wrongdoer in this example is Finagle Financial for having misrepresented itself to its investors. It is also important to note that Gotham uses information that is publicly available to all investors. It would be difficult for investors to argue that they were harmed because they failed to do due diligence in researching their investment with Finagle Financial.

Now think about the shareholder that Gotham borrowed from. Remember that short selling is basically a bet between the borrower and the lender. The lender was under no compulsion to lend their shares to Gotham. Furthermore, the lender had access to the same information that Gotham had. If the lender had done their due diligence and investigated Finagle Financial's reports and statements, they would not have taken the bet. Instead, they would have realized Finagle Financial was overvalued and would have sold their shares. It would be difficult for this particular shareholder to argue that they were harmed because they made an ill-advised and uninformed bet with Gotham. Also, it is crucial to note that the lender has exactly the same number of shares in the company as they started with.

For Discussion

1. Explain how deceptive reporting practices produces a market inefficiency.
2. Tim Worstall, in an article praising companies like Gotham, writes, "The incentives to uncover fraud and abuse are greater when you can make a profit by selling something that you don't already own."[17] What does he mean by this?
3. Gotham's corporate name alludes to the morally ambiguous superhero vigilante: Batman. While Gotham does identify corporate wrongdoing and benefits from it, some see Gotham as causing harm to other investors by reducing the value of their shares and by taking advantage of an information asymmetry. Do you think Gotham is taking advantage of an information asymmetry relative to other shareholders, and is it being deliberately predatory toward unknowing and innocent investors? Explain your answer in terms of Heath's ten commandments and stakeholder values.
4. Most companies do not allow its employees to borrow shares from its investors for the purpose of short selling. What reasons can you give for this policy?
5. Suppose you held shares in a company targeted by a short seller such as Gotham. Would you accept an offer to borrow your shares? Or would you take such an offer as a signal to sell those shares while they are overvalued? How would you decide?

corporation negligently causes the death of a person, for instance, we should remove it from society. As mentioned, very few charters in history have been revoked. It is therefore extremely difficult to predict what would happen if lawyers or politicians were to take Bakan's advice and attempt to start dissolving corporations that they found miscreant. It is possible that corporations wield too much power in society and the charter revocation laws themselves might be appealed and overthrown. But at present, charter revocation laws exist and serve as the ultimate potential check on corporate power. If corporations behave in a manner that is detrimental to society, society can make them cease to exist.

The consumer boycott, shareholder activism, and charter revocation are all exciting possibilities that exist outside of the normal corporate decision-making apparatus and can serve as correctives when that internal apparatus makes a mistake. It is worth remembering, however, what was said at the beginning of this section: stories of corporate malfeasance that would elicit these types of responses are news stories precisely because they are unusual. Most of the time, internal decision-making procedures will be sufficient to avoid calamity. But in the event that calamity does occur, it is important to be aware of the alternatives that exist.

Summing Up

If a business is able to incentivize the right kind of behaviour from those who work on its behalf (that is, behaviour that is prudentially rational and ethically justifiable), then all is well and good. But if a business does not take care, and ends up incentivizing the wrong kind of behaviour from those who work on its behalf (that is, behaviour that is detrimental, unethical, or illegal), then things can go badly for the business in a hurry. Hostile work environments, lawsuits, criminal investigations, and loss of public trust are generally bad for profit-seeking businesses.

We respond to incentives in predictable ways. But that does not justify illegal, unethical, or grossly self-serving behaviour. We are on the proverbial hook for how we respond to incentives, and people will hold us accountable, especially if their money is on the line. Incentives matter.

For Discussion and Review

1. Corporate assets are held by the corporation itself, not its individual shareholders. Explain how sole corporate ownership benefits both the corporation and the shareholders.
2. Identify examples of corporations that are not intended to make a profit for their shareholders. What do these corporations value?
3. How does the principal–agent problem relate to moral hazard and perverse incentives?
4. Does corporate structure lend itself to the production of moral hazard? Explain your answer.

5. Think of a time you faced a work- or school-related perverse incentive. What was the incentive that could be exploited? What kept you from (or led you to) taking advantage of the incentive?

6. Explain how consumer activism such as boycotts can lead to changes in corporate focus.

7. Research another instance of shareholder activism that led to the resignation of board members or executives. What motivated the assertion of shareholder rights against the directors? Was the outcome beneficial to the shareholders in the short term or the long term?

8. Revoking a corporation's charter can be seen as punishing the innocent shareholders and employees along with the persons guilty of wrongdoing. How is this similar to the tragedy of the commons?

Further Reading

Demirag, Istemi, ed. *Corporate Social Responsibility, Accountability, and Governance: Global Perspectives.* London, UK: Routledge, 2017.

Liao, Carol. "The Next Stage of CSR for Canada: Transformational Corporate Governance, Hybrid Legal Structures, and the Growth of Social Enterprise." *McGill International Journal of Sustainable Development Law and Policy* 9, no. 1 (2013): 53–85.

Organisation for Economic Co-operation and Development. *OECD Corporate Governance Factbook 2019.* www.oecd.org/corporate/corporate-governance-factbook.htm.

Salterio, Steven E., Joan E.D. Conrod, and Regan N. Schmidt, "Canadian Evidence of Adherence to 'Comply or Explain' Corporate Governance Codes: An International Comparison." *Accounting Perspectives* 12, no. 1 (March 2013): 23–51.

Tricker, Bob. *Corporate Governance: Principles, Policies, and Practices.* 3rd edn. Oxford, UK: Oxford University Press, 2015.

CHAPTER 10
Strategic Negotiations

By the end of this chapter you should be able to

- List various strategic moves to facilitate negotiation.

- Evaluate zero-sum and fixed-pie thinking from a strategic standpoint.

- Distinguish and evaluate positional bargaining and integrative bargaining.

- Apply game-theory reasoning to social action problems.

In many of the previous chapters, we developed the idea that each one of us has a conception of what it means to live well, and we quite often disagree about what that looks like. We claimed that different people can have different values and can give ethically defensible reasons for holding them. These differences can give rise to ethical disagreements, which, if left unresolved, will get in the way of organizational success. Our goal should be to resolve these kinds of issues co-operatively and constructively. Therefore, it is in our interest to learn how to navigate, negotiate, and make ethically defensible strategic moves. Consider the following example.

Suppose a professor has a strict policy concerning term tests: students who miss a test need compelling documentation to support a request to write it later. Four students had been out socializing the night before and missed the early-morning test. They thought they could game their professor and agreed to tell her that the car they had been in had had a flat tire, and that the test was over by the time they made it to campus. The professor asked to see the receipt for the tire repair, but the students said they had simply changed the tire themselves. Nevertheless, the professor agreed to have them all write a make-up test. The four students were quite pleased with themselves. When the time came for the make-up test, the professor sat each student in a different room and handed each of them a single sheet of paper with just one question on it: "Which tire was flat?"

There are two morals to this example. First, do not set out to "game" someone without first thinking through the full consequences of your decisions. The students failed to look ahead to what the professor might do and reason backwards to the conclusion that they should probably not pick a battle that they could not win. Second, learn to recognize when you are in a strategic interaction and adjust your decision making accordingly. The interaction between the professor and the students was a strategic one, but the students failed to recognize it as such and, because of this, made a hubristic decision and betrayed their professor's trust. Trust is hard to rebuild after an ill-conceived stunt like this.

See **Chapter 6** and **Appendix B** for more about game theory.

We introduced *zero-sum games* in **Chapter 6**. Zero-sum games have a clear winner and loser, with one player's success coming at the expense of the other player.

Strategic Moves

Our decisions are rarely made in isolation of others making similar decisions, and we can avoid strategic traps if we are able to recognize when our interests and decisions are entangled with those of others. Game theory can teach us a lot about how to negotiate using strategic moves.

Strategic moves are not necessarily sneaky or underhanded. They are simply tools to transform the negotiating game into a scenario where you have a good chance of getting what you want, while still leaving your **interlocutor** with something they want. It is important to remember that negotiations are rarely zero-sum. Even if you can have perfectly aligned interests with another person, you may still find yourself needing to make strategic moves while negotiating with them. For example, if you choose to partner with another person to create value for your respective shareholders, you will still need to negotiate how the rewards of your creative labour are divided up. Of course, there will be times when your interests with an interlocutor will only partially align, which makes negotiating a higher stakes game. Things can go badly for us if we misread a situation or misplay a strategic move.

interlocutor
A party with whom you are engaged in a game or negotiation. This term is more appropriate than *adversary* or *opponent* because not all negotiations are adversarial in nature. Even in those cases where negotiations *are* adversarial, it is important to keep in mind that your adversary is not always your enemy.

CONCEPT CHECK

10.1 What is an interlocutor?

a. It is a person who takes part in a dialogue.

b. It is another name for a locksmith.

c. It is a person who avoids conflict at all costs.

d. It is a location tracker.

Credibility

credibility
A person has credibility if they are willing to act, have the power to act, and have the means with which to act on their stated intentions. Credibility also means having a reputation for following through on stated intentions.

If you are going to make an effective strategic move, you must have a certain degree of **credibility** with your interlocutor. Having credibility means that your interlocutor knows that you have the willingness, power, and means with which to make good on your stated intentions. If your interlocutor knows (or senses) that you are not willing to act, or do not

BACKGROUND

Credibility versus Trust

Credibility is not the same thing as *trust*. If you trust someone, you have confidence that you can place something of value in their care. For example, if Jim trusts Greg, Jim knows that he can lend Greg his car and be confident that Greg will not turn around and sell it to an auto wrecker. Credibility, in contrast, is simply having a reputation for following through on a promise or threat. For example, let us say that Greg asks to borrow Jim's car. Let us also say that Greg promises to sell Jim's car to an auto wrecker, and has a reputation for doing that sort of thing. In this case, Greg's promise is credible, but Jim should not trust him with his car.

CONCEPT CHECK

10.2 What is the relationship between credibility and trust?

a. One can be trustworthy without being credible.

b. One can be credible without being trustworthy.

c. This is a trick question. They are the same concept.

d. If you are trustworthy, you cannot be credible at the same time.

have the power to act, or do not have the means with which to carry out your stated intentions, you will have no credibility and will therefore be at a disadvantage in any subsequent attempt to negotiate.

Credibility, when combined with honesty and integrity, is a catalyst to good negotiating. Honesty and integrity mean the negotiation will be carried out in good faith, but credibility means that the parties can accept and deliver what was agreed, knowing that the interests of all parties have been addressed, if not met. Without credibility, the parties run the risk of having all the good intentions go unfulfilled. If that risk becomes a reality, then a new set of negotiations to manage the breaches, defaults, and contingencies is required. Since at least one party will have suffered harm, a **win-win outcome** will no longer possible, so these additional negotiations will be adversarial rather than co-operative.

win-win outcome
An outcome that is satisfactory or better for all parties involved; the parties all improve their situation or attain a net benefit.

CONCEPT CHECK

10.3 What does it mean to have credibility in making a strategic move?

a. It means that you can convince your interlocutor that you are able and willing to make good on your intentions.

b. It means having more information than your interlocutor.

c. It involves not trusting your interlocutor.

d. It means that you are unable to convince your interlocutor that you are acting in the interests of your organization.

Making Strategic Moves

There is a maxim that surrounds any negotiation: *until everything is settled, nothing is settled.* Any partial agreement can fall apart until there is complete agreement. All of the strategic moves described in this section are designed to keep you from losing ground with respect to your interests. Most of these are applicable at the beginning stages of negotiation, but some are designed to hold partial agreements together long enough to arrive at a final one.

Limit Your Options

One strategic move is to limit *your* options. This seems counterintuitive, because it takes away some of your flexibility in negotiating. The strategic advantage comes from dispelling any ideas your interlocutor has about you needing a deal at any cost. It also sets parameters for the negotiations, keeping them from expanding beyond the original purpose of meeting in the first place.

One way of limiting your options is to adopt a strategy of *automatic fulfillment*. This is a **categorical** response to your interlocutor's actions. If a certain condition is violated,

categorical
Something that does not permit an exception for any reason.

the violation triggers an automatic, non-negotiable response intended to protect your interests and block further attempts to push you into a weaker position. Here is an example.

One of the authors of this text was in a position to advise senior management on the choice of database software to embed within a product. The company needed to provide a definite price to its customers. Any negotiation that did not deliver cost certainty would not succeed. In preliminary negotiations, Vendor *A* promised the company a lower initial price than its competitors to include the database software in its product, but expected a significant ongoing royalty based on how many database transactions took place each year. In a separate preliminary negotiation, Vendor *B* was willing to license the software for a slightly higher but fixed initial price with a limit on the number of client processes that could access the database server. Vendor *A*'s introduction of an ongoing royalty was an automatic deal-breaker because it meant the company could not provide cost certainty to its customers—a necessary condition for continued negotiations. The company went ahead with Vendor *B*.

Delegation is another strategy that can work to your advantage. You can delegate a part of the negotiation to an independent third party such as an arbitrator or regulatory body. It takes both parties out of this part of the negotiation and leaves it to someone who must follow established, well-understood procedures and policies to arrive at an appropriate set of obligations and exchanges. This kind of move is advantageous only if you know the third party's decision is not going to work against your interests, and it limits the moves your interlocutor can make to undermine your interests. Note that by doing this you are not necessarily undermining your interlocutor's interests. You are just limiting the scope of the negotiation to the things that you are willing to negotiate on, and deferring part of it to a competent and independent authority whose decision will become part of the final agreement.

CONCEPT CHECK

10.4 Which of the following is an example of delegation?

a. Greg is selling an expensive bike to Tim, and suggests that they use a direct deposit.

b. Greg is selling an expensive bike to Tim, and suggests that they use an online escrow service to facilitate the financial transaction.

c. Greg is selling an expensive bike to Tim, and suggests that they use cash.

d. Greg is selling an expensive bike to Tim, and Tim tricks Matt into watching his dog.

Another way to limit your options is to *burn bridges*. This can happen in two ways. The first way is to give up something of value—perhaps a business relationship with one of your interlocutor's competitors—as a signal that you will change something initially unrelated to the negotiation in order to move forward with the negotiation. For example, suppose your company is negotiating a purchase agreement with a company called Titiro-Hiko for some custom-purpose signal-processing devices. Titiro-Hiko also provides corporate data and voice communication services, but you currently purchase those services from their main competitor. Since your contract with Titiro-Hiko's main competitor is expiring in a year, you can invite Titiro-Hiko to make an offer for providing your communication services in order to secure a better price for the signal-processing devices. In other words, you signal to Titiro-Hiko that you are willing to *burn bridges* with their competitor if Titiro-Hiko is willing to cut you a deal.

The second way you can burn a bridge comes into play once you have arrived at a particular negotiating position: you can cut off any means of backing away from it. This kind of bridge-burning indicates that you are not willing to give back anything that has already been agreed to. It is a way of transforming something that has been negotiated into something that is no longer negotiable so progress can be made on the remaining issues. Both forms of burning bridges require that the negotiation start from scratch again if either party backs away from the partial agreement because what had been tentatively agreed in part turned out to be unacceptable after new considerations were added.

Finally, if things are not progressing in a way that addresses your interests, you can cut off communication for a period of time. This allows you (and your interlocutor) a chance to process what has taken place, re-evaluate strategies and priorities, or receive further instructions from superiors on how—or even whether—to continue negotiating. This means that you have to be willing to receive and acknowledge a message from your interlocutor. This strategy is useful if you know your interlocutor has to conclude negotiations quickly, as this will increase the chances of them relenting on one or more of the key sticking points in the negotiation.

Sometimes this means concluding the negotiation without an agreement, so before you cut off communication, you have to be prepared to move forward without one. Thus it is important to have a strong BATNA (best alternative to a negotiated agreement). We talk about this later in this chapter.

Adjust Your Expectations

You can also make a strategic move by changing the game itself. You do this in part by focusing on a satisfactory outcome, not necessarily a maximal one. This means striking a balance between several things that are simultaneously important, so the most desirable outcome for you may not be the one that your interlocutor expects it to be. Perhaps both of you will value your working relationship highly enough that you and your interlocutor will work toward something that is less than what someone using a pure maximizing strategy might negotiate. This is more likely to happen if both parties view the business relationship as an ongoing collaboration rather than a series of competitive one-off transactions.

For example, suppose your customer is developing a new product that relies on a component (say, a microprocessor) from your company. They are the first company to use this component in a commercial product. You have already agreed to a lower price from the customer as part of sharing the risk of using a new component. While your customer is not in the advertising business, you see that you can still use them to promote your component. You offer to reduce the price of the component a little further, reducing your company's monetary return on this particular deal, in exchange for having your company's logo displayed discreetly on the product and prominently at the trade show where the product is announced. While this reduces the expectations for the profit you will make from this customer, it also primes the market for your component, and may increase the demand for it as your customer's competitors develop new competing products. You have made a strategic move that might give you an advantage in other negotiations. It also indicates that your company has an interest in making your customer's product work well. You have given something up to benefit your initial customer, but you may gain more customers as a result.

Your reputation as a *collaborator* (that is, someone who fulfils their promises) or a *defector* (someone who does not) will affect how your interlocutor engages in negotiations. Reputations are not built on the basis of a single exchange, but over the course of several transactions. More importantly, reputations develop in the open as other parties observe your interactions. Suppose you are an independent accountant serving small businesses in your area. You earn a reputation for doing good work. Once your clients learn that you provide consistently good value, you can charge a bit more than your competitors for your services without losing your client base, since the risk of shifting the work to someone without an established reputation and facing an audit for improper accounting is not worth a small reduction in expenses. You also have an incentive to not overcharge because it costs more to replace a lost client than it does to retain one. There is an equilibrium that satisfies both parties' goals. Moreover, because your clients know you provide good value, they may well recommend your services to someone else, and your business will grow as a result. A good reputation lets you cultivate beneficial business relationships, ones where the negotiations acknowledge that there is more than just striking the best possible deal for your side at stake.

Another way to adjust expectations is to leverage strategic *irrationality* to attain a more favourable position. One of the writers enjoys playing cards with friends. They are not concerned so much with winning the game according to its rules as they are with having fun, and sometimes it is more fun to make sure someone else loses the game than to win it themselves. With respect to the rules of the card game, they are playing irrationally. But they are not playing the card game. They are only using the structure of the card game to play another larger game with a different individual payoff. This is a low-risk kind of irrationality, because it does not jeopardize future opportunities to play cards with those friends. However, there are scenarios where you can show willingness to risk a loss by acting irrationally in a negotiation, provided that your interlocutor will also lose something of value if you do act irrationally. The challenge here is to make a credible claim. If your interlocutor believes that you will act irrationally, that forces them to respond in a way that will minimize their potential loss rather than maximize a potential gain.

A scenario of this sort occurred in an ITV game show called *Golden Balls*. The game starts with four players, and two are eliminated through the preliminary stages of play. The final phase of the game has the structure of a prisoner's dilemma, except the two remaining players can negotiate before deciding how to act. A pot of money is available to be won. The players each secretly choose to either split the pot with the other, or to steal it from the other. If both players choose to steal the pot, nobody wins anything. If both players choose to split the pot, each takes half of the pot. If one player chooses to steal while the other player chooses to split, then the player who chose to steal wins the entire pot (the other player gets nothing).

In one episode of the game, one of the players (Nick Corrigan) declared that he was going to steal the pot (a threat) and then divide it evenly with the other player (Ibrahim Hussein) after the game if Ibrahim chose to split (a promise).[1] If Nick's threat was credible, Ibrahim had no winning move; he had to accept Nick's promise to divide the pot if he were to get anything at all, and the only way to have a pot to divide is to risk the loss and elect to split rather than steal. Game Table 10.1 shows the structure of the game.

See **Chapter 6** for more on the concept of *prisoner's dilemma*.

See **Appendix B** for explanation of how to read game tables.

	Ibrahim	
	Split	Steal
Split	£6,800 , £6,800	0 , £13,600
Steal	£13,600 , 0	0 , 0

Nick

Game Table 10.1 *Golden Balls* Payoff

The **dominant strategy** for both players is to steal, but if each plays their dominant strategy both players lose and leave with nothing. A rational negotiation on the basis of getting something rather than nothing would typically result in an agreement to split the pot—and Ibrahim proposed this. This seems like a reasonable strategy on the face of things since both players would leave the game with £6,800. But this is an unstable solution. If Nick agreed to Ibrahim's proposal and chose to split, he would risk being double-crossed by Ibrahim. "Reasonableness" aside, Nick made it clear that he was not going to go along with Ibrahim's suggestion. Instead, he dared Ibrahim to steal as well and risk getting nothing. So Ibrahim, in the hope of salvaging something in the face of a promise coupled with a credible threat, chose to split the pot. It turned out Nick's threat was not credible because he, too, chose to split the pot. Nick's apparently irrational declaration was an instance of **rational irrationality** since it had its desired effect: it forced Ibrahim to play as Nick wished, so he could then play to win something.

You can also willingly and strategically put yourself in a position to lose something if you fail to live up to the terms of a negotiated agreement. In other words, you demonstrate that you have an interest not only in completing the contract, but also doing so in a way that satisfies your customer. Putting yourself in this position involves making a *contract* with your interlocutor to not only do what was agreed in the negotiation, but also to pay a significant penalty if you do not live up to your end of the bargain. You then have an incentive to deliver on what was agreed, and your interlocutor knows that. But it is also in your interlocutor's interest that you satisfy the terms of the agreement, so the interlocutor has no incentive to thwart your efforts in an attempt to trigger the penalty. What could this kind of move look like?

Suppose Good & Wells is a construction company with a reputation for completing projects on time and on budget. Good & Wells provides reliable estimates for proposed projects, but competing companies have recently started submitting bids with significantly lower cost estimates. If cost is the only criterion for awarding a contract, Good & Wells will not get any more business. However, none of its competitors have delivered what was promised in those low-estimate projects, so its clients have had to spend more money than anticipated (and perhaps was available) to complete those projects. Good & Wells can also play the low-bid game,

dominant strategy
In game theory, we say that Act *A* strictly dominates Act *B* when Player 1 always does better by playing Act *A* no matter what Player 2 chooses to do.

rational irrationality
The use of apparently irrational tactics or strategies to help ensure that a (rational) goal will be attained.

See **Appendix B** for more on the concept of *dominant strategy*.

but that will make it no better than its competitors, and it will quickly lose its reputation for being a reliable company. So what it can do is make a strategic move: risk imposing a penalty upon itself by attaching a performance bond to each tendered project proposal. If Good & Wells fails to deliver the project within the agreed schedule and budget, the client keeps the bond. This provides prospective clients with a realistic cost estimate that can be budgeted for without any surprise additional costs. If there are cost overruns, the performance bond will cover those costs.

This leaves the competing construction companies with a choice. If they do not start doing the same thing, they will not win as many contracts because they are not willing to back up their contracts with a performance guarantee, so Good & Wells gets more business. If those companies do start offering performance bonds, then everyone benefits. Every construction company will operate in a way that promotes honest bidding because failure to do so has a real cost. A strategic move like this does more than change one negotiation for Good & Wells. It also changes any future negotiation with any construction company in the area. And it begins with the irrational—from the perspective of a rational maximizer—promise to impose a penalty on yourself for failing to fulfill a contract.

CONCEPT CHECK

10.5 What is irrational rationality?

a. It is a refusal to consult reason.

b. It involves deviating from rational expectations in order to produce a desired response from your interlocutor.

c. It involves an economy of scale.

d. It requires a blatant disregard for your opponent's autonomy.

Resisting Strategic Moves

Of course, strategic moves may be met by strategic countermoves. Some of these look just like strategic first moves. For example, you can threaten an irrational no-win scenario if your interlocutor is not moving in a direction that helps you meet your goals. Again, credibility is important. If your threat is not credible, a strategic irrational countermove will not have any effect. You can also cut off communication yourself, frustrating your interlocutor's attempt to express any movement or renewed interest on their part, at least until you are ready to respond.

If you see that a burned bridge leaves your interlocutor in a vulnerable position, you can also offer a retreat of sorts—on your terms. If your interlocutor accepts, then you have undermined the credibility of some of their strategic threats, and can use that knowledge to push the negotiations toward satisfying your interests. This runs the risk of turning the negotiations into a zero-sum game, but if you can make a strategic escape worth something to your interlocutor as well as yourself, then there is still room for both parties to come to an agreement.

You can also whittle away your interlocutor's unwillingness to give you something that you want through what Thomas Schelling has called **salami tactics**.[2] The idea is to get what

salami tactics
Dismantling the opposition of one's interlocutor by gradually securing apparently insignificant concessions. By the time your interlocutor realizes what has happened, it is too late for them to claw back on the concessions they have made. Sometimes this is called the *foot-in-the-door* technique.

you want from your interlocutor, not all at one time, but through a series of discrete and trivial requests. You achieve your larger objective by dividing it into smaller, easily attainable goals. The trick to succeeding at this strategy is to make each request trivial for your interlocutor to fulfill.

The salami tactic is much like the fable of the camel's nose.[3] A person is travelling through the desert with a camel, and stops for the night. As the sky is clear and the air is dry, the night becomes cool enough to be uncomfortable without some kind of shelter. The camel, being a wise and conniving creature that saves speech only for its own purposes, comments to the traveller, "Friend, the evening is cool, much cooler than the ones to which I am accustomed. But if I keep my nose warm, I believe that I shall be able to rest comfortably. Would you do me the kindness of letting me keep my nose in the tent?" The traveller, not being one who likes dealing with a stubborn camel in the morning, grants the request. A few moments later, the camel shivers and snorts, and then remarks in an entirely offhand manner, "Friend, this is great comfort. But my ears are sensitive to the cool and it is keeping me from sleep. I perceive that you are a gentle soul, so I ask that you, in your compassion, permit me to bring that much of my head into the tent." The traveller acquiesces. After a few more exchanges, the camel is sleeping comfortably inside the tent while the traveller is shivering in the cold, wondering how the camel had won the comforts of the tent. (Of course, the sleeping camel has now cut off communication, and can feign sleep longer than the traveller is willing to rant about being cold. In the morning it will be to the camel's advantage to be silent.)

In the fable of the camel's nose, the camel skilfully deploys salami tactics to secure shelter for the night.

CONCEPT CHECK

10.6 What is a salami tactic?

a. It is a trick to use to get free salami on your sub sandwich.

b. It is a way to keep some people from eating your Meat Lover's pizza.

c. It is a series of discrete but trivial requests to get what you want from your interlocutor.

d. It involves establishing dominance quickly in a negotiation.

To avoid falling victim to salami tactics, treat your interlocutor's strategic transgressions as matters of degree. Prepare a series of responses of increasing severity, but proportionate to the severity of the transgression. You want to make it not worth your interlocutor's effort to continue down that path, while offering an opportunity for them to move away from the offending position.

This kind of strategy played out on the global scene during the late 2010s. In June 2018, US President Donald Trump introduced heavy tariffs on imports of Canadian steel and aluminum. Then on 1 July, Canadian Prime Minister Justin Trudeau and his government responded with tariffs of equal value on select American products imported to Canada. This response was proportionate and discriminating. It aimed for maximum political impact by focusing on goods produced in areas that voted for Trump's party in the 2016 election. Canada's countermeasures were not intended to escalate the trade war, but were designed to offset the value of the tariffs on both sides of the border. Knowing that Trump was not a trustworthy interlocutor,[4] the Canadian government made a strategic move to stop further harm to the Canadian economy. In game-theory terms, this is a **tit-for-tat** strategy.

Finally, you can ask to be a *confidential exception* to one of your interlocutor's policies. If your interlocutor has a particular reputation that they wish to uphold, but the negotiations are pushing against that, you can offer to not tell anyone else about the special deal you received. If your interlocutor grants you the exception, you have another valuable piece of information: your interlocutor's policies themselves are negotiable. Now, it would be a breach of confidentiality (and since you have been entrusted with valuable information, also a breach of fiduciary duty) to let other companies know that you have received such an exception. However, if you are the one offering an exception while acting as an agent for someone else (for example, you are negotiating for a company with shareholders), you cannot keep the details of that agreement from the persons you are representing.

Strategic Sanctions

Sometimes a party to a negotiation decides that co-operation is not going to benefit them as much as acting unilaterally will, particularly if they believe that the other parties are not going to co-operate either. In a context of fear and distrust it is easy to think, "If I don't take advantage of them first, they're going to take advantage of me." The first move, then, can be described as a **pre-emptive strike** against the other parties.

---

tit-for-tat
A strategy of reciprocation in which a player chooses to mirror an opponent's gameplay. For example, if an opponent chooses to defect in a prisoner's dilemma, the player will respond by choosing to defect in the next game. Similarly, co-operation in one game will be met by co-operation in the next.

Fiduciary duties are discussed in **Chapters 3**, **4**, and **9**.

pre-emptive strike
In anticipation of non-co-operative play by your interlocutor, you might open with a non-co-operative move. This is most effective when you are reasonably certain that your interlocutor is planning a hostile attack, and your move has the ability to dismantle their capacity to carry out this attack.

While this move can bring an abrupt end to the negotiation, if all of the other parties are thinking strategically, it will only work once. Your reputation will be harmed if you defect, and that will affect future interactions. The other parties might choose to preclude repeating a pre-emptive strike simply by not inviting you to the table for a while. This kind of sanction leaves you having to justify whether the single victory was worth the downstream cost of not being able to make further gains in co-operation with others.

Sometimes the sanction takes the form of a poison-pill clause in future agreements. A defection automatically triggers this provision, which is intended to undermine the value of a strategic move against the other parties. Poison pills are often incorporated into shareholder agreements to prevent hostile parties from acquiring a controlling interest in a company. For example, if a company receives an unsolicited takeover bid, a poison pill could trigger the automatic issuance of more shares. This dilutes the value of individual shares—a harm to the current shareholders—but may make the takeover prohibitively expensive. Another kind of poison pill might terminate all parties' rights. For example, if the authors of this book believed that one of the authors would be disrespectful of the others to the extent that they would claim the work as their own and try to sell it independently, the group could put a clause in their authorial agreement that such a move immediately places the content in the public domain. This prevents the one person from unjustly enriching themselves at the expense of the others. (For the record, the authors did not do this.)

> **poison-pill clause**
> A clause in an agreement stipulating that certain hostile moves by the other party will automatically trigger a provision that will defuse the effect of the other party's move.

Strategic Moves and Social Action Problems

Strategic moves can help us avoid social action problems. Social action problems, for the most part, are the result of a strategic interaction gone awry: each player does what is in their self-interest, and everyone is worse off for it. The trick is to learn to recognize when a strategic interaction is about to devolve into a social action problem and take the appropriate steps to thwart it.

Back in Chapter 6 we introduced the free-rider problem and described it as a social action problem. One way to overcome a free-rider problem is through collective co-operation. This requires agreeing to an enforcement mechanism so everyone has an incentive to deliver on their commitments rather than reap the benefits of others' contributions without making any of their own. The enforcement mechanism also must include its own enforcement—the threat of punishment for not enforcing an agreement must be sufficient to make it worth the other team members' effort to enforce the free-rider's compliance with the agreement. The goal here is to make the temptation to shirk one's agreed duty too expensive to act on. The best outcome for each individual is the one where everyone satisfies their commitments.

> **collective co-operation**
> A strategy to avoid free-rider problems by using mechanisms to ensure the co-operation of group members.

Incentivizing collective co-operation through credible enforcement mechanisms is a crucial step in thwarting social action problems. Consider the following examples.

Acing the Exam Strategically

Peter Froelich, a computer science professor at Johns Hopkins University in Baltimore, Maryland, had a policy of grading students relative to the top performer in the class. The top performer received a grade of 100 per cent on the assessment, and everyone else's grade was awarded proportionately to that. This also meant that if the top score on a test was zero, it would earn a grade of 100 per cent, though this was never clearly stated. He operated under this

CASE STUDY

Strategic Moves Used by Ontario Teachers and the Ford Government

The negotiations between the Ontario government and the teachers' unions in 2019 and 2020 represent an ongoing process which, being carried out before the public, lets us see certain strategic considerations. The news sources will doubtless continue to provide examples of the various strategies we have discussed.

The Ontario government, under Premier Doug Ford, made plain its desire to reduce the costs of education, and it also knew that a strategy to accomplish this would be the threat of unilateral legislation putting a cap on the amount of any wage increase. However, the government is constrained by court rulings that any legislated cap first requires consultation with the affected workers, so it engaged in attempts to have consultations with the relevant teachers' unions. The unions in turn resisted such meetings, claiming that they were not genuine but were aimed at preparing the way to impose a cap.[5]

Imposing a cap before negotiations is certainly a form of limiting one's options. In this case the government is not burning bridges, but it is limiting what the unions' response could be. This move can also be seen as a pre-emptive strike, particularly if legislation capping salaries passes before contracts are negotiated, so the unions have an interest in blocking that move. Of course, if public sentiment turned strongly against an overly stringent cap, it is possible for the government to have limited its options unduly. There are other ways by which the government can limit its options—total budget amounts, regulations concerning class size, course requirements, rules about sick days, saving unused sick days for eventual retirement, and the like.

Another strategy is to change the conditions under discussion. The government has made the limit on class sizes in some schools higher, thus apparently reducing the number of teachers needed to teach those classes. This, too, is a pre-emptive strike to which the teachers cannot respond directly. But they can make it a matter of public concern by pointing out the effects on the quality of education.

The public's views in this area are important, since the government knows it could lose power if the voters decided that children's education has been harmed. But some commentators point to teachers' summer break and perceived shorter workday as a way of arguing that teachers are overpaid

---

See the discussion of perverse incentives in **Chapter 9**.

policy from 2005 to 2012, when students finally acted on this hidden incentive.[10] Students in one class used social media to coordinate a boycott of the final exam—though that did not stop some of them from (wisely) preparing for it just in case someone decided to break the boycott.

The strong incentive is to defect from the agreed-upon boycott, and it would take only one student to ruin the plan by writing the exam, in which case *everyone* would have to write the exam whether they were prepared for it or not in order to get a non-zero grade. The students recognized that they were facing a social action problem and acted together

and underworked,[6] trying to sway public opinion against the teachers. Such pronouncements misrepresent the working life of a teacher, but that detail seems to be lost on the voters who support the government in this matter.

Meanwhile, the province has made a small increase in absolute terms to the total education budget, allocating $24.66 billion for 2019–20, or $130 million more than it did for the previous year.[7] This announcement allows the government to say it is spending more on education, even though "3475 teaching positions will be eliminated by attrition,"[8] and "[p]er-pupil funding will be $12,246 for 2019–20, down from $12,300 this school year."[9] In negotiations like these, public opinion is an important part of the forces that decide the issue. The government wants to appeal to the public's interest in saving costs without significantly reducing quality, while the union wants to highlight the existing high quality, hard work, and devotion of teachers and emphasize that the government's plans will reduce student choices. Both sides of the dispute want to persuade the voting public of the superiority of their position and will frame the dispute in a way that serves their agenda.

An important ethical point to consider is that although blame should be assigned for any work stoppage, it should not always be attributed to the side that stops the work (for example, the striking workers, or the government that lock outs the workers). The strategic moves that led to the work stoppage must be examined to determine who was bargaining in good faith. Then the public can apply pressure to the blameworthy party to change their stance.

For Discussion

1. Explain how publicly fomenting the sentiment that teachers are overpaid and underworked is a strategic move.
2. How do the confirmation bias and attribution error (Chapter 3) affect how we assess the value of the work of other people (in this case, teachers)?
3. List all of the groups of stakeholders in a teachers' strike. What are the interests of each group? What are the underlying values of each group?
4. Examine the list you made in question three. What are the common interests among the stakeholder groups? What are the shared values of the various stakeholder groups?
5. Do you think it is possible to negotiate with another person or party if there are no shared interests or values? Explain.

to thwart it through coordination and co-operation. The students gathered outside the classroom where the test was to be written and a couple of them guarded the door until it was clear that no one was going to write it. Professor Froelich was surprised that the students managed to co-operate strategically to take advantage of the incentive, but still honoured his grading scheme: since every student received a zero on the final exam, the highest grade was zero, and therefore every student received a grade of 100 per cent on the final exam.

CONCEPT CHECK

10.7 What is one way to prevent collective co-operation from collapsing into a social action problem?

a. All co-operating parties agree to an enforcement mechanism, ensuring co-operation.

b. Everyone agrees to make just one person do all the work.

c. Go nuclear at every opportunity.

d. Buy out everyone's interests and sell back access at an inflated price.

Inflationary Incentives

Higher-education consultant Alex Usher has noted that educational institutions are engaged in a similar kind of cycle of escalating incentives to increase enrolment. Universities in Ontario have offered merit scholarships to attract high-performing students. Since the early 2000s, they have increased the value of these scholarships to stay ahead of the other universities in order to get a larger share of the provincial tuition subsidy. Usher observes, "All institutions are making themselves worse off because their net tuitions are all declining, yet no one can disengage because they are afraid they would lose share to others. And into the deal we get a complete devaluation of the word 'merit' because institutions are giving these awards to about 70% of incoming freshmen."[11]

What began as a strategic move to gain an advantage over the other universities turned—predictably—into a no-win, no-escape social action problem for all of the universities. No one university has the incentive to unilaterally disengage from this process of escalation; it is not entirely clear what strategic move can be made by a university to encourage other universities to disengage as well. The only plausible way out of this social action problem is through governmental regulatory intervention. In short, the government must step in to save the universities from themselves. The irony of suggesting the government step in to stop the social action problem is, unfortunately, that the government incentivized the **arms race** in the first place.

Heavy Lifting and Heavy Metal

Sometimes an arms race is mean-spirited rather than unintentional. For example, some smaller gyms do not have sophisticated music or video systems for their members to enjoy while they work out. One of the authors was a member of such a gym a few years ago. In this particular gym, there was a small sound system that was tuned to a local radio station. Musical tastes are intensely personal, so one radio station will not be acceptable to all of the members. One dissatisfied member took things into their own hands and brought their cellphone into the weight room. They did not bother to bring earbuds with them; they simply played the music loudly on their cellphone for everyone to hear. Their cellphone was not powerful enough to drown out the radio station, so it was just a noisy racket. Predictably, things escalated quickly. Another member brought in a very large, battery-operated stereo system that had enough power to drown out the cellphone and the gym's music system. The cacophony of conflicting

arms race
An escalation between competitors for supremacy. Although the phrase was originally used to describe a competition between nations for weapons superiority, the phrase can refer to any situation where each player refuses to back down because they fear they will lose if their opponent does not back down as well. Neither player has the incentive to move first.

sounds made it impossible for anyone to enjoy their workout. One self-serving move provoked others to respond in kind, ruining the experience for everyone.

A social action problem can become entrenched once ego and spite enter into the picture. Once people stop acting in good faith, there is no incentive on anyone's part to change their self-defeating strategy. In such a scenario, it would take a person of Herculean strength to detach themselves from their ego and seek a conciliatory way out. The only way out of this pattern of escalating selfishness would be for management to step in with the threat of expulsion from the gym for nuisance behaviour. The point is that co-operative and collaborative ways out of a social action problem are only possible if people act in good faith.

Ethical Disputes

Each one of us has a conception of what it means to be good. Each one of us has an idea of what makes an action right or wrong. And we are not always in agreement. We live in a pluralistic society, and the odds are that we will find ourselves working with others who subscribe to different ethical principles and embrace different values; hence, there is the possibility of disagreement when it comes to making ethical decisions in the workplace. These disagreements can get in the way when trying to make good decisions for the organization or the business that we are a part of. If left unchecked, these disagreements can become a liability, causing every decision to be made on prudential grounds alone without considering the impact those decisions have on persons and society.

We introduced you to an ethical decision-making model in Chapter 3 (with worksheets in Appendix A). If applied correctly, this decision-making model will help us put rigour to our thinking, and will help us better understand the nature of the ethical disagreement. We will be able to state the facts of the case, articulate our underlying values, and identify the ethical assumptions that each of us brings to the proverbial table. However, it is not enough to simply understand the nature of the disagreement. We must also learn how to negotiate with those who disagree with us. Ethical disputes do not need to be zero-sum; compromise is possible in many cases, and is often the better solution.

> Being willing to compromise does not mean acquiescence. Being willing to compromise means that you avoided an impasse and did not fall prey to zero-sum thinking. My-way-or-the-highway thinking can be hugely disruptive to an organization, and will prematurely cut off other ways of thinking about an issue.

Positions and Interests

Each party in a negotiation brings their own preconceptions and thought patterns along with them. The goal of a negotiation is to come to a mutually satisfying agreement. Some patterns of thinking make arriving at an agreement easier than others.

Zero-Sum Thinking

Zero-sum thinking is a bit like double-entry accounting. Every increase in one account is exactly offset by a decrease in another account. It is also like the pot in a game of poker, where everything a person wins comes directly from another player at the table. Each gain for one party comes with a corresponding and equal loss from the others. The goal of a zero-sum thinker in a negotiation is to walk away with everything and leave opponents with nothing. Zero-sum thinking can quickly turn a negotiation into an unhealthy competition.

When zero-sum thinking is misapplied, the parties to a negotiation treat each other as enemies—with all of the acrimony that entails. For example, consider a negotiation between

Zero-sum thinking is counterproductive. If no one else has anything to trade, you will not be able to trade, either.

Party *A* and Party *B*, and let us assume that the negotiation includes something of moral significance to Party *A*. If Party *B* adopts a zero-sum attitude and extracts a concession of moral significance from Party *A*, then Party *A* has incurred a significant loss. It may even be the case that Party *A*'s perceived value of the loss is greater than Party *B*'s perceived value of the concession. No one wins in this situation as any semblance of trust is destroyed and any hope of future co-operation or goodwill is decimated.

Zero-sum thinking should not be applied to ethical disagreements in business or the workplace. Because morality is unquantifiable, it does not divide parties into winners and losers. Ethics evaluates actions in terms of praiseworthiness and blameworthiness, permissibility and impermissibility. Ethics also has to account for any dirty hands that occur. But note well that assigning moral blame to one party does not come with a corresponding assignment of praise to the other—in other words, *negotiations involving ethical conflicts are never zero-sum games*. If the parties can overcome zero-sum thinking with respect to the ethical concerns in a negotiation, then all parties can come away knowing that, for all the other gains and losses, it was a deal done in good faith with candour and a concern for integrity. Overcoming zero-sum thinking in one part of the negotiation may also be a springboard to finding co-operative outcomes in other parts of the negotiation.

> The idea of dirty hands is discussed in **Chapter 3**.

Fixed-Pie Thinking

> **fixed-pie thinking**
> Assuming that the pool of benefits available from negotiating are fixed, so that any gain made by one party will be a loss for the other. This is problematic when it is in fact possible to find arrangements that would increase the pool of benefits available to both parties.

Distributing resources has been compared to slicing up a pie. Some people, anticipating a piece of the pie, hope for the largest piece available. If they expect the division to be equal, they watch to make sure their piece is not smaller than the others. This is **fixed-pie thinking**.

The two-player *ultimatum game* demonstrates fixed-pie thinking. Let us say that Player One is given ten dollars and must divide it between themself and Player Two. Player Two then has the option to accept or reject the offer. If Player Two accepts the offer made by Player One, then both players receive their allotted amounts. However, if Player Two rejects the offer, then neither player gets anything. So, for example, let us say that Irina is given the ten dollars and is instructed to make an offer to Maciej. There are many different ways that Irina could divide the ten dollars between herself and Maciej. She could, for example, offer four dollars to Maciej

Irina \ Maciej	Accept	Reject
Offer $1	$9 , $1	0 , 0
...	...	...
Offer $5	$5 , $5	0 , 0
...	...	...
Offer $9	$1 , $9	0 , 0

Game Table 10.2 Ultimatum Game Payoff Table

and keep six dollars for herself. Or she could offer two dollars to Maciej and opt to keep eight dollars for herself. The gameplay is represented in the truncated Game Table 10.2.

A close inspection of Table 10.2 should convince us that both players have a dominant strategy. On the assumption that something is better than nothing, Maciej's dominant strategy is to accept any offer from Irina. Knowing this, Irina will play her dominant strategy and keep nine dollars and only offer one dollar to Maciej (the upper-left quadrant). This is the outcome that game theory predicts. But what if Irina sees herself as a co-operator and not a competitor? We have noticed in our many years of playing this game in the classroom that students overwhelmingly play the ultimatum game as co-operators and split the pot 50/50. In those rare occasions that Player One offers just one dollar, the offer is soundly rejected by Player Two. Our hypothesis is that internalized norms of fairness motivate a fair division of the "pie."

Fixed-pie thinking can result in the **fixed-pie fallacy**. The fixed-pie fallacy is an error in reasoning that occurs when a person wrongly assumes that a resource is finite or fixed. Wealth, success, happiness, and jobs in a labour market are often mistaken as finite resources. It is wrong to assume that wealth is a finite resource. Overall wealth increases over time as economies grow. For this reason, it is also wrong to assume that the overall number of jobs in an economy is fixed. The fixed-pie fallacy can result in unhealthy competition in the

fixed-pie fallacy
An error in reasoning that occurs when a person wrongly assumes that a resource is finite or fixed.

workplace. Think about what can happen in the workplace when co-workers think that their success is only possible if their co-workers fail. Or think about the consequences of assuming that there is a fixed amount of happiness and that one person's happiness comes at the expense of another person's happiness. The fixed-pie fallacy can lead us to many wrong conclusions.

The point to take away is that sometimes a resource is fixed and finite, and in such a case fixed-pie thinking is appropriate. But fixed-pie thinking is not appropriate when a resource is wrongly assumed to be fixed and finite. In such a case, there has been an error in reasoning and the conclusions that are drawn from it can be a barrier to a successful negotiation.

CONCEPT CHECK

10.8 Which of the following illustrates the fixed-pie fallacy?

a. The fallacy is committed when the person who cuts the pie also distributes the pieces of pie to their co-workers.

b. The fallacy is committed when a resource is a public good.

c. The fallacy is committed when both parties agree to steal someone else's pie.

d. The fallacy is committed when it is wrongly assumed that the resource being negotiated for is fixed and finite.

If the metaphorical pie is too small to make bargaining for a slice worthwhile, then the negotiators have to look for a way to make that pie larger so each party can get something satisfying out of the deal. This may mean broadening the scope of negotiations to include other things of value to the parties, or thinking creatively about the problem in order to find a more general, wider-ranging solution to a whole class of related problems. This larger scope effectively "grows the pie" so each party can get more than they would have otherwise.

Consider an arena that hosts a competitive hockey league. There is a fixed amount of ice time in a week, and the arena does not have the funding to have staff on hand overnight. Meanwhile, because the arena is well-used, the teams have to use different arenas scattered across a large area to get enough time to practice. The teams, through the league, could offer to pay for staff as well as ice time in order to increase the amount of practice time the teams have at their home arena. If the offer is accepted, the ice-time pie has grown, the number of hours of labour required has gone up, teams' practices have become more consistent, the arena generates more revenue, and no one has had anything taken away from them. (This does not account for the effects of shift work on the health of employees; this requires a more creative solution.) The idea of growing the pie is not only to make efficient use of a resource, but to make more of the resource to use efficiently.

Types of Bargaining

If we get trapped in zero-sum and fixed-pie thinking, any attempt to find a co-operative and collaborative resolution to an ethical dispute in the workplace will be greatly hindered. Learning how to negotiate with the interests of your interlocutor in mind is an important skill to learn. There are two ways to approach negotiations. The first is called *positional bargaining*; the second is called *integrative* or *interest-based bargaining*.

Positional bargaining is often associated with zero-sum and fixed-pie thinking. Each party comes to the negotiation table with the same attitude: get as much of the pie as you can. Positional bargaining shows up in many kinds of negotiations, such as proposed joint ventures, investment agreements, and labour contracts. The parties know what they want to get out of the negotiation, and they will work hard to make sure that they get it, even if some of the objectives are incompatible with those of the other parties. Holding one's ground becomes more important than coming to an agreement.

Integrative bargaining helps avoid this kind of impasse. Instead of defending positions, the interlocutors set out what they hope to get from the agreement and identify the values or reasons that are behind taking those positions in the first place. This brings out the parties' interests and not just their desired outcomes. If there is some common interest, then there is a good starting point for finding a mutually agreeable outcome. The tone of the negotiation changes from *How do I get what I want?* to *How do we get what we each want?* The negotiations are integrated with parties' interests, not entrenched positions. As a result, the parties are more likely to negotiate what they need without necessarily getting everything they may want. If integrative negotiations are coupled with creative thinking about expanding the benefit for all parties, everyone is more likely to come away with something they wanted, and perhaps more of it than they thought possible going into the negotiation. This kind of mutually beneficial agreement is often described as a win-win outcome.

positional bargaining
An adversarial approach to bargaining in which the interlocutors focus on getting what they want without regard for one another's interests. This is also called *position-based bargaining*.

integrative bargaining
A co-operative approach to bargaining in which the interlocutors seek common ground and mutual benefit based on an understanding of one another's goals and interests. This is also called *interest-based bargaining*.

CONCEPT CHECK

10.9 What is positional bargaining?

a. It involves staking out a position and demanding that your opponent bend to your demands. This type of bargaining ignores common underlying interests.

b. It involves geocaching your values and forcing your interlocutor to guess what is in your head. This type of bargaining confounds underlying interests.

c. It involves staking out a position, and then acquiescing on the first counter-demand. This kind of bargaining produces common underlying interests.

d. It involves staking out a position that you know is unpalatable to your stakeholders. This kind of bargaining ignores common underlying interests.

10.10 Which of the following best describes integrative bargaining?

a. It involves advancing your interests at all costs.

b. It involves a hostile takeover of a competitor.

c. It involves seeking out underlying interests of all parties to a negotiation.

d. It involves alerting the press to the grand opening of a store where there will be a lot of bargains.

Moving from Positional to Integrative Bargaining

When the negotiating parties get stuck in positional bargaining and finally become aware that things are going nowhere, they need to change their approach. This involves introspection and evaluation of internal factors rather than attributing intransigence and bad faith to the other party. The questions to consider here are things like:

- Why am I holding to my principles?
- How does sticking to a principle advance my goals?
- Are my principles clear—both to me and to the other party?
- Will sticking to my principles cause me more harm than benefit in the long run?

If it becomes clear that holding tightly to your principles is keeping you from your negotiating goals, then the principles and goals may be incompatible. You may never reach an agreement on this set of principles.

This does not mean you have to give up your principles when negotiating. Instead, you can adopt a principle of co-operation and look for other shared principles. These are often expressed as interests or values, and basic interests can be captured by many different principles. Continue the process by asking yourself questions like these:

- What do I believe is important here?
- What does my interlocutor believe is important?
- What is our disagreement about?
- Is a compromise possible?
- What happens if compromise is not possible?

Once the interests or values are disclosed, you may find compatible, if not common, interests. Start working there. What can both parties offer to serve these interests? Then look to see how what is offered needs to be extended to address the most important considerations. Take time to stop and reflect on both the process and the progress. If you continue in this way, you will either come to the framework of an agreement, or you will have made a potential ally who has good stuff to offer, but not for the problem at hand. If you wind up negotiating with your interlocutor again, you will have a respectful relationship and a shared method to use in the new negotiation, and you will avoid the combative nature of positional bargaining entirely.

When No Agreement Is Possible

If negotiations just wind up frustrating both sides, it may be time to decide that there will be no agreement. It is unwise to go into a negotiation without a plan for responding to an offer you cannot accept. This should not be thought of as a kind of Plan B, which requires going back to the proverbial drawing board. Rather, this aspect of the plan is part of a potential exit strategy for the current Plan A. It also should not be thought of as a kind of fallback position. If negotiations have not advanced, you are not retreating from an established position; it only means that you have not moved from the starting point. This part of the plan merely maps out another direction to take, one that would have been reasonable if the opportunity to negotiate had never arisen. This part of the negotiation plan is known as **best alternative to a negotiated agreement** (BATNA).

best alternative to a negotiated agreement (BATNA)
A second-best plan that sets out what you will do if you cannot get what you need from a negotiation.

A BATNA allows you to begin moving in a different direction rather than remain stuck in a stalled (and increasingly heated) negotiation. The strategic benefit of a BATNA comes from being able to make a move when your interlocutor thinks you are blocked. This might provide an incentive for them to re-open negotiations on more favourable terms to you, since they will know you are capable of taking "no" for an answer. But be aware that your interlocutor is also likely to have a BATNA of their own, and that may mean that there is no next round of negotiating on the matter at hand.

When the negotiation is of moral significance to any of the parties, a BATNA is essential. It allows you to stand your ground if it looks like you will be asked to do something against your organization's code of ethics or a legal obligation, and it may save you from agreeing to something you cannot in good conscience—or even in accordance with statute—accept. A BATNA leaves you with a morally defensible alternative to proceeding with a deal that, should it ever come into public view, will not look good for you.

> Sometimes it can be necessary to take a stand against the unethical activities of the organization you work for. We discuss both internal mechanisms and whistle-blowing in **Chapter 11**.

Skills and Attitudes

Even though negotiations may be impersonal and goal-oriented, the interpersonal and professional skills of the negotiators also shape the proceedings. More competitive negotiators are good for positional bargaining, but ones who are able to see alignments and commonalities may foster a more co-operative integrative negotiation. The best negotiators know how to shift between the two styles to keep things moving on behalf of their principals.

Regardless of one's preferred negotiating style, there are certain things that any successful negotiator must bring to the table:

- beneficence
- non-malfeasance
- ability to maintain confidentiality
- ability to recognize and avoid conflicts of interest
- respectability
- credibility
- competence

Some of these are moral values, some are professional, and some are personal. These attributes and skills do not guarantee that all of your negotiations will end well, but you are not likely to come to a mutually beneficial agreement on anything if you lack any of these. A lack of competence makes you ineffective in defending the interests of those you represent. If you act in ways that intentionally harm your interlocutor (that is, you commit malfeasance or wrongdoing), they have no reason to continue with negotiations. If you are not respectable, you will be seen as unprofessional, and this will reflect badly on your organization. Overlooking potential **conflicts of interest** may cause legal headaches for both parties down the road. Any failing here will harm your reputation, and perhaps your organization's reputation as well. If you cause harm to your organization, you may find yourself undergoing an involuntary and unfavourable career transition without a chance to negotiate a severance.

> **conflict of interest**
> A situation in which your personal interests and goals conflict with the interests and goals you must maintain in your professional or public role.

CASE STUDY

From Positional to Integrative Bargaining: General Motors Oshawa Assembly

General Motors (GM) announced in November 2018 that it was going to close its Oshawa, Ontario assembly facility—one of the largest automobile plants in the world—in December 2019. Having operated a plant in Oshawa since 1918, GM had invested heavily in the plant, including a multi-billion-dollar refit during the 1980s and a reduced-emission paint facility in 2006.[12]

As might be expected, the community was not happy. Closing the plant would mean losing almost 3000 jobs across the company, most of those in Oshawa. This would be a huge economic blow to everyone in the city, challenging the abilities of families, downstream businesses, and the municipal government to manage the after-effects. Moreover, after a century of ongoing investment in new and flexible technology by GM, it looked like both implicit and explicit promises were being broken.

From the company's point of view, closing the plant was a strictly economic decision. The plant was producing only half of what it had been designed to make, in part because of costs, and in part because of the changing market for automobiles. Unifor, the union to which the hourly workers belong, saw things differently: they had a pre-existing agreement with GM that the plant would operate until September 2020.[13] From the union's point of view, the plant was GM's most flexible manufacturing facility and could switch from making one model to another quickly. The plant was the only automotive plant in North America that could make both cars and trucks. Additionally, there was a lot of support for the plant from both federal and provincial governments. Together, the Government of Canada and the Government of Ontario invested an equivalent of US$9.5 billion in the restructuring of the company following its bankruptcy in 2009 in order to preserve some GM jobs in Ontario.[14] From the union's perspective, all of these factors—the versatility of the plant along with government support—should have made the plant more attractive to operate, not less. Nonetheless, since the company's obligation is to make money, sustaining a money-losing plant runs counter to this obligation. The conflicting views, goals, and values seemed to be irreconcilable.

After Unifor ran a media campaign that was critical of GM,[15] the union and the company met to try to work out a transition agreement.[16] In May 2019, they jointly announced that GM would spend $170 million retooling the plant to make parts for its other factories, with an eye toward doing work for other companies as well. Some of the site will be used for a test track for vehicles incorporating new technologies. Kirsten Dziczek, the vice-president of industry, labour, and economics at the Center for Automotive Research in Ann Arbor, Michigan, observed, "Getting that kind of money is more than a stay

Applying the Concepts

None of what has been said here is of value unless it can be put to use in situations other than contrived textbook examples. Here are some examples where the tools of strategic ethical negotiations were used.

of execution and does allow them to fight for another day. That's better than closing."[17] GM Canada president Travis Hester, at a joint news conference with Unifor president Jerry Dias, proclaimed, "We are now so much more than a vehicle manufacturing facility. We are integrated into the future of our business, the future of our development and into an entire business model for parts manufacturing and accessory, aftermarket parts and component sets that will sustain us for at least ten years."[18]

In February 2020, GM announced that it was "committed to be in Oshawa for the long-term."[19] Although the shift in the GM business model preserved some jobs at the assembly plant, around 2600 people lost their jobs when vehicle production ended on 18 December 2019.[20]

The two options first being considered in 2018 were either to close the plant entirely, or to continue producing various vehicles. The disadvantage of the first option would be the financial loss to the workers, their families, and the community. The disadvantage of the second would be the financial loss to the corporation. The negotiations between GM and Unifor ultimately succeeded in finding an integrative and imaginative alternative to closing the plant: instead of making cars, the plant will now make parts; instead of selling exclusively to other units of GM, it will now sell to other companies.[21]

For Discussion

1. What kind of strategic move did Unifor make in response to the original announcement of the Oshawa plant's closure? Was it effective?
2. What were the interests of the company and the union? What interests did they have in common?
3. Is the negotiated solution described in this case study enough to be called an integrative solution? Or do we need to wait to see if further uses of this expensive manufacturing system lead to even more jobs?
4. Could a system have been put in place several years ago to plan for a reduced output of cars? If so, what might it have looked like?
5. Can you think of any better solution? (Hint: Work through the ethical decision-making model presented in Chapter 3.)
6. What is the appropriate weight of saving jobs and reducing impact to the community versus profit for GM? Justify your answer.
7. Contrast this case with the conflict between Ontario's government and its teachers earlier in this chapter. Do you think the teachers' unions and the Government of Ontario were interested in an integrative solution? Explain your answer.

Social Media and Privacy

Students interviewing for a co-operative (co-op) work term at a particular company were asked to give the company access to their Facebook profiles. This is not permitted in Canada, but it places those who point this out in a difficult position: either they provide their social media history to someone without any assurance of receiving a job offer or having that information protected from further distribution, or they are dropped from consideration in favour of a student who will give access to their Facebook profile. It is difficult for someone to prove to a judge or jury that a job was not offered because they did not accede to an illegal request during the interview, and trying to prove this takes more money for lawyers than a student can afford. There is no accessible legal recourse for the students who are otherwise qualified for the job but were not considered because they defended their own privacy rights.

Each student being interviewed has to make a strategic choice about how they are going to proceed, and they will proceed on the basis of how much they value their privacy and how much illegal activity they will allow the interviewer to get away with. This means the motivations for choosing how to proceed will vary from person to person. When understood as a prisoner's dilemma, this particular game has a single Nash equilibrium: every student reveals their Facebook profile to the interviewer. But this strategy is sub-optimal given that it comes at a personal cost of privacy. (As an exercise, construct the game table yourself.)

Some employers have tried less direct, more secretive ways to see candidates' Facebook profiles rather than ask outright for access to them. Jaganathan was a co-op student on a work term, and Wei was his manager. (Names have been changed to protect the parties' identities.) Wei discovered that Jaganathan's friend Paulo had applied to a co-op job for the following work term. Wei asked Jaganathan if he and Paulo were friends on Facebook. Jaganathan replied that they were. Wei then asked Jaganathan to add him as a friend so he could see Paulo's activity before deciding to offer him an interview. Jaganathan knew that he could not be readily fired for denying Wei's request. There was no fruitful negotiation to be had, since Jaganathan had a moral obligation toward Paulo to protect his information. Jaganathan asked for time to think things over. He went home and acted on his BATNA: he deleted his Facebook account.

Nash equilibrium
The best outcome a player can hope for, given the choices available to the other player(s).

See **Appendix B** for more on the Nash equilibrium.

Summing Up

We must resist the temptation to think that our ethical perspectives are always right and that others must bend their will to ours. Progress in the public sphere is made through co-operation and collaborative decision making. This decision-making process will invariably involve negotiations. The principles behind successful negotiations are simple. But that does not mean that negotiations will be easy, especially when ethical conceptions of what makes an action right or wrong are brought into the mix.

In this chapter, you have seen several strategies and techniques for keeping negotiations moving forward despite obstacles. You have also seen that not all negotiations have successful endings. Some ethical disputes, for instance, are without resolution and require a more confrontational approach. Whistle-blowing, which we consider in the next chapter, is one such confrontational approach.

For Discussion and Review

1. Has anyone tried to "game" you like the students in the opening example tried to "game" their professor (see page 205)? If so, how did you respond? Now that you have learned some things about strategy, would you respond differently? Explain how your strategy could counter your interlocutor's move.

2. Zero-sum thinking seems to be popular in the business world. What explains this phenomenon?

3. What might happen if each party in a negotiation comes to the table with both fixed-pie and zero-sum thinking? As a disinterested third party charged with ensuring a negotiated outcome occurs, what advice might you be able to give the two parties, and why would you give it?

4. How are arms-race scenarios related to moral hazard (see Chapter 6)? Explain using an example.

5. Have you or someone you know ever been able to use integrative bargaining? If so, how successful was the strategy?

6. Is any negotiation strategy inherently more ethical than others? Explain your answer.

7. Explain in your own words why it is important to have a BATNA in any negotiation.

8. Construct the game table for Facebook disclosure where the students value privacy over being considered for the position (see pages 227–8). What is the Nash equilibrium under these conditions? How is this situation similar to the example in the chapter regarding the students who all earned full marks by not writing the final exam (see pages 215–17)?

Further Reading

Alfredson, Tanya, and Azeta Cungu. "Negotiation Theory and Practice: A Review of the Literature." *EASYPol* module 179. Food and Agriculture Organization of the United Nations, 2008. http://www.fao.org/docs/up/easypol/550/4-5_Negotiation_background_paper_179EN.pdf.

Bazerman, Max H., and Margaret A. Neale. *Negotiating Rationally.* New York: Free Press, 1992.

Dietmeyer, Brian J., and Rob Kaplan. *Strategic Negotiation: A Breakthrough Process for Effective Business Negotiation.* Chicago: Dearborn Trade, 2004.

Dixit, Avinash K., and Barry J. Nalebuff. *The Art of Strategy: A Game Theorist's Guide to Success in Business and Life.* New York: Norton, 2008.

Fisher, Roger, William Ury, and Robert Patton. *Getting to Yes: Negotiating Agreement without Giving In.* Rev. edn, New York: Penguin, 2011.

CHAPTER 11
Whistle-Blowing and Codes of Ethics

By the end of this chapter you should be able to

- Explain what professional codes of ethics are and how they relate to public morality.

- Describe the motivations for whistle-blowing, along with the obstacles or undesirable consequences one might face should one decide to blow the whistle.

While there is a presumption of loyalty of an employee to an employer, this does not mean the employee must acquiesce to the employer in all things. It is quite the contrary. If a business is engaged in illegal or unethical behaviour, an employee is completely justified in bringing such activity to light. Depending on the nature of the activity, it may be an employee's legal or social duty to report this activity.

Up to this point in the text, we have emphasized the benefits of co-operation and collegiality in decision making. We have described the pernicious nature of social action problems and talked about strategic moves to thwart them. One strategic move that we saw in the last chapter is to respond with *rational irrationality*, though this involves a degree of trust and a commitment to co-operation with others. Because everyone has a particular conception of what makes an action right or wrong, there are bound to be ethical disagreements in the public sphere. With this in mind, we talked about how to negotiate at the level of underlying interests in order to seek a compromise when possible. In short, we have focused on positive ways to make ethical decisions and constructive ways to address ethical disagreements. This chapter differs in that it assumes that everything has been done to redress unethical—or illegal—activity, but that the problematic behaviour persists and requires a confrontational response.

Professional Expectations and Codes of Ethics

Whatever your chosen field of work, people will expect certain things from you and will hold you accountable to some sort of standard. Many professional bodies expect their members to comply with a professional **code of ethics**. Almost every profession establishes such guidelines for its members. These types of codes can be found in high-stakes, high-prestige environments such as medicine and legal practice, but also in more humble disciplines where you might not expect to find them, like archaeology, cosmetology, political science, and landscaping. Each of these professions encounters unique ethical dilemmas as part of their work and has developed community standards regarding the most appropriate ways to respond to them.

The ethical obligations of professionals have equivalents in other organizational settings. Corporations typically expect their employees to comply with a corporate code of ethics. The same is true for many universities, non-governmental organizations (NGOs), charities, governments, etc. A code of ethics is aspirational in nature and represents the **ethos** of an organization. A code of ethics should make expectations clear, provide a standard of conduct, and empower its constituents to make ethical decisions. It provides a framework for thinking about how to act in a way that is consistent with the organization's moral expectations, without getting into the details of what to do in each possible scenario.

code of ethics
A set of principles intended to guide the members of a profession or organization in carrying out their roles in accordance with ethical norms.

ethos
Describes the values that an organization considers to be its defining characteristics; it is a way of characterizing the spirit or culture of an organization. Here we are concerned with *ethos* in this ethical sense, not its rhetorical sense.

CONCEPT CHECK

11.1 What is a code of ethics?

a. It is aspirational in nature and represents the ethos of an organization.

b. It is a bunch of rules that makes people poor.

c. It is a bunch of rules that nobody follows.

d. It is a legally binding document.

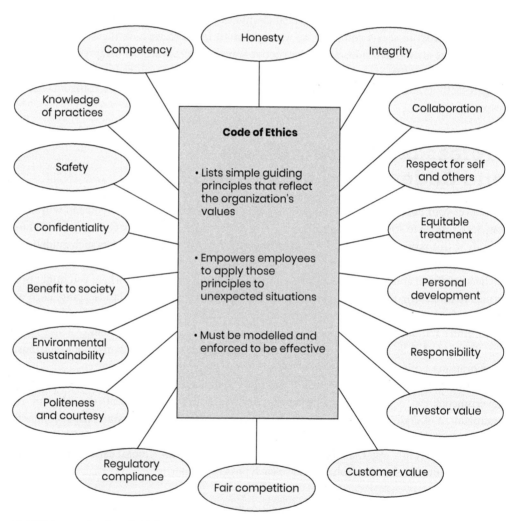

FIGURE 11.1 Code of ethics and values. A code of ethics captures the values that the organization wants to hold. The values shown in this diagram are typical of what businesses aspire to and expect their employees to uphold, although each organization's specific core values will differ. A code of conduct builds on these values to provide specific rules for behaviour and operation.

Some industries and organizations also have formal codes of conduct to guide behaviour. These are procedural, rule-oriented, and promote conformity. One significant problem with codes of conduct is that a set of rules cannot capture every possible scenario, and they can produce absurd results when they are applied uncritically in situations that were not anticipated when the rules were set down. Codes of conduct do not promote careful thinking about ethical matters. For this reason, we focus on codes of ethics, which are meant to guide decision making when the rules of a code of conduct do not apply. Interpreting a code of ethics takes careful thinking.

code of conduct
A set of rules specifying the behaviour expected of the members of a profession or other organization, in addition to disciplinary measures the organization may use in case of code violations.

We have distinguished numerous times in this text between private and public morality. Recall that public morality consists in the ethical considerations that you must make while acting as an agent on behalf of a principal. A professional or corporate code of ethics will inform these ethical considerations. But how should breaking a code of ethics be managed? Or what happens if an agent acting on behalf of a principal deliberately flouts a code of ethics, or worse, deliberately engages in illegal activity? If the system has well-functioning mechanisms, then the behaviour will be caught and punished. But such systems are frequently imperfect and the behaviour may go undetected. Misdeeds can only be corrected if they are first brought to light.

See **Chapter 3** for more on the distinction between public and private morality.

CONCEPT CHECK

11.2 What is the ethos of an organization?

a. It is the attempt by an organization to brand itself in a positive way.

b. An ethos describes the values that an organization considers to be its virtues, and is a way of characterizing the spirit of an organization.

c. It is the attempt by an organization to become credible by having celebrity endorsements.

d. An ethos is an attempt to justify maximizing profits.

Internal Reporting Mechanisms

One way to bring code violations to light is through an organization's internal mechanisms. Large organizations usually have an ethics officer or internal legal counsel who can advise on and adjudicate ethical concerns within an organization. Smaller ones may not have anyone explicitly charged to address ethical concerns, but that does not relieve them of the need to address as many ethical concerns as they can within the organization.

ethics officer
An individual charged with the task of ensuring that the employees and procedures of a corporation comply with its code of ethics.

An organization's code of ethics (provided it has one) will tell you how to raise an ethical concern. If the concern arises in the workplace, but your employer has no information about a process for resolving it, then start with your immediate manager. If the issue you are concerned with involves your immediate manager, the next appropriate step would be to contact your manager's manager, and so on.

Some people work in an environment that does not have such a clearly defined corporate structure. Even if you do not operate within a conventional business setting, there may still

CASE STUDY

The Problem of Accepting Gifts While Performing Your Job

On 26 November 2012, Swedish furniture company IKEA held an exclusive media preview party at its new store in Winnipeg, Manitoba. The company invited journalists, bloggers, and social media personalities to share in the celebration, which included "beer and champagne, live music, and a gift bag of free IKEA stuff, in addition to the chance to shop at the store with a 15 per cent discount."[1] Some members of the media accepted not only the invitation, but also the gifts that IKEA generously offered.

The problem is that the Canadian Association of Journalists has a code of ethics that tells its members, "We do not solicit gifts or favours for personal use. . . . We do not accept the free or reduced-rate use of valuable goods or services offered because of our position."[2] As journalism instructor Duncan McMonagle put it, "If you're dumb enough to go to IKEA and take a freebie from them and then go and pretend that you're reporting in a disinterested way, you're not that smart."[3]

CBC Manitoba sent a reporter along to the event to see who showed up and to ask IKEA about the ethics of giving gifts to members of the media. IKEA's spokesperson claimed that the event was benign, noting, "It's really to help, just kind of giving an opening look—showcase our products in a really good way and let people come and enjoy it."[4] Nick Russell, who wrote a book on media ethics, observed, "[W]hat IKEA is trying to do is make friends, to socialize the media so that they all feel warm and cuddly about IKEA, and that's not healthy."[5]

What happened? IKEA made an invitation to members of the media. Many members accepted the offer. But IKEA also knew that once the offer had been accepted, it had gained the reporters' favour, and that potentially would turn into an implicit bias toward IKEA in reports about the company and its new Winnipeg store. In exchange for the cost of the food, beverages, entertainment, and product, IKEA tried to influence those whose words and opinions were widely distributed without investing in a costly advertising campaign. The members of the media who took IKEA up on their offer had been gamed—their role in society had been undermined to serve IKEA's corporate goals rather than the goals of a free and independent press.

For Discussion

1. CBC Manitoba sent a reporter to ask about the ethics of having a media preview event. What could the reporter do to stay within the Canadian Association of Journalists' code of ethics during the event?

2. Do you think that the journalists who accepted IKEA's gifts would be able to report impartially or fairly on future stories about IKEA? Think in terms of human cognition and relationships and explain your answer.

3. Describe the interaction between IKEA and the members of the media as an informal strategic negotiation (see Chapter 10). What did IKEA offer, and what do you think the company was hoping to gain? Do you think they were successful? Explain.

4. Is it morally acceptable to violate a code of ethics at an event as long as you are not the first one to do it? Why or why not?

5. How can a code of ethics help you avoid compromising your integrity as a professional when such a code cannot give guidance about each specific situation?

be resources in place to pursue ethical concerns. For example, if the ethical concern involves a member of a self-regulating professional association, that association will likely have guidelines around behaviour and reporting. Groups like the Chartered Professional Accountants of Canada (CPA Canada), Professional Engineers Ontario (PEO), and the Medical Council of Canada (MCC) all have a stake in the behaviour of their members and will assist you with concerns.

In situations where there may have been a breach of ethics, it is important not to jump to premature conclusions or evaluations. Present your concerns without assigning blame, and explain as clearly as you can why you believe the matter poses an ethical problem that needs a resolution. Give the organization an opportunity to investigate and commit to letting you know when (but not necessarily how, if it involves matters of confidence) it has been resolved. If there is no movement after a reasonable period of time, remind them of the ethical concern and the shadow it could cast on the organization if it becomes public knowledge. Reassure them that you are not threatening to go public, only that you are concerned about what would happen if the matter did become public.

Be persistent. A large majority of ethical concerns can be resolved by way of these internal mechanisms. Most people want to do the right thing and many ethical lapses are due to an honest lack of awareness about the issue. This is why it is important to speak up and bring issues to the attention of the relevant parties in your workplace when you notice a problem. Use all of the internal mechanisms available to you until either the issue is resolved or the parties have given reasons why the ethical issue cannot be resolved within existing constraints. If it becomes clear that the organization is not interested in addressing the ethical problem, then—*and only then*—are you justified in "blowing the whistle" to attract the attention of an outside party.

> Ensuring the compliance of its members with ethical standards is part of the justification for allowing the professions to be self-regulating.

> Use the first two steps of the ethical decision-making model presented in **Chapter 3** to help you here.

> There may be ethical issues that cannot be resolved without leaving another ethical issue behind. See the discussions of *moral tragedy* in **Chapter 2** and *dirty hands* in **Chapter 3**.

Overcoming Internal Obstacles

As we have indicated, internal mechanisms for resolution almost always exist, but this does not mean that they always function well. Sometimes complaints are quietly ignored by the manager who receives them. This type of behaviour on the part of managers is potentially immoral, but the situation is often more complicated than that. Just as you, as a potential whistle-blower, must take many factors into consideration, so too does the manager to whom you initially report the concern. Correcting ethical lapses can potentially be expensive or embarrassing for the company. It may also give rise to a separate ethical issue elsewhere in the company that you are not aware of. None of this is meant to justify managers ignoring issues that are brought to their attention, but rather to capture the reality that many potential whistle-blowers experience in the workplace. This uncertainty about whether or not your complaint will be taken seriously can lead some whistle-blowers to keep quiet. This is not a desirable outcome. If no one points out ethical problems, they will not be resolved. So, this section will briefly look at three factors that can influence an individual's decision to report wrongdoing to their superiors.

Leadership

The first factor that can influence an employee's decision to report ethical wrongdoing is leadership. *Leadership* is a notoriously difficult word to define and can mean many different things to different people. The qualities discussed here are by no means an exhaustive list of what it means to be a good leader, but leadership plays an important role as the first point of contact for many ethical issues, so we believe it is worthwhile to explore a few common features of good leadership here.

In a business setting, good leaders will have strong communication skills, be compassionate, and be able to execute the changes that they set their mind to. All three of these characteristics will play an important role in whether or not internal reporting mechanisms function well. Is the boss easy to contact, or never in the office and unresponsive to emails? Do they show an interest in the well-being of their employees, or are they abrasive and unapproachable? Are they effective planners who are able to lay out the appropriate steps needed and get things done, or do projects frequently fizzle out and get forgotten? At each of these points, it is easy to see how an employee might be encouraged or discouraged as a result of reporting an issue to their manager.

Peer Influences

Two other factors that influence the decision to report ethical issues are peer support and peer pressure. Employees typically discuss ethical issues with friends and co-workers before they bring those concerns to management. What would you do if your friend pointed out an issue to you? Would you encourage them to do the right thing or to keep quiet? What if they do report the issue and the manager starts treating them unfairly? Would you stand up for your co-worker, or would you consider such retribution a risk that they brought on themselves? As we will learn later in this chapter, the decision to escalate from internal reporting procedures to whistle-blowing can come at immense personal cost. Knowing that one's friends will remain steadfast can greatly influence the types of hard decisions this chapter describes.

Professionalism

Lastly, beyond your immediate circle of friends and co-workers, there is sometimes a distinct professional culture that can influence an individual's decision about reporting an ethical issue. To illustrate this, consider a caricature of two very different professions: journalism and being a soldier. Journalism has a culture of speaking truth to power, and journalists are constantly exposed to public criticism of their opinions. Such an employee might be more inclined to pursue perceived injustices and not be dissuaded by the public scrutiny that might follow. Conversely, the military has a more rigid culture in which there are frequently good reasons not to disclose information and one is expected to follow orders. An employee in this type of environment might be less inclined to speak up when they see a potential problem. Both of these examples are caricatures, and most industries will exist somewhere in between the two, but they serve to illustrate the effect that culture can have on individuals. An employee needs to consider the kind of culture that exists in their industry and how it might affect them.

How to Think about Whistle-Blowing

Suppose that you have exhausted all of your organization's internal mechanisms for reporting potential ethics violations, and you have no evidence that the problem has been addressed. Do you have to do anything more? If so, what, and how?

A Public Act

Whistle-blowing has been described as "making public matters that organizations have ignored or wish to keep hidden but which constitute a significant wrong or an immediate danger."[6] Whistle-blowing draws attention to matters of public interest, not interpersonal ones. Whistle-blowing is a matter of last resort, to be used only when all other attempts to resolve an issue have been exhausted.

whistle-blowing
Releasing information to the public about an organization's wrongdoing that the organization has kept from the public and is not doing anything to address.

CONCEPT CHECK

11.3 Which of the following describes an aspect of whistle-blowing?

a. It keeps quiet matters of unethical or illegal activity.

b. It makes public unethical or illegal matters that an organization has ignored or wishes to keep hidden.

c. It raises concerns about ethical or legal matters to management.

d. It provides legal protection, since all whistles come with a warranty.

While it is a person's duty to society to draw attention to a wrongdoing that affects the public good, if that wrongdoing can be resolved using internal channels, then the organization may be perceived as flawed and perhaps guilty—but still proactive. There is no public involvement. Whistle-blowing, by contrast, is a public act. It involves public shame and perhaps government intervention (either through law enforcement or regulation) to force the organization to answer for its wrongdoing.

BACKGROUND

Internal versus External Whistle-Blowing

Whistle-blowing means drawing public attention to a threat of harm resulting from the activities of a business, or to actual observed wrongdoing perpetrated by the business. Some writers have a broader view of whistle-blowing than we do. They use the phrase *internal whistle-blowing* to describe using an organization's formal channels to address an ethical issue, and *external whistle-blowing* to describe what we call *whistle-blowing* in this chapter.

Luko Durda/Alamy

Tracy Fleury of Team Canada delivers a stone at the 2020 Continental Cup in London, Ontario. Curling has a code that expects players to call their own fouls, such as touching a moving stone or releasing the stone after it crosses the hog line. Whistle-blowing is a bit like calling a foul on your own team, but in a much more important context.

CONCEPT CHECK

11.4 Which of the following describes an aspect of whistle-blowing?

a. It draws attention to matters of public interest, not interpersonal ones.

b. It focuses on private morality, not public morality.

c. It encourages unhealthy competition in the workplace.

d. It is an example of pre-emptive reasoning.

A Conflict between Public and Private Morality

Whistle-blowing occurs when somebody makes an illegal, unethical, or otherwise incorrect practice public. Whistle-blowing is often done by an insider or somebody who works for the organization that is enacting the wrongdoing. As we will discover, whistle-blowing often means sacrificing personal and professional status for the sake of doing the right thing.

This is the crux of the whistle-blowing dilemma: the battle between our private and public moralities. Private morality refers to the values that we hold as individuals in our personal lives. We all have our own views on what is right or wrong—and this is perfectly appropriate in the personal sphere. Public morality refers to the organization's values that we must uphold as employees of that organization.

The question of whether to blow the whistle arises from a conflict between our private and public moralities. Our private morality might tell us that an organization's actions are wrong, but our public morality requires us to be loyal to the organization. If you decide that the wrongdoing is egregious enough that you have no choice but to become a whistle-blower, your private morality has overcome your public morality. If you choose to stay with the organization and keep quiet, your public morality has overcome your private morality. The tension between these two duties can be extremely difficult to navigate and it can be stressful trying to reach a decision. Fortunately, decisions are not always so stark, and exploring other options might uncover a compromise between the two.

BACKGROUND

Edward Snowden

Perhaps one of the best-known whistle-blowers in recent years has been Edward Snowden. In the early 2000s, Snowden worked for the USA's National Security Agency (NSA) and witnessed a massive expansion of state surveillance apparatus. Most of what the NSA was doing was technically legal, but Snowden still felt uncomfortable with the actions he saw; he decid-

Edward Snowden blew the whistle on surveillance activities of the National Security Agency in the United States.

ed to leak documents to the press revealing the nature and scope of the new programs.[7] The public shared his discomfort with what they learned. Subsequently, Snowden had to flee the USA to avoid prosecution under the Espionage Act and currently lives in exile in Russia.

CONCEPT CHECK

11.5 Which of the following describes an aspect of whistle-blowing?

a. It means ignoring professional obligations.

b. It means marginalizing stakeholders.

c. The choice to blow the whistle means that our private morality has overcome our public morality.

d. It means that we can do whatever we want to do.

A Matter of Public Duty

While the standards of public morality expect you to act in the interests of your organization, you may be a part of multiple organizations whose interests conflict. For example, if you have a professional engineering designation and work for a large engineering firm, you are a representative of both the corporation and your professional association. You are expected to serve the interests of both at the same time. This will be discussed further in the next section.

You may also recognize that you have a public duty to blow the whistle as a private member of society and not out of any obligation raised by being an agent for an organization. Regardless of which normative ethical theory you subscribe to, there is usually some responsibility toward other members of the moral community to protect them from harm when it is possible to do so; however, this duty may also come into conflict with the duties of public morality as an agent of a business or organization. No matter which way you look at things, whistle-blowing will involve a conflict of ethical obligations, and dirty hands are almost inevitable. Whistle-blowing rarely has a happy ending.

> Refer to **Chapter 2** for a discussion of ethical theories, and **Chapter 3** for a discussion of *dirty hands*.

CONCEPT CHECK

11.6 Which of the following describes an aspect of whistle-blowing?

a. It inevitably involves a conflict of ethical obligations.

b. It is the denial that there are competing ethical obligations.

c. It is the refusal to accept moral responsibility.

d. It involves moral defeat.

11.7 What is meant by *dirty hands*?

a. It is the idea that a morally justified course of action can still have a negative impact on the well-being of another party.

b. It is the idea that doing the right thing is futile.

c. It is the idea that doing the wrong thing is always the easiest.

d. It is a form of moral defeat.

To Blow the Whistle or Not to Blow the Whistle?

There are a few serious considerations to account for when you find yourself in a situation where you might blow the whistle. You might want to consider what incentives there might be, whether you are protected under applicable law, whether you have a duty to your profession, and what personal costs you might endure for blowing the whistle. We will go through each of these in turn.

Some regulatory agencies provide a reward to whistle-blowers if wrongdoing is confirmed. The Internal Revenue Service of the USA offers up to 30 per cent of recovered tax payments to whistle-blowers,[8] while the Ontario Securities Commission offers between fifty thousand and five million dollars, depending on the particular case, for information on breaches of the provincial Securities Act or Commodity Futures Act.[9] These agencies do not set aside a pool of money for paying whistle-blowers. The only reason a reward can be paid is that the agency has recovered some money—either what was owed, or a fine of some sort. However, there are stringent conditions for receiving such a reward and they place heavy demands on the whistle-blower to provide information and testimony. With the exception of these rare instances, there is no financial reward for blowing the whistle, so there is little incentive to do it.

This lack of incentive is compounded by a lack of protection. Protections for whistle-blowers under Canadian law are widely agreed to be outdated and inadequate. There are more protections for public-sector workers (that is, government workers) compared to private-sector workers, but even public-sector workers sorely lack protection under the Public Servants Disclosure Protection Act.[10] For example, public-sector workers have the option of requesting remedies to reduce the personal cost of whistle-blowing, but this is done through a tribunal that, as of 2017, had offered no remedies for whistle-blowers.[11] Private-sector workers, who are the majority of the workforce, have almost no protections at all.[12] A report released in 2017 suggested changes to the Public Servants Disclosure Protection Act,[13] but there was little follow-up and there remain virtually no protections for private-sector workers. What protection there is comes from the Criminal Code of Canada, which prohibits reprisals against whistle-blowers who report violations of applicable law.[14]

CONCEPT CHECK

11.8 What does it mean to say that whistle-blowing will inevitably involve dirty hands?

a. It means that you have failed in your legal obligations.

b. Since whistle-blowing will inevitably involve a conflict of ethical obligations, no matter what you choose to do, you will fail to fulfill one of your obligations.

c. It means that you cannot fulfill your duty to maximize profit.

d. It means that your public morality conflicts with your company's ethos.

The case of Quebec civil servant Louis Robert shows how difficult things can get for a whistle-blower who has legal protection. Robert had worked as an agronomist for the Quebec Ministry of Agriculture, Fisheries, and Food (MAPAQ) for 32 years when he made the decision to speak out against the way private companies had been interfering with MAPAQ's research into pesticide use. Although the law states that Robert should not have faced any repercussion as a result of his actions, he was fired in January 2019. The government minister in charge claimed that other factors led to the firing, but later that year a government ombudsman report cast doubt on that claim and Robert was offered his job back.[15] Should we be encouraged that Robert's legal protections were eventually upheld? Or worried that his boss showed a willingness to ignore the law and retaliate against a whistle-blower?

Despite there being few formal protections for whistle-blowers, you might have a duty to your profession to report illegal or unethical behaviour. Professions like accounting, engineering, and medicine are all governed by professional bodies that set codes of ethics and behavioural expectations for their members. Members who do not uphold the code of ethics and behave inappropriately may have their licence revoked or be removed from the professional body entirely. The loss of professional status would be career-ending.

It is important to take the code of ethics of your profession seriously and familiarize yourself with the expectations it places upon you independent of your organization's expectations of you. Having a duty to report illegal or unethical behaviour under your professional code of ethics may help you make a decision about blowing the whistle.

Finally, you must consider the potentially crushing personal costs to whistle-blowing. First, it is highly unlikely that you will be able to continue working with the organization that you blow the whistle on. Whistle-blowing is an act that is usually viewed as being disloyal, and your organization will believe that you are no longer trustworthy. It may also be extremely difficult to find another job once you leave your current organization. Whistle-blowing is done in the public eye, so you will likely attract local, and potentially regional and national, news coverage. Thus, your name and image will be associated with being disloyal to organizations or even your profession. Given this kind of negative publicity, other organizations will hesitate to hire you. It is important to note that, because of these factors, whistle-blowing is potentially career-ending and it may take a while for you to find a new job. Personal considerations like how much money you have saved, whether you have family to look after, and whether you are willing to retrain for another profession come into play.

CONCEPT CHECK

11.9 Which of the following describes an aspect of whistle-blowing?

a. It a perverse incentive to vilify your employer.

b. It is the first thing you do when confronted with an ethical issue.

c. It means that management has to send you to a resort for corporate alignment training.

d. It is a matter of last resort.

CASE STUDY

Evan Vokes and TransCanada Corporation

Evan Vokes was a materials engineer in pipeline standards for TransCanada Corporation. His work primarily concerned troubleshooting day-to-day problems with pipeline welding and materials. When Vokes began working for TransCanada in 2007, the company was already under fire from the Canadian National Energy Board (NEB) about compliance with safety codes. Around that time, TransCanada had been served three court orders from the NEB demanding that the company comply with certain pipeline construction regulations that they had violated. It was part of Vokes's job to ensure TransCanada complied with the court orders. For five years Vokes worked hard to get TransCanada to comply with the codes, suggesting changes and persisting even in the face of having his suggestions rejected.

In 2011, Vokes was fed up with what he saw to be a general "culture of non-compliance."[16] Time and again, he would see senior management prioritize speedy project completion over quality construction and inspection. The use of substandard materials was widespread, and it was a common practice for pipeline construction contractors to hire their own pipeline inspectors rather than have TransCanada hire them. This gave rise to a conflict of interest: because the inspectors were not operating independently of the construction contractors but working directly for them, they were susceptible to pressure to meet the contractors' goals of delivering a pipeline on time and on budget, not to meet the NEB's goals of public safety. Consequently, there was a risk that inspections would be cursory and incomplete, and the inspection reports would provide an inadequate basis for granting safety approval for the pipeline. Independent inspectors would be free from this pressure.

In an interview conducted for the Council of Canadians, Vokes identified how incentives for project managers and TransCanada executives are part of the problem. He explained that bonuses for executives and project managers are tied to financial performance; a financially performing pipeline is a finished pipeline with as much oil as possible rushing through it. Pipelines built with expensive, high-quality materials eat into bonuses, as do time-consuming external safety inspections. If it is this kind of system that makes a company tick, says Vokes, "It's just going to happen." Safety will inevitably fall to the wayside.[17]

Vokes voiced his concerns internally at first. He met with TransCanada's vice-president of operations, then later wrote a very frustrated letter to TransCanada's CEO, Russ Girling. A few days after Vokes wrote to the CEO, he was put on a mandatory stress leave. This was in November 2011. Unwilling to give up, Vokes decided to take his complaints to external parties. Between March and 1 May 2012, he submitted evidence of wrongdoing to the Association of Professional Engineers and Geoscientists of Alberta, the NEB, and the US Department of Transportation Pipeline and Hazardous Materials Safety Administration (PHMSA). On 8 May 2012, Vokes was fired from TransCanada.[18]

In June 2012, the NEB responded to Vokes's complaints by launching an internal audit of TransCanada. After some delay and disorganization, by October that year, the NEB issued a public letter to TransCanada indicating that many of Vokes's allegations (though they do not name Vokes in the letter) were valid and that action would be taken if TransCanada continued to break

Continued

compliance with specific regulations concerning welding inspections, the training of inspectors, and engineering standards.

Years later, the NEB also linked an explosion that happened in 2013 along the Bison pipeline that runs through Cree hunting grounds in Alberta to rejected advice that Vokes had offered TransCanada. The NEB acknowledged that Vokes had correctly identified safety issues with that stretch of pipeline but that TransCanada had neglected to address them.[19] This connection the NEB made was despite the regulators' initial audit back in 2012, which stated that Vokes's complaints did "'not represent immediate threats to the safety of people or the environment."[20] With respect to this incident, Vokes himself said that it was a miracle that no one ended up getting severely injured.[21]

Unlike many other whistle-blower stories in Canada, this story has a somewhat positive ending: Vokes's story was validated and he received public recognition for the risks he took and sacrifices he made. Nevertheless, Vokes lost his job and has since been unable to find permanent work. It also remains unclear how much good Vokes's whistle-blowing actually accomplished. Subsequent releases of internal documents and emails between the NEB and TransCanada showed both a slow and disorganized response on the part of the NEB to Vokes and questionable auditing practices. For instance, it turns out that TransCanada was actually given a heads-up about the audit before it commenced. This would have given the corporation time to address issues that they might not want on record. As well, some have argued that the NEB was particularly soft on TransCanada given the extent of its construction violations.[22]

Vokes himself is very disappointed about the extent to which pipeline building in Canada and the USA complies with construction codes. He says that even after appearing before the Canadian Senate to testify about the safety of pipelines in Canada, he received no support from the Canadian government and feels his testimony fell on unlistening ears. As for the USA, Vokes points out that pipeline construction is even more deregulated now than it was when he was working for TransCanada. The signing of the Pipeline Safety, Regulatory Certainty, and Job Creation Act of 2011 meant that, beginning in 2014, US pipeline companies were no longer obligated to abide by construction codes if those codes are not "made available to the public, free of charge, on an Internet website."[23] As it happens, the industry standard for pipeline construction code is a print manual that is available for purchase only. While the print manual is not expensive, it does not technically meet the "freely available" criterion simply because it must be purchased.[24]

For Discussion

1. Explain the problems that can arise if construction inspectors, who are responsible for ensuring safety, are not independent of the construction companies, who are responsible for delivering a project on time and on budget. How can this produce a conflict of interest?

2. It seems that Vokes was willing to sacrifice gains both to himself and the company he works for in order to produce the greater good. What ethical theory does this remind you of, and why?

3. Consider those who could be harmed by a faulty pipeline (consider plants and animals, too), who could gain financially from an inexpensively yet poorly constructed pipeline, or who has a reputation that could be harmed. Who are the morally relevant stakeholders in this case, and what do they stand to gain or lose?

4. It is clear that the parties involved have a conflict of values. What do they value, and how do those values conflict?

5. Who do you think is in the moral right here: TransCanada, Vokes, or the NEB? Why do you think this?

What Are My Options?

You may comprehend the extremely high personal costs of whistle-blowing yet still feel strong pressure to report the illegal or unethical behaviour. This is both admirable and understandable. The pressure to report may be so strong that you choose to blow the whistle regardless of its consequences. However, you may also feel that the consequences of whistle-blowing are too great and choose to remain complicit in the organization's wrongdoings. Finally, you may choose to make a compromise by walking away from the situation. You would do this by quitting your current organization and finding work elsewhere, but staying quiet about the illegal or unethical behaviour. This act would remove you from the troubling situation but would not remedy the situation itself.

If you choose to blow the whistle regardless of the consequences, you must recognize that it takes a tremendous amount of courage, **integrity**, and sense of justice to do so. You must be courageous, as the organization that you work for has more power than you do. They can—and likely will—vilify you in the media, fire you outright, or make your job very difficult until you choose to quit.

You must also be courageous to take on the extremely high personal costs of whistle-blowing discussed above. Integrity comes into play because, once you blow the whistle, you are effectively saying that your private morality trumps your public morality in this instance. You need to be confident in the assessment of the situation you have made. You must repeat your story over and over again, thinking that you are doing the right thing by reporting illegal or unethical behaviour.

You must commit to potentially lengthy media coverage that may invade your personal life, and you will not be able to rescind your comments or respond to all the sources of criticism. Again, since whistle-blowing is public, once you have already blown the whistle it is difficult for you to decide that the personal sacrifices are too much and retreat. Finally, you must have a strong sense of justice and know for yourself that you are doing the right thing by making all of these personal sacrifices. You will likely be driven by this sense of justice to blow the whistle and make things better for the remaining employees and the affected public.

Phaedra Al-Majid is one whistle-blower who has faced many tribulations. In December of 2010 it was announced that Qatar would host the 2022 FIFA World Cup. Qatar's suitability to host such an event was questionable for a number of reasons, giving rise to speculation as to how they had secured the decision. Al-Majid, a former employee of the Qatar bid team, brought one possible explanation to light. She gave testimony and evidence to FIFA's internal ethics panel, making allegations of bribery and corruption. For her bravery, Al-Majid has faced a double misfortune. First, no actions have been taken or punishments given out as a result of the misconduct she witnessed. Second, there have been credible threats made against her life and the life of her family leading her to seek FBI protection—which never came. To this day, Al-Majid fears for her safety.[25]

integrity
Holding firmly to what one knows to be right in the face of temptations to compromise one's principles for personal gain or in the face of pressure exerted by those who are less scrupulous.

The maxim known as *Zymurgy's First Law of Evolving System Dynamics* states, "Once you open a can of worms, the only way to re-can them is to use a larger can."

CONCEPT CHECK

11.10 Whistle-blowing requires:

a. a small amount of courage, a large amount of hostility, and a good lawyer.

b. a respectable amount of integrity, tremendous passion, and a willingness to look the other way.

c. a tremendous amount of courage, integrity, and sense of justice.

d. hostility, slyness, and stamina.

Whistle-blowing incurs a high personal cost. Any protections against formal reprisals do not protect the whistle-blower from informal ones such as smear campaigns, charges of disloyalty, and being excluded from the profession.

Whistle-blowing demands a lot of an individual. Given that there are very few or no protections for whistle-blowers in Canada, it makes sense that many of us would choose to stay quiet and dutifully go about our jobs. This is, of course, an option. You may decide that, for example, your personal obligations to your family are more important right now, or you may like your profession a lot and not want to change professions. It is important to recognize that being complicit does not necessarily mean that you are a coward. Staying quiet is a perfectly rational decision given the high costs of whistle-blowing.

Richard Grundy/CBC

Sylvie Therrien was fired from her job as a fraud investigator in Canada's Employment Insurance system in 2013. Her whistle-blowing claim was that her job was not to find fraud but to find reasons to disqualify persons from receiving benefits.[26] She engaged in a years-long battle with the federal government to get her job back.

Finally, your private morality may make it impossible for you to stay complicit, but you may also not be prepared to bear the costs of whistle-blowing. Thus, an option for you is to quit your position with your current organization and work elsewhere. If you decide to take this route, be prepared to reply when future employers ask you why you left your current organization. You do not want to expose the illegal or unethical behaviour and you do not want to sound as if you are disloyal to an organization, but you also do not want to lie. There are many creative ways that you could explain your departure to future employers that fulfill these criteria. You might say something like, "I disagreed with the organization's policies . . . ," or you might cite some unrelated but irritating part of working for that organization like, "I was often required to work overtime without notice."

Summing Up

Whistle-blowing is the last resort to correcting a wrong. Whistle-blowing is the process by which illegal or unethical behaviour is reported to a third party such as a regulatory body, the police, or the media. The decision to blow the whistle cannot be made lightly, and involves personal, professional, and legal considerations. Whistle-blowing almost always results in dirty hands. This is because the costs of blowing the whistle are life-changing and not necessarily in a positive way.

For Discussion and Review

1. Codes of conduct are often lists of rules about what must and must not be done in specific situations. They leave little room for interpretation or imagination. Codes of ethics are typically more general and require careful interpretation in each situation where the right thing to do is not immediately obvious. What kinds of behaviour are the two kinds of codes likely to produce?
2. Find five corporate or professional codes of ethics. What do they have in common? Would you expect these to be general features of any code of ethics? Why or why not?
3. How important is whistle-blowing to you? (Think about this both as a person in a position to blow the whistle and as a person being harmed by the behaviour that was not known about until someone blew the whistle.)
4. Explain how whistle-blowing relates to the distinction between public and private morality (see Chapter 3).
5. Could blowing the whistle to expose a genuine problem count as an unethical act? Try to think of some examples. (Recall the discussion of moral tragedy in Chapter 2 and dirty hands in Chapter 3.)
6. Should whistle-blowers have formal legal protection from retribution? Why or why not?

7. Should there be a financial (or similar) reward for whistle-blowing if the public is being harmed by the wrongful action? Why or why not? (Recall the discussions of perverse incentives and moral hazard in Chapter 6.)

8. Is there ever an obligation to blow the whistle? What personal consequences might follow from not blowing the whistle? How would you apply the ethical decision-making model (see Chapter 3 and the worksheets in Appendix A) to this kind of situation?

Further Reading

Boot, Eric R. *The Ethics of Whistle-Blowing*. Abingdon, UK: Routledge, 2019.

Bron, Ian. "Vile Wretches and Public Heroes: A Survey of Canadian Whistle-blowing Literature." *Canadian Public Administration* 62 no. 2 (June 2019): 356–61. https://doi.org/10.1111/capa.12324.

Kaptein, Muel. "Toward Effective Codes: Testing the Relationship with Unethical Behavior." *Journal of Business Ethics* 99 no. 2 (March 2011): 233–51.

Latan, Hengky, Charbel Jose Chiappetta Jabbour, and Ana Beatriz Lopes de Souza Jabbour. "To Blow or Not to Blow the Whistle: The Role of Rationalization in the Perceived Seriousness of Threats of Wrongdoing." *Journal of Business Ethics* (2019). https://doi.org/10.1007/s10551-019-04287-5.

McKinney, Joseph A., Tisha L. Emerson, and Mitchell J. Neubert. "The Effect of Ethical Codes on Ethical Perceptions of Actions toward Stakeholders." *Journal of Business Ethics* 97 no. 4 (December 2010): 505–16.

CHAPTER 12
Concluding Thoughts

In this text we have argued that you can make money and be professionally successful and still be ethical while doing it. You do not need to trade in your personal or corporate integrity in order to achieve business success in a free-market economy. Conversely, you do not have to give up doing business in order to live a morally upright life. We have aspired not only to argue for these points, but also to provide tools to help you equip yourself to live successfully and ethically in the workplace and society. This concluding chapter gives an overview of how we have attempted to achieve these goals. We begin by recapping the major ideas guiding our approach to business ethics and summarizing the way these ideas have played out across the content of Chapters 1 through 11. We then explain how engaging with the ideas we have presented can position you to work through challenging situations in the workplace with ethical panache.

Insofar as our actions affect the well-being of another person, ethics has something to say. Our actions in the course of doing business are no exception to this rule. If you only take one message away from this text, this should be it. Everything else we have said is rooted in the core idea that people doing business must listen to what ethics has to say, and that those who ignore the voice of ethics do so at their own peril. To make the same point more positively, allowing ethics to guide our business activities can help us combine success with a clear conscience, two things most of us value fairly highly. The authors of this text have painted a picture of ethical business according to three main interconnected ideas: pro-market ethics, pro-social business, and strategic co-operation in decision making. Let us briefly review each of these ideas.

Pro-Market Ethics

Business is a human activity that serves a social function—people who can participate freely in a co-operative, coordinated, or transactional setting can improve their well-being through economic exchanges that also improve the well-being of others. The fact that business activity has this function explains why society has good reason to encourage it; we should structure our institutions in a way that promotes effective business activity because we collectively benefit from such activity. The existence of a free-market economy is justified by these benefits, as we argued at greater length in Chapter 1. Although business activity in a free-market system involves competition, and competition goes against some of our everyday moral norms, we permit competition in this context because it increases efficiency; businesses in competition with each other tend to produce the things people want at prices that are more reasonable and with less waste.

A similar argument supports the practice of disruptive innovation, "a process whereby a smaller company with fewer resources is able to successfully challenge established incumbent businesses."[1] When a company disrupts a market by introducing an innovative and more cost-effective way of achieving customers' goals, this causes harm to the companies already established in that market. Nevertheless, we accept and encourage such disruption because of the gains in efficiency it produces.

All other things being equal, efficiency is a good thing, and waste is a bad thing. To that extent, rules that promote the proper functioning of the market are ethical rules. According to Joseph Heath's *market-failures approach* to business ethics—an approach we adopted in various places in this text—businesses are obligated to respect the norms that promote healthy market functioning. In Chapter 1 we summarized Heath's approach in what we called the *ten commandments of business ethics*. Throughout the text we gave attention to some of these pro-market rules when they were particularly relevant to the issues being discussed. In Chapter 7 we discussed the environmental and social costs of economic activity. These are negative externalities, and Heath's first commandment says people involved in business are obliged to minimize them. We talked about informational asymmetries in numerous chapters—7, 8, 9, and 10 in particular. In the context of advertising—Chapter 8—reducing informational asymmetries between firms and customers allows customers to make informed, autonomous choices. This is Heath's third commandment. The commandment to not engage in opportunistic behaviour toward customers is also relevant in Chapter 8. Any attempts to deceive, manipulate, or marginalize through advertising are patently unethical. We also talk about the principal–agent problem in numerous places in the text, particularly in Chapter 9. This is where Heath's command about not exploiting the diffusion of ownership comes into play.

When those in business follow these pro-market rules, they help ensure that market transactions are carried out efficiently. When these rules are violated, inefficiency results; people are hindered from getting the things they want at the best possible prices. Because the social function of business in a free-market context is to ensure an efficient distribution of goods, businesses that break pro-market norms are not playing fair, and deserve to be censured. Fair play in competition requires a strong degree of aligned interests with respect to the rules of the game. Without rules of fair play, business can devolve into something that is harmful to society. The ethical take-away for people in business is play fair; be a good sport; and do not engage in business practices that hinder market functioning.

> Recall from **Chapter 2** that under utilitarianism, doing what is morally right involves maximizing utility and minimizing disutility.

Pro-Social Business

As just argued, an efficient distribution of resources has great value for society, and the market promotes efficiency. Therefore, business activity should respect the norms that govern healthy market functioning. But other things are valuable in addition to efficiency, and so ethics has more to say to business than what the market-failures approach contains. In different ways, Chapter 4 (Corporate Social Responsibility), Chapter 5 (Fairness and Non-Discrimination), and Chapter 7 (Environment, Ethics, and Business) explore what traditional ethical theories contribute to the discussion. Chapter 4 makes the case that a firm's social responsibility extends beyond simply meeting its fiduciary obligations to shareholders and respecting the letter of the law. A business must recognize a broader base of stakeholders, including members of the society in which it operates and the environment on which all our lives depend. Chapter 5 envisions the place of business within a just and fair society, explaining the harms that result from inequality and discrimination in business. Business is not just for the young and able-bodied; no one should be precluded from the marketplace simply because of their age or their disabilities. In a similar way, business is not just for those who come from the right race, the right sexual orientation, the right religion, and the right class; no one should be precluded from the marketplace because of their race, religion, creed, gender, or sexual orientation. Chapter 7 examines the challenges of doing business while acknowledging the harmful effects it can have on the environment and the persons who depend on it to sustain their livelihoods.

An *efficient* distribution of resources might not be a fair distribution. Nor is efficiency in meeting the preferences of individuals who engage in business transactions always the best thing for society or for the environment. These are further reasons why people who engage in business must listen to what ethics has to say. Sometimes efficiency-based norms lead to the same conclusions as ethical principles. Minimizing negative externalities for pro-market reasons, for instance, may lead to better protection for the environment. Avoiding information asymmetries in advertising and marketing practices aligns nicely with the Kantian view that deception is intrinsically immoral. But efficiency-based norms do not always yield ethically optimal outcomes. For example, it might be efficient for a firm to discriminate against members of underprivileged groups, but doing so would not be consistent with the values of justice and fairness that are core to civil society. So, again, ethics places demands on business activity that go beyond purely market-based considerations.

Everything we have said so far might be accepted, and yet the cynic might still ask, "Isn't this idea of 'ethical business' unrealistic? Isn't business ethics a contradiction in terms?" Let us take a minute to revisit the reasons a person might think this way. News headlines set in bold 216-point capital letters screaming "Professor Grades Test Fairly" do not capture anyone's imagination. This is just reporting what ought to be done. The activities of most professionals and businesses are not newsworthy because they are done in ways that are not detrimental to the well-being of others. Breaking these moral norms, however, often does make headlines, and headlines get noticed. This creates a kind of collective confirmation bias toward believing that all businesses are unethical. But the negative examples we hear about in the news are exceptional cases. The list of businesses behaving badly, though it seems long, is still much shorter than the list of businesses behaving well. Paying attention only to the relatively short list of bad cases and ignoring the longer list of good examples can lead us to feel discouraged and hopeless. We end up thinking that it is only being realistic to expect that businesses will act in unethical ways, and we lose sight of the potentially great contributions that ethical businesses can and do make.

> In **Chapter 3** we discuss the confirmation bias along with other biases that can affect our ability to make good decisions.

Giving in to this discouragement can lead to admitting *moral defeat*. To admit moral defeat is to give up on any attempt to justify decisions on an ethical basis, and to make any subsequent decisions based on our narrow self-interest, for prudential reasons alone. To combat these tendencies toward cynicism and discouragement, we have attempted throughout this text to highlight examples of successful pro-social business—ethically exemplary people succeeding at their business ventures and turning a profit. Our aim has been to provide encouragement and guidance; if we look around, we can find many positive cases to learn from and

In **Chapter 6**, we explain how even self-interest, when it is not narrowly focused but "enlightened," opens up to include the interests of other people and makes room for co-operation. We also show how narrow self-interest, which does not consider the impact a decision will have on others, often turns out not really to be in our interest after all, when we consider the bigger picture.

good examples to follow. Doing the ethically right thing may not make headlines as readily, but at least it creates the possibility of being in the news for legitimate business successes rather than for moral failings. Carrying out business in a pro-social way not only passes the light-of-day test, but allows the entrepreneur to fall asleep at night with a clear conscience. These benefits sometimes turn out to be worth gold (in that reputational capital is increased), but in the final estimation are worth more than gold.

Strategic Co-Operation

In writing this text, we wanted to do more than merely describe, in a theoretical way, how pro-market ethics and pro-social business can work together. Our hope has been to go further by showing how these ideas can be put into practice and make a real difference for the better in people's lives and in our society. The text does not aspire to be a detailed instruction manual on how to make money ethically. Given the great diversity of business practices and social contexts, it would be impossible for us to be that specific. Nevertheless, we have provided a set of useful tools and ways of thinking that, if applied in specific business contexts, should help our readers to figure out for themselves how to be ethical disruptors—innovative yet co-operative and pro-social businesspeople.

Recall that ethical disruptors are opportunistic, but not in a way that unjustly exploits or undermines other persons. Ethical disruptors will anticipate problems and opportunities, and will subsequently carve out a niche in previously underdeveloped markets. But their interests remain aligned with relevant stakeholders, broadly conceived. This recognition of aligned interests constrains their market innovations. By constraining their behaviour in this way, ethical disruptors still play according to the rules of the game established by both social and market norms. Ethical disruptors do not disrupt the ethical norms of the markets, but disrupt those markets in ways that are consistent with ethics.

This text has provided three main resources for doing business ethically: a model for ethical decision making, a set of game-theory and strategic negotiation tools, and a kit of critical thinking skills.

Chapter 2 set the stage by discussing the major normative ethical theories advocated by contemporary ethicists, in order to help readers better understand and appreciate the language and key concepts of ethics. These ethical theories help us to identify the sorts of values that are properly ethical, as opposed to merely prudential. The diversity of established ethical theories also supports the view—known as *moral pluralism*—that distinct but equally legitimate ethical values can conflict with one another. This is especially relevant when different people with different ways of seeing the world have to work and make decisions together. In Chapter 3, we showed how to use ethical theories in the context of a *model for ethical decision making*. The abilities to understand the ethical interests of legitimate stakeholders, recognize when conflicting interests give rise to ethical issues, and strategize courses of action that will address these issues are key to the decision-making model we recommend. In our treatment of case studies in Chapters 2 through 11, we attempted to demonstrate how to use the decision model in the context of real-life situations in business. Increasing your ability to apply the principles captured in this model will give you guidance in dealing with ethical conflicts in the workplace.

BACKGROUND

Moral Pluralism

We all have our own ideas about what is morally right and wrong. These differences are rooted in intuitions captured by the different normative ethical theories, each of which has something important to say, while giving priority to different important moral values. Moral pluralism allows us to consider what matters to all relevant stakeholders in light of all of the applicable ethical theories. This gives us the opportunity to make a better decision on ethical grounds than we might have produced otherwise.

We have also provided, as a second resource to help equip our readers to live as ethical disruptors, a set of game-theory and strategic negotiation tools. Chapter 6 discussed social-contract theory and the difference between narrow and enlightened self-interest in order to contextualize some basic game-theory ideas. *Social action problems*, which often take the form of a *prisoner's dilemma*, illustrate how people following their narrow self-interest end up worse off than if they had learned to coordinate and co-operate with others. We then considered a number of real-life social action problems, and began to consider ways to "solve" such problems; that is, to find ways to secure the benefits of co-operation. Chapter 10 picked up this theme, explaining how an interest-based (integrative) approach to bargaining can help us to overcome *zero-sum thinking*. The strategies discussed in Chapter 10 share the goal of working toward solutions that are mutually beneficial. Trade makes us better off, and it is wrong to think of it as a zero-sum game. We often have aligned interests, even when we are in competition with each other. If we focus on locating areas where our own interests align with those of our interlocutors, we can find ways of increasing the pool of utility for everyone (*win-win* outcomes), instead of assuming that my gain is always a loss for my interlocutor and vice versa. Developing your abilities to locate common ground and to negotiate strategically to secure the benefits of co-operation will make you a valuable partner to your business partners—and even to your competitors.

> Appendix B has a detailed account of how to read a game table and how to play the best-response strategy.

Third, we have provided a kit of critical thinking skills and have demonstrated how these critically important skills can be applied to help us avoid various pitfalls that we are subject to because of our cognitive and social biases. In Chapter 3 we examined how limited evidence (either because it is not available or it is deemed not acceptable) and reactive interpretations can give rise to *confirmation biases* and *attribution errors* that prevent us from seeing things in their larger context. We also learned that these judgments are often made quickly, without reflection or analysis, and that it takes effort to overcome the bias blind spot in order to recognize and mitigate the effect of these cognitive shortcuts. Learning to be aware of your biases and how to take steps to counteract them will also serve you in other areas, such as creating a business strategy or designing a new product. This is because you will be less likely to minimize or overlook the impact your biases have on relevant stakeholders.

Throughout the text we promote an approach to ethical decision making that is collaborative and co-operative, and that values fairness. That said, we are being disingenuous to others and ourselves if we think that ethics is a matter of common sense and that doing the right thing is easy. It is not. Unfortunately, not everyone plays fair or thinks ethics is relevant, which is why whistle-blowing is such an important option to consider. Whistle-blowing is necessarily confrontational, and doing the right thing by calling out those who are violating laws, regulations, or codes of ethics will likely come at a huge personal cost. We discussed these issues in Chapter 11.

From the Gallery into the World

It is possible to make a financial gain in a way that meets the ethical requirements that enable society—and thus business—to flourish. But ethical decision making is a skill and, just like any other skill, it takes diligence and continuous practice to become competent. Furthermore, ethical decision making is a unique skill in that it requires the courage to resist the temptation to defect from market- and justice-based norms. Ethical decision making in business involves recognizing interdependence, anticipating opportunities for ethical disruption, and appreciating the moral constraints placed on how we do business.

Choosing the ethical path is not easy, and takes courage, integrity, and determination. It may feel at times that being ethical in the public sphere is putting you at a disadvantage. But take a sober second thought before stepping over the ethical boundaries set out by society: is my worry about losing out reflective of reality, or is it just my perception? Moving from "Others are behaving unethically" to "I should therefore be unethical" is a dangerous (and fallacious) inference. Thinking this way, in fact, can generate a type of social action problem: when everyone makes that inference, everyone is worse off for it. More than that, moral defeat should never be an option; the costs to ourselves and to others of giving up on ethics are simply too great.

We have now completed a tour of a gallery of important and connected ideas about business, humanity, economics, society, and ethics. This is just an introductory tour. There are other places to learn more about these ideas separately if you want. But if we want business, society, and individuals to flourish, we need to help each other see these connections, and to increase our awareness of the ways our actions have consequences that go beyond the ones we are most interested in. Even though our tour is ending, your journey continues. You now have some tools to help you navigate the world of business without bypassing ethical concerns. The sign saying "Here be dragons" at the borders of moral morasses should no longer be frightening. You have the means to lead others through those underexplored territories. We hope that these tools serve you—and others—well.

For Discussion and Review

1. How would you now respond to someone who claims that the phrase "business ethics" is a contradiction in terms? Elaborate.
2. "A market-efficiency argument without ethical considerations is _____." Fill in the blank and elaborate.

3. What does it mean to be an ethical disruptor? Can you think of an example of an industry in which disruptive innovation is an ethical imperative? Explain.

4. We have argued that the goal of Heath's ten commandments is to make markets fair and efficient. Consider the following claim: profit exists only because of market inefficiencies. Do you agree or disagree? Elaborate.

5. As a follow-up to question four, what is the moral status of seeking profit?

6. We made the claim that seeking profit is the only socially acceptable social action problem. Explain what this claim means and whether you agree or disagree with it.

7. "If you do not like the game, change the rules." What would this look like in the context of business? Who sets the rules? How can the rules be changed fairly and ethically?

8. "Lie, cheat, and steal. Do whatever it takes to succeed." What can we do to ensure that this type of advice is rejected as careless and ill-considered?

9. "I only care about fairness if it is to my advantage." Is this attitude consistent with what you now know about business ethics?

10. Choose one concept from this text that you found challenging. What did you find challenging about it? How have your ideas (or beliefs) changed as a result? Elaborate.

APPENDIX A

Ethical Decision-Making Model Worksheets

The decision-making model set out in Chapter 3 describes a process and suggests some questions to ask as you work toward resolving an ethical issue. However, it does not tell you how to weigh the competing criteria, obligations, and constraints as you work toward a decision. The following worksheets are designed to help you capture the information you need as you work through the decision-making process. Please note that Step 2 has two worksheets.

Step 1: Identify Relevant Facts

Set out the factual statements that describe the case. (Add or remove rows as needed. Put a checkmark in the relevant box when the answer is "yes.")

Factual statement	Morally relevant? (yes/no)	Prudentially relevant? (yes/no)
	☐	☐
	☐	☐
	☐	☐
	☐	☐
	☐	☐
	☐	☐
	☐	☐
	☐	☐
	☐	☐
What questions did you ask here?		

Step 2a: Identify Relevant Stakeholders

Gather information about who is being—or will be—affected and how. (Add or remove rows as needed.)

Potential stakeholder	What they stand to gain or lose	Has a proximal interest? (yes/no)	Has a genuine interest? (yes/no)
		☐	☐
		☐	☐
		☐	☐
		☐	☐
		☐	☐
		☐	☐
		☐	☐
		☐	☐
		☐	☐
		☐	☐

What questions did you ask here?

Step 2b: Identify Ethical Issues

Determine what the main ethical issues are. (Add or remove rows as needed.)

Potential ethical issue	Is this central to the problem? (yes/no)	Why is this a problem?
	☐	
	☐	
	☐	
	☐	
	☐	
	☐	
	☐	
	☐	

What questions did you ask here?

What is the main ethical issue, and why?

Step 3: Identify Stakeholder Values and Conflicts

Look for conflicting stakeholder values that need to be considered as you make your decision. (Add or remove rows as needed, but make sure you leave room for two or three values per stakeholder.)

Relevant stakeholder	Values important to this stakeholder	Is this a prudential value? (yes/no)	Is this a moral value? (yes/no)
		☐	☐
		☐	☐
		☐	☐
		☐	☐
		☐	☐
		☐	☐
		☐	☐
		☐	☐
		☐	☐
		☐	☐
		☐	☐
		☐	☐
		☐	☐
		☐	☐

What questions did you ask here?

Step 4: Create Resolution Strategies and Identify Consequences

This is both a creative and analytical step. Identify the consequences of doing nothing, and of any courses of action that do not shift the responsibility for managing the problem to another party. (Make sure you leave room for five alternatives in addition to the status quo.)

Status quo (do nothing)	Description:		
	Consequences		Values considered
Short term	Positive		
	Negative		
Long term	Positive		
	Negative		
Alternative 1	Description:		
	Consequences		Values considered
Short term	Positive		
	Negative		
Long term			
Alternative 2	Description:		
	Consequences		Values considered
Short term	Positive		
	Negative		
Long term	Positive		
	Negative		
Alternative 3	Description:		
	Consequences		Values considered
Short term	Positive		
	Negative		
Long term	Positive		
	Negative		
Alternative 4	Description:		
	Consequences		Values considered
Short term	Positive		
	Negative		

Long term	Positive	
	Negative	
Alternative 5	Description:	
Consequences		Values considered
Short term	Positive	
	Negative	
Long term	Positive	
	Negative	

Step 5: Assess the Resolution Strategies

Describe the main moral considerations and prudential benefits or constraints that weigh in favour of or against each course of action. (Make sure you leave room for five alternatives in addition to the status quo.)

	Moral considerations	Prudential considerations	How good a solution is this, and why?
Status quo (do nothing)			
Alternative 1			
Alternative 2			
Alternative 3			
Alternative 4			
Alternative 5			

Step 6: Recommend and Defend a Resolution Strategy

Taking into account both moral and prudential constraints, identify the best and second-best resolutions to the problem. Remember that the second-best option may not look anything like the preferred option.

Which action do you recommend?

Why is this the best solution?

What is the second-best solution?

What makes the second-best solution not as good as the first?

APPENDIX B

A Primer on Game Theory

What Is Game Theory?

Game theory allows us to model and analyze rational behaviour in **strategic interactions**. We can think of a strategic interaction as an individual decision made in a group context where others are making similar individual decisions. For example, your decision to drive your car to school or work is not made in isolation. Instead, it is made against the backdrop of other motorists deciding to do the same; when a critical mass of people decide to drive, the result is a high volume of traffic on the roads.

A traffic jam is an excellent example of a social action problem. Everyone individually does what is in their self-interest (driving their car), and everyone collectively is worse off for it (sitting in in a traffic jam). We talk a lot about social action problems in this textbook. They are pernicious problems and we do well when we understand why they happen. Game theory is well-suited to help us understand the logic of social action problems.

Games and Those Who Play Them

For the sake of simplicity we will call a strategic interaction a **game**. The word *game* in this context is understood very broadly. It can refer to games of amusement like chess, Monopoly, or Pokémon Go. It can refer to social interactions—like whether to let the person beside you exit the bus first, or to elbow your way in front of them. It can also refer to international relations that affect people around the globe—like dozens of countries deciding to sign an environmental treaty aimed at reducing the use of plastic.

Those who play games are called *players*. Again, the word *player* should be interpreted as broadly as possible. A player in a strategic interaction could be an individual person, a business, a charitable organization, a sports club, a government, or a nation. We want to use the word *player* because it is more neutral than words like *opponent* or *rival*. Not all games are rivalrous and zero-sum. In many types of games, players have partially aligned interests, and it makes sense to use a more inclusive term in contexts where co-operation is possible or even encouraged.

Modelling Games

Game theory allows us to rigorously model strategic interactions. A good game-theory model has two characteristics. First, a good model will be simple enough for us to understand. The world is a complex place and human decision making is complicated by psychological, social, and environmental factors. By simplifying our assumptions, a game-theory model can help us focus on what is important to us in a strategic interaction. Second, a good model will be sophisticated enough to teach us something about strategic interactions.

The games that we consider in this text consist of just two players. However, we sometimes generalize our conclusions about two-player games to make a broader point. Each player in a

strategic interaction
A situation where players must decide what to do based on what they think other players will choose to do.

game
For the purposes of game theory, a game is a strategic interaction between at least two players, with a definite outcome for each player.

See **Chapter 7** for a discussion of rivalrousness, and **Chapter 6** and **Chapter 10** for a discussion of zero-sum games.

payoffs
The outcome for each player. The payoff is a number that represents everything of measurable value to the player receiving the payoff. The payoff is a function of both players' choices.

Go to www.oup.com/he/Andres to find links to excellent online video demonstrations of how to use game tables.

game must choose an action from among many (like rock, paper, or scissors). Each game has payoffs. The payoffs of the game denote what is important to the players individually and are typically represented as numbers. The numbers can represent time, money, usefulness, points, happiness, or anything else that is measurable. The numbers can also represent the ranking of one's preferences. For example, if Bob prefers cycling to running, cycling would be represented with a number greater than the number representing running. This is all very abstract, so let us construct a game table and demonstrate out how to read it.

How to Read a Game Table

A game table identifies the players, the choices available to them, and the payoffs that result when both players make their choices. To see how to construct a game table and read the payoffs, let us construct a simple model of rush-hour traffic. The simplest type of game to model can be represented in a 2 × 2 table. See Game Table 1.

The choices of Rowe and Colombe are represented in Game Table 1. Rowe's choices are represented row by row. In this particular game, Rowe can choose to *bike* to work or take a *taxi*. Rowe's payoffs are to the left of the comma in each of the four quadrants. Colombe's choices are represented column by column. In this particular game, Colombe can choose to *walk* to school or *drive*. Colombe's payoffs are to the right of the comma in each quadrant.

Payoffs are a function of the choices that both players make. Here is how to read the player's payoffs for Game Table 1:

- Upper-left quadrant: If Rowe chooses to *bike* and Colombe chooses to *walk*, both players receive 3 units of happiness.
- Lower-left quadrant: If Rowe chooses to take a *taxi* and Colombe chooses to *walk*, Rowe receives 5 units of happiness and Colombe receives 0 units of happiness.

	Colombe	
	Walk	**Drive**
Rowe **Bike**	3 , 3	0 , 5
Taxi	5 , 0	1 , 1

Game Table 1 Rush-Hour Traffic

Rowe and Colombe are trying to decide how to get to work in the morning. Rowe can choose either to *bike* or take a *taxi*. Colombe can choose either to *walk* or *drive*. Their respective payoffs are represented in each quadrant. For this example, we can just think of the numbers as representing units of happiness. (The larger the number, the more happiness one has.)

- Upper-right quadrant: If Rowe chooses to *bike* and Colombe chooses to *drive*, Rowe receives 0 units of happiness and Colombe receives 5 units of happiness.
- Lower-right quadrant: If Rowe chooses to take a *taxi* to work and Colombe chooses to *drive* to work, both players receive 1 unit of happiness each.

Thinking of the payoffs in terms of units of happiness may seem odd, so here is another way to conceptualize what we are trying to capture with those values. If Rowe decides to ride a bike to work, and Colombe decides to walk to work, then both get some exercise and neither must sit in rush-hour gridlock. So we simply say, for the sake of ease of comparison, that Rowe and Colombe each receive 3 units of happiness. Compare this level of happiness to the scenario where both players decide to use a vehicle to get to work (Rowe takes a taxi, and Colombe drives). In this scenario, both Rowe and Colombe are much less happy—with only 1 unit of happiness each. Why the decrease in happiness? Driving is stressful, parking costs money, burning fuel is bad for the environment, and more vehicles on the road mean more congestion. As an old TomTom billboard message read, "You are not stuck in traffic. You are traffic."[1]

Dominance Reasoning

So how should Rowe and Colombe play the game? The answer no doubt seems obvious: if both Rowe and Colombe are happier when Rowe rides a bike and Colombe walks (see upper-left quadrant in Game Table 1), then surely this is what they should choose. But this choice is not the actual outcome of the game if both Rowe and Colombe play their rationally optimal strategy.

Let us reflect on Rowe's gameplay first. If Colombe chooses to *walk*, Rowe will do better by choosing to take a *taxi*. This is because a payoff of 5 points for Rowe is better than a payoff of 3 points. Similarly, if Colombe chooses to *drive*, Rowe will again do better by choosing to take a *taxi*. This is because a payoff of 1 point for Rowe is better than a payoff of 0 points. We can keep track of this by using blue circles to circle the 5 and the 1, as per Game Table 2. No matter what Colombe does, Rowe should choose to take a *taxi*. So, we say that Rowe's **dominant strategy** is to take a *taxi*.

dominant strategy
In game theory, we say that Act *A* strictly dominates Act *B* when Player 1 always does better by playing Act *A* no matter what Player 2 chooses to do.

Game Table 2 Rush-Hour Traffic—Rowe's Dominant Strategy
The blue circles show Rowe's dominant strategy. No matter what Colombe chooses to do, Rowe does better by choosing to take a *taxi*. Since 5 is greater than 3, we draw a blue circle around it in the lower-left quadrant. Since 1 is greater than 0, we draw a blue circle around it in the lower-right quadrant.

Colombe

	Walk		Drive	
Bike	3	, 3	0	, ⑤
Taxi	⑤	, 0	①	, ①

Rowe (row label)

Game Table 3 Rush-Hour Traffic—Colombe's Dominant Strategy

The red circles show Colombe's dominant strategy. No matter what Rowe chooses to do, Colombe does better by choosing to *drive*. Since 5 is greater than 3, we draw a red circle around it in the upper-right quadrant. Since 1 is greater than 0, we draw a red circle around it in the lower-right quadrant.

Turning our attention to Colombe's gameplay, we notice upon close examination that it is better for Colombe to *drive* no matter what Rowe chooses to do. If Rowe chooses to *bike*, Colombe will do better by choosing to *drive*. This is because a payoff of 5 points for Colombe is better than a payoff of 3 points. Similarly, if Rowe chooses to take a *taxi*, Colombe will again do better by choosing to *drive*. This is because a payoff of 1 point for Colombe is better than a payoff of 0 points. We can keep track of this by drawing red circles around the 5 and the 1 in the right-hand column, as per Game Table 3. So no matter what Rowe does, Colombe should choose to *drive*. In this case we say that Colombe's dominant strategy is to *drive*.

The rational thing to do, according to game theory, is to play the dominant strategy—if in fact there is a dominant strategy. So in our rush-hour traffic game, the rational thing for Rowe to do is to take a *taxi*, and the rational thing for Colombe to do is to *drive* (see lower-right quadrant in Game Table 4). This is also known as Nash equilibrium, which you will learn about in the next section.

Nash Equilibrium

Nash equilibrium
An outcome of the game where no player has the incentive to unilaterally change strategies. In other words, it is the best a player can hope for, given the rational choice of the other player.

When both players play their dominant strategies, we have what is called Nash equilibrium. Nash equilibrium is a crucially important concept in game theory. A Nash equilibrium is a set of strategies for each player, such that when each player plays their rationally optimal strategy, no player can make themselves better off by unilaterally changing their strategy. If both players have a dominant strategy, we will always find Nash equilibrium using dominance reasoning.

It is important to keep in mind that Nash equilibrium need not be jointly best for both players. Let us see what this means by revisiting Game Table 6.1 from Chapter 6, which is reproduced here as Game Table 5.

Colombe

	Walk	Drive
Bike	3 , 3	0 , (5)
Taxi	(5) , 0	(1) , (1)

(Rowe on left axis)

Game Table 4 Rush-Hour Traffic—Rationally Optimal Strategies

The lower-right quadrant shows the outcome of the game when both players choose their rationally optimal strategies. This outcome is called Nash equilibrium.

John L.

	Co-operate	Double-cross
Co-operate	Safe and secure , Safe and secure	Murdered , Complete dominance
Double-cross	Complete dominance , Murdered	Nasty, brutish, short , Nasty, brutish, short

(Thomas H. on left axis)

Game Table 5 Responses to the Social Contract

Both Thomas and John have a choice to make: co-operate with each other and form a civil society, or double-cross each other and remain in lawless chaos. If both Thomas and John agree to *co-operate*, then they can rest assured that they will live out their lives safe and secure. However, if both players choose to *double-cross*, then their lives will be nasty, brutish, and short.

We initially used words to describe the payoffs for both players. We can clarify things by replacing these words with numbers in Game Tables 6, 7, and 8. Remember that these numbers represent all that is important to the player.

Both Thomas and John have the same decision to make: to *co-operate* or *double-cross*. And the payoff structure is the same for both players. However, these two facts do not alter how we

John L.

	Co-operate	Double-cross
Co-operate	5 , 5	−10 , 10
Double-cross	⑩ , −10	⑴ , −1

Thomas H.

Game Table 6 Responses to the Social Contract—Thomas's Dominant Strategy

The blue circles show Thomas's dominant strategy. Since 10 is better than 5, we draw a blue circle around it in the lower-left quadrant. Since −1 is better than −10, we draw a blue circle around it in the lower-right quadrant. Two blue circles in the bottom row indicate that the dominant strategy for Thomas is to *double-cross*.

analyze the game. On close inspection we see that Thomas has a dominant strategy. Since a payoff of 10 is better than a payoff of 5, and since a payoff of −1 is better than a payoff of −10, Thomas will choose to *double-cross*. See Game Table 6.

The same form of reasoning applies to John. Since a payoff of 10 is better than a payoff of 5, and since a payoff of −1 is better than a payoff of −10, John will also choose to *double-cross*. See Game Table 7.

John L.

	Co-operate	Double-cross
Co-operate	5 , 5	−10 , ⑩
Double-cross	⑩ , −10	⑴ , ⑴

Thomas H.

Game Table 7 Responses to the Social Contract—John's Dominant Strategy

The red circles show John's dominant strategy. Since 10 is better than 5, we draw a red circle around it in the upper-right quadrant. Since −1 is better than −10, we draw a red circle around it in the lower-right quadrant. Two red circles in the right-hand column indicate that the dominant strategy for John is to *double-cross*.

John L.

	Co-operate	Double-cross
Co-operate	5 , 5	−10 , ⟨10⟩
Double-cross	⟨10⟩ , −10	⟨−1⟩ , ⟨−1⟩

Thomas H.

Game Table 8 Responses to the Social Contract—Nash Equilibrium
The lower-right quadrant shows the Nash equilibrium. Choosing the rationally optimal strategies that result in Nash equilibrium; however, that does not mean both players will be better off. In fact, they would be better off collectively if they both chose to co-operate (upper-right quadrant.)

Both Thomas and John have the same dominant strategy: *double-cross*. The payoff for both players is −1. We can confirm this in Game Table 8, where both payoffs are circled in the lower-right quadrant: this indicates Nash equilibrium. If both players have a dominant strategy, an analysis of the players' dominant strategies will always result in a quadrant that has both payoffs circled.

Though it is rational for each player to choose to *double-cross*, it is clear that both players would be better off collectively if they both chose to *co-operate* instead. If both chose their **dominated strategy**, each would receive a payoff of 5 instead of −1. But there is no incentive for either Thomas or John to unilaterally change their strategy. If Thomas decides to unilaterally change strategies and *co-operate*, John can exploit this by choosing to *double-cross*. Similarly, if John decides to unilaterally change strategies and *co-operate*, Thomas can exploit this by choosing to *double-cross*. Despite the fact that Thomas and John would be better off if they both agreed to *co-operate*, this will not happen unless they agree to some external mechanism to punish the defector. This type of situation is an example of a social action problem.

> The game tables in **this appendix** have just one Nash equilibrium. It is useful to note, however, that it is possible for some games to have more than one Nash equilibrium.

dominated strategy
If a player has a choice between Strategy A and Strategy B, and Strategy A is the *dominant* strategy, then we say Strategy B is the *dominated* strategy.

Using Game Theory to Model Social Action Problems

Recall that a social action problem is a situation where everyone (individually) does what is in their self-interest and everyone (collectively) is worse off for it. As a formal tool, game theory is well suited to help us think about social action problems.

In Chapter 7 we stated that the tragedy of the commons is an example of a social action problem, and used the pending water crisis in western Kansas as an example. The payoffs in Game Table 7.1 represented the revenue each corn farmer could expect to earn from dryland

Farmer 2

		Convert to Dryland (co-operate)		Continue Irrigating (defect)	
Farmer 1	Convert to Dryland (co-operate)	$133,000 per square mile	$133,000 per square mile	$133,000 per square mile	$400,000 per square mile
	Continue Irrigating (defect)	$400,000 per square mile	$133,000 per square mile	$400,000 per square mile	$400,000 per square mile

Game Table 9 The Farmer's Tragedy—Part 1

Both farmers have a dominant strategy. Since more revenue is better than less revenue, there is no financial incentive for either farmer to stop using irrigated fields. Both farmers will play their dominant strategy and continue irrigating their fields, which results in the Nash equilibrium of this game.

farming ($133,000 per section of land) versus irrigated land ($400,000 per section of land). This is reproduced in Game Table 9 for ease of reference.

Game Table 9 does a very good job revealing the (short-term) financial incentives that each farmer has for choosing to *continue irrigating*. It does not, however, clearly show how devastating short-term financial incentives can be for the environment. The future will be very bleak for both farmers if they simply continue to focus on how much money they can make in the short term. This is because of the pending water crisis that will soon be upon them if they continue extracting water from the Ogallala Aquifer at the current rates.

To remedy the shortsightedness of short-term financial incentives, we can reconstruct this game table to reflect payoffs that represent a mix of short-term and long-term financial incentives, and the long-term environmental impact of water use in farm management practices. See Game Table 10.

The dominant strategy remains the same for both farmers: *continue irrigating*; the Nash equilibrium is shown in the lower-right quadrant. If both farmers continue to irrigate their fields at current rates they will make more money in the short term, but this will precipitate a water crisis much sooner than originally anticipated, which will have a significant impact on their ability to make money in the future. If both farmers co-operate and convert their fields to dryland, they will both do better in the long term (as per the upper-left quadrant). They will make less money in the short term, but the water crisis will be pushed back by a couple of generations, meaning they can continue to make money into the future. If one farmer decides to co-operate and cut back on water consumption but the other decides to continue irrigating, the co-operator will be at a significant disadvantage. The co-operator will make less money not only in the short term but also in the long term, because the defector's water consumption is hastening a water crisis. The unfortunate reality, however, is there is no incentive for any farmer to unilaterally start converting to dryland farming.

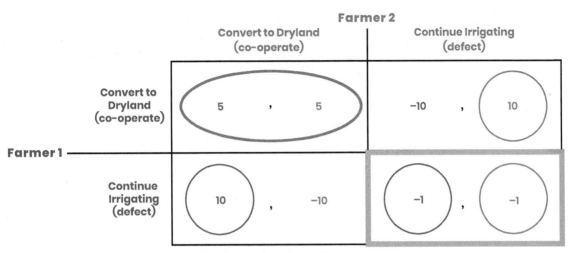

Game Table 10 The Farmer's Tragedy—Part 2

This game has the same structure as all the games in this appendix: both players have a dominant strategy, yet both players would be better if they chose to play their *dominated* strategy instead (in this case, *convert to dryland*; see the upper-left quadrant). This is a *tragedy of the commons,* which is an example of a social action problem.

You might be thinking that this setup is contrived. There are many more than two farmers in western Kansas. Further, it is impossible to say with any amount of certainty how water management in farming practices will change in the future, and how that will affect future earnings from growing corn. This is all true, but models are necessarily idealizations. An idealized model purposefully strips away some information to focus our attention on other, more relevant, information. In this case, we want to focus our attention on the underlying incentives each player faces. Notice that both farmers do better by co-operating. Indeed, given the payoff structure of this model, the socially optimal outcome occurs when both farmers cut back on their water consumption and convert their fields to dryland farming. Once again, however, the tragedy is that neither farmer has the incentive to unilaterally change their current farming practices.

This is the harmful effect of a social action problem. We will do well to understand what motivates and drives people to engage in what is ultimately socially defeating behaviour. How do we avoid social action problems? We started an answer to that question in Chapter 10.

Further Reading

Dixit, Avinash K., Susan Skeath, and David H. Reiley. *Games of Strategy.* New York: W.W. Norton, 2015.

APPENDIX C

Concept Check Answers

Chapter 1

1.1: A, 1.2: A, 1.3: C, 1.4: D, 1.5: B, 1.6: B, 1.7: B, 1.8: D

Chapter 2

2.1: A, 2.2: B, 2.3: D, 2.4: B, 2.5: C, 2.6: B, 2.7: C, 2.8: B, 2.9: B, 2.10: A

Chapter 3

3.1: D, 3.2: B, 3.3: D, 3.4: C, 3.5: A, 3.6: B, 3.7: C, 3.8: A, 3.9: B, 3.10: D, 3.11: C, 3.12: C, 3.13: B

Chapter 4

4.1: B, 4.2: A, 4.3: C, 4.4: B, 4.5: D, 4.6: D, 4.7: B, 4.8: A, 4.9: C, 4.10: B

Chapter 5

5.1: C, 5.2: B, 5.3: A, 5.4: B, 5.5: A, 5.6: D, 5.7: A, 5.8: A, 5.9: C, 5.10: B

Chapter 6

6.1: A, 6.2: B, 6.3: C, 6.4: D, 6.5: B, 6.6: C, 6.7: D, 6.8: B, 6.9: D

Chapter 7

7.1: A, 7.2: B, 7.3: B, 7.4: D, 7.5: C, 7.6: A, 7.7: A, 7.8: D, 7.9: A, 7.10: B

Chapter 8

8.1: D, 8.2: C, 8.3: A, 8.4: C, 8.5: B, 8.6: A, 8.7: D

Chapter 9

9.1: A, 9.2: C, 9.3: B, 9.4: A, 9.5: D, 9.6: B, 9.7: B, 9.8: D, 9.9: C, 9.10: A

Chapter 10

10.1: A, 10.2: B, 10.3: A, 10.4: B, 10.5: B, 10.6: C, 10.7: A, 10.8: D, 10.9: A, 10.10: C

Chapter 11

11.1: A, 11.2: B, 11.3: B, 11.4: A, 11.5: C, 11.6: A, 11.7: A, 11.8: B, 11.9: D, 11.10: C

NOTES

Introduction

1. "Waterloo Named Canada's Most Innovative University for 26th Consecutive Year," University of Waterloo, last modified 12 October 2017, https://uwaterloo.ca/news/news/waterloo-named-canadas-most-innovative-university-26th; "Canada's Top School by Reputation 2019," *Maclean's*, last modified 11 October 2018, https://www.macleans.ca/education/university-rankings/canadas-top-school-by-reputation-2019.
2. "Global Entrepreneurship and Digital Innovation," University of Waterloo, last modified 14 February 2018, https://uwaterloo.ca/global-entrepreneurship-disruptive-innovation.

Chapter 1

1. United States Holocaust Memorial Museum, "Documenting Numbers of Victims of the Holocaust and Nazi Persecution," *Holocaust Encyclopedia*, last modified 4 February 2019, https://encyclopedia.ushmm.org/content/en/article/documenting-numbers-of-victims-of-the-holocaust-and-nazi-persecution.
2. Paul E. Lovejoy, "The Impact of the Atlantic Slave Trade on Africa: A Review of the Literature," *Journal of African History* 30 (1989): 368.
3. "Education, Outreach, and Public Planning," National Centre for Truth and Reconciliation, last modified 2019, https://education.nctr.ca.
4. Charles L. Stevenson, *Ethics and Language* (New Haven: Yale University Press, 1944).
5. Linda Drouin, "Rhinoceros Party Promises Pie in the Face," *Ottawa Citizen,* 26 April 1979, 8.
6. Milton Friedman, "The Social Responsibility of Business Is to Increase Its Profits," *The New York Times Magazine,* 13 September 1970.
7. Albert Z. Carr, "Is Business Bluffing Ethical?" *Harvard Business Review* 46 no. 1 (Jan./Feb 1968): 143–53. https://hbr.org/1968/ 01/is-business-bluffing-ethical.
8. Ibid.
9. Joseph Heath, *Morality, Competition, and the Firm: The Market Failures Approach to Business Ethics* (New York: Oxford University Press, 2014).
10. Ibid., 103–5.
11. Harvey S. Rosen, John-François Wen, Tracy Snoddon, Bev Dahlby, and Roger S. Smith, *Public Finance in Canada*, 3rd Canadian edition (McGraw-Hill Ryerson, 2008), 26.
12. Bombardier Inc., *2018 Financial Report*, 14 February 2019, https://ir.bombardier.com/modules/misc/documents/44/15/81/81/15/Bombardier-Financial-Report-2018-en.pdf, inside front cover.
13. Ibid.
14. Steve Kupferman, "A Timeline of Bombardier's Excuses for Not Building Toronto's New Transit Fleet," *Toronto Life,* 6 January 2017,http://www.torontolife.com/city/transportation/timeline-bombardiers-excuses-not-building-torontos-new-transit-fleet/.
15. Bombardier Inc., *2019 Financial Report*, 13 February 2019, https://ir.bombardier.com/modules/misc/documents/92/58/57/85/15/Bombardier-Financial-Report-2019-en.pdf, 11.
16. Mark Milke, "Bombardier and Canada's Corporate Welfare Trap," Fraser Institute, last updated 31 January 2014, https://www.fraserinstitute.org/article/bombardier-and-canadas-corporate-welfare-trap.
17. Heath, *Morality, Competition, and the Firm*, 37.
18. US National Institutes of Health, "Familial Lipoprotein Lipase Deficiency," *U.S. National Library of Medicine*, https://ghr.nlm.nih.gov/condition/familial-lipoprotein-lipase-deficiency.
19. Kelly Crowe, "The Million-Dollar Drug," *CBC News*, 17 November 2018, newsinteractives.cbc.ca/longform/glybera.
20. Ibid.
21. Ibid.
22. Ibid.
23. Ibid.
24. Michael Hayden, qtd. in Crowe, "The Million-Dollar Drug."
25. John Kastelein, qtd. in Crowe, "The Million-Dollar Drug."
26. Crowe, "The Million-Dollar Drug."
27. Sander van Deventer, qtd. in Crowe, "The Million-Dollar Drug."
28. Crowe, "The Million-Dollar Drug."
29. Ibid.
30. van Deventer, qtd. in Crowe, "The Million-Dollar Drug."
31. Kastelein, qtd. in Crowe, "The Million-Dollar Drug."

Chapter 2

1. Immanuel Kant, *Groundwork for the Metaphysic of Morals*, ed. Jonathan Bennett, last modified 2008, https://www.early-moderntexts.com/assets/pdfs/kant1785.pdf, 24.
2. Ibid., 29.
3. W.D. Ross, *The Right and the Good*, ed. Philip Stratton-Lake (Oxford, UK: Clarendon Press, 1930), 21.
4. United Nations General Assembly, *Universal Declaration of Human Rights*, 10 December 1948, 217 A (III), http://www.un.org/en/ universal-declaration-human-rights/.
5. Daniel Kahneman and Angus Deaton, "High Income Improves Evaluation of Life but Not Emotional Well-Being,"

Proceedings of the National Academy of Sciences of the United States of America 107, no. 38: 16489–93.

6. Maureen Sander-Staudt, "Care Ethics," in *Internet Encyclopedia of Philosophy*, last modified 2011, https://www.iep.utm.edu/care-eth.

7. Jean Keller and Eva Kittay, "Feminist Ethics of Care," in *The Routledge Companion to Feminist Philosophy,* eds Ann Garry, Serene J. Khader, and Alison Stone (New York: Routledge, 2017), 540–55.

8. Carol Gilligan, *In a Different Voice* (Cambridge, MA: Belknap Press, 1982); Gail Golding and Tony Laidlaw, "Women and Moral Development: A Need to Care," *Interchange* 10 (1979): 95–103.

9. Gilligan, *In a Different Voice.*

10. Sander-Staudt, "Care Ethics."

11. Margaret Little, "Seeing and Caring: The Role of Affect in Feminist Moral Epistemology," *Hypatia* 10, no. 3 (Summer 1995): 123.

12. Little, "Seeing and Caring," 124.

13. Virginia Held, "The Ethics of Care as Normative Guidance: Comment on Gilligan," *Journal of Social Philosophy* 45, no. 1 (Spring 2014): 114.

14. Sander-Staudt, "Care Ethics."

15. Keller and Kittay, "Feminist Ethics of Care."

16. Held, "The Ethics of Care," 113.

17. Ingrid Robeyns, "The Capability Approach," in *Stanford Encyclopedia of Philosophy*, Fall 2016 edition, ed. Edward N. Zalta, last modified October 2016, https://plato.stanford.edu/entries/capability-approach.

18. Amartya Sen, "Well-Being, Agency, and Freedom: The Dewey Lectures 1984," *Journal of Philosophy* 82, no. 4 (April 1985): 169–221; Amartya Sen, "Why Health Equity?" *Health Economics* 82, no. 8 (December 2002): 660.

19. Amartya Sen, *Inequality Reexamined* (Oxford, UK: Clarendon Press, 1992), 45.

20. Peter Vallentyne, "Debate: Capabilities versus Opportunities for Wellbeing," *Journal of Political Philosophy* 13, no. 3 (September 2005): 359–71.

21. Martha C. Nussbaum, "Capabilities as Fundamental Entitlements: Sen and Social Justice," *Feminist Economics* 9, nos. 2–3 (January 2003): 33–59; Thomas W. Pogge and Thomas C. Pogge, "Can the Capability Approach Be Justified?" *Philosophical Topics* 30, no. 2 (Fall 2002): 167–228; Roland Pierik and Ingrid Robeyns, "Resources versus Capabilities: Social Endowments in Egalitarian Theory," *Political Studies* 55, no. 1 (March 2007): 133–52.

22. Martha C. Nussbaum, *Frontiers of Justice: Disability, Nationality, Species Membership* (Cambridge, MA: Harvard University Press, 2006), 76–8.

23. Philippa Foot, "The Problem of Abortion and the Doctrine of Double Effect," *Oxford Review* 5 (1967): 5–15.

24. Daisuke Wakabayashi, "Self-Driving Uber Car Kills Pedestrian in Arizona, Where Robots Roam," *The New York Times* 3 (2018): 19.

25. "Anti-Corruption in Canada," Global Compliance News, accessed 18 January 2020, https://globalcompliancenews.com/anti-corruption/handbook/anti-corruption-in-canada/

26. Legislative Services Branch, "Consolidated Federal Laws of Canada, Corruption of Foreign Public Officials Act," Corruption of Foreign Public Officials Act, 17 January 2020, https://laws-lois.justice.gc.ca/eng/acts/c-45.2/page-1.html#h-112316.

27. William S. Burroughs, *Naked Lunch: The Restored Text*, eds James Grauerholz and Barry Miles (New York: Grove Press, 2004), 11.

Chapter 3

1. Kenneth J. Arrow, "A Difficulty in the Concept of Social Welfare," *Journal of Political Economy* 58, no. 4 (August 1950): 328–46.

2. "Promoting Fair Competition in the Restaurant and Mobile Food Industry," Competition Bureau of Canada, last modified 14 February 2018, http://www.competitionbureau.gc.ca/eic/site/cb-bc.nsf/eng/04260.html.

3. Mary Gentile, *Giving Voice to Values: How to Speak Your Mind When You Know What's Right* (New Haven: Yale University Press, 2010), 34–44.

4. Ibid., 172–4.

5. Daniel Kahneman, *Thinking Fast and Slow* (London, UK: Penguin, 2012).

6. Jonathan Haidt, "The Emotional Dog and Its Rational Tail: A Social Intuitionist Approach to Moral Judgment," *Psychological Review* 108, no. 4 (October 2001): 818–9, doi:10.1037/0033-295X.108.4.814.

7. Kahneman, *Thinking Fast and Slow*, 236–7.

8. Shannon Proudfoot, "Survey Finds Many Canadians Believe Poor are 'Part of the Problem,'" *National Post*, accessed 19 January 2020, http://www.nationalpost.com/Survey finds many Canadians believe poor part problem/4365289/story.html.

9. Public Health Agency of Canada, Government of Canada, 24 April 2019, https://www.canada.ca/en/public-health/services/publications/science-research-data/inequalities-working-poor-canadians-infographic.html.

10. Pete Evans, "It's Next to Impossible to Pay the Rent Working Full Time for Minimum Wage, New Report Calculates," *CBC News*, 18 July 2019, https://www.cbc.ca/news/business/ccpa-rents-minimum-wage-1.5216258.

11. Irene Scopelliti et al., "Bias Blind Spot: Structure, Measurement, and Consequences," *Management Science* 61, no. 10 (October 2015): 2468, doi:10.1287/mnsc.2014.2096.

12. Carey K. Morewedge et al., "Debiasing Decisions: Improved Decision Making with a Single Training Intervention," *Policy Insights from the Behavioral and Brain Sciences* 2, no. 1 (October 2015): 129–40, doi:10.1177/2372732215600886.

13. Richard H. Thaler and Cass R. Sunstein, *Nudge: Improving Decisions about Health, Wealth, and Happiness* (New Haven: Yale University Press, 2018).

14. Xenophon, *Cyropaedia The Education of Cyrus*, edited by F. M. Stawell, translated by Henry Graham Dakyns (The Project Gutenberg, 2011), https://www.gutenberg.org/files/2085/2085-h/2085-h.htm#2H_4_0004.

15. Ibid.

16. "Canada Had to Give up Dairy Access to Get a Deal on NAFTA, Says Negotiator," *CBC News*, 4 October 2018, https://www.cbc.ca/news/politics/powerandpolitics/usmca- nafta-dairy-supply-management-1.4851411.

17. "New USMCA Trade Deal 'Devastating' to Canada's Dairy Industry, Farmer Says," *CBC News*, 1 October 1, 2018, https://www.cbc.ca/news/canada/manitoba/usmca-trade-deal-dairy-farmer-1.4845229.

18. Jessica Conditt, "'Red Dead Redemption 2': Separation of Crunch and Art," *Engadget*, last modified 25 October 2018, https://www.engadget.com/2018/10/25/red-dead-redemption-2-review-crunch-rockstar; Ben Gilbert, "Grueling, 100-Hour Work Weeks and 'Crunch Culture' Are Pushing the Video Game Industry to a Breaking Point. Here's What's Going On," *Business Insider*, last modified 9 May 2019, https://www. businessinsider.com/video-game-development-problems-crunch-culture-ea-rockstar-epic-explained-2019-5.

19. Kevin Webb, "A Top Video-Game Executive Accused of Farting on Subordinates and Hitting Their Genitals as a Joke Has Been Suspended without Pay, but Some Employees Want Him Gone Entirely," *Business Insider*, last modified 14 December 2018, https://www.businessinsider.com/riot-games-suspends-coo-scott-gelb-bro-culture-2018-12.

20. Matt Weinberger, "If You Want to Make Video Games for a Living, Get Ready for Long Hours and a Lot of Unpaid Overtime," *Business Insider*, last modified 16 March 2016, https://www.businessinsider.com/if-you-want-to-work-in-the-gaming-industry-beware-38-of-all-game-developers-put-in-unpaid-overtime-last-year-2016-3.

21. Ibid.

22. Gilbert, "Grueling, 100-Hour Work Weeks."

23. Ibid.

Chapter 4

1. Albert Z. Carr, "Is Business Bluffing Ethical?" *Harvard Business Review*, 1 August 2014, https://hbr.org/1968/01/is-business-bluffing-ethical.

2. Milton Friedman, *Capitalism and Freedom* (Chicago: University of Chicago Press, 1982), 112.

3. Gregory Beyer, "Why Business Leaders Are Obsessed with Sun Tzu's Ancient Military Guide, 'The Art of War,'" *HuffPost Canada*, last modified 6 December 2017, https://www.huffingtonpost.ca/2014/03/24/why-business-leaders-are-0_n_5003283.html.

4. Kevin O'Leary, qtd. in Rose Simone, "'Business Is War,' Kevin O'Leary Tells University of Waterloo Students," *Waterloo Region Record*, 5 February 2015, https://www.therecord.com/news-story/5322749--business-is-war-kevin-o-leary-tells-university-of-waterloo-students.

5. *Dodge* et al. v. *Ford Motor Co.* et al., 204 Mich 459, Supreme Court of Michigan, 7 February 1919, https://h2o.law.harvard.edu/cases/3965.

6. Adam Smith, *An Inquiry into the Nature and Causes of the Wealth of Nations*, ed. Sálvio Marcelo Soares (MetaLibri, 29 May 2007), https://www.ibiblio.org/ml/libri/s/SmithA_WealthNations_p.pdf, 349.

7. Vanessa Correia, Ph.D. dissertation, University of Waterloo, 2020.

8. lbelanger225, "Global 500," *Fortune*, 15 January 2020, https://fortune.com/global500/search/.

9. "Walmart," Wikipedia, Wikimedia Foundation, 16 January 2020, https://en.wikipedia.org/wiki/Walmart.

10. "Bangladesh Fire Kills 112 at Wal-Mart Supplier," *CBC News*, CBC/Radio Canada, 22 February 2019, https://www.cbc.ca/news/world/bangladesh-fire-kills-112-at-wal-mart-supplier-1.1179644.

11. David Barstow, "Wal-Mart Hushed Up a Vast Mexican Bribery Case," *The New York Times*, 21 April 2012, https://www.nytimes.com/2012/04/22/business/at-wal-mart-in-mexico-a-bribe-inquiry-silenced.html?_r=1&pagewanted=all.

12. Ibid.

13. Bloomberg.com (Bloomberg), accessed 20 January 2020, https://www.bloomberg.com/news/articles/2018-08-02/walmart-is-said-to-be-deadlocked-with-u-s-over-bribery-probe.

14. Lauren Debter, "Walmart Will Cough Up $282 Million to Put Years-Long Bribery Investigation Behind It," *Forbes*, accessed 20 June 2019, https://www.forbes.com/sites/laurendebter/2019/06/20/walmart-will-cough-up-282-million-to-put-years-long-bribery-investigation-behind-it/#218364df4ac5.

15. "Sustainability," Walmart Canada, accessed 20 January 2020, https://www.walmartcanada.ca/responsibility/sustainability.

16. Ibid.

17. Walmart Inc. 2018 *Global Responsibility Report Summary*, PDF file. https://corporate.walmart.com/media-library/document/2018-grr-summary/_proxyDocument?id=00000162-e4a5-db25-a97f-f7fd785a0001.

18. John Elkington, *Cannibals with Forks: The Triple Bottom Line of 21st Century Business* (Gabriola Island, BC: New Society Publishers, 1998).

19. Wayne Norman and Chris MacDonald, "Getting to the Bottom of 'Triple Bottom Line,'" *Business Ethics Quarterly* 14, no. 2 (April 2004): 243–62.

20. Moses Pava, "Why Corporations Should Not Abandon Social Responsibility," in *Ethical Issues in Business: Inquiries, Cases, and Readings*, 2nd edn, ed. Peg Tittle (Broadview Press, 2017), 295–303.

21. Tim Hindle, "Triple Bottom Line," *The Economist*, last modified 17 November 2009, https://www.economist.com/news/2009/11/17/triple-bottom-line.

22. Ibid.

23. Laura Musikanski, "Triple Bottom Line Reporting," Network for Business Innovation and Sustainability (May 2008), http://www.nbis.org/nbisresources/reporting_csr/triple_bottom_line_reporting_%20l_musikanski.pdf, 8.

24. Timothy F. Slaper and Tanya J. Hall, "The Triple Bottom Line: What Is It and How Does It Work?" *Indiana Business Review* 86, no. 1 (Spring 2011): 4–8.

25. Norman and MacDonald, "Getting to the Bottom."

26. Slaper and Hall, "The Triple Bottom Line."

27. Norman and MacDonald, "Getting to the Bottom."

28. Archie B. Carroll, "The Pyramid of Corporate Social Responsibility: Toward the Moral Management of Organizational Stakeholders," *Business Horizons* 34, no. 4 (July–August 2003): 39–48.

29. Archie B. Carroll and Mark S. Schwartz, "Corporate Social Responsibility: A Three-Domain Approach," *Business Ethics Quarterly* 13, no. 4 (October 2003): 503–50.

30. TD Bank Group, "TD Only Canadian Bank among DJSI's Most Sustainable Companies," 25 September 2019, https://www.newswire.ca/news-releases/td-only-canadian-bank-among-djsi-s-most-sustainable-companies-855920461.html.

31. Dow Jones Sustainability Index, "DJSI Index Family," accessed 31 January 2020, https://www.robecosam.com/csa/indices/djsi-index-family.html.

32. TD Bank Group, "TD Only Canadian Bank."

33. TD Bank Group, "TD Commitment to Gender Equality Recognized by Bloomberg," 16 January 2019, https://newsroom.td.com/featured-news/td-commitment-to-gender-equality-recognized-by-bloomberg.

34. Bloomberg, "Bloomberg-Gender Equality Index Doubles in Size, Recognizing 230 Companies Committed to Advancing Women in the Workplace," 16 January 2019, https://www.bloomberg.com/company/press/2019-bloomberg-gender-equality-index/; Bloomberg, "Gender-Equality Index," accessed 31 January 2020, https://www.bloomberg.com/impact/products/gender-equality-index/

35. TD Bank Group, "Performance Summary for Investors," *2018 Environmental, Social and Governance (ESG) Report,* 19 January 2020, https://www.td.com/document/PDF/corporate responsibility/2018-ESG-Report.pdf, p. iii.

36. David Sanders, "Top 50 Safest Commerical Banks 2019," *Global Finance Magazine,* 8 November 2019, https://www.gfmag.com/magazine/november-2019/50-safest-commercial-banks; the 2018 Global Finance ranking appears in TD Bank Group: "Performance Summary for Investors."

37. *Bloomberg Gender-Equality Index 2020,* "Frequently Asked Questions," May 2019. https://data.bloomberglp.com/company/sites/46/2020/01/GEI_2020-FAQs.pdf, p. 2.

38. Joseph Heath, *Morality, Competition, and the Firm: The Market Failures Approach to Business Ethics* (New York: Oxford University Press, 2014), 205.

Chapter 5

1. John Rawls and Erin Kelly, *Justice as Fairness: A Restatement* (Cambridge, MA: Belknap Press, 2001).

2. "Alarm over Voter Purges as 17m Americans Removed from Rolls in Two Years," *The Guardian*, last modified 1 August 2019, https://www.theguardian.com/us-news/2019/aug/01/voter-purges-us-elections-brennan-center-report.

3. Jordan Weissman, "McDonald's Can't Figure Out How Its Workers Survive on Minimum Wage," *The Atlantic*, 16 July 2013, https://www.theatlantic.com/business/archive/2013/07/mcdonalds-cant-figure-out-how-its-workers-survive-on-minimum-wage/277845.

4. Nancy Krieger, "Racial and Gender Discrimination: Risk Factors for High Blood Pressure?" *Social Science & Medicine* 30, no. 12 (1990): 1273–81.

5. "What Is Harassment?" Canadian Human Rights Commission, June 2019, https://www.chrc-ccdp.gc.ca/eng/content/what-harassment-1.

6. Brian Thompson, "The Racial Wealth Gap: Addressing America's Most Pressing Epidemic," *Forbes*, last modified 18 February 2018, https://www.forbes.com/sites/brianthompson1/2018/02/18/the-racial-wealth-gap-addressing-americas-most-pressing-epidemic.

7. Ibid.

8. Alain Noël and Florence Larocque, "Aboriginal Peoples and Poverty in Canada: Can Provincial Governments Make a Difference?" Annual Meeting of the International Sociological Association's Research Committee 19, Montreal, QC, 20 August 2009, 13–4, http://www.cccg.umontreal.ca/RC19/PDF/Noel-A_Rc192009.pdf.

9. Emily Badger, "Whites Have Huge Wealth Edge over Blacks (but Don't Know It)," *New York Times*, 18 September 2017, https://www.nytimes.com/interactive/2017/09/18/upshot/black-white-wealth-gap-perceptions.html.

10. Natasha Beedie, David Macdonald, and Daniel Wilson, "Towards Justice: Tackling Indigenous Child Poverty in Canada" *Upstream*, July 2019, https://www.afn.ca/wp-content/uploads/2019/07/Upstream_report_final_English_June-24-2019.pdf, 9.

11. Government of Canada, "Aboriginal Income Disparity in Canada," Aboriginal Affairs and Northern Development Canada, 7 October 2013, https://www.aadnc-aandc.gc.ca/DAM/DAM-INTER-HQ-AI/STAGING/texte-text/rs_re_brief_incomedisparity-PDF_1378400531873_eng.pdf

12. Sheila Block, "Canada's Population Is Changing but Income Inequality Remains a Problem," *Behind the Numbers*, 8 November 2019, http://behindthenumbers.ca/2017/10/27/population-changing-income-inequality-remains/.

13. The Conference Board of Canada, "Racial Wage Gap," April 2017, https://www.conferenceboard.ca/hcp/provincial/society/racial-gap.aspx.

14. Office of the Auditor General of Canada, "Socio-Economic Gaps on First Nations Reserves—Indigenous Services Canada," *2018 Spring Reports of the Auditor General of Canada*, report 5, 29 May 2018, http://www.oag-bvg.gc.ca/internet/English/parl_oag_201805_05_e_43037.html.

15. Kristine Phillips, "Utah Republican Argues Against Equal Pay for Women: It's 'Bad for Families' and Society," *Washington Post*, 19 February 2017, https://www.washingtonpost.com/news/post-nation/wp/2017/02/19/utah-republican-argues-against-equal-pay-for-women-its-bad-for-families-and-society/?utm_term=.9cf03d91704d; Katie Gibbons, "BBC Pay Gap Justified as Men Pay for Their Families, Says Actor Tom Chambers," *The Times*, 26 July 2017, https://www.thetimes.co.uk/article/bbc-pay-gap-justified-as-men-pay-for-their-families-says-actor-tom-chambers-rqc5th5vq.

16. Sarah Jane Glynn, "Bread-Winning Mothers Continue to Be the U.S. Norm," Center for American Progress, 10 May 2019, https://www.americanprogress.org/issues/women/reports/2019/05/10/469739/breadwinning-mothers-continue-u-s-norm/.

17. Marianne Bertrand and Sendhil Mullainathan, "Are Emily and Greg More Employable than Lakisha and Jamal? A Field Experiment on Labor Market Discrimination," Working Paper Series 9873 (National Bureau of Economic Research, July 2003), doi:10.3386/w9873.

18. Ibid., 2.

19. Ibid., 2–3.

20. Claudia Goldin and Cecilia Rouse, "Orchestrating Impartiality: The Impact of 'Blind' Auditions on Female Musicians," *American Economic Review* 90, no. 4 (September 2000): 715–41.

21. Rachel Siegel, "'They Can't Be Here for Us': Black Men Arrested at Starbucks Tell Their Story for the First Time," *The Washington Post*, 28 March 2019, https://www.washingtonpost.com/news/business/wp/2018/04/19/they-cant-be-here-for-us-black-men-arrested-at-starbucks-tell-their-story-for-the-first-time/.

22. Associated Press, "Black Men Arrested at Philadelphia Starbucks Feared for Their Lives," *The Guardian*, 19 April 2018, https://www.theguardian.com/business/2018/apr/19/starbucks-black-men-feared-for-lives-philadelphia.

23. Ibid.

24. Catherine Thorbecke, "Black Men Arrested at Starbucks Settle with City for $1 Each and $200K for a Non-Profit Student Program," *ABC News*, 2 May 2018, https://abcnews.go.com/GMA/News/black-men-arrested-phila-starbucks-settle-city-200k/story?id=54893753; Hayden Field, "The 2 Men Wrongfully Arrested at Starbucks Negotiate for a $200,000 Program to Support Young Entrepreneurs," *Entrepreneur,* 3 May 2018, https://www.entrepreneur.com/article/312941.

25. "About the AODA," Accessibility Services Canada, last modified 19 August 2019, https://accessibilitycanada.ca/aoda.

26. Government of Ontario, "Understanding Barriers to Accessibility," Ministry of Community and Social Services, last modified 29 February 2012, https://web.archive.org/web/20120702031258/http://www.mcss.gov.on.ca/en/mcss/programs/accessibility/understanding_accessibility/understanding_barriers.aspx.

27. Ibid.

28. "Understanding Barriers to Accessibility," Council of Ontario Universities, 2018, http://www.accessiblecampus.ca/understanding-accessibility/what-are-the- barriers.

29. Ibid.

30. Ibid.

31. Lonnie Golden, "Irregular Work Scheduling and Its Consequences," Briefing paper #394 (Economic Policy Institute, 9 April 2015), https://www.epi.org/files/pdf/82524.pdf, 8.

32. Ibid., 9.

33. "Religious Rights (Fact Sheet)," Ontario Human Rights Commission, last modified 2018, http://www.ohrc.on.ca/en/religious-rights-fact-sheet.

34. Government of Canada, "Sexual Harassment—Overview," Employment and Social Development Canada, 29 July 2019, https://www.canada.ca/en/employment-social-development/programs/employment-standards/sexual-harassment.html.

35. "#MeToo, 1 Year Later: Canadian Sexual Assault Crisis Centres Report Record Number of Calls," *Global News*, 5 October 2018, https://globalnews.ca/news/4519574/metoo-1-year-later-canada/.

36. "The #MeToo Movement in Canada," Canadian Women's Foundation, accessed 27 January 2020, https://canadianwomen.org/the-facts/the-metoo-movement-in-canada/.

37. "Sexual Harassment in Employment (Fact Sheet)," Ontario Human Rights Commission, last modified 2011, http://www.ohrc.on.ca/en/sexual-harassment-employment-fact-sheet.

38. Ibid.

39. "Racial Harassment: Know Your Rights," Ontario Human Rights Commission, last modified 2012, http://www.ohrc.on.ca/sites/default/files/Racial%20harassment_English_accessible.pdf.

40. Ibid.

41. Rupa Banerjee, Jeffrey G. Reitz, and Phil Oreopoulos, "Do Large Employers Treat Racial Minorities More Fairly? A New Analysis of Canadian Field Experiment Data," University of Toronto, 25 January 2017, http://www.hireimmigrants.ca/wp-content/uploads/Final-Report-Which-employers-discriminate-Banerjee-Reitz-Oreopoulos-January-25-2017.pdf.

42. Olivia McEvoy, "Diversity . . . Is It Good for Business, Really?" *Accountancy Ireland* 49, no. 2 (April 2017): 24–8, https://www.charteredaccountants.ie/docs/default-source/Publishing/accountancy-ireland-archive/accountancy-ireland-april-2017.pdf?sfvrsn=4.

43. Vivian Hunt, Dennis Layton, and Sara Prince, "Why Diversity Matters" (McKinsey & Company, January 2015), https://www.mckinsey.com/business-functions/organization/our-insights/why-diversity-matters.

44. "Why Is Diversity in the Workplace Important?" BrightHR, last modified 2018, https://www.brighthr.com/articles/equality-and-discrimination/equality-and-diversity-in-the-workplace.

45. "BMO Bank of Montreal Spots Economic Opportunities in Canada," *World Finance*, last modified 7 September 2015, https://www.worldfinance.com/banking/bmo-bank-of-montreal-spots-economic-opportunities-in-canada.

46. Nicholas Sokic, "BMO's $3-Billion Fund for Women-Owned Businesses Taps into Segment Growing Faster Than Any Other," *Financial Post,* updated 4 November 2019, https://business.financialpost.com/entrepreneur/fp-startups/bmos-3-billion-fund-for-women-owned-businesses-taps-into-segment-growing-faster-than-any-other.

47. "BMO Bank of Montreal Spots Economic Opportunities in Canada," *World Finance*; Dana Flavelle, "BMO Boosts Lending to Women Entrepreneurs by $2 Billion," *Toronto Star,* 26 November 2014, https://www.thestar.com/business/2014/11/26/bmo_boosts_lending_to_women_entrepreneurs_by_2_billion.html.

48. Veronica Silva, "Women Entrepreneurs Not Appreciated for Their Innovation, New Study Suggests," *Research Money,* 28 February 2018, https://researchmoneyinc.com/articles/women-entrepreneurs-not-appreciated-for-their-innovation-new-study-suggests/.

49. Sokic, "BMO's $3-Billion Fund."

50. Ibid.

51. Ibid.

52. Canada, Canadian Charter of Rights and Freedoms, Part I of the Constitution Act, 1982, being Schedule B to the Canada Act, 1982 (UK), 1982, c. 11, 1982, https://laws-lois.justice.gc.ca/eng/Const/page-15.html.

53. Canada, Canadian Human Rights Act, RSC 1985, c. H-6, 1985, s. 2, http://laws-lois.justice.gc.ca/eng/acts/h-6/page-1.html.

54. Ibid., s. 26(1).

55. Canada, Employment Equity Act, SC 1995, c. 44, s. 2, http://laws-lois.justice.gc.ca/eng/acts/e-5.401/page-1.html.

56. Social Development Canada, "Canada's First Federal Accessibility Legislation Comes into Force," Government of Canada News, 12 July 2019, https://www.canada.ca/en/employment-social-development/news/2019/07/canadas-first-federal-accessibility-legislation-comes-into-force.html.

57. Ibid.

58. Ontario, Accessibility for Ontarians with Disabilities Act, 2005, SO 2005, ch. 11, s. 2, https://www.ontario.ca/laws/statute/05a11.

59. Government of British Columbia, "Building a Better B.C. for People with Disabilities," accessed 4 February 2020, https://www2.gov.bc.ca/gov/content/governments/about-the-bc-government/accessibility; Essential Accessibility, "An Overview of Canada's Accessibility Laws: A Look at the Old and the New," 13 June 2019, https://www.essentialaccessibility.com/blog/canadian-accessibility-laws/.

60. Social Development Canada, "Government of Canada," Summary of Part 2 of the Canada Labour Code, Government of Canada, 18 August 2015, https://www.canada.ca/en/employment-social-development/services/health-safety/reports/summary.html.

61. Ibid.

62. Ibid.

63. "History of the ILO," International Labour Organization, last modified 2019, https://www.ilo.org/global/about-the-ilo/history/lang--en/index.htm.

64. "About the ILO", International Labour Organization, last modified 2018, http://www.ilo.org/global/about-the-ilo/lang--en/index.htm.

65. International Labour Organization, Discrimination (Employment and Occupation) Convention, 1958 (No. 111), Art. 2, https://www.ilo.org/dyn/normlex/en/f?p=NORMLEXPUB:12100:0::NO::P12100_ILO_CODE:C111. The USA, Japan, Malaysia, and Singapore are among the 12 ILO member states that have not adopted this convention.

66. David Gaider, quoted in Tyler Wilde, "GDC 2013: BioWare's David Gaider Asks, 'How about We Just Decide How Not to Repel Women?' *PC Gamer,* 29 March 2013, https://www.pcgamer.com/bioware-david-gaider-sex-in-video-game.

Chapter 6

1. Thomas Hobbes, *Leviathan* (McMaster University, 2000), https://socialsciences.mcmaster.ca/econ/ugcm/3ll3/hobbes/Leviathan.pdf, 78.

2. Ibid., 79.

3. Tom Baker, "On the Genealogy of Moral Hazard," *Texas Law Review* 75, no. 2 (December 1996): 250–2, https://scholarship.law.upenn.edu/faculty_scholarship/872.

4. Michael Lista, "A Doctor's Deception," *Toronto Life*, August 2019, https://torontolife.com/city/greed-betrayal-medical-misconduct-north-york-general.

5. Ibid.

6. Jerome Solomon, "Cut-Blocking Is Legal, but Is It Ethical?" *Houston Chronicle*, 6 November 2011, https://www.chron.com/sports/solomon/article/Cut-blocking-is-legal-but-is-it-ethical-2254311.php.

7. Joe Bugel, qtd. in Solomon, "Cut-Blocking Is Legal."

8. Les Steckel, qtd. in Mark Oppenheimer, "In the Fields of the Lord," *Sports Illustrated* 118, no. 4 (4 February 2013): 38–43, https://www.si.com/vault/2013/02/04/106280215/in-the-fields-of-the-lord.

9. Meghna Chakrabarti and Alex Schroeder, "An Unbridgeable Divide? Pennsylvania's (Ongoing) Story of Gerrymandering and Redistricting," *On Point*, WBUR-FM, 7 October 2018, http://www.wbur.org/onpoint/2018/10/07/pennsylvania-gerrymandering-redistricting-congressional-map-7th-district.

10. Rene Lynch, "Yo, Parents! Back Away from the Easter Eggs! (or the Hunt's Off)" *Los Angeles Times*, 5 April 2012,

http://articles.latimes.com/2012/apr/05/nation/la-na-nn-easter-egg-hunt-20120406.

11. "Misbehaving Parents Ruin Easter Egg Hunt," National Public Radio, 27 March 2012, https://www.npr.org/2012/03/27/149449351/misbehaving-parents-ruin-easter-egg-hunt.

12. Elizabeth Roman, "Easter Bunny Arrives by Ambulance and Toddlers Get Knocked Over during Easthampton Egg Hunt," *Springfield Republican* (Massachusetts), 2 April 2012, https://www.masslive.com/news/index.ssf/2012/04/easter_ bunny_arrives_by_ambula.html.

13. Farhad Manjoo, "There Is No Harvard Cheating Scandal," *Slate*, 4 September 2012, http://www.slate.com/articles/news_and_politics/hey_wait_a_minute/2012/09/harvard_cheating_scandal_everyone_has_it_wrong_the_students_should_be_celebrated_for_collaborating_on_an_unfair_test.html.

14. Ibid.

15. Howard Gardner, "When Ambition Trumps Ethics," *Washington Post*, 31 August 2012, https://www.washingtonpost.com/opinions/when-ambition-trumps-ethics/2012/08/31/495c694a-f384-11e1-892d-bc92fee603a7_story.html.

16. Rebecca D. Robbins, "The Class of 2014 by the Numbers," *Harvard Crimson*, 2014, https://features.thecrimson.com/2014/senior-survey.

17. Global Affairs Canada, "Canada's Fight against Foreign Bribery," 5 August 2019, https://www.international.gc.ca/trade-agreements-accords-commerciaux/topics-domaines/other-autre/corr-19.aspx?lang=eng.

Chapter 7

1. "Sip It Slowly," *The Economist*, 3 October 2013, https://www.economist.com/news/united-states/21586874-farmers-kansas-are-starting-adapt-declining-stocks-groundwater-sip-it-slowly.

2. Ibid.

3. Ibid.

4. The price used in these calculations is based on the price of corn in Kansas in January 2020.

5. R. Edward Freeman, Jeffery G. York, and Lisa Stewart, "Environment, Ethics, and Business," Bridge Paper (Business Roundtable Institute for Corporate Ethics, 2008), http://www.corporate-ethics.org/pdf/ environment_ethics.pdf.

6. Ibid., 12.

7. Ibid.

8. Ibid., 13.

9. Ibid.

10. Ibid., 14.

11. Mia Rabson, "Federal Electric-Vehicle Rebate Uses Half of Its Three-Year Budget in Eight Months," *CTV News,* 27 January 2020, https://www.ctvnews.ca/autos/federal-electric-vehicle-rebate-uses-half-its-three-year-budget-in-eight-months-1.4785600.

12. The Canadian Press, "Electric Vehicle Sales Expected to Tumble after Doug Ford Nixes Rebate, Industry Group Says," *CBC News*, 13 July 2018, https://www.cbc.ca/news/canada/toronto/ev-rebates-sales-1.4745965.

13. The Canadian Press, "Canada Launched an Electric-Car Rebate with a 3-Year Budget. Eager Buyers Gobbled Nearly Half in 8 Months," *CBC News*, 28 January 2020, https://www.cbc.ca/news/canada/british-columbia/electric-car-rebate-canada-half-its-3-year-budget-in-8-months-1.5443129; Rabson, "Federal Electric-Vehicle Rebate Uses Half of Its Three-Year Budget in Eight Months."

14. Rabson, "Federal Electric-Vehicle Rebate Uses Half of Its Three-Year Budget in Eight Months."

15. Ian Bickis, "Canada's EV Charging Network Growing Up as Numbers and Power Improve," *CTV News*, 4 April 2019, https://www.ctvnews.ca/autos/canada-s-ev-charging-network-growing-up-as-numbers-and-power-improve-1.4365685.

16. Tesla, Inc. "Supercharging," 24 January 2020, https://www.tesla.com/support/supercharging.

17. Lizzie Wade, "Tesla's Electric Cars Aren't as Green as You Might Think," *Wired*, 31 March 2016, https: //www.wired.com/2016/03/teslas-electric-cars-might-not-green-think.

18. Ibid.

19. "Cleaner Cars from Cradle to Grave," Union of Concerned Scientists, accessed 28 January 2020, https://www.ucsusa.org/resources/cleaner-cars-cradle-grave.

20. Ronald H. Coase, "The Problem of Social Cost," *Journal of Law & Economics* 3 (October 1960): 1–44.

21. David Hall, "Self-Determination and The Struggle: Kyle Powys Whyte on Standing Rock," *The Pantograph Punch*, 26 January 2017, https://www.pantograph-punch.com/post/self-determination-struggle-kyle-whyte-standing-rock.

22. Nicky Woolf, "North Dakota Oil Pipeline Protesters Stand Their Ground: 'This Is Sacred Land,'" *The Guardian*, 29 August 2016, https://www.theguardian.com/us-news/2016/aug/29/north-dakota-oil-pipeline-protest-standing-rock-sioux.

23. Sam Levin, "Dakota Access Pipeline: The Who, What and Why of the Standing Rock Protests," *The Guardian*, 3 November 2016, https://www.theguardian.com/us-news/2016/nov/03/north-dakota-access-oil-pipeline-protests-explainer.

24. US Army, "Army Will Not Grant Easement for Dakota Access Pipeline Crossing," 4 December 2016, https://web.archive.org/web/20161204235307/https://www.army.mil/article/179095/army_will_not_grant_easement_for_dakota_access_pipeline_crossing.

25. Steven Mufson and Juliet Eilperin, "Trump Seeks to Revive Dakota Access, Keystone XL Oil Pipelines," *Washington Post*, 24 January 2017, https://www.washingtonpost.com/news/energy-environment/wp/2017/01/24/trump-gives-green-light-to-dakota-access-keystone-xl-oil-pipelines.

26. Hall, "Self-Determination and the Struggle."

27. Kyle Powys Whyte, qtd. in Hall, "Self-Determination and the Struggle."

28. Alleen Brown, "Five Spills, Six Months in Operation: Dakota Access Track Record Highlights Unavoidable Reality—Pipelines Leak," *The Intercept*, 9 January 2018, https://theintercept.com/2018/01/09/dakota-access-pipeline-leak-energy-transfer-partners.

29. Brigham A. McCown, "Whatever Happened to the Dakota Access Pipeline?" *Forbes*, 4 June 2018, https://www.forbes.com/sites/brighammccown/2018/06/04/what-ever-happened-to-the-dakota-access-pipeline/#6013013d4055.

30. Associated Press, "Keystone Pipeline Shut after Spilling 1.4 Million Litres of Oil in North Dakota," *CBC News*, 1 November 2019, https://www.cbc.ca/news/business/keystone-spils-over-1-million-litres-oil-north-dakota-1.5343509.

31. Whyte, qtd. in Hall, "Self-Determination and the Struggle."

32. Canada Energy Regulator, "Pipeline Profiles: Trans Mountain," Government of Canada, updated June 2019, https://www.cer-rec.gc.ca/nrg/ntgrtd/pplnprtl/pplnprfls/crdl/trnsmntn-eng.html.

33. Conversations for Responsible Environmental Development, "A History of Spills and Leaks," last updated March 2013, http://credbc.ca/wp-content/uploads/2013/03/KMInfographic2-02.png.

34. Kyle Benning and Simon Little, "Protesters Target Construction at Kinder Morgan's Burnaby Pipeline Terminal," *Global News*, 28 October 2017, https://globalnews.ca/news/3830748/protesters-target-construction-at-kinder-morgans-burnaby-pipeline-terminal.

35. Trans Mountain Corporation, "Kinder Morgan Canada Limited Suspends Non-Essential Spending on Trans Mountain Expansion Project," 8 April 2018, https://www.transmountain.com/news/2018/kinder-morgan-canada-limited-suspends-non-essential-spending-on-trans-mountain-expansion-project.

36. Kathleen Harris, "Liberals to Buy Trans Mountain Pipeline for $4.5B to Ensure Expansion Is Built," *CBC News*, 29 May 2018, https://www.cbc.ca/news/politics/liberals-trans-mountain-pipeline-kinder-morgan-1.4681911.

37. Joan Bryden, "Federal Court Quashes Trans Mountain Expansion; Ottawa Forging Ahead with Purchase," *Global News*, 31 August 2018, https://globalnews.ca/news/4418485/trans-mountain-pipeline-quashed-federal-court; CP (The Canadian Press), "Trans Mountain Scores a Win as Federal Court Dismisses First Nations' Challenges," *The Calgary Herald*, 4 February 2020, https://calgaryherald.com/business/energy/alert-federal-court-of-appeal-dismisses-challenge-to-trans-mountain-pipeline.

38. CP, "Trans Mountain Scores a Win."

39. Justine Hunter, "Federal Court of Appeal Clears a Hurdle for the Trans Mountain pipeline," *Globe and Mail*, 4 February 2020, https://www.theglobeandmail.com/canada/article-court-upholds-trans-mountain-pipeline-approval/;CP,"Trans Mountain Scores a Win."

Chapter 8

1. Minette E. Drumwright and Patrick E. Murphy, "The Current State of Advertising Ethics: Industry and Academic Perspectives," *Journal of Advertising* 38, no. 1 (January 2009): 89.

2. David Mikkelson, "Cards against Humanity Bulls***," Snopes, 8 November 2014, https://www.snopes.com/news/2014/12/18/bullish-investment.

3. Shlomo Sher, "A Framework for Assessing Immorally Manipulative Marketing Tactics," *Journal of Business Ethics* 102, no. 1 (August 2011): 107.

4. Ibid., 99.

5. Roger Crisp, "Persuasive Advertising, Autonomy, and the Creation of Desire," *Journal of Business Ethics* 6, no. 5 (July 1987): 413–18.

6. Ibid., 417–8.

7. Robert L. Arrington, "Advertising and Behaviour Control," *Journal of Business Ethics* 1, no. 1 (February 1982): 6.

8. Ibid., 7.

9. Ibid., 11.

10. Adria Vasil, interview with Laura Lynch, "'It's Pretty Staggering': Returned Online Purchases Often Sent to Landfill, Environmental Journalist Says," *The Current*, CBC Radio One, 12 December 2019, https://www.cbc.ca/radio/thecurrent/the-current-for-dec-12-2019-1.5393783/thursday-december-12-2019-full-episode-transcript-1.5394272#segment3.

11. Courtney Reagan, "That Sweater You Don't Like Is a Trillion-Dollar Problem for Retailers. These Companies Want to Fix It," *CNBC*, 12 January 2019, https://www.cnbc.com/2019/01/10/growing-online-sales-means-more-returns-and-trash-for-landfills.html.

12. Ibid.

13. Aaron Saltzman, "Here's What Really Happens to All Those Gifts You Return to the Store," *CBC News*, 14 January 2017, https://www.cbc.ca/news/business/christmas-gifts-returns-1.3932253.

14. "Canadian Code of Advertising Standards," Ad Standards, July 2019, https://adstandards.ca/code/the-code-online.

15. "The Broadcast Code for Advertising to Children," Ad Standards, 2015, https://adstandards.ca/wp-content/uploads/2018/09/broadcastCodeForAdvertisingToChildren.pdf.

16. Nawel Ayadi, Corina Paraschiv, and Xavier Rousset, "Online Dynamic Pricing and Consumer-Perceived Ethicality: Synthesis and Future Research," *Recherche Et Applications En Marketing (English Edition)*32, no. 3 (2017): 49–70, https://doi.org/10.1177/2051570717702592.

17. "Dynamic Pricing," IONOS Digitalguide, accessed 14 February 2020, https://www.ionos.ca/digitalguide/online-marketing/online-sales/dynamic-pricing/.

18. Lilach Bullock, "5 Pricing Tips to Raise Your e-Commerce AOV," Smart Insights, 27 January 2020, https://www.smartinsights.com/ecommerce/ecommerce-strategy/5-pricing-tips-raise-your-e-commerce-aov/.

19. "Busted: Easyhome," *Marketplace*, season 37, episode 9, Canadian Broadcasting Corporation, 2 April 2010, https://watch.cbc.ca/media/marketplace/season37/episode-9/38e815a-00cd9d9e466.

20. "'Strong' 2014 Chevy Silverado Anthem Debuts July 4," General Motors, 2 July 2013, https://media.gm.com/media/

us/en/chevrolet/vehicles/silverado/2014.detail.html/content/Pages/news/us/en/2013/Jul/0702-silverado-july4.html.

21. Susan Krashinsky, "Labatt Rolls Out a Kokanee Ad in the Shape of a Feature-Length Movie," *Globe and Mail*, last modified 11 May 2018, https://www.theglobeandmail.com/report-on-business/industry-news/marketing/labatt-rolls-out-a-kokanee-ad-in-the-shape-of-a-feature-length-movie/article9098818.

22. Rae Ann Fera, "A Big-Screen Brand-Content Play: Behind Kokanee's Cinematic Debut, 'The Movie Out Here,'" *Fast Company*, 14 March 2013, https://www.fastcompany.com/1682573/a-big-screen-brand-content-play-behind-kokanees-cinematic-debut-the-movie-out-here.

23. Randy Stein, qtd. in Jennie Punter, "Alliance Films Sets Pic Promoting Beer," *Variety*, 7 June 2012, https://variety.com/2012/film/news/alliance-films-sets-pic-promoting-beer-1118055186.

24. Duncan Macleod, "Coca-Cola Heist," *Inspiration Room*, 31 January 2009, http://theinspirationroom.com/daily/2009/coca-cola-heist.

25. "How Coke Got College Freshmen to Make New Friends Just by Changing the Cap of Its Bottles," *Digital Synopsis*, 2 June 2014, https://digitalsynopsis.com/advertising/coke-friendly-twist-bottles.

26. Vauhini Vaura, "Coca-Cola's Happiness Machines," *The New Yorker*, 15 May 2014, https://www.newyorker.com/business/currency/coca-colas-happiness-machines.

27. Marion Nestle, interview by Roberto A. Ferdman, "How Coca-Cola Has Tricked Everyone into Drinking So Much of It," *Washington Post*, 5 October 2015, https://www.washingtonpost.com/news/wonk/wp/2015/10/05/how-coca-cola-gets-its-way.

28. Ibid.

29. Vaura, "Coca-Cola's Happiness Machines."

30. "Dumb Ways to Die," Metro Trains Melbourne, 14 October 2012, https://www.youtube.com/watch?v=IJNR2EpS0jw.

31. Asher Moses, "Aussie Viral Video, 'Dumb Ways to Die,' Lives On," *The Age*, 29 October 2012, https://www.theage.com.au/technology/aussie-viral-video-dumb-ways-to-die-lives-on-20121129-2ahm0.html.

32. Leah Waymark, qtd. in Simon Crerar, "Cute Melbourne Safety Video Dumb Ways to Die Becomes Internet Smash," *Herald Sun*, 18 November 2012, https://www.heraldsun.com.au/news/cute-dumb-ways-to-die-melbourne-safety-video-becomes-internet-smash/news-story/ee8b402e469be46369cc9c0ff904ea4a.

33. "200 Million Downloads: Be Safe around Big Numbers," Metro Trains Melbourne, 18 April 2016, http://www.dumbwaystodie.com/200-million-downloads.

34. Leah Waymark, qtd. in Stephen Cauchi, "No Dumb Luck: Metro Claims Safety Success," *The Age*, 14 February 2013, https://www.theage.com.au/national/victoria/no-dumb-luck-metro-claims-safety-success-20130214-2eelt.html.

35. Erin J. Strahan, Steven J. Spencer, and Mark P. Zanna, "Subliminal Priming and Persuasion: Striking While the Iron Is Hot," *Journal of Experimental Social Psychology* 38, no. 6 (November 2002): 566.

36. Thijs Verwijmeren et al., "Warning: You Are Being Primed! The Effects of a Warning on the Impact of Subliminal Ads," *Journal of Experimental Social Psychology* 49, no. 6 (November 2013): 1128.

37. Adam W. Craig et al., "Suspicious Minds: Exploring Neural Processes during Exposure to Deceptive Advertising," *Journal of Marketing Research* 49, no. 3 (June 2012): 369–70.

38. Derren Brown, Advertising Agency Task, (posted Sept 12, 2012; originally from *Mind Control*, season 4, episode 1, March 2003), https://www.youtube.com/watch?v=YQXe1CokWqQ.

39. Steve Genco, "How Advertising Really Works," Intuitive Consumer Blog, last modified 4 October 2013, https://intuitiveconsumer.com/blog/how-advertising-really-works/.

40. Jay Brooks, "Beer in Ads #1393: Anyway, You Didn't Burn the Schlitz," Brookston Beer Bulletin, 3 December 2014, https://brookstonbeerbulletin.com/beer-ads-1393-anyway-didnt-burn-schlitz.

41. Rebecca Cope, "Gap Kids under Fire for New Gender-Stereotyping Adverts," *Harper's Bazaar*, 3 August 2016, https://www.harpersbazaar.com/uk/fashion/fashion-news/news/a37769/gap-kids-under-fire-for-new-gender-stereotyping-adverts.

42. Catherine Jacquet, "Domestic Violence in the 1970s," United States National Library of Medicine, 15 October 2015, https://circulatingnow.nlm.nih.gov/2015/10/15/domestic-violence-in-the-1970s.

43. "Edmonton Salon Ad Irks Family Violence Groups," *CBC News*, 30 August 2011, https://www.cbc.ca/news/canada/edmonton/edmonton-salon-ad-irks-family-violence-groups-1.1091406.

44. Will Heilpern, "18 Awful Vintage Ads from the 20th Century Which Show How Far We Have Progressed," *Business Insider Nordic*, last modified 17 April 2016, https://nordic.businessinsider.com/vintage-sexist-and-racist-ads-2016-4.

45. Amy B. Wang, "Nivea's 'White Is Purity' Ad Campaign Didn't End Well," *Washington Post*, 5 April 2017, https://www.washingtonpost.com/news/business/wp/2017/04/05/niveas-white-is-purity-ad-campaign-didnt-end-well.

46. Tiffany Elle Burgess, "The Dove Ad Just Proved What We Already Knew: We Need a Seat at the Table," *Huffington Post*, 11 October 2017, https://www.huffpost.com/entry/the-dove-ad-just-proves-what-we-already-knewwe_b_59dce0c8e4b0a1bb90b8312f.

47. Duncan Macleod, "Reebok Reetone," The Inspiration Room, 13 March 2010, http://theinspirationroom.com/daily/2010/reebok-reetone.

48. Mountain Equipment Co-op, "Our Roots," last updated 1 January 2020, https://www.mec.ca/en/explore/our-roots.

49. Van Badham, "Female Genital Mutilation Is Alive in Australia. It's Just Called Labiaplasty," *The Guardian*, 26 August 2015, https://www.theguardian.com/commentisfree/2015/

aug/26/female-genital-mutilation-is-alive-in-australia-its-just-called-labiaplasty.

50. Ibid.

51. Tom Houghton, "Building Firm Advert Featuring Naked Woman Banned as It's 'Sexist and Demeaning to Women,'" *The Mirror*, 22 June 2017, https://www.mirror.co.uk/news/uk-news/building-ad-naked-woman-shower-10665746.

Chapter 9

1. Luís M. B. Cabral, *Introduction to Industrial Organization* (Cambridge, MA: MIT Press, 2002), 36.

2. David Dayen, "Bank vs. America—Protests Outside, Inside BofA Shareholder Meeting," *Shadowproof*, 9 May 2012, https://shadowproof.com/2012/05/09/bank-vs-america-protests-outside-inside-bofa-shareholder-meeting.

3. Joel Bakan, *The Corporation* (New York: Free Press, 2005), 157–8.

4. Richard Blackwell, "Canadian Pacific Proxy Battle Heats Up," *The Globe and Mail*, 13 March 2012, https://www.theglobeandmail.com/globe-investor/canadian-pacific-proxy-battle-heats-up/article4095947.

5. Yvan Allaire and François Dauphin, "A 'Successful' Case of Activism at the Canadian Pacific Railway: Lessons in Corporate Governance," *Harvard Law School Forum on Corporate Governance*, 23 December 2016, https://corpgov.law.harvard.edu/2016/12/23/a-successful-case-of-activism-at-the-canadian-pacific-railway-lessons-in-corporate-governance.

6. Blackwell, "Canadian Pacific Proxy Battle."

7. Letter from William Ackman to Canadian Pacific Railway shareholders, proxy circular, 4 April 2012, qtd. in Allaire and Dauphin, "A 'Successful' Case of Activism."

8. Allaire and Dauphin, "A 'Successful' Case of Activism."

9. Yvan Allaire and François Dauphin, "How Pershing Square Found Success at Canadian Pacific Railway," *Financial Post*, 2 February 2015, https://business.financialpost.com/opinion/how-pershing-square-found-success-at-canadian-pacific-railway.

10. Allaire and Dauphin, "A 'Successful' Case of Activism."

11. Brent Jang and Jacquie McNish, "CN Suspends Hunter Harrison's Pension Payments," *The Globe and Mail*, 23 January 2012, https://www.theglobeandmail.com/globe-investor/cn-suspends-hunter-harrisons-pension-payments/article1359484.

12. Allaire and Dauphin, "How Pershing Square Found Success."

13. Scott Deveau, "CN to Suspend Benefits for Former CEO Hunter Harrison," *Financial Post*, 23 January 2012, https://business.financialpost.com/transportation/cn-to-suspend-benefits-for-former-ceo-hunter-harrison.

14. Allaire and Dauphin, "How Pershing Square Found Success."

15. Gotham City Research LLC, "Disclaimer," n.d., https://www.gothamcityresearch.com/termsofservice.

16. Tim Worstall, "Gotham, Valiant, Short Sellers, to Make $60 Million Off Lets Gowex Collapse," *Forbes*, 7 July 2014, https://www.forbes.com/sites/timworstall/2014/07/07/gotham-valiant-short-sellers-to-make-60-million-off-lets-gowex-collapse.

17. Ibid.

Chapter 10

1. "The Golden Rule," *Radiolab*, WNYC, 25 February 2014, https://www.wnycstudios.org/story/golden-rule. The story contains a link to a video clip of the exchange.

2. Thomas C. Schelling, *Arms and Influence* (New Haven: Yale University Press, 1966), 66–7.

3. A version of this fable is published as "The Miller and the Camel: An Arab Parable," in *Child's Companion and Juvenile Instructor* (Religious Tract Society, 1860), https://babel.hathitrust.org/cgi/pt?id=coo.31924007182979, 318–9.

4. Rosemary Barton, "'Oh My God, What Did I Say?' How Justin Trudeau Learned to Deal with Donald Trump," *CBC News*, 11 August 2019, https://www.cbc.ca/news/politics/wherry-book-power-peril-barton-1.5242449.

5. Mike Crawley, "Ford Government Sets the Stage for Capping Public Sector Raises," *CBC News*, 9 May 2019, https://www.cbc.ca/news/canada/toronto/doug-ford-union-negotiation-wage-cap-legislation-1.5126776.

6. Howard Levitt, "Excessive Teachers' Wages a Boondoggle We Can't Ignore," *Financial Post*, 2 October 2012, https://business.financialpost.com/executive/careers/why-excessive-teachers-wages-are-a-boondoggle-we-cant-afford.

7. Kristin Rushowy, "Ford Government Hikes Education Spending, Chops Support for School Boards with Needy Students," *Toronto Star*, 26 April 2019, https://www.thestar.com/politics/provincial/2019/04/26/ford-government-hikes-education-spending-chops-support-for-school-boards-with-needy-students.html.

8. Jacquie Miller, "Fact-Checking Doug Ford: We Analyze His Claims on Class Sizes, Math and Student Protests," *Ottawa Citizen*, 9 May 2019, https://ottawacitizen.com/news/local-news/fact-checking-doug-ford-we-analyze-his-claims-on-school-sizes-math-and-student-protests.

9. Rushowy, "Ford Government Hikes Education Spending."

10. Andrea Michalowsky, "Computer Science Students Successfully Boycott Class Final," *Johns Hopkins News-Letter*, 31 January 2013, http://www.jhunewsletter.com/article/2013/01/computer-science-students-successfully-boycott-class-final-76275.

11. Alex Usher, "Ending the Merit Scholarship Arms Race," *Higher Education Strategy Associates*, 25 September 2014, http://higheredstrategy.com/ending-the-merit-scholarship-arms-race/.

12. "GM's Oshawa Plant Is Closing: Here's What You Need to Know," *CBC News*, 26 November 2018, https://www.cbc.ca/news/canada/gm-shawas-closure-1.4921660.

13. Ibid.

14. "Summary Report on Canada's Support for the Restructuring of General Motors and Chrysler in 2009," Industry Canada,

2014, http://publications.gc.ca/collections/collection_2015/ic/Iu44-94-2014-eng.pdf, 3, 5.

15. "Unifor Airs Super Bowl Ad Despite GM's Cease and Desist Letter," *CBC News*, 3 February 2019, https://www.cbc.ca/news/canada/toronto/gm-unifor-oshawa-super-bowl-ad-1.5004190.

16. Canadian Press, "Unifor Reports Productive Talks with General Motors on Oshawa Plant," *CBC News*, 20 March 2019, https://www.cbc.ca/news/canada/toronto/gm-oshawa-unifor-talks-negotiations-1.5063873.

17. Kirsten Dziczek, qtd. in John Irwin, "GM Oshawa 2.0 Marks a First for the Automaker," *Automotive News Canada*, 27 May 2019, https://canada.autonews.com/automakers/gm-oshawa-20-marks-first-automaker.

18. Travis Hester, qtd. in Irwin, "GM Oshawa 2.0."

19. Scott Bell, qtd. in "'We're Committed to Be in Oshawa for the Long-Term': GM Canada President," *BNN Bloomberg*, 11 February 2020, https://www.bnnbloomberg.ca/we-re-committed-to-be-in-oshawa-for-the-long-term-gm-canada-president-1.1388577.

20. Mike Walker, "Man Wins Last Truck Built in Oshawa Assembly Plant in 'Bittersweet' Raffle," *CTV News*, 5 February 2020, https://toronto.ctvnews.ca/man-wins-last-truck-built-in-oshawa-assembly-plant-in-bittersweet-raffle-1.4798719.

21. Bell, "'We're Committed to Be in Oshawa for the Long-Term.'"

Chapter 11

1. "Winnipeg Media Chided for Taking IKEA Freebies," *CBC News*, 27 November 2012, https://www.cbc.ca/news/canada/manitoba/winnipeg-media-chided-for-taking-ikea-freebies-1.1183866.

2. "Ethics Guidelines," Canadian Association of Journalists, June 2011, http://caj.ca/content.php?page= ethics-guidelines.

3. Duncan McMonagle, qtd. in "Winnipeg Media Chided."

4. Maegan Sheskey, qtd. in "Winnipeg Media Chided."

5. Nick Russell, qtd. in "Winnipeg Media Chided."

6. Damien Grace and Stephen Cohen, *Business Ethics*, Canadian edition, ed. William R. Holmes (Toronto: Oxford University Press, 2014), 154.

7. Glenn Greenwald, Ewen MacAskill, and Laura Poitras, "Edward Snowden: The Whistleblower behind the NSA Surveillance Revelations," *The Guardian*, last modified 11 June 2013, https://www.theguardian.com/world/2013/jun/09/edward-snowden-nsa-whistleblower-surveillance.

8. "Whistleblower Informant Award," United States Internal Revenue Service, last modified 15 July 2019, https://www.irs.gov/compliance/whistleblower-informant-award.

9. "Whistleblower Program," Ontario Securities Commission, OSC Policy 15-601, last modified 4 October 2018, https://www.osc.gov.on.ca/documents/en/Securities-Category1/rule_20181004_15-601_whistleblower-program-policy-only.pdf.

10. Canada, Public Servants Access Disclosure Act, SC 2005, c. 46, 2018, https://laws-lois.justice.gc.ca/eng/acts/P-31.9.

11. Transparency International Canada, "Enhancing Whistleblower Protection," submission to "Help Shape Canada's Action Plan on Open Government 2016–18," Open Government Portal, 12 May 2016, https://open.canada.ca/en/idea/enhancing-whistleblower-protection.

12. Ibid.

13. Julie Ireton, "Report Calls for Revamping of Whistleblower Law," *CBC News*, 19 June 2017, https:// www.cbc.ca/news/canada/ottawa/whistleblower-report-law-canada-1.4167847.

14. Canada, Criminal Code, RSC 1985, c. C-46, 1985, s. 425.1, https://laws.justice.gc.ca/eng/acts/C-46/page-89.html.

15. Max Harrold, "Government Whistleblower Louis Robert Returns to Work," *CTV News* Montreal, 6 August 2019, https://montreal.ctvnews.ca/government-whistleblower-louis-robert-returns-to-work-1.4538858.

16. Evan Vokes, qtd. in Julie Dermansky, "TransCanada Whistleblower Evan Vokes Details Lack of Confidence in Keystone XL," DeSmog, 22 September 2013, https://www.desmogblog.com/2013/09/22/transcanada-whistleblower-evan-vokes-details-lack-confidence-keystone-xl.

17. Council of Canadians, "Whistleblower Warns about Energy East," YouTube, 9 July 2015, https://www.youtube.com/watch?v=HUSKh1nIPV8&t=33s.

18. Charles Rusnell, Timothy Sawa, and Joseph Loiero, "Whistleblower Forced Investigation of TransCanada Pipelines," *CBC News*, 17 October 2012, https://www.cbc.ca/news/canada/whistleblower-forced-investigation-of-transcanada-pipelines-1.1146204.

19. Mike De Souza, "TransCanada Blames 2013 Pipeline Rupture on Miscommunication," Reuters, 9 November 2015, https://ca.reuters.com/article/businessNews/idCAKCN0SZ04120151110.

20. "TransCanada Reproached by NEB over Pipeline Compliance," *CBC News*, 12 October 2012, https://www.cbc.ca/news/business/transcanada-reproached-by-neb-over-pipeline-compliance-1.1261686.

21. Mike De Souza, "TransCanada Dismissed Whistleblower. Then Their Pipeline Blew Up," *National Observer*, 5 February 2016, https://www.nationalobserver.com/2016/02/05/news/transcanada-dismissed-whistleblower-then-their-pipeline-blew.

22. Mike De Souza, "They Told Me to Take Money and Run, Says Pipeline Whistleblower," *National Observer*, 18 March 2016, https://www.nationalobserver.com/2016/03/18/news/they-told-me-take-money-and-run-says-pipeline-whistleblower; Dermansky, "TransCanada Whistleblower Evan Vokes."

23. United States Congress, Pipeline Safety, Regulatory Certainty, and Job Creation Act of 2011, HR 2845, 112th Congress (2012), sec. 24.

24. Dermansky, "TransCanada Whistleblower Evan Vokes."

25. Richard Conway, "FIFA Whistleblower Phaedra Al-Majid Fears for Her Safety," *BBC Sport*, 20 December 2014, https://www.bbc.com/sport/football/30122601.

26. Erica Johnson, "'Process Is Torturous': Federal Whistleblower Says Canada Doesn't Protect People Who Speak Out," *CBC News*, 2 September 2018, https://www.cbc.ca/news/canada/british-columbia/delays-in-whistleblower-protection-system-1.4803588.

Chapter 12

1. Clayton M. Christensen, Michael E. Raynor, and Rory McDonald, "What Is Disruptive Innovation?" *Harvard Business Review*, December 2015, https://hbr.org/2015/12/what-is-disruptive-innovation.

Appendix B

1. Carlton Reid, "You Are Not Stuck in Traffic, You Are Traffic," *Forbes*, 3 December 2018, https://www.forbes.com/sites/carltonreid/2018/12/03/you-are-not-stuck-in-traffic-you-are-traffic.

Glossary

1. "What Is Harassment?" Canadian Human Rights Commission, June 2019, https://www.chrc-ccdp.gc.ca/eng/content/what-harassment-1.
2. Adam Smith, *An Inquiry into the Nature and Causes of the Wealth of Nations*, ed. Sálvio Marcelo Soares (MetaLibri, 29 May 2007), https://www.ibiblio.org/ml/libri/s/SmithA_WealthNations_p.pdf, 349.
3. Government of Canada, "Sexual Harassment—Overview," Employment and Social Development Canada, 29 July 2019, https://www.canada.ca/en/employment-social-development/programs/employment-standards/sexual-harrassment.html.

GLOSSARY

accessibility The degree to which a business or service is available to be used by all intended audiences.

accommodation A fairness-based approach to justice that aims to make full participation in society possible for everyone.

act utilitarianism The version of utilitarianism that directs us to weigh and compare the utility of individual actions. See *utilitarianism* and *rule utilitarianism*.

advertising Any means of promoting a product or service for sale to the general public or target market. Advertising is not necessarily purchased by the seller. Even the display of a slogan or an image on a piece of clothing purchased by a consumer is an advertisement.

altruism A person is altruistic if they care about the well-being of someone else for its own sake, not because of how it benefits the person doing the caring.

arms race An escalation between competitors for supremacy. Although the phrase was originally used to describe a competition between nations for weapons superiority, the phrase can refer to any situation where each player refuses to back down because they fear they will lose if their opponent does not back down as well. Neither player has the incentive to move first.

Arrow's impossibility theorem Arrow's theorem shows that an ideal voting structure (a reasonable procedure for forming a collective ordering of preferences in relation to alternatives) is impossible.

attribution error The tendency to give too much weight to internal reasons, and too little weight to external reasons, when making judgments about other people.

autonomous desire A desire that an individual willingly identifies with or has freely chosen to have.

autonomy A person's capacity to make decisions about their own life, in line with their own beliefs and values.

best alternative to a negotiated agreement (BATNA) A second-best plan that sets out what you will do if you cannot get what you need from a negotiation.

blind-spot bias Admitting that other people are affected by biases, but refusing to acknowledge the effect of biases on oneself. Also referred to as *bias blind spot*.

board of directors Elected representatives of a company's shareholders entrusted with the responsibility to direct the company according to the wishes of its shareholders. In some places, this board is called a *board of trustees* or a *supervisory board*.

bystander intervention Active opposition to discriminatory behaviour given by someone who is not themself the target of the behaviour but who observes it.

capability approach An ethical theory that focuses on promoting human abilities to attain the elements of a good life.

categorical Something that does not permit an exception for any reason.

categorical imperative According to Kant, the most basic or fundamental rule expressing our ethical duty.

caveat emptor (buyer beware) It is the customer's responsibility to examine the product before purchasing it, to become aware of any defects or unsuitability of the product for their use.

character The sum of a person's various dispositions to act in ways that enable their *flourishing* (*virtues*) or hinder their flourishing (*vices*).

charter revocation The government revoking the charter of a corporation would essentially mean the cessation of the corporation's legal existence.

Coase theorem In the absence of transaction costs, the participants in a perfectly competitive market will find the most efficient distribution of a resource, regardless of who is given ownership of the resource.

code of conduct A set of rules specifying the behaviour expected of the members of a profession or other organization, in addition to disciplinary measures the organization may use in case of code violations.

code of ethics A set of principles intended to guide the members of a profession or organization in carrying out their roles in accordance with ethical norms.

collective co-operation A strategy to avoid free-rider problems by using mechanisms to ensure the co-operation of group members.

Condorcet paradox Aggregating rational individual preference orderings can produce circular (irrational) collective preferences.

confirmation bias The tendency to give credence to information that supports our beliefs, and to give less credence to information that would count against what we already think is true.

conflict of interest A situation in which your personal interests and goals conflict with the interests and goals you must maintain in your professional or public role.

conservatism A political theory that prioritizes the preservation of a certain way of life over individual liberty.

consumer boycott Consumers may attempt to alter the perceived negative behaviour of a corporation by refusing to purchase its products or services, thereby communicating their disapproval of the behaviour.

corporate officers Those in positions of the highest level of management in a corporation. These include the *chief executive officer (CEO)*, *chief financial officer (CFO)*, and the *chief operating officer (COO)*.

corporate social responsibility (CSR) The accountability of a business to society, and the way businesses seek to promote the well-being of legitimate stakeholder groups including, but also extending beyond, their shareholders.

credibility A person has credibility if they are willing to act, have the power to act, and have the means with which to act on their stated intentions. Credibility also means having a reputation for following through on stated intentions.

dark green approach An environmental strategy that allows environmental issues identified by experts to dictate company policy.

debiasing Taking intentional and reflective steps to reduce the impact of cognitive biases on reasoning.

default co-operative attitude The strategy of playing co-operatively unless the other player defects from the co-operative strategy.

deliberative decision making Conscious, reflective mental processing of factors relevant to choice and action. Kahneman refers to this as System 2 thinking.

deontological monism The view that there is a single, absolute, ethical duty. For Kant, this is the categorical imperative.

deontological pluralism The view that there are multiple, distinct basic duties.

deontological theories of ethics Theories that claim ethically right actions are those that fulfill one's duty.

descriptive ethics The study of what people actually believe concerning what is ethically right or wrong.

dirty hands A situation where we do a morally good thing, but still end up doing some kind of harm or injustice.

distal interest A person has a *distal interest* in a decision if their well-being is only indirectly affected by the outcome of that decision.

dominant strategy In game theory, we say that Act *A* strictly dominates Act *B* when Player 1 always does better by playing Act *A* no matter what Player 2 chooses to do.

dominated strategy If a player has a choice between Strategy *A* and Strategy *B*, and Strategy *A* is the *dominant* strategy, then we say Strategy *B* is the *dominated* strategy.

efficiency An activity or a system is efficient if it attains its goal(s) without wasting time or resources.

enlightened self-interest What is best for oneself, including consideration of the interests of others.

environment The surroundings within which something exists. Typically this refers to the natural habitat, including land, water, atmosphere, and climate, but can also refer to political or economic circumstances, or a particular setting in which events and activities occur.

environmental protections Initiatives put in place to protect and benefit the natural environment.

equality Individuals have equality if they have the same rights and the same opportunity to access social goods such as education, health care, the justice system, and public infrastructure.

equity Individuals are treated equitably if they are given what is needed for them to realize a full human life, considering their circumstances.

equity initiatives Programs and policies aimed at increasing and promoting equity.

ethical considerations The factors that need to be taken into account when making decisions because they involve moral rights, obligations, issues of fairness, virtue, or other ethically relevant concerns.

ethical decision-making process A series of steps intended to guide your thinking as you assess a situation and formulate a well-reasoned ethical decision about a best course of action in that situation.

ethical objectivism The view that what is ethically right or wrong is an objective matter. rather than determined subjectively on the basis of what people believe is ethically right or wrong.

ethical pluralism Multiple distinct and potentially incommensurable views of what is ethically right or wrong can be equally warranted, and worthy of respect.

ethical relativism The view that the ethical beliefs and values people hold determine what is ethically right or wrong for those people. This is sometimes called *moral relativism.*

ethics of care An ethical theory that holds care and caring relationships as the central ethical value. Also known as *care ethics.*

ethics officer An individual charged with the task of ensuring that the employees and procedures of a corporation comply with its code of ethics.

ethnocentric harassment Harassment that targets the race, colour, ancestry, place of origin, ethnic origin, creed, or citizenship of the individual being harassed.

ethos Describes the values that an organization considers to be its defining characteristics; it is a way of characterizing the spirit or culture of an organization. Here we are concerned with *ethos* in this ethical sense, not its rhetorical sense.

explicit bias Tendencies of association that the holder of the bias is aware of.

fallible A fallible person is someone for whom it is possible to make a mistake. If we are being realistic, we will see that this includes all of us. For this reason, we should be humble.

fiduciary A person commissioned to act in the interests of another party called the *principal.*

fiduciary duty A duty of care owed by a trustee to a beneficiary.

First Fundamental Theorem of Welfare Economics Resources will be distributed Pareto-efficiently in a perfectly competitive market. In other words, trading will make the distribution of resources socially optimal.

fixed-pie fallacy An error in reasoning that occurs when a person wrongly assumes that a resource is finite or fixed.

fixed-pie thinking Assuming that the pool of benefits available from negotiating are fixed, so that any gain made by one party will be a loss for the other. This is problematic when it is in fact possible to find arrangements that would increase the pool of benefits available to both parties.

flourishing The Greek word *eudaimonia*, used by Aristotle, is often translated as *happiness*, but *flourishing* better captures its meaning. To *flourish* is to realize your human potential to its full extent—in other words, to actualize yourself as the kind of being you are or are meant to be.

free-rider problem A free-rider problem emerges when someone (the free-rider) benefits from the co-operative activities of others without themself contributing to produce the benefits. This puts a strain on the rest of the group and threatens to undermine the co-operative outcome.

game For the purposes of game theory, a game is a strategic interaction between at least two players, with a definite outcome for each player.

game of chicken A game-theory depiction of a situation where the competing players have little to gain by winning and a great amount to lose by losing, and are motivated toward mutual self-destruction by perversely preferring to maintain their pride or reputation for being "tough."

game theory A formal system for modelling the actions of rational decision makers (the *players*) in strategic social interactions (*games*). The outcome depends on the combined actions of all of the players. The players individually choose the action they will take on the basis of the information they have available and the outcomes they are willing to accept.

gender essentialism The view that certain observed behavioural differences between men and women are rooted in biological or psychological traits, unique to what is thought to be male and female. Gender essentialism is problematic for several reasons.

gender wage gap The difference in average wages between women and men, all else being equal. The gap can describe the average difference in a given workplace, a sector, or over the whole of a country's economy.

genuine interest A person's claim or interest in a decision is *genuine* if the decision infringes on something they are entitled to.

harassment According to the Canadian Human Rights Commission, harassment "includes any unwanted physical or verbal behaviour that offends or humiliates you."[1]

hostile work environment A work environment is *hostile* when discriminatory behaviour makes it uncomfortable or frightening for individuals to work in that environment.

humanity formulation The version of the categorical imperative that states that one must always treat a human person as an end in themselves and never merely as a means.

humble objectivism The view that there are facts about what is right or wrong, but that we are as likely as anyone else to be mistaken about these facts. In this way, humble objectivism differs from both ethical relativism and from moral imperialism.

hybrid approach An environmental strategy that draws on particular aspects of the light green, market green, stakeholder green, and deep green approaches.

implicit bias Tendencies of association that the holder of the bias is not aware of.

incentives Reasons for acting that appeal to a person's self-interest. *Perverse incentives* have the effect of motivating the agent to act in ways contrary to the interests of the principal(s). *Benign incentives* align the agent's self-interest with the interests of the principal(s).

incommensurate To say that the practices of one culture are incommensurate with those of another culture is to say that the practices of the first culture cannot be measured using the standards or norms of the second culture.

information asymmetry A situation where one party has information that another party does not have. The person with more information has an advantage over the less informed party in any kind of debate, negotiation, or transaction.

insider trading The illegal act of members of the board of directors or corporate officers enriching themselves by using their early access to information relevant to changes in share price.

instrumental value Something that is useful to achieve some goal. For example, money has instrumental value because it is useful for purchasing food.

integrative bargaining A co-operative approach to bargaining in which the interlocutors seek common ground and mutual benefit based on an understanding of one another's goals and interests. This is also called *interest-based* bargaining.

integrity Holding firmly to what one knows to be right in the face of temptations to compromise one's principles for personal gain or in the face of pressure exerted by those who are less scrupulous.

interlocutor A party with whom you are engaged in a game or negotiation. This term is more appropriate than *adversary* or *opponent* because not all negotiations are adversarial in nature. Even in those cases where negotiations *are* adversarial, it is important to keep in mind that your adversary is not always your enemy.

internalization The internalization of a belief or attitude takes place when that belief becomes a stable part of one's psychological makeup or character.

intrinsic value Something that is valued for its own sake, not because it is useful for some other purpose.

invisible hand The belief that a free and competitive market will spontaneously coordinate buyers and sellers, acting in self-interested ways, in the most efficient way possible. The metaphor comes from Adam Smith's *The Wealth of Nations*.[2]

justice approach Ethical theories that emphasize impersonal and universal determinations of rights and merits while neglecting the personal and relational aspects of ethics.

liberalism A political theory that holds individual liberty as its central value.

light green approach An environmental strategy that relies on public policy to guide environmental initiatives undertaken by the company.

light-of-day test An assessment of whether you would be comfortable with your decision or action becoming public knowledge. If not, your decision or action fails the light-of-day test.

manipulation To control or use someone for your own purposes, without their awareness of the fact that they are being so controlled.

marginal social cost The complete social cost of the production of a unit of something. Marginal social cost is greater than the direct cost of producing a unit of something. Marginal social cost takes both negative and positive externalities into account.

marginalization Treating people as insignificant and not worthy of moral consideration.

market economy An economic system in which the competitive interactions of businesses control prices and distribution of goods within society.

market-failures approach According to the market-failures approach to business ethics, which derives from Joseph Heath, businesses are obligated to respect norms that promote the efficient functioning of the market. A market failure occurs when something or someone causes a market to operate less efficiently than it could have.

market green approach An environmental strategy focused on responding to environmental concerns and preferences of the company's consumer base.

maxim A general action-guiding rule or principle.

moral context A set of relational and situational factors that yield distinctive ethical requirements on your action. The most important contexts we discuss are the personal and the professional (fiduciary) contexts.

moral hazard The phenomenon known as moral hazard emerges when people who believe they have protection from the full consequences (though not necessarily full protection from any consequences) of risky behaviour will take more risks.

moral imperialism The desire to hold other people—who hold moral views different from yours—accountable to your own moral standard (or to the standard of your group); the refusal to acknowledge the legitimacy of moral views when they differ from your own.

moral intuition A persistent and powerful moral belief possessed by a person immediately, without being consciously justified in terms of other reasons or factors. Kahneman calls intuitive thinking of this sort System 1 thinking.

(moral) right A justified claim or entitlement to have something or to be treated in a certain way.

moral tragedy A situation in which a choice must be made between alternatives, each of which involves violating an important ethical requirement.

narrow self-interest What is best for oneself, irrespective of the interests of others.

Nash equilibrium An outcome of the game where no player has the incentive to unilaterally change strategies. In other words, it is the best a player can hope for, given the rational choice of the other player.

negative externality An uncompensated cost that is imposed on a person by the actions of one or more other people. For example, if your neighbour hosts a wild backyard party with live music and fireworks, you will suffer the cost of air, noise, and light pollution, among other vexatious things.

negative incentive An incentive that threatens to punish bad behaviour rather than motivates by rewarding positive behaviour.

negative right Requires other people to refrain from interfering with your actions or possessions. Examples include property rights and the rights to life, freedom of religion, and freedom from slavery.

normative ethics The study of what makes something ethically right (praiseworthy) or wrong (blameworthy). A normative ethical theory will tell us how we should act.

norms General social rules that we are expected to follow. These rules tell us what kind of behaviours are or are not acceptable.

objective discipline An objective discipline studies objective facts—that is, facts that do not depend on human perception or opinion.

overt discrimination Discrimination that takes place openly, in a way that is acknowledged and perhaps even formally encoded into policies.

ownership rights The right of ownership to something. According to the Coase theorem, it does not matter to whom the ownership rights of a resource are given. Give the ownership rights to one party, and allow them to negotiate with the other interested parties, and all parties involved will come to an efficient distribution of the resource.

Pareto efficiency A particularly stringent form of efficiency, in which all resources are allocated and no one can be made better off by trading without making someone else worse off.

payoffs The outcome for each player. The payoff is a number that represents everything of measurable value to the player receiving the payoff. The payoff is a function of both players' choices.

peak production The maximum yield or production of a resource, after which point the yield will decline.

perverse incentive A kind of "loophole" in a structure that allows an incentive designed to encourage beneficial behaviour to be used instead in a way that undermines the purpose of the incentive.

planned economy An economic system in which a centralized government dictates prices and the production and distribution of goods within society. This type of economy is also known as a *state-owned* or a *command economy*.

poison-pill clause A clause in an agreement stipulating that certain hostile moves by the other party will automatically trigger a provision that will defuse the effect of the other party's move.

positional bargaining An adversarial approach to bargaining in which the interlocutors focus on getting what they want without regard for one another's interests. This is also called *position-based* bargaining.

positive right Entails that other people have an obligation to do something for you or provide you with something. Positive rights include the rights to education and health care, among other things.

practical ethics The branch of ethics that seeks to help people to use ethical concepts to make good decisions and act well in real-life situations. Practical ethics is also called *applied ethics*.

pre-emptive strike In anticipation of non-co-operative play by your interlocutor, you might open with a non-co-operative move. This is most effective when you are reasonably certain that your interlocutor is planning a hostile attack, and your move has the ability to dismantle their capacity to carry out this attack.

prima facie duty A duty that is binding on us but that may be overridden by the demands of other duties in certain circumstances. *Prima facie* literally means *on the face of things*, and so a prima facie duty is accepted as holding on the face of things, or until proven otherwise.

priming A way of influencing people's decisions by instilling words or images in their memory. Once primed in this way, people are more likely to respond in ways preferred by the one doing the priming, under certain circumstances.

principal In a *fiduciary relationship*, the principal is the party whose interests are formally represented by the agent acting as a *fiduciary*. In the context of corporations, the owners are the principals, and the executives and other employees are the agents.

principal–agent problem A problem that arises when the actions and interests of agents are not aligned with those of the principals. In a corporate context, usually the managers, executives, and officers are agents and the shareholders are principals. A major function of corporate governance is to ensure that the corporation does not fall prey to principal–agent problems.

prisoner's dilemma A prisoner's dilemma is a scenario in which two alleged criminals, acting rationally and according to their self-interest, confess to the crime (that is, defect) and end up with longer jail sentences than if they had simply kept quiet (that is, co-operated with each other).

private morality The personal ethical norms and values of an individual.

profit motive The desire to increase financial wealth by engaging in economic activity.

proximal interest A person has a *proximal interest* in a decision if their well-being is directly affected by the outcome of that decision.

prudential considerations The factors that need to be taken into account when making decisions because they affect someone's self-interest.

public morality The set of ethical norms and values that constrain a fiduciary given their relationship to a principal.

publicly traded corporation A corporation whose shares are publicly traded on a stock exchange.

pyramid of corporate social responsibility Responsibilities of business are organized hierarchically with economic obligations as the foundation, followed by legal, ethical, and finally, at the top of the pyramid, discretionary or philanthropic obligations.

rational irrationality The use of apparently irrational tactics or strategies to help ensure that a (rational) goal will be attained.

reputational capital The way the reputation of a business, organization, or an individual acts as a factor that increases profitability.

rights-based deontological ethics An approach to ethics that links the idea of duty to ensuring that people's rights are respected.

rivalrous A resource is rivalrous if one party's use or consumption of it means that another party or parties cannot consume or use it.

rule utilitarianism The version of utilitarianism that requires us to follow rules that tend to promote high levels of net utility. See *utilitarianism* and *act utilitarianism*.

salami tactics Dismantling the opposition of one's interlocutor by gradually securing apparently insignificant concessions. By the time your interlocutor realizes what has happened, it is too late for them to claw back on the

concessions they have made. Sometimes this is called the *foot-in-the-door* technique.

self-refuting A claim is self-refuting if the truth of the claim entails that the claim itself is false. Here is the clearest example: "This sentence is false." If the sentence in quotation marks is true, then it must be false, because it states that it is false. Philosophers call this the *liar sentence*; it leads to the logical problem known as the *liar paradox*.

self-regulation The activities of a profession or an organization aimed at ensuring compliance of its members with legal and ethical standards.

self-serving bias An excessively favourable view of oneself that results in inaccurate thinking or perception.

sentimentality To appeal to sentimentality is to seek to influence people's choices by playing on their strong emotional connotations rather than giving them reasons for making those choices.

sexual harassment The Canadian government defines sexual harassment as "any conduct, comment, or contact of a sexual nature that is likely to cause offence or humiliation to any employee; or that might, on reasonable grounds, be perceived by that employee as placing a condition of a sexual nature on employment or on any opportunity for training or promotion."[3]

shadism A form of personal discrimination based on the relative lightness or darkness of a person's skin. This is distinct from racism, but is just as pernicious.

shareholder Someone who has a financial interest in a company through the purchase (and therefore ownership) of shares.

shareholder activism Those holding shares in a corporation may seek to alter the behaviour or direction of a corporation in a variety of ways, including submitting proposals for action for discussion at shareholder meetings, voting against director candidates nominated by the board, and so forth. Note that if a person sells all their shares, then they are not able to participate in other forms of shareholder activism.

shielding from negative consequences When a corporation takes on legal responsibility for its employees, it is *shielding* those employees from (some of) the negative consequences of their actions.

social action problem A situation where, if each individual in that situation does what is in their self-interest, the result will be that everyone is worse off than they would have been had each individual acted otherwise. Also known as a *collective action problem*.

social contract The idea that people mutually agree to forgo what is in their narrow self-interest for the sake of what is in their enlightened self-interest, namely to give up some of their individual liberty in exchange for social security and stability.

social injustice Social injustice exists where people or groups of people are left out or disadvantaged in a social system such that they do not have the opportunities they are owed.

social licence The idea that society permits something (for instance, particular business activities) to take place, and that society has the right to disallow that thing if it sees fit.

social utility Utility measured across the whole of society, accounting for both the benefits and harms that come from the action.

socialism A political theory that views equality as the fundamentally important value.

socially optimal outcome The result of the players' choices that yields the greatest utility available to them collectively.

stakeholder A party with an interest in the decisions and actions of a business.

stakeholder green approach An environmental strategy that reflects the concerns not only of consumers but of stakeholders more generally.

stakeholder theory The view that businesses should strive to satisfy the interests of all important stakeholders.

status quo The *status quo* is the way things are at present, and the way things will remain if nothing is done to change the situation.

strategic interaction A situation where players must decide what to do based on what they think other players will choose to do.

strategic move An attempt to convince others to adopt a co-operative attitude and to thwart those who would be tempted to defect from a co-operative strategy.

strong fiduciary responsibility Businesses, acting as fiduciaries of their investors, have no other responsibility than to maximize profit.

subliminal advertising Bypassing a person's critical self-reflective capacities to generate a desire for a product or service.

supply chain The various stages and parties involved in generating a product and getting it to customers.

sustainability A business is *sustainable* if it can be maintained for the long term in an appropriate balance with important financial, social, and environmental constraints.

ten commandments of business ethics A list of ten rules given by Joseph Heath that express requirements of the market-failures approach to business ethics.

three-domain model A presentation of the responsibilities of business as three interconnected domains: economic, legal, and ethical.

tit-for-tat A strategy of reciprocation in which a player chooses to mirror an opponent's gameplay. For example, if an opponent chooses to defect in a prisoner's dilemma, the player will respond by choosing to defect in the next game. Similarly, co-operation in one game will be met by co-operation in the next.

tragedy of the commons A situation in which a commonly owned or accessible resource is depleted or ruined because of overuse by individuals acting in their self-interest without regard for the sustainability of the resource.

transaction costs Costs incurred during an economic transaction like transferring ownership rights between agents (a person, a company, or a regulatory body). These costs derive from gathering information, establishing who the negotiating parties are, negotiating contracts, and enforcing contracts.

triple-bottom-line reporting A way of measuring success in business performance that uses social and environmental measures in addition to financial profit.

universalizability formulation The version of the categorical imperative that states that one may act only on a maxim that one would accept as a universal law. In other words, if we want a maxim to be applicable universally, then acting in accordance with that maxim must be a rational exercise of moral duty for everyone, without partiality or exception.

unscrupulous interest A person's claim or interest in a decision is *unscrupulous* if the decision does not infringe on anything they are entitled to.

utilitarianism An ethical theory that sees the right action as the one that maximizes the net utility of the relevantly affected parties.

veil of ignorance A hypothetical state of ignorance, in which people thinking about what a just society would look like imagine they do not know what their own place in society will be.

vice A bad or negative character trait that inhibits human flourishing.

virtue A good or positive character trait that contributes toward human flourishing.

virtue ethics An ethical theory according to which good action has to be understood in relation to good character and to the overall purpose of human life.

weak fiduciary responsibility In addition to their fiduciary responsibility to maximize profit, businesses can have additional important obligations and goals.

wealth gaps Wealth gaps are calculated by adding total assets, then subtracting financial liabilities. From this we can measure net worth.

whistle-blowing Releasing information to the public about an organization's wrongdoing that the organization has kept from the public and is not doing anything to address.

win-win outcome An outcome that is satisfactory or better for all parties involved; the parties all improve their situation or attain a net benefit.

zero-sum game A game in which any gain for Player *A* involves an exactly proportionate loss for Player *B*, and vice versa.

INDEX